Medical Treatment

Decisions and the Law

Medical Treatment
Decisions and the Law

Robert Francis QC

and

Christopher Johnstone

3 Serjeant's Inn
London

Butterworths
London, Dublin and Edinburgh

2001

United Kingdom	Butterworths, a Division of Reed Elsevier (UK) Ltd, Halsbury House, 35 Chancery Lane, LONDON WC2A 1EL and 4 Hill Street, EDINBURGH EH2 3JZ
Australia	Butterworths, a Division of Reed International Books Australia Pty Ltd, CHATSWOOD, New South Wales
Canada	Butterworths Canada Ltd, MARKHAM, Ontario
Hong Kong	Butterworths Hong Kong, a division of Reed Elsevier (Greater China) Ltd, HONG KONG
India	Butterworths India, NEW DELHI
Ireland	Butterworth (Ireland) Ltd, DUBLIN
Malaysia	Malayan Law Journal Sdn Bhd, KUALA LUMPUR
New Zealand	Butterworths of New Zealand Ltd, WELLINGTON
Singapore	Butterworths Asia, SINGAPORE
South Africa	Butterworths Publishers (Pty) Ltd, DURBAN
USA	Lexis Law Publishing, CHARLOTTESVILLE, Virginia

© Reed Elsevier (UK) Ltd 2001

A CIP Catalogue record for this book is available from the British Library.

ISBN 0 406 904 901

Typeset by YHT Ltd, London
Printed and bound in Great Britain by The Bath Press, Bath

Visit Butterworths LEXIS *direct* at http://www.butterworths.com

To *Joanna*, *Lily*, *Cathy*, *Anna*, *Helen* and *Nick*

FOREWORD

Undoubtedly the most significant development in the family justice system in the last decade has been the development of the law and practice in relation to incapacitated patients. The decision of the House of Lords in *Re F (mental patient: sterilisation)* [1990] 2 AC 1 that an application for a declaration of lawfulness should be issued in the Family Division has added to the already daunting responsibilities of the judge a considerable additional dimension. Of course that is not because of the volume of the work, indeed the number of applications going to contested hearing in any year is extremely small, but because of its intense difficulty. The operation to sterilise a disabled and vulnerable young woman; the force-feeding of the anorexic adolescent; the caesarean section to save a baby on the threshold of life; the ending of the life of a PVS patient: these are all instances of judgments which must be taken, not by reference to some well recognised precedent or rule of law, but in an endeavour to do right in a dilemma that has no right answer. The critics who see only of touch judges might ponder the burden of the responsibility and the pressure of the emotions that surround such decisions. Nor are the moral and ethical dilemmas which the cases raise faced only by the judge. They are fully shared by the medical professionals and the legal practitioners to whose judgment intensely difficult decisions are brought long before the issue reaches the judge.

So an authoritative text on this developing field of law is badly needed. I know that Butterworths have nourished the plan to publish for some years. They could not have commissioned more experienced or distinguished authors. Robert Francis QC has appeared in almost all the significant cases and the authority that characterises his advocacy is equally evident in his writing. Having myself some years ago written the chapter on this topic for the current edition of *Rayden* I am well placed to assess and admire the comprehensive and lucid quality of this welcome edition to every family lawyer's library.

The Rt Hon Lord Justice Thorpe
January 2001

CONTENTS

PART I
GENERAL PRINCIPLES

Chapter 1
Consent – General

Chapter 2
Consent – Adults

Contents

Chapter 5
Abortion

Chapter 6
Caesarean Sections

Chapter 7
Feeding

Contents

Chapter 8
Religious Objections to Treatment

Chapter 9
Permanent Vegetative State

Contents

Chapter 10
Treatment of Suicidal Patients

Part III
APPENDICES

Appendix 1
Consent – General

Appendix 2
Consent – Adults

Appendix 3
Deciding for Others

Contents

Table of Cases

H

J

K

L

M

N

O

P

R

S

T

V

W

X

Y

Z

Table of Statutes, Statutory Instruments and European/International Conventions

STATUTES

Introduction

This book owes its genesis to the recent expansion of court involvement in the medical decision-making process. A glance through the table of cases we have referred to will indicate that the vast majority were decided within the last 15 years. Before then the common law appeared to concentrate on the application of the law of negligence to medical treatment. Indeed, until the publication of *Medical Law: Text with Materials* by Professors Kennedy and Grubb in 1989 many lawyers might have been forgiven for being somewhat sceptical as to whether there was such a subject, as opposed to medical negligence law. The reasons are not hard to find. Until relatively recently – at least in this country – the standards to be applied to medical treatment were left almost entirely to the medical profession. The courts intervened rarely, and then reluctantly. The standard of care imposed on the medical profession, as a result of the *Bolam*[1] case was largely the standard they thought it right to adopt. Behind this stand-offish approach was a desire not to inhibit medical progress to the disadvantage of the community as a whole:

> 'we should be doing a disservice to the community at large if we were to impose liability on hospitals and doctors for everything that happens to go wrong. Doctors would be led to think more of their own safety than of the good of their patients. Initiative would be stifled and confidence shaken. A proper sense of proportion requires us to have regard to the conditions in which hospitals and doctors have to work.'[2]

Since then the immense and rapid advances in medical science have provoked a more anxious and less trusting reaction to medical matters. Patients have become accustomed in other fields to having and being able to exercise rights, to express their views, however inexpert, and to being able to pick and choose between options which they demand they are given. They see no reason why they should not be able to do so in relation to medical treatment. The law has responded, slowly and often tortuously to these concerns. It has advanced way beyond the ability retrospectively to examine the standard of care applied in the case of treatment which has gone wrong, and is now willing to intervene in matters of medical treatment and care before it is given or during it. Often this has the result of, quite literally, placing the lawyer at the bedside at the shoulder of the doctor. Not everyone welcomes this, but there is no doubt that we are only at the beginning of this development.

---

1 *Bolam v Friern Hospital Management Committee* [1957] 1 WLR 582.
2 *Roe v Minister of Health* [1954] 2 QB 66 at 83 per Denning LJ.

1

At the front line of these developments is the process whereby decisions are made about medical treatment. In most cases what is to be done is decided between doctor and patient without the intervention of any third party and without the shadow of any special legislation falling upon them. In matters of difficulty or controversy, however, recourse is now made on an increasingly regular basis to the courts.

The purpose of this book is modest. Some types of treatment cause day-to-day challenges for doctors, hospital managers, patients, their families as well as lawyers. Often problems arise in these areas at very short notice; many require application to the court for approval in one form or another. We have identified those areas where reference to the courts is most likely to be needed. We have sought to set out relatively briefly, and, we hope, without an excessive degree of academic analysis, what we understand to be the law applicable to these problems, first by reference to the general principles, and secondly by applying those principles to each problem in the subsequent chapters. Where we have thought it helpful to do so we have appended informative material relevant to the subject and precedents.

We hope this will prove of use not only to lawyers who are asked to advise any client involved in a difficult treatment decision, but also to doctors and medical managers, who may need to have available an easily accessible reference to a particular topic. For these reasons the book is more of an anthology of different situations, rather than an attempt at an exhaustive survey of all circumstances in which medical treatment decisions have to be made. For example, we have not sought to deal with the generality of the Mental Health Act 1983, an area already well covered by established texts, or matters coming within the remit of the Human Fertilisation and Embryology Authority, a subject worthy of a book to itself. Readers will no doubt think of other areas which are not covered. We hope that they may find some assistance from the general principles described in these pages in any event, and, if they do not, can only hope they find consolation in the comparative brevity of this work!

As we hope the book may be of help to the layman as well as the lawyer it is necessary to make clear a few caveats about the content of this book. As will be readily apparent, medical science continually springs new ethical and legal challenges on the world which throw new light on previously accepted legal principles. While the law is often rightly accused of lagging behind scientific and social developments, it is capable of producing novel solutions very rapidly indeed. The development of the declaratory jurisdiction to assist patients lacking the capacity to authorise their own treatment in *Re F (mental patient: sterilisation)*[3] is one example, the resolution offered to the challenges presented by the PVS patient in *Airedale NHS Trust v Bland*[4], in litigation which was concluded from the beginning of the first instance hearing to judgment in the House of Lords in 12 weeks, is another. Therefore, great care should be taken to avoid being tempted to assume that principles set out in previous cases, and described here, will be followed in the future, even in a similar case, if the result is seen to be undesirable or unjust. In this of all areas of law,

---

3 [1990] 2 AC 1.
4 [1993] AC 789.

a flexibility of approach is constantly required, and a responsiveness to the needs of society likely to be shown by the courts. This is, of course, why it is such an exciting and productive part of the law in which to study and work.

We cannot end this introduction without expressing our heartfelt thanks to Lord Justice Thorpe for kindly agreeing to write the foreword. We must also acknowledge the assistance from many of our colleagues who – often unwittingly – have helped us develop some of the ideas in this book. Last, but certainly not least, we must acknowledge our indebtedness to our families who have had to suffer the absences and late hours known to all those who are foolish enough to attempt producing any publication.

PART I

GENERAL PRINCIPLES

CHAPTER 1

Consent – General

CONTENTS

A FRAMEWORK

Introduction

The legality of all medical treatment is founded on the existence of **[1.1]**
consent or some other lawful authority. The general principle is that no
form of medical treatment can be given without the consent of the patient
or, if the patient is not a competent adult, either the consent of some
other person or court with authority to give it, in the case of a child, or by
reason of the common law doctrine of necessity in the case of an
incompetent adult. The very structure of the last sentence displays the
convoluted structure of the law in this area, which is a result of its
piecemeal, largely accidental development. The most common case,
however, involves obtaining authority to treat by way of consent.

This chapter addresses those cases in which consent is or can be obtained. **[1.2]**
Although the provision of medical treatment and the consent to it may
form a legal contract, it need not do so. However, there is sufficient
similarity in the process that must be gone through: there must be a
proposal to treat or offer in contractual parlance, a communication of
that proposal or offer, understanding of what is proposed, consent to or
acceptance of it, and communication of the consent or acceptance by a
patient possessing the relevant capacity. The ingredients necessary for a
contract which will often be missing in the context of the National Health
Service will be consideration for the offer of treatment, and intention to
form legal relations in the contractual sense.

Proposal to treat

Formulation of proposal

It is axiomatic that no treatment will be undertaken unless a medical **[1.3]**
practitioner proposes to provide it. This is not the place to examine the
medical thought process that leads to a decision to offer treatment, but it
will usually be necessary for the doctor to have examined the patient,
undertaken any preliminary investigations and enquiries, including the
taking of a history, and on the basis of the material so obtained come to
a diagnosis, provisional or firm. From this he will deduce the appropriate
form of treatment to offer.

Treatment demanded by the patient

A doctor cannot be compelled to provide treatment which he does not **[1.4]**
consider to be in the patient's best interests[1]. This is so even if other
practitioners consider the treatment desirable. This sensible rule is very
necessary: it would clearly be highly undesirable for both doctor and patient
if an unwilling doctor could be forced to provide treatment he believed to
be harmful to the patient or the effectiveness of which he doubted. The rule
is consistent with the contractual rule that specific performance will not be
granted to enforce the provision of personal services. Doctors do need,
however, to be aware of the need to refer a patient for a second opinion, if
it is obvious that the patient wishes to receive treatment which is known to
be available in other responsible and competent hands. A doctor is not
entitled to restrict a patient's choice of treatment to satisfy his own
conscience, and might be found liable in an action for negligence if his

advice did not conform with a responsible and accepted medical practice or
was not sustainable on rigorous logical scrutiny[2].

1 *Re J (a minor) (child in care: medical treatment)* [1993] Fam 15.
2 The duties of a doctor as defined by the GMC include an obligation to make sure that
personal beliefs do not prejudice patient's care; see App 1.3: GMC: *Guidance on duties of
doctor.*

Irrational decisions by care providers to refuse treatment

[1.5] There is no English authority on whether a doctor can be required to
provide treatment which he refuses to give on irrational or discriminatory
grounds. Two principles would appear to clash: that against forcing
someone to give personal service[1], and the public law principle requiring
rational decisions to be made by those exercising public administrative
functions[2]. The courts have jurisdiction to compel a health authority to
provide treatment where an irrational or, in some circumstances, unfair,
decision to refuse it has been made[3]. If such a refusal arose because of an
irrational decision of the only doctor available to provide treatment, then
it is likely that the courts would act to ensure that treatment was
provided, if this was practicable.

1 *Re J (a minor) (child in care: medical treatment)* [1993] Fam 15.
2 *Associated Provincial Picture Houses Ltd v Wednesbury Corpn* [1948] 1 KB 223; *R v
North and East Devon Health Authority, ex p Coughlan* [1999] Lloyd's Rep Med 306.
3 See *ex p Coughlan* (n 2 above); *R v North West Lancashire HA, ex p A* [2000] 1 WLR 977,
CA (Health Authority had acted unlawfully in the rigid operation of a policy which
resulted in a refusal to provide gender re-assignment surgery under the National Health
Service Act 1977).

Alternative forms of treatment

[1.6] If there are alternative forms of treatment available the doctor will need
to consider which is in the best interests of the patient. Sometimes there
is little to choose in terms of outcome, in which case he will doubtless
decide to offer the treatment with which he is most familiar or is most
readily available. Whether he has to give the patient a choice may depend
on the demands of competent medical practice in the precise circumstances. It was confirmed in *Gold v Haringey Health Authority*[1] that there
was no duty to advise of alternative forms of treatment where that was in
accordance with a responsible body of opinion. However, the latest GMC
guidance states baldly that:

> 'Patients have a right to information about their condition and *the
> treatment options available to them*.'[2]

This guidance may mean that it will now be universally accepted professional practice to give advice on the alternative forms of treatment,
subject only to the qualifications mentioned in the guidance. Therefore it
might well be negligent not to offer such advice now.

1 [1988] QB 481.
2 See App 1.4: *GMC: Seeking patients' consent – the ethical considerations*, paras 4 to 6
below [emphasis added].

Risks of treatment

[1.7] A doctor owes a duty of care to inform a patient about those risks of
which any competent medical practitioner undertaking such treatment

would warn a patient[1]. Further, there will be a duty to warn of any risk which is so grave that it is obvious that the patient has the right to know of it, whatever may be the accepted medical practice[2]. However, a failure to give such a warning does not render the treatment unlawful in the sense of being an assault, so long as the patient is given a general understanding of the nature of the treatment being proposed[3]. Any action will be in negligence. It should be noted that the latest GMC guidance accepts that patients have a right to information and in effect requires doctors to give them a wide range of information, tailored to their needs and priorities[4]. A paternalistic view of what it is right for the patient to know has been decisively rejected. The standard form of consent suggested by the Department of Health requires the professional to declare that the options available have been explained[5]. The doctrine of 'informed consent' rejected by the House of Lords[6] may now have been incorporated in English law by way of accepted professional practice.

1 *Sidaway v Board of Governors of the Bethlem Royal Hospital and the Maudsley Hospital* [1985] AC 871.
2 *Sidaway v Board of Governors of the Bethlem Royal Hospital and the Maudsley Hospital* [1985] AC 871.
3 *Chatterton v Gerson* [1981] QB 432; *Freeman v Home Office (No 2)* [1984] QB 524.
4 See App 1.4: *Seeking patients' consent: the ethical considerations*, paras 4 to 6 below.
5 See App 1.1: *Patient Consent to Examination or Treatment* (DoH, 1990), below.
6 *Sidaway v Board of Governors of the Bethlem Royal Hospital and the Maudsley Hospital* [1985] AC 871.

Resources

Problems may arise where the form of treatment the doctor would like to offer is unavailable in his hospital or practice because of a lack of resources over which he has no control. Generally health authorities are at liberty to allocate resources in the best way they see fit in the fulfilment of their statutory duties[1], although this power is under constant challenge in the courts[2]. An individual doctor is unlikely to be criticised where he is not given the relevant resources, but in such circumstances he will have to consider whether the patient should be referred to a centre which has them. **[1.8]**

1 *R v Secretary of State for Social Services, ex p Hincks* (1980) 1 BMLR 93; *R v Cambridge Health Authority, ex p B* [1995] 1 WLR 898.
2 See for example, *R v North Derbyshire Health Authority, ex p Fisher* [1997] 8 Med LR 327, (1997) 38 BMLR 76, CA, Dyson J (Health Authority refusal to fund beta interferon treatment on the grounds of insufficient resources successfully challenged on ground that Health Authority policy failed to pay sufficient heed to NHS Executive circular asking Health Authorities to facilitate introduction of the drug).

Known comparative outcomes

Should a doctor put himself forward to perform treatment if there is a practitioner elsewhere who does it better or is known to have a better record of outcome? If a centre has a higher mortality or morbidity rate than others, should it cease the treatment in question? The medical profession has been struggling towards ethical answers to these difficult questions, and the matter is currently the subject of a public inquiry[1], but the following principles are suggested as forming the basis of prudent practice: **[1.9]**

- Doctors and all those responsible for the provision of health services ought to keep their results under review and apply to them accepted clinical audit systems.
- Where it is possible to compare outcomes with a national or other accepted standard, this should be done.
- Where the performance of the doctor or the centre is below a generally accepted deviation from the standard, serious consideration should be given to whether it is in the interests of patients to be offered treatment by that doctor or at that centre or whether patients should be referred elsewhere until the cause of the deviation has been identified and remedied.
- Comprehensible information about performance should be available for patients, even where the outcomes are within the accepted range.

1 The Bristol Royal Infirmary Inquiry.

Communication of the proposal

[1.10] No consent can be obtained without the nature and effect of the proposed treatment being communicated to the patient or other person giving consent. The treatment need not be described in complete detail, but sufficient must be stated to enable the person consenting to understand in broad terms what is to be done[1].

1 *Sidaway v Board of Governors of the Bethlem Royal Hospital and the Maudsley Hospital* [1985] AC 871.

[1.11] The communication may be oral or in writing: in practice it is always oral, but may be supplemented by something in writing. Where a surgical or other invasive procedure is contemplated it is usual and prudent practice for a consent form to be used. The standard NHS form is no substitute for a thorough discussion with the patient about what is proposed. Even so, care should be taken to ensure that the treatment is accurately described on the form[1]. Whether or not a form is used a note should be made in the patient's medical records of what the patient was told. It is no longer of any assistance in risk management for the doctor to enter 'consent ✔' in the notes and expect this to be accepted as proof that an adequate description of the procedure was given.

1 However, note Gage J in *Abbas v Kenney* [1996] 7 Med LR 47 who held that *on the facts* a patient had consented to a more extensive operation being performed if the need arose despite it not being referred to expressly in the consent form.

[1.12] It should be noted that the duty to communicate a proposal to provide treatment applies to all forms of treatment, not only operations and major medical treatment. A pulse should not be taken before the intention to do so has been communicated or without the patient's consent. The more radical or serious the treatment the greater the detail required.

Consent – state of mind

Intention

[1.13] For treatment to be provided lawfully to a competent adult patient, he or she must consent, ie agree to and acquiesce in the treatment being proposed. This requires an intention on the part of the patient to consent. However, it may be that an intention can be deduced from words or conduct which the reasonable observer would construe as manifesting intentional consent.

Language/hearing/literacy
It may be a statement of the obvious, but clearly the patient who is unable **[1.14]** to understand the language in which the treatment information is given or unable to hear it, or read it because of illiteracy, disability or unconsciousness cannot give a valid consent.

Comprehension
Does the requirement that the patient be given sufficient information to **[1.15]** enable him to understand the nature and effect of the proposed treatment import a requirement that he must actually understand everything he has been told? We think not. Capacity to understand is required [see below] but to require proof of actual understanding of what has been said is to create a dangerously high hurdle to overcome before necessary treatment is given[1]. So long as the patient realises that some form of treatment is proposed and that this will be as described by the doctor, and he agrees to submit to this, we consider that a sufficient intent to consent has been established. Many patients will be unable to or will choose not to understand the full technical detail of what is being proposed.

1 In the context of information to be given by police officers on arrest the Divisional Court in *Wheatley v Lodge* [1971] 1 WLR 29, DC determined that what is required is not that the person being arrested actually comprehends what is being said but merely that the officer has acted reasonably on the basis of the information he knew about the person being arrested. (The officer – reasonably – had failed to realise that he was deaf).

Communication of consent
A consent which is not communicated is no consent at all. It can be **[1.16]** manifested to the person seeking consent in three ways.

Written consent
In practice consent for all elective invasive treatment of any significance **[1.17]** is obtained in writing signed by the patient[1]. This is not a legal requirement, but is clearly a matter of prudence. The discipline of being required to present a form to the patient, and to explain the need for it, provides some assurance that the patient has been provided with details of what is proposed and has actually consented to it. However, while it is a prudent step to take, the existence of such a form is no guarantee that consent has in fact been obtained. The patient may have been asked to sign a form without reading it, or without an adequate or any explanation being given. Therefore, such a form has evidential value but is not conclusive proof of a proper consent procedure.

1 See NHS consent form in App 1.1: *Patient Consent to Examination or Treatment* (DoH 1990).

Oral consent
Most routine medical treatment is given by virtue of consent which has **[1.18]** been obtained informally and orally. There is nothing objectionable in law about this and everything to commend it in practice and common

sense in relation to treatment and care which carries minimal risks or is repetitive and routine.

Conduct

[1.19] Consent can often be inferred from the patient's conduct. An arm proffered to a nurse brandishing a syringe is sufficient consent – even if the patient insists on looking the other way. Before conduct – whether active or acquiescent – can be taken to be consent, however, it must be shown that by words or conduct the practitioner has informed the patient of the nature and effect of what he wishes to do, and that the conduct is an intentional response to that information.

B INFORMATION ABOUT RISKS

No doctrine of informed consent

[1.20] No information about the risks of the proposed treatment is required for a legally valid consent to be obtained. A failure to give any or any adequate information about the possible adverse effects of treatment or about its likelihood of success or failure does not render the practitioner liable to an allegation of assault, criminal or civil, even where competent professional practice requires such information to be given[1]. The common law purpose of the doctrine of consent is to provide a framework for justifying necessary medical treatment rather than to enforce a requirement that proper information be given to the patient, which is the realm of the duty of care and the cause of action of negligence.

1 *Chatterton v Gerson* [1981] QB 432.

Duty of care

[1.21] The obligation to provide proper information about risks is protected by the law of negligence. The doctor owes a duty to his patient to provide such information about the risks of the proposed treatment as would be provided by any competent and responsible practitioner in the circumstances[1]. There is no distinction between advice given in relation to therapeutic and non-therapeutic procedures[2]. There are circumstances in which the risk is so obviously important that any prudent doctor would warn of it: then the courts are entitled to hold that there was a duty to do so, even if the medical practice was not to do so[3]. This application of the *Bolam* test has been the subject of much criticism, but has survived to date. In other jurisdictions[4], however, the duty is to warn of such risks as it would be reasonable to expect of a doctor in the circumstances and which a patient would reasonably expect to receive. This imports an element of objectivity into the duty and permits the court to reject accepted medical practice where this offends against its notions of reasonableness.

As has been noted briefly above, the General Medical Council has now issued very detailed advice on consent[5], which at least provides strong encouragement, and in many cases may require, a standards of disclosure to patients which would amount to compliance with the doctrine of informed consent as understood in other jurisdictions.

It is suggested that in an age of increasing demands for patient autonomy, the prudent practitioner or health authority will ensure that there is a constant review of the information that is given to patients in respect of common procedures, and perhaps the less common but complex ones, and that steps are taken to ensure that patients are informed of all significant risks. It would also be prudent for any specific risks that are mentioned to be recorded in the patient's medical records. This is not merely a legal defence precaution, but in a busy hospital with different doctors attending patients, will help to avoid needless repetition of alarming facts to the patient. It also recognises the likelihood that the courts will give increasing emphasis to an objective standard of reasonableness in preference to a professionally created standard.

1 *Sidaway v Board of Governors of the Bethlem Royal Hospital and the Maudsley Hospital* [1985] AC 871.
2 Such as sterilisations: *Gold v Haringey Health Authority* [1988] QB 481.
3 *Sidaway v Board of Governors of the Bethlem Royal Hospital and the Maudsley Hospital* [1985] AC 871.
4 *Rogers v Whitaker* (1992) 109 ALR 625, (1993) 4 Med LR 79 (Australia); *Canterbury v Spense* 464 F 2d 772 (1972) (USA); *Reibl v Hughes* (1980) 114 DLR (3d) 1 (Canada).
5 See App 1.4: *Seeking patients' consent: the ethical considerations* (GMC, 1999), paras 4 to 6 below.

Duty to answer questions

There is a very clear duty on the part of those seeking a patient's consent **[1.22]** to answer truthfully and accurately any questions asked[1]. This is so even where it is feared that the answers may dissuade the patient from treatment it thought to be in his best interests, or will give rise to unhelpful anxiety. Lord Bridge in *Sidaway* stated:

> ' ... when questioned specifically by a patient ... about risks involved in a particular treatment proposed, the doctor's duty must, in my opinion, be to answer both truthfully and as fully as the questioner requires.'[2]

The amount of information which must be provided by a practitioner in response to a specific question was considered obiter at first instance by Sir Maurice Drake[3] who agreed with the contention in *Clerk and Lindsell*[4] that:

> ' ... in answering express queries about treatment, practitioners are not obliged to give the patient **all** the information in their possession. The answers given must ... be judged in the context of good professional practice rather than what "reasonably prudent patient" might want to know.'

The duty to provide information and should be assessed in the context of 'what the particular patient wanted to know'[5].

1 See *Sidaway v Board of Governors of the Bethlem Royal Hospital and the Maudsley Hospital* [1985] AC 871 per Lord Diplock at 895D and per Lord Bridge at 898.
2 *Sidaway v Board of Governors of the Bethlem Royal Hospital and the Maudsley Hospital* [1985] AC 871 at 898.
3 *Poynter v Hillingdon Health Authority* (1997) 37 BMLR 192 (information to provided to parents concerning the risk of brain damage following heart transplant surgery in a 15 month-old baby).
4 *Clerk and Lindsell on Torts* (17th ed), p 433.

5 On the particular facts, the judge concluded that it was arguable that the surgeons would have been entitled to withhold information of a risk of permanent brain damage which was smaller than 1% even if they had been asked a direct question about such a risk. However, we suggest that the safer practice is to provide information even of small risks if asked a direct question concerning a particular adverse outcome.

Information about alternative forms of treatment

[1.23] The courts in general will be reluctant to impose liability on doctors who fail to identify alternative procedures. However, the courts may well impose a duty to inform of alternative procedures in circumstances where the risks of the alternative procedure are substantially lower than the procedure in fact proposed or where the procedure proposed has a particularly severe complication which would be avoided using the alternative procedure. In those circumstances, even if a body of medical opinion would support not informing the patient about the alternative, the case could be considered as falling into the exception set out in *Sidaway* as being so grave a risk that the patient is entitled to know of it regardless of 'accepted' medical practice. Alternatively the courts may be prepared to carve out a second *Bolam* exception based on the need to inform patients of alternative procedures in the circumstances outlined above[1]. In any event medical practice, as reflected by the advice of the General Medical Council, seems to be in favour of the available alternatives being offered to patients.

1 In *Haughian v Paine* [1987] 4 WWR 97 the Saskatchewan Court of Appeal (albeit applying the doctrine of informed consent) held that a surgeon should advise the patient of the consequences of leaving an illness untreated and of alternative means of treatment and their risks. As this was not done the patient did not give informed consent to his surgery.

C VITIATING FACTORS

[1.24] A consent is not valid if it is obtained:

- by fraud;
- by duress;
- from a person who lacks capacity.

A doctor should satisfy himself that none of these factors apply[1].

1 This requirement was set out in *Re T (adult: refusal of treatment)* [1993] Fam 95 in relation to refusals, but the same principle must apply to consents.

Fraud

[1.25] Consent obtained by some fundamental deception such as to the nature of the act or the identity of the person who is to provide the treatment is no consent at all, and provides no justification for treatment which would otherwise be an assault[1]. The test is whether the deception is of a nature which means that the decision is not really that of the patient at all[2]. Therefore any consent given by a patient who in doing so relies on a false representation on these matters made by the person seeking consent is invalid. The deception must be material, ie must be one which the patient might reasonably be expected to rely on or which he makes known he is in fact relying on. It must also relate to the nature of the treatment or the identity of the person to provide it. Examples might be:

- consent obtained by or for a person pretending to be a doctor;
- a materially inaccurate account of the surgeons outcome figures;
- a false description of the procedure, eg stating that the patient is to have her appendix removed, when the intention is to perform a hysterectomy;
- consent obtained for an ulterior motive, such as an indecent assault, or to bolster research results.

However, surprisingly a deception about the qualifications of the practitioner has been held by the Court of Appeal (Criminal Division) in *R v Richardson*[3] not to vitiate consent:

- The appellant was a registered dental practitioner until 30 August 1996, but was suspended from practice by the General Dental Council. Whilst still suspended, she carried out dentistry on a number of patients in September 1996.
- The Court of Appeal held that the deception concerning her status as a registered practitioner was not a deception as to the 'identity' of the person who is to provide treatment. Therefore it did not vitiate consent in criminal law.

1 In *Chatterton v Gerson* [1981] QB 432, Bristow J said that to prove trespass to the person it had to be shown that the consent was 'unreal'.
2 See Lord Donaldson in *Re T (adult: refusal of treatment)* [1993] Fam 95 at 113.
3 [1999] QB 444; [1998] 3 WLR 1292.

Duress and undue influence

Consent cannot be validly obtained from a person not acting under their own free will, ie where the will of the patient is overborne by circumstances over which he has no control[1]. Thus if the patient is detained against his will and feels forced to consent to treatment in order to escape detention the consent will not be recognised. Similarly, if undue influence is brought to bear by a third party. Doctors need to be aware of social and other factors in the patient's background which may make him liable to be forced by others to submit to or refuse treatment. This may be a far from easy task. The matters to be considered were set by Lord Donaldson of Lymington MR[2]: **[1.26]**

> 'A special problem may arise if at the time the decision is made the patient has been subjected to the influence of some third party. This is by no means to say that the patient is not entitled to receive and indeed invite advice and assistance from others in reaching a decision, particularly from members of the family. But the doctors have to consider whether the decision is really that of the patient. It is wholly acceptable that the patient should have been persuaded by others of the merits of such a decision and have decided accordingly. It matters not how strong the persuasion was, so long as it did not overbear the independence of the patient's decision. The real question in each such case is "Does the patient really mean what he says or is he merely saying it for a quiet life, to satisfy someone else or because the advice and persuasion to which he has been subjected is such that he can no longer think and decide for himself?" In other words "Is it a decision expressed in form only, not in reality?"'

When considering the effect of outside influences, two aspects can be of crucial importance. First, the strength of the will of the patient. One who is very tired, in pain or depressed will be much less able to resist having his will overborne than one who is rested, free from pain and cheerful. Second, the relationship of the "persuader" to the patient may be of crucial importance. The influence of parents on their children or of one spouse on the other can be, but is by no means necessarily, much stronger than would be the case in other relationships. Persuasion based upon religious belief can also be much more compelling and the fact that arguments based upon religious beliefs are being deployed by someone in a very close relationship with the patient will give them added force and should alert the doctors to the possibility – no more – that the patient's capacity or will to decide has been overborne. In other words the patient may not mean what he says.'

1 *Re T (adult: refusal of treatment)* [1993] Fam 95.
2 *Re T (adult: refusal of treatment)* [1993] Fam 95 at 113.

Capacity

[1.27]   The person consenting must have the relevant mental capacity to do so. Capacity consists of the ability to[1]:

- receive and retain treatment information;
- to believe it;
- to weigh the information in order to reach a decision;
- to communicate his decision.

A patient lacking any of these abilities will lack capacity to consent to treatment. The application of this broad principle is considered in detail below by separate reference to adults and children. Consent given by a person not possessing the relevant capacity has no effect and cannot be used to justify the provision of treatment.

It is not clear whether a doctor who mistakenly, but in the circumstances reasonably, believes that the patient has capacity commits an assault if he provides treatment relying that belief. Staughton LJ doubted that such a belief would be a defence in the case of a purported refusal[2]:

'Some will say that, when there is doubt whether an apparent refusal of consent is valid in circumstances of urgent necessity, the decision of a doctor acting in good faith ought to be conclusive. In this case there was an application at the judge's lodgings at 11 o'clock at night, a procedure which may not always be available. However, I cannot find authority that the decision of a doctor as to the existence or refusal of consent is sufficient protection, if the law subsequently decides otherwise. So the medical profession, in the future as in the past, must bear the responsibility unless it is possible to obtain a decision from the courts.'

To hold a doctor liable in such circumstances may seem harsh in the case of a refusal of consent; it would be even more unjust in the case of a mistaken reliance on a purported consent. The answer in criminal law would appear to be that a person should be judged on his honest, albeit mistaken, view of the facts[3]. Further, an accusation of assault in such circumstances could usually be answered by showing that the treatment given was in the patient's best interests[4] in any event.

1 *Re C (adult: refusal of medical treatment)* [1994] 1 WLR 290; *Re T (adult: refusal of treatment)* [1993] Fam 95.
2 *Re T (adult: refusal of treatment)* [1993] Fam 95 at 122.
3 *R v Williams (Gladstone)* [1987] 3 All ER 411; *Albert v Lavin* [1982] AC 546.
4 For the principles justifying treatment of incompetent patients, see below.

D SCOPE OF AUTHORITY

Treatment may be carried out as authorised by the consent. This justifies **[1.28]** the provision only of the treatment actually described in the consent. Unless the consent expressly or impliedly allows for it, no variation is authorised.

This is not to say that no different treatment may be carried out even though no consent has been given for it:

- If it emerges that the proposed treatment is not possible, eg where the cancerous tumour proves to be inoperable, the doctor may stop the procedure which has been authorised and undertake conservative treatment consequent on his inability to pursue the procedure originally contemplated.
- If an emergency arises while the patient is unconscious during an authorised procedure, and it is necessary to act immediately to save life or prevent a deterioration in health, the doctor may provide the treatment necessary to this end. What he may not do is to extend the scope of what has been authorised merely because he finds an unexpected condition which he considers it to be in the patient's interests to deal with.

Many consent forms contain an expression designed to permit a surgeon to perform such treatment other than that specified which is necessary to treat the patient's condition[1]. Only very cautious reliance should be placed on such a provision. It cannot be a justification for embarking on treatment of a type not discussed with the patient, and only remotely connected with what was authorised. It should be regarded as authorisation for no more than treatment necessarily ancillary to that which has been authorised.

1 See App 1.1: *Patient Consent to Examination or Treatment* (DoH, 1990), below.

E DURATION OF AUTHORITY

Consent is inevitably intended to cover some future event: retrospective **[1.29]** consent can have no legal effect[1]. The consent may be for an injection to be offered almost immediately, or it may be for an operation to be performed in several weeks' time. In either case the consent may be presumed to be intended to last until the procedure is performed, unless the patient has specified some time limit or condition under which the consent will be revoked. Where this is done, and it will be an unusual occurrence, the doctor taking the consent must be careful to record what is required.

A consent will not survive a material change of circumstance. The following are examples where the consent might cease to be valid:

- Where the consent specifies a particular doctor to perform the procedure and he is unavailable.
- Where new information, either generally about the procedure, or specifically about the patient, comes to light which materially alters the risks of the procedure of which the patient has or ought to have been told[2].
- Where the clinical condition of the patient changes or the diagnosis changes so that in the opinion of the responsible doctor the procedure consented to is no longer necessary in the patient's interests.

1 It may have an evidential effect in relation to a causation issue by showing that the patient would have consented if asked.
2 The effect on the legal validity of the consent will depend on whether the information on the risks is of a character that ignorance of it results in the consent not being real: see above.

[1.30] Consent will survive a patients' loss of capacity. Indeed this is applied in all surgical procedures under general anaesthetic: the consent to the operation remains valid although the patient has been rendered unconscious by the anaesthetic. A difficulty may arise if following a loss of capacity circumstances change to an extent where normally a further consent would be required. The rule is that the doctor may only undertake different treatment if it is necessary as a matter of urgency and it is not possible to wait until the patient has recovered capacity. If the patient is unlikely to recover capacity at all, then the doctor may act immediately in the patient's best interests, subject to the principles governing the treatment of incapacitated patients[1].

1 See Chap 3, *Deciding for Others* below.

F WITHDRAWAL OF AUTHORITY

[1.31] A patient possessing the appropriate mental capacity may withdraw a consent at any time before the treatment so authorised has been given. The consent obviously ceases to have effect from that moment.

If consent is withdrawn after treatment has started, the doctor must stop, but cannot be required to leave the patient in an unacceptable state. For example, he must be enabled to sew up the surgical wound if he has started an operation: a patient cannot insist on a doctor leaving him with a serious injury. Consent is no defence to the infliction of serious injury for no good purpose[1].

In order for a withdrawal of consent to be effective it must be communicated to those providing the treatment. Carers and others cannot be held liable for providing treatment in innocent ignorance of the withdrawal of consent.

If the patient has communicated a withdrawal of consent to a person other than the actual treatment provider, that person may be under a duty to relay that change to those actually providing treatment. If he fails to do so he may be responsible and liable for the unauthorised continuation of treatment. For obvious reasons such circumstances could arise only rarely as usually the patient will be in a position to communicate directly with those actually treating him. There could, however, be cases where the patient is able to communicate a withdrawal of consent to some particular aspect of an operation to a member of the hospital staff before being anaesthetised, and this is not passed on to the surgeon. In such a case the surgeon acting in good faith on the previous consent would not be liable to the patient for the unwanted procedure, but the person to whom the withdrawal of consent had been given – and his or her employer – would be liable.

1 *R v Brown* [1994] 1 AC 212.

CHAPTER 2

Consent – Adults

CONTENTS

A ADULT

[2.1] An adult is a person aged 18 years or more. Certain aspects of the law of consent apply only to adults and these are dealt with below.

B CAPACITY

Definition of capacity and its assessment

[2.2] The person consenting must have the relevant mental capacity to do so. Capacity consists of the ability:

- to receive and retain treatment information;
- to believe it;
- to weigh the information in order to reach a decision[1]; and
- to communicate his decision.

A patient lacking any of these abilities will lack capacity to consent to treatment.

   The level of ability required of an adult will vary according to the gravity of the decision to be taken[2]. This rather unclear principle enables an attending doctor to make a subjective assessment of the level of ability present. This must not be confused with the level of understanding actually achieved. Many patients give valid consent without actually understanding precisely what the doctor has told them, however carefully and clearly he may have done so.

The patient is not obliged to use those abilities to arrive at a rational decision: indeed a patient is entitled to refuse treatment, and therefore to consent to it for any reason, good or bad, rational or irrational. In *Re MB (an adult: medical treatment)* the width of this freedom was emphasised[3]:

> 'Irrationality is here used to connote a decision which is so outrageous in its defiance of logic or of accepted moral standards that no sensible person who had applied his mind to the question to be decided could have arrived at it. As Kennedy and Grubb (*Medical Law* (2nd ed, 1994)) point out, it might be otherwise if a decision is based on a misperception of reality eg where the blood is poisoned because it is red.'

This is just as well, as many patients doubtless consent to necessary and beneficial treatment on entirely illogical or unjustified grounds.

1 *Re C (adult: refusal of medical treatment)* [1994] 1 WLR 290; *Re T (adult: refusal of treatment)* [1993] Fam 95.
2 *Re T (adult: refusal of treatment)* [1993] Fam 95 at 113.
3 *Re MB (an adult: medical treatment)* [1997] 2 FCR 541, [1997] 2 FLR 426, [1997] 8 Med LR 217.

Temporary incapacity – the *Re MB* gloss

Capacity may be lost temporarily: the obvious example is temporary **[2.3]** unconsciousness. Less obviously extreme panic or pain can result in a loss of capacity, as can a phobia precipitated by a specific stimulus. Such phenomena do not of themselves amount to incapacity, but they may amount to such a serious impairment or disturbance of mental functioning as to render a patient incapable of making a decision[1].

It is suggested that doctors need to exercise considerable caution before satisfying themselves that temporary phenomena of this type have given rise to a loss of capacity. The Court of Appeal emphasised that regard had to be paid to the gravity or otherwise of the decision in question. Therefore they cannot be used as an excuse for running patients' lives without their consent. Furthermore, the circumstances which are likely to provoke extreme pain, panic or even a phobia are usually predictable, and the wishes of the patient in such an eventuality can and should be established at a time when calm and rational discussion is possible. A doctor who knows that a patient has a needle phobia, but fails to discuss with the patient in advance the need to use a needle, and thus fails to ascertain what his wishes might be is probably failing in his duty to advise the patient of the treatment required and to obtain his consent. That may expose the doctor to liability in negligence if not assault.

It is also suggested that the concept of temporary incapacity allows for a degree of subjective judgment in emergencies which could undermine the autonomy of patients very substantially. It is rare for patients to present with permanent incapacities of mind. It must be much more frequent for them to appear in pain or panic. It would doubtless surprise many women in labour to be told that they were in danger of being deprived of their freedom to make decisions about the management of that labour by reason of the pain they were suffering. It might be argued that it is in just such circumstances that a patient most values the right to decide what should be done to her or his body. It is also in just such circumstances that the pressure is greatest on the attending doctor – or midwife – to 'do something' and thus to regard any hesitation on the part of the patient as evidence of an inability to make a decision rather than of reluctance on the patient's part to allow something abhorrent to be done to her. Therefore it is suggested that over reliance on temporary incapacity is dangerous and should be avoided if at all possible by intelligent anticipation of the circumstances in which it might arise.

1 *Re MB (an adult: medical treatment)* [1997] 2 FLR 426, [1997] 2 FCR 541, [1997] 8 Med LR 217.

Presumption of capacity

[2.4] All adults are presumed to possess the capacity to consent to medical treatment unless the contrary is shown. This principle only becomes relevant in practice where a reported consent is being considered by a doctor who has to treat the patient after he has become unconscious or incapacitated, or in a retrospective analysis of the legality of treatment in a particular case. Where in such circumstances there is no evidence about a patient's capacity, the presumption will apply.

The existence of the presumption is of little help to the doctor who is seeking a patient's consent. He must assess the patient in front of him. If there is anything in the patient's presentation which gives rise to a question of whether he possesses the relevant capacity, then he must investigate it. A doctor cannot ignore the possibility of incapacity and expect to be able to rely on the patient's consent if it transpires that there was no capacity.

The absolute nature of an adult's consent

[2.5] The consent of an adult patient is always enough to justify a willing doctor providing lawful treatment. It cannot be challenged by anyone else, whatever legal or moral claim to interest in the outcome they may have. Thus it is clearly established that the father of a fetus has no right to seek to prevent the mother consenting to the termination of the pregnancy[1]. The court cannot override an adult's consent, if the proposed treatment would otherwise be lawful.

1 *Paton v British Pregnancy Advisory Service Trustees* [1979] QB 276; *C v S* [1988] QB 135.

Treatment must be lawful

[2.6] The mere demand by a patient for a particular treatment which the doctor is willing to give does not automatically render it lawful. Treatment will be considered unlawful if it is deemed so by statute; for example, an abortion not authorised by the Abortion Act 1967. Further, treatment will be unlawful at common law if it is against public policy[1]. This is more difficult to define, but it may be thought that the amputation of a limb purely for some claimed psychological need would offend against public policy. As a matter of general principle any form of physical mutilation is unlawful unless it is for good reason. Obviously bona fide medical treatment provides such a reason. However, consensual sado-masochistic practices leading to serious injury do not[2]. While this is a problem unlikely to be encountered in routine medical practice, there may be questions over cosmetic treatment intended to disfigure the patient in some way considered to be unacceptable in the public interest. It is not easy to determine which activities fall on which side of the line, but consensual tattooing, even if undertaken by unqualified individuals appears to be lawful[3]. This principle will have to be kept in mind when consideration is given to new and ethically controversial treatments such as advanced techniques for reproduction and cloning, etc.

1 See by way of analogy *R v Brown* [1994] 1 AC 212.
2 *R v Brown* [1994] 1 AC 212, [1993] 2 WLR 556, [1993] 2 All ER 75, HL.
3 *R v Brown* (above); *R v Wilson* [1997] QB 47, [1996] 3 WLR 125, [1996] 2 Cr App Rep 241, CA (Crim Div) (accused branded his wife's buttocks with his own initials at her instigation and with her consent: held that the action taken by the accused could be seen as similar to tattooing, which did not attract a criminal sanction).

C REFUSAL

It is the corollary of the right to authorise treatment that there is a right **[2.7]** to refuse it. To the extent that the right to refuse treatment is denied, so is the autonomy of the individual[1].

A refusal may be for any reason, good or bad, or for no reason at all. The fact that the refusal is considered by others to be irrational or morally repugnant in no way invalidates it or avoids the need to respect it[2].

The only qualification to the right to refuse treatment is that a refusal cannot be used as a backdoor method of insisting on treatment which the doctor is unwilling to provide. No doctor, and no health authority, can be required to provide a patient with treatment which is not clinically indicated and is not considered by them to be in the patient's interests[3]. Thus, a patient who is advised to have a treatment consisting of two inseparable elements cannot by consenting to only one of them require the doctor to provide it unless he is willing to do so.

This does not excuse the treating doctor from dealing with the patient as he finds him. If he starts a treatment with the patient's consent, and the consent is subsequently withdrawn, the treatment cannot proceed, and the doctor must provide whatever proper treatment the patient allows him to undertake in order to ameliorate the position. Thus a patient who refuses a blood transfusion which is needed for an operation to proceed cannot be forced to have the operation or the transfusion, and conservative treatment must be resorted to, even though, in the opinion of the surgeon, surgery is the best treatment for the patient.

1 *S v S; W v Official Solicitor (or W)* [1972] AC 24 at 43 per Lord Reid, HL: 'The real reason is that English law goes to great lengths to protect a person of full age and capacity from interference with his personal liberty. We have too often seen freedom disappear in other countries not only by coups d'etat but by gradual erosion: and often it is the first step that counts. So it would be unwise to make even minor concessions.'
2 *St George's Healthcare NHS Trust v S* [1999] Fam 26, CA.
3 *Re J (a minor) (child in care: medical treatment)* [1993] Fam 15.

D CHANGE OF MIND

[2.8] An adult with full capacity is entitled to withdraw a consent already given at any time before the treatment concerned has been provided. Even if the treatment has started, and the patient retains capacity he may demand that it be stopped. While, as stated above, the doctor cannot be required to treat the patient so as to leave him in an unacceptable state, it is doubtful whether he can insist upon finishing a procedure he has started, if a patient still possessing full capacity requires him to stop. There may be a difference between the doctor being required to *do* something which will have an unacceptable result, and being required to *stop* doing something which will avoid it. In practice, of course, this is unlikely to arise, and a doctor reasonably believing that a patient is likely to act in this way if provided with treatment is justified in refusing to do so.

   For a withdrawal of consent to have effect it is necessary for it to be communicated to the person providing treatment. A surgeon who continues to operate in ignorance of a withdrawal communicated to a junior doctor on the ward is unlikely to attract personal liability, although the junior doctor, and his or her employer most certainly will for a breach of the duty of care to the patient[1].

1 *Re J (a minor) (child in care: medical treatment)* [1993] Fam 15.

E ADVANCE DIRECTIVES

General principle

[2.9] Consent is often given in advance of the proposed treatment. In the case of surgery under general anesthetic it has to be. Equally it is possible for a patient to express a present intention to refuse treatment in specified circumstances. There is now no doubt that if certain conditions are fulfilled that doctors and others are bound in law to comply with such statements. In other words, to proceed with treatment prohibited by a valid advance directive is unlawful and renders those providing the treatment liable to a charge or claim for assault and battery.

Requirements

[2.10] The general conditions that must be fulfilled are as follows:

- The patient must have the capacity to refuse medical treatment.
- There must have been no vitiating influence such as duress, undue influence or fraud.
- The scope and effect of the refusal must have been intended to cover the circumstances actually prevailing at the time when the need for treatment arises. For example, a refusal of blood transfusions in the belief that alternative suitable forms of treatment are available will be negated if, in the particular circumstances, there is no such alternative.
- The patient must have been in possession of knowledge of the nature and effect of the decision being taken. Therefore an advance refusal made in ignorance that the effect of withholding the treatment objected to will be certain death will not bind the doctors unless there is

clear evidence that the patient was aware of this consequence, or was at least clearly willing to take that risk.

Form

An advance statement may be oral or in writing. There is no legal   **[2.11]** requirement as to form so long as the requirements referred to above are met. It is obviously prudent for any patient desiring to ensure that his wishes are respected to record his intentions in writing and to give a copy of the document to any doctor likely to be treating him in the future, and also to his general practitioner. Any doctor receiving such a document should ensure that a copy is lodged with the patient's records, and that all doctors who may be treating the patient are informed.

While any form of words will suffice if it makes the intentions of the patient clear, many patients will want to be offered some form on which they can indicate their choices. a form of directive is illustrated in Appendix 2.1: Draft *Advanced Directive* below.

Informed refusal?

Where consent is being obtained for treatment the doctor may be under   **[2.12]** a duty to warn the patient of the risks involved. Failure to do so may render the doctor liable in negligence, but does not invalidate the consent, unless the doctor deceives the patient in a way which results in his true will not being expressed. It is unclear whether the same principle applies to advance refusals. A patient may express an advance refusal to specific treatment under mistaken beliefs as to the risks and benefits of the treatment, either because he has not asked any qualified person for advice, or because erroneous advice has been given. For example, an advance directive may be signed because of a false rumour relayed by a friend that a particular form of treatment was very dangerous, without having discussed the matter with a person qualified to know. A person with strong religious beliefs may hold views about the effects of certain types of treatment quite at odds with the opinions of the medical profession. There is no direct authority on the point. It is arguable that an intention to refuse treatment expressed under a mistaken belief as to the facts is invalid because it is not a statement intended to govern the actual factual situation at the time when the perceived need for treatment arises. However, to override an advance refusal on this ground would be to deny the individual's right to make decisions for himself, on whatever information he chooses to base them. If, therefore, the doctor wishes to ignore an advance directive because he is aware that the statement was made under a belief as to the risks and benefits of the treatment, which he considers to have been mistaken, he may be exposing himself to criticism. In view of the uncertainty it would be prudent to seek a court declaration in such a case before proceeding. The court in some such cases might find it easy to be persuaded that the advance refusal did not cover the factual situation facing the doctor.

Knowledge

In order for an advance directive to be effective in practice the doctor   **[2.13]** confronted with the incapacitated patient must obviously be aware of its existence. It has been suggested above that patients wishing to make such statements should ensure they are in writing and disseminated to all those likely to need to know about them. What are doctors meant to do when presented with a patient and they do not know if a directive has been made? It is suggested that as a matter of practice, if not law, any doctor proposing to treat an incapacitated patient should make reasonable enquiries into whether there is such a statement. What is reasonable will depend on the nature of the patient's condition and the proposed treatment. It is more easily anticipated that some patients will be reluctant to accept treatment for some conditions, eg radical surgery to palliate an inevitably fatal cancer, than for others. Greater efforts to establish whether the patient has left any statement might be required in such a case than in a case of more routine care.

It might be thought that a doctor would be able to raise as defence to any charge of assault the assertion that he acted in good faith in ignorance of an advance refusal of treatment. Doubtless this should be the law but at least one Lord Justice has doubted that this is the position in a passage cited above[1].

If ignorance may be no defence then it must be incumbent on doctors and health managers to have in place systems which minimise the chance of an advance statement being missed. It is sometimes argued that the risks involved in treating in ignorance of an advance directive are not as great as providing treatment to an ill person because damages for the latter could never be more than nominal. This is not so. First, to treat in such circumstance could lead to criminal charges. Secondly, as the act is unlawful damages are at large and could arguably be assessed on the basis that the injury was the invasive treatment itself[2]. Further, where the treatment gave rise to complications, even non-negligent ones, there would undoubtedly be a right to compensatory damages.

1 See Staughton J in *Re T (adult: refusal of treatment)* [1993] Fam 95 at 122.
2 In *Malette v Shulman* [1991] 2 Med LR 162, a Jehovah's Witness was in an accident. She had a card requesting no blood transfusions which was shown to the treating doctor. Nonetheless he administered blood transfusions to the patient. The transfusion probably saved her life. She made a good recovery from her injuries. The Ontario Court of Appeal affirmed the first instance judge's determination that the doctor's actions constituted an assault and that the award made of $20,000 was appropriate.

Duration

[2.14]   In theory an advance directive is of indefinite duration. In practice its life will be limited by the requirement that it is intended to cover the circumstances as they are at the time treatment is being considered. Many such statements are intended to cover specific illnesses and will expire if the patient either fails to develop the feared condition or recovers from it unexpectedly. The emergence of new forms of treatment may also invalidate the directive. Accordingly, patients who make directives should be advised of the need to review them on a regular basis, preferably in conjunction with their general practitioner or other appropriate medical adviser.

Records

[2.15]   As recently made clear by the Court of Appeal[1], for their own protection health authorities and doctors should seek unequivocal assurances in writing that a refusal represents an informed and settled decision and that the patient understands the nature of the proposed treatment, the reasons for it being recommended, the risks, and likely prognosis involved in the decision to refuse it. Where the patient is not prepared to provide such a written assurance, a careful record must be made of the advice given to the patient about the need for treatment and the risks of refusing it, together with the patient's reasons for refusal.

1 *St George's NHS Healthcare Trust v S* [1999] Fam 26, CA.

CHAPTER 3

Deciding for Others

CONTENTS

A FOR ADULTS WITH CAPACITY

General rule

There is a frequently held misconception that the competent patient's **[3.1]** next of kin has some right to be consulted or even to decide on treatment. This is not so. No-one other than the patient can make a decision about his treatment so long as he is an adult and has the relevant capacity. Whether others are consulted at all will be governed by the duty of confidentiality owed to the patient and the consequent need to obtain the patient's permission to do so.

Obstetric treatment in the interests of a viable foetus no exception

It is now authoritatively established that the competent adult patient's **[3.2]** right to personal freedom from physical invasion extends to cases where the exercise of that freedom may prejudice the well-being of a viable foetus[1]. For a full treatment of this subject see Chapter 6, para **[6.2]**ff below.

1 See *Re MB (an adult: medical treatment)* [1997] 2 FLR 426, [1997] 2 FCR 541, [1997] 8 Med LR 217; and *St George's Healthcare NHS Trust v S* [1998] 3 WLR 936.

B DECIDING FOR ADULTS WITHOUT CAPACITY

General rule

Where a patient lacks the capacity to make a decision for himself, no **[3.3]** other person has any power in law to consent or refuse treatment on his behalf. In particular the next of kin or other close family members have no such power, although as a matter of good practice they are frequently consulted about what is best for the patient. Further, the courts have no power to consent to treatment in respect of an adult[1], in the sense of rendering lawful that which would be unlawful without consent.

1 Cf the court's powers in relation to children.

Necessity in the patient's best interests

[3.4] The absence of a power to obtain a consent to treatment on behalf of an incapacitated patient does not mean that the doctor is unable to help him. Indeed, he remains under a duty of care to his patient. The law requires him to provide such treatment and care as are in the patient's best interests. This principle is derived from the legal doctrine of necessity and translates into the medical context by requiring the doctor to provide such treatment as he considers to be in the patient's best interests and necessary in relation to the preservation or improvement of his health[1].

1 *Re F (mental patient: sterilisation)* [1990] 2 AC 1.

Temporary incapacity

[3.5] Where the patient is permanently incapacitated then the doctor may provide any treatment he considers necessary in the patient's best interests: there would be no point in delay. Where, however, the incapacity is or may be temporary, the doctor must decide whether the treatment is necessary to prevent a deterioration in health or to effect an improvement in it before the patient is likely to recover the capacity to make his own decision. He may provide only the treatment or care which is necessary to be undertaken before the likely recovery of capacity.

Scope of power to treat

[3.6] This principle is sufficient justification for all forms of treatment and care required for an incapacitated adult patient. Thus a decision as to the location in which a mentally incompetent stroke victim should be cared for is to be decided by those responsible for his care by reference to his best interests[1] in the same way as a decision to perform surgery. A patient lacking the capacity to consent to treatment who has been admitted informally to a mental hospital under s 131 of the Mental Health Act 1983 may be provided wi ∴ such treatment for their condition as is in their best interests. This may include the detention of the patient in hospital where this is justified by necessity in his best interests, in circumstances where, without that justification, the detention would amount to unlawful imprisonment.[2]

1 *Re S (hospital patient: court's jurisdiction)* [1996] Fam 1, [1995] 3 WLR 78, [1995] 3 All ER 290.
1 *R v Bournewood Community and Mental Health NHS Trust, ex p L* [1999] 1 AC 458.

Determination of best interests

[3.7] In general the doctor is obliged to assess the patient's best interests in accordance with a competent and responsible standard of medical practice, ie in the same way as he performs all other parts of his duty to his patient. If he proceeds to treat the patient in accordance with his own assessment, he may be judged at a later date in accordance with that standard[1]. However, there will be some cases where precedent, medical practice or general prudence require him to seek a declaration of the court[2]. It was arguable on the basis of House of Lords authority that the court is meant to do no more than satisfy itself that the doctors have assessed the patient's interests in accordance with the standards of the medical profession, as opposed to imposing its own view of the case[3]. The difficulty with that approach was that it did nothing to resolve a disagreement between two conflicting responsible views, competently formed. Both points of view will be found to be lawful, and no decision will have been taken for the patient unable to decide for himself or herself[4].

The Court of Appeal in *Re SL*[5] has resolved this problem. In cases where a declaration is sought the court should adopt a two-stage approach. First, it should consider whether the treatment proposed is *Bolam* reasonable, namely would a responsible body of medical practitioners accept this treatment as being appropriate for this patient. Second, the court should determine whether in fact the treatment is in the patient's best interests. The President stated:

> 'In these difficult cases where the medical profession seeks a declaration as to lawfulness of the proposed treatment, the judge, not the doctor, has the duty to decide whether such treatment is in the best interests of the patient. The judicial decision ought to provide the best answer not a range of alternative answers. There may, of course, be situations where the answer may not be obvious and alternatives may have to be tried. It is still at any one point the best option of that moment which should be chosen[6].
>
> ... The question ... for the judge, was not was the proposed treatment within the range of acceptable opinion among competent and responsible practitioners, but was it in the best interests of S?'

It is submitted that this approach is in accordance with the practice followed in cases where there has been a real dispute about the correct result[7].

Thus the court can and does impose its own view: it is obliged to determine the case on the facts and the evidence before it. These may be very different to those known to the doctors at the time of their initial decision. Nonetheless, a doctor who acts in accordance with recognised and accepted medical practice is unlikely to find himself open to criticism. The *Bolam* test is useful to medical practitioners and other professionals as a standard by which they go about their business, and the court can judge retrospectively whether they have complied with that standard. However, where the court has to make a finding as to the patient's best interests, the judge will look at all the evidence before the court and make an unequivocal finding as to where those interests lie, in just the same way as a finding of more concrete fact is made.

However, the Court of Appeal has not interpreted the application of the best interests test quite in this way. It has recently been said that the true analysis is that doctors owe not one, but two duties to their patients: to treat them with the standard of care required by *Bolam*, and to treat them in their best interests[8]. It may be questioned whether this is consistent with the judgements in *Sidaway*[9] in which it was emphasised that the doctor owes just one duty. It is in any event difficult to conceive of circumstances in which the *Bolam* standard of care required the doctor to act other than in the patient's best interests.

1 In accordance with the standard set out in *Bolam v Friern Hospital Management Committee* [1957] 1 WLR 582.
2 See Chap 4, *Sterilisation* and Chap 9, *Permanent Vegetative State* below.

3 See *Re F (mental patient: sterilisation* [1990] 2 AC 1 at 52 per Lord Bridge, at 66–68 per Lord Brandon, at 69 per Lord Griffiths and at 78 per Lord Goff. See also the speech of Lord Browne-Wilkinson in *Airedale NHS Trust v Bland* [1993] AC 789 at 884.

4 One judge of the Family Division in a treatment case concerning a proposed hysterectomy has indeed made declarations that two opposing courses of action would be lawful: *Re NK (No 2)* (4 April 1990, unreported) Scott Baker J.

5 [2000] 1 FCR 361.

6 Smith Bernal Transcript, p 13.

7 See *Re S (hospital patient: foreign curator)* [1996] Fam 23, Hale J; *Re LC (medical treatment: sterilisation)* [1997] 2 FLR 258, Thorpe J; and *Re S (adult sterilisation)* [1999] 1 FCR 277, [1998] 1 FLR 944, Johnson J.

8 *Re A (medical treatment: male sterilisation)* [2000] 1 FCR 193, 53 BMLR 66, [2000] 02 LS Gaz R 30, sub nom *Re A (male sterilisation)* [2000] 1 FLR 549, CA.

9 *Sidaway v Board of Governors of the Bethlem Royal Hospital and the Maudsley Hospital* [1985] AC 871. At p 893 Lord Diplock said emphatically: 'In English Jurisprudence the doctor's relationship with his patient which gives rise to the normal duty of care to exercise his skill and judgment to improve the patient's health in any particular respect in which the patient has sought his aid, has hitherto been treated as single comprehensive duty covering all the ways in which a doctor is called upon to exercise his skill and judgment in the improvement of the physical or mental condition of the patient for which his services either as a general practitioner or specialist have been engaged. This general duty is not subject to dissection into a number of component parts to which different criteria of what satisfy the duty of care apply, such as diagnosis, treatment, advice (including warning of any risks of something going wrong however skilfully the treatment is carried out).

What are the interests to be considered?

[3.8] Doctors will be proposing treatment or care firstly because of their assessment of the patient's *medical* interests and needs. This will be derived from their examination, investigation and diagnosis in the usual manner. However:

> 'Best interests are not limited to best medical interests'.[1]

They go much wider. As Thorpe LJ stated in *Re SL (adult patient) (medical treatment)*[2]:

> 'In deciding what is best for the disabled patient the judge must have regard to the patient's welfare as the paramount consideration. That embraces issues far wider than the medical. Indeed it would be undesirable and probably impossible to set bounds to what is relevant to a welfare determination.'

Just as a judge in addressing this question of best interests consider broader welfare and social issues, so must a treating doctor. A competent patient will consider these for himself when deciding whether or not to consent to treatment. It is relevant to consider the patient's domestic circumstances in determining, for example, whether an appropriate level of family or domestic support for the treatment is available to allow for a reasonable chance of recovery[3].

In rare cases the interests of others may be a factor, but only in so far as these are of potential benefit to the patient: thus organ donation may be appropriate if it may ensure a close bond with a caring relative or indeed the survival of the carer[4].

The *financial* interests of the patient are unlikely to be legitimately taken into account, but it is possible to envisage rare cases where this might be so: if there was a choice between equally valid two forms of treatment one which would make fewer demands on the patient's estate in terms of the cost of care to be provided, it might be acceptable to take this into account. However, it would be unwise in most cases for the doctor to become involved in such matters. This is not to suggest that they should be unaware of the dangers of others having ulterior motives for the views they express about the patient's interests[5]. What will always be unacceptable is seeking to adjust the timing of treatment or its withdrawal for the convenience, financial or otherwise, of others.

1 *Re MB (an adult: medical treatment)* [1997] 8 Med LR 217 at 225 per Butler-Sloss LJ.
2 [2000] 1 FCR 361, CA.
3 See, for example *Re T (a minor) (wardship: medical treatment)* [1997] 1 WLR 242. Although this case concerned a child, the court took into account the practical difficulties caused by the parents' reluctance to allow the proposed operation to be performed.
4 *Re Y (mental patient: bone marrow donation)* [1997] Fam 110.
5 See, for example *Re S (hospital patient: foreign curator)* [1996] Fam 23.

The use of force and restraint

Treatment which is in the best interests of an incapacitated patient may   [3.9] be given even if he is uncooperative; if it is his best interests to receive such treatment in spite of resistance, it is lawful to use reasonable force to do so, so long as the use of force itself does not change the balance of interest against the treatment itself. Similarly, if it is necessary to restrain a patient or even detain him for the purpose of providing treatment, it is lawful to do so[1]. The extent of force required and the balance of advantage to detriment is as much a matter for professional judgment as any other aspect of treatment in such a case[2]. Judicial concern has been expressed that the detention justified by the doctrine of necessity lacks the safeguards of the Mental Health Act 1983. Lord Steyn has said of this principle[3]:

> 'The general effect of the decision of the House is to leave compliant incapacitated patients without the safeguards enshrined in the Act of 1983. This is an unfortunate result. The Mental Health Act Commission has expressed concern about such informal patients in successive reports. The common law principle of necessity is a useful concept, but it contains none of the safeguards of the Act of 1983. It places effective and unqualified control in the hands of the hospital psychiatrist and other health care professionals. It is, of course, true that such professionals owe a duty of care to patients and that they will almost invariably act in what they consider to be the best interests of the patient. But neither habeas corpus nor judicial review are sufficient safeguards against misjudgments and professional lapses in the case of compliant incapacitated patients. Given that such patients are diagnostically indistinguishable from compulsory patients, there is no reason to withhold the specific and effective protections of the Act of 1983 from a large class of vulnerable mentally incapacitated individuals. Their moral right to be treated with dignity requires nothing less. The only comfort is that counsel for the Secretary of State has assured the House that reform of the law is under active consideration.'

It is open to question whether detention justified by reference to the doctrine of necessity would be in compliance with the Human Rights Act 1998 and Art 5 of the European Convention. Article 5 provides:

'(1)　Everyone has the right to liberty and security of person. No-one shall be deprived of his liberty save in the following cases and in accordance with a procedure prescribed by law: ...

(*e*) the lawful detention of persons for the prevention of the spreading of infectious diseases, of persons of unsound mind, alcoholics, or drug addicts or vagrants ...

(4)　Everyone who is deprived of his liberty by arrest or detention shall be entitled to take proceedings by which the lawfulness of his detention shall be decided speedily by a court and his release ordered if his detention is not lawful ...'

It is arguable that there is no procedure prescribed by law, and that there is no adequate right to have the lawfulness of the detention reviewed[4]. Therefore is it suggested that where possible acts capable of being construed as non-statutory detention should be avoided if at all possible.

1 *R v Bournewood Community and Mental Health NHS Trust, ex p L* [1999] 1 AC 458.
2 *Re MB (an adult: medical treatment)* [1997] 8 Med LR 217 at 225 per Butler-Sloss LJ.
3 See n 1 above.
4 See *Winterwerp v Netherlands* (1979) 2 EHRR 387, ECtHR; *Ashingdane v United Kingdom* App No 8225/78 28 May 1985, Fennell, *Doctor Knows Best? Therapeutic Detention under Common Law, the Mental Health Act and the European Convention* [1998] 6 Med L Rev 322 at 345 to 353; *Mental Health Act Code of Practice 1999* (HMSO), paras 2.7 and 2.8.

C DECIDING FOR CHILDREN

Framework

[3.10]　In English law a child is any person under the age of 18. As might be expected English law recognises that children do not possess the same capacity to make decisions as adults. As will be seen, however, much depends on the age of the child.

Consent to medical treatment can be obtained from a number of sources and treatment should not be undertaken without some such consent or authority. The persons from whom consent may be obtained are:

- those with parental responsibility: usually one or both of the parents, unless the responsibility has been allocated by the court in some different way or to a third party[1];
- the child in question if he or she is over the age of 16 or is otherwise of sufficient maturity and comprehension to take a decision of the relevant gravity;
- the court exercising its inherent or statutory jurisdiction over children.

In the absence of any such authority it is unlawful to treat a child unless the circumstances are of such urgency that it is not possible to obtain such consent and it is in the child's best interests to have the treatment: the treatment will be justified by the doctrine of necessity.

Authority for medical treatment may be refused by any of those who have the power to consent. The effect of such refusal depends on who makes it. Whereas a consent by any of those with the power to do so will be sufficient authority to proceed with the treatment, this is not so with a refusal. There is an hierarchy of authority:

- the refusal of the child patient, of whatever age, will not prevail in law against the consent of a person with parental responsibility or the court;
- the refusal of the parent will not prevail against the consent of a child of 16 and over or even of a younger child if of sufficient maturity and understanding for the purpose;
- the refusal of the child (of any age) or of the parents will not prevail against the authority of the court exercising its inherent or statutory jurisdiction[2].

It follows that authority for treatment of a child is much easier to obtain than a prohibition of it. As English law stands it is permissible with the relevant authority to treat a child against his or her will and to use the restraint reasonably necessary for that purpose. The legitimacy of this position under the Human Rights Act 1998 has yet to be tested.

1 However, note certain categories of procedure should not be performed without the court's permission: see for example, Chap 4, *Sterilisation* and note in relation to circumcision where if parents are in dispute court approval should be sought (discussed below).
2 *Re W (a minor) (medical treatment: court's jurisdiction)* [1993] Fam 64, [1992] 3 WLR 758, [1992] 4 All ER 627, CA.

Capacity to consent to treatment

Children of 16 years of age and over
The Family Law Reform Act 1969, s 8 provides: **[3.11]**

> (1) The consent of a minor who has attained the age of 16 years to any surgical, medical or dental treatment which, in the absence of consent, would constitute a trespass to his person, shall be as effective as it would be if he were of full age; and where a minor has by virtue of this section given an effective consent to any treatment it shall not be necessary to obtain any consent for it from his parent or guardian.
> (2) In this section 'surgical, medical or dental treatment' includes any procedure undertaken for the purposes of diagnosis, and this section applies to any procedure (including, in particular, the administration of an anaesthetic) which is ancillary to any treatment as it applies to that treatment.
> (3) Nothing in this section shall be construed as making ineffective any consent which would have been effective if this section had not been enacted.

Therefore the consent of any child over the age of 16 is as valid as if given by an adult patient. Parliament has created the presumption that such children have the relevant capacity. Therefore the test of capacity is the same, and reference should be made to the adult consent section above[1]. Clearly a child of such limited capacity as would fail the 'adult' test would not be able to provide a valid consent.

1 See Chap 2, *Consent – Adults*, paras **[2.2]** to **[2.6]**.

Children under the age of 16

[3.12] Until relatively recently it was assumed that children younger than 16 had no capacity to consent to treatment and that in all cases the authority had to be provided by their parents or someone in a similar position of authority. However, controversy surrounding the provision of contraceptive advice to children caused the capacity of children to be considered by the House of Lords in *Gillick v West Norfolk and Wisbech AHA*[1]. That case established that children of *any* age may have the capacity to consent to treatment without the consent or even knowledge of their parents. What is required is that they are of sufficient maturity and understanding to take a decision of the seriousness of that in question[2]. In other words they must be able to understand the general nature and effect of what is proposed and be able to balance the factors for and against the treatment in the same way as an adult. As stated by Lord Scarman[3].

> 'I would hold that as a matter of law the parental right to determine whether or not their minor child below the age of 16 will have medical treatment terminates if and when the child achieves a sufficient understanding and intelligence to enable him or her to understand fully what is proposed. It will be a question of fact whether a child seeking advice has sufficient understanding of what is involved to give a consent valid in law. Until the child achieves the capacity to consent, the parental right to make the decision continues save only in exceptional circumstances.'

In *Re R (a minor) (wardship: consent to treatment)* Lord Donaldson MR stated that[4]:

> 'What is involved is not merely an ability to understand the nature of the proposed treatment ... but a full understanding and appreciation of the consequences both of the treatment in terms of intended and possible side effects and, equally important, the anticipated consequences of a failure to treat.'

This seems to suggest that in fact the *Gillick* competence test may be more difficult to pass than the adult capacity test.

The closer a child is to the age of 16 the more likely the determination that he or she is *Gillick* competent. However, it must be stressed that – as with the test for an adult's competence[5] – the test for *Gillick* competence varies according to the nature and gravity of the decision which is to be taken[6].

Re E (a minor)[7] provides an example where the nature of the decision precluded an otherwise apparently *Gillick* competent child – who was nearly 16 – from achieving competence in relation to a particular decision.

E was a 15¾ year old Jehovah's witness with leukaemia: blood transfusions were a necessary part of conventional treatment; he refused to consent to blood transfusions. His parents also refused to consent. In relation to *Gillick* competence Ward J concluded[8] that E was a 'boy of sufficient intelligence to be able to take decisions about his own well-being, but I also find that there is a range of decisions of which some are outside his ability fully to grasp their implications'. He did not have full understanding of the whole implications of a refusal of blood transfusions. Thus he was not of sufficient understanding and intelligence and maturity to give a full and informed consent.

The House of Lords has emphasised that they expected that doctors would consult parents in most cases, but that this could only be done in relation to a child of the relevant degree of understanding and maturity with the child's consent: if such a child wishes to keep the matter confidential that is his or her entitlement.

If a child has the relevant capacity he or she obviously has no duty to exercise the power of consent in any particular manner. As will be seen however, the ability to refuse consent is circumscribed.

Who is to judge whether the child has the relevant capacity? In the first place this can only be the attending doctors who must form an opinion on the matter in accordance with accepted practice. If parents or others with a legitimate interest disagree with the medical assessment, then it is likely that the dispute will have to be referred to the court to decide. In such a case, of course, the reality is that the court will make the final decision about what is in the child's best interests – see below. There may be cases of particularly serious treatment where the doctors may feel doubt about whether the child has the capacity to make the decision even if the parents do not disagree. Again the doctors may wish to refer the matter to court[9].

1 [1986] AC 112, [1985] 3 WLR 830, [1985] 3 All ER 402.
2 Note Convention on the Rights of the Child, Art 12(1): 'States Parties shall assure to the child who is capable of forming his or her own views the right to express those views freely in all matters affecting the child, the views of the child being given due weight in accordance with the age and maturity of the child.'; Art 14(1): 'States Parties shall respect the right of the child to freedom of thought, conscience and religion.' This Convention has been increasingly referred to as an aid to interpretation in Strasbourg decisions and opinions; see for example, *Keegan v Ireland* (1994) 18 EHRR 342, referring at para 50 to Art 7 (right to be cared for by his or her parents); *Costello-Roberts v United Kingdom* (1993) 19 EHRR 112 ECtHR, referring at para 35 to Art 16 (right to respect for private life).
3 [1986] AC 112 at 188H, HL.
4 [1992] Fam 11 at 26A, CA.
5 See Chap 2, *Consent – Adults*, para **[2.2]**.
6 UN Convention on the Rights of the Child, Art 14(2): 'States Parties shall respect the rights and duties of the parents and, when applicable, legal guardians, to provide direction to the child in the exercise of his or her right in a manner **consistent with the evolving capacities of the child**.'
7 [1993] 1 FLR 386 (Ward J).
8 [1993] 1 FLR 386 at 391A.
9 It is unlikely that this will arise very often: few parents who agree to treatment will not authorise it themselves if there is doubt about the child's capacity. The most likely situation for this to happen would be where the parents themselves lack capacity.

Parents and those with parental responsibility

The mother of a child, and – if married to the mother, or an order of the court has so provided – the father[1], have the power to consent to treatment unless deprived of it either through lack of personal capacity or because the entitlement has been modified or removed by order of a court. **[3.13]**

The duty of such a person is to give or withhold consent in the best interests of the child and without regard to their own[2].

A parent's capacity to consent to the treatment of their child will be assessed in the same way as for a patient personally. Therefore an adult parent will be presumed to have capacity unless shown not to satisfy the test of capacity for an adult[3]. A parent under the age 18 will be assessed by reference to the *Gillick* test. If a parent lacks capacity then he or she will be unable to give a valid consent. It is likely in such circumstances that a social service authority will have been given parental responsibility by a family court. If this has not occurred a doctor seeking consent to treat the child should approach the appropriate authority or seek approval directly from the court.

Where someone other than a parent may have been awarded parental responsibility, such as another relation or a public authority[4], doctors should approach that person for authority to treat rather than the natural parents. Depending on the circumstances it may be good practice to approach the latter to consult them in any event, but they are unable to give valid consent.

Whilst the general position is that the consent of one parent is sufficient, the position concerning circumcision is different:

> '*in the absence of agreement* of those with parental responsibility, [it] ought not to be carried out or arranged by a one-parent carer although she has parental responsibility under s 2(7) of the Children Act 1989. Such a decision should not be made without the specific approval of the court.'[5]

1 Children Act 1989, ss 2 to 4.
2 *Re J (a minor) (wardship: medical treatment)* [1991] Fam 33.
3 See Chap 2, *Consent – Adults*, para [2.2]ff.
4 See Children Act 1989, s 5.
5 *Re J (child's religious upbringing and circumcision)* [2000] 1 FLR 571 at 577 per Butler-Sloss P.

The courts

[3.14] An approach may be made to the court for authority to treat a child either because no person with capacity to consent to treatment can be found, or because there is a dispute requiring court intervention. The court's jurisdiction may be invoked in various ways:

[3.15] *Specific issue order under the Children Act 1989* – This may be appropriate where there is a discrete dispute concerning specific short-term treatment. It may be less easy to define the issue in the case of long-term treatment or treatment which is likely to vary according to circumstances.

[3.16] *Order in wardship proceedings* – Such an order will be necessary in the case of any child who is already a ward of court where the treatment is likely to have serious consequences. No serious step should be taken in the life of a ward without the authority of the court[1]. Apart from such a case wardship will hardly ever be the appropriate means of proceeding. It is not necessary to make a child a ward of court for the purpose of obtaining court authority for proposed treatment. Indeed it might be suggested that it is wrong to seek an order which in effect deprives those with parental responsibility of their authority in all areas of the child's life when less invasive legal procedures are available. It should be noted that in any event the policy of the Children Act 1989 is to discourage wardship applications: for instance a social services authority requires the permission of the court to make a wardship application[2] and has other powers under the Act which should mean that such an application is usually unnecessary. While doctors would not require permission to bring such an application, to make one would in many cases appear to be unacceptably in excess of what is necessary to cater for the child's medical needs.

1 *Re S (a minor)* [1976] Fam 1, CA; *Re G-U (a minor) (wardship)* [1984] FLR 811 (termination of pregnancy).
2 Section 100(3) of the Children Act 1989 states: 'No application for any exercise of the court's inherent jurisdiction with respect to children may be made by a local authority unless the authority have obtained the leave of the court.'

Order under the inherent jurisdiction of the court – The court's inherent **[3.17]** jurisdiction is preserved by the Children Act 1989. Generally it is this jurisdiction which will be invoked by doctors anxious to obtain authority to perform important treatment when no other form of authority can be found. An application can be mounted swiftly and the procedure is sufficiently flexible to cover all eventualities. Unlike the position with adults[1] there is no limit on the court's power to make an interim order.

The child's welfare is the paramount consideration for a court in deciding whether to give its consent to treatment and no other consideration will take priority[2].

1 See para **[3.11]** above.
2 *Re B (a minor) (wardship: medical treatment)* [1981] 1 WLR 1421; *Re B (a minor) (wardship: sterilisation)* [1988] AC 199 at 202.

Power to refuse treatment
The uninformed observer might be forgiven for expecting that, as with **[3.18]** adults, the principles governing refusal of treatment would be the same as those for authorising treatment. However, this is not the case. The fundamental principle is that the authority of any one party with the power to consent trumps the refusal of any other, unless a court otherwise directs. It might be argued therefore that the system is biased in favour of children receiving treatment to avoid their being deprived of care which it is in their best interests to receive.

Children over the age of 16 or possessing Gillick capacity
Children recognised by the law as having the capacity to authorise **[3.19]** treatment for themselves may refuse it. However, unlike the position with competent adults, such a refusal, whether given by a child over the age of 16[1] or a younger, *Gillick* competent child[2], is not binding on the doctors if another person with the capacity to consent to treatment does so[3]. In effect this means that any person with parental responsibility can authorise the imposition of treatment on an unwilling child. The Court of Appeal has felt able to confine the effect of *Gillick* to a restriction on the power of veto a parent has over the treatment given to his or her child, and the effect of the Family Law Reform Act 1969 to the power to consent rather than the power to refuse.

Of course, the fact that someone other than the patient can authorise treatment does not necessarily mean that it would be right, let alone obligatory, to do so in respect of an unwilling patient. Whether or not a child is *Gillick* competent will not ultimately determine the application, but the judge must give due weight to the child's views when approaching best interests and a competent refusal must weigh heavily in the scales. Thus there may be cases in which the balance may be tipped in favour of refusal of treatment because the child's refusal is a competent refusal.

Lord Donaldson of Lymington MR said in *Re W (a minor) (medical treatment: court's jurisdiction*[4]:

> 'Hair-raising possibilities were canvassed of abortions being carried out by doctors in reliance upon the consent of parents and despite the refusal of consent by 16 and 17 year olds. Whilst this may be possible as a matter of law, I do not see any likelihood taking account of medical ethics, unless the abortion was truly in the best interests of the child. This is not to say that it could not happen. This is clear from the facts of *Re D (a minor) (wardship: sterilisation)* [1976] Fam 185, where the child concerned had neither the intelligence nor understanding either to consent or refuse. There medical ethics did not prove an obstacle, there being divided medical opinions, but the wardship jurisdiction of the court was invoked by a local authority educational psychologist who had been involved with the case. Despite the passing of the Children Act 1989, the inherent jurisdiction of the court could still be invoked in such a case to prevent an abortion which was contrary to the interests of the minor.'

And as stated by Balcombe LJ[5]:

> 'Since Parliament has not conferred complete autonomy on a 16 year old in the field of medical treatment, there is no overriding limitation to preclude the exercise by the court of its inherent jurisdiction and the matter becomes one for the exercise by the court of its discretion. Nevertheless, the discretion is not to be exercised in a moral vacuum. Undoubtedly, the philosophy ... is that, as children approach the age of majority, they are increasingly able to take their own decisions concerning their medical treatment. In logic there can be no difference between an ability to consent to treatment and an ability to refuse treatment ... Accordingly the older the child concerned the greater the weight the court should give to its wishes, certainly in the field of medical treatment. In a sense this is merely one aspect of the application of the test that the welfare of the child is the paramount consideration. It will normally be in the best interests of a child of sufficient age and understanding to make an informed decision that the court should respect its integrity as a human being and not lightly override its decision on such a personal matter as medical treatment, all the more so if that treatment is invasive. In my judgment, therefore, the court exercising the inherent jurisdiction in relation to a 16 or 17 year old child who is not mentally incompetent will, as a matter of course, ascertain the wishes of the child and will approach its decision with a strong predilection to give effect to the child's wishes ... Nevertheless, if the court's powers are to be meaningful, there must come a point at which the court, while not disregarding the child's wishes, can override them

in the child's own best interests, objectively considered. Clearly such a point will have come if the child is seeking to refuse treatment in circumstances which will in all probability lead to the death of the child or to severe permanent injury.'

Thus there will be cases where it is considered in the child's best interests to impose treatment, such as where his or her life can only be saved by it, despite the child's 'competent' objection to the treatment[6]. Equally there will be cases where it is considered impracticable or unethical to impose the treatment. In most such situations, difficult though they are, it will be possible for the doctors and the parents between them to work out what is for the best. In rare cases there will remain a sufficient degree of doubt to justify a reference to the court.

A proposal for any such compulsory treatment must now be scrutinised with the Human Rights Act 1998 in mind. Article 8(1) protects the moral and bodily integrity of a person from unjustified assault[7]. It thus includes a right not to be subjected to compulsory medical interference[8]. However this is a right which, by virtue of Art 8(2) may be justifiably interfered with on grounds of health or morals: as stated by Ursula Kilkelly[9]:

> 'Compulsory medical treatment . . . will not infringe the Convention as long as there is proportionality between the interference which it creates and the need to protect the public interest which it serves. This has been found to be particularly important where children are concerned, because they have limited possibilities to protect their own rights.'[10]

The Art 8 protection should in fact mean that courts when performing the 'best interests' assessment will ensure that only in exceptional circumstances – for example, where it is necessary to save life – will the wishes of a child over the age of 16 or a *Gillick* competent child be overridden. Thus, the disparity between the law's approach to a child's right of refusal and to his right to consent is likely to narrow: the courts will be more likely to accept a child's refusal of treatment in circumstances in which he has the capacity – whether by statute or *Gillick* – to consent to the same treatment.

1 *Re W (a minor) (medical treatment: court's jurisdiction)* [1993] Fam 64.
2 *Re R (a minor) (wardship: consent to treatment)* [1992] Fam 11.
3 For example, see *Re K, W and H (minors) (consent to treatment)* [1993] 1 FLR 854, Thorpe J.
4 [1993] Fam 64.
5 *Re W (a minor) (medical treatment: court's jurisdiction)* [1992] 2 FCR 785 at 810, [1993] Fam 64 at 88.
6 See, for example, *Re M (child: refusal of medical treatment)* [1999] 2 FCR 577 where doctors were authorised to carry out a heart transplant on a 15½ year old girl who refused to consent to the operation. The risks of the child's resentment against the imposition of treatment and the risks of the procedure itself had to be set against 'not simply the risk but the certainty of death'. Fortin, *Children's Rights and the Developing Law* (Butterworths, 1998: Update 4, Chap 5), has commented in support of the *Re M* approach that: 'It insults a perfectly normal teenager's intelligence to argue that she is not *Gillick* competent. She might better appreciate that the court, under its inherent jurisdiction, though obliged to consider her wishes, is also obliged to act in her best interests and keep her alive, if possible, throughout her minor status.'

7 *X and Y v The Netherlands* (1985) 8 EHRR 235; *Peters v Netherlands* 77A DR 75 (1994) at 79, indicating that unwanted medical intervention (the taking of urine samples) is an infringement of Art 8. And see also reference to *X v Austria* and the European Court of Justice decision in the HIV case cited at fns 1 and 2 of Nys, *Physician Involvement in a Patient's death – a Continental European Perspective* (1999) Med L Rev 7(2) 209.

8 *Re A (children) (conjoined twins: surgical separation)* [2000] 4 All ER 961, [2000] 3 FCR 577, [2000] 1 FLR 1, [2001] Fam Law 18, CA.

9 Kilkelly, *The Child and the European Convention on Human Rights* (Dartmouth Publishing, 1999).

10 Kilkelly, *The Child and the European Convention on Human Rights* (Dartmouth Publishing, 1999) at p 150 citing *JR, GR, RR & YR v Switzerland* No 22398/93 Dec 5/4/95, DR 81, p 61.

Children under the age of 16 not possessing *Gillick* capacity

[3.20] As such children lack the capacity to consent it also follows that they can not validly refuse treatment which is otherwise lawfully authorised. In effect they can be compelled to accept treatment either under the authority of a person with parental responsibility or of the court exercising its inherent jurisdiction over children.

Parents

[3.21] As has been seen, parents have the power to override their children's refusal of treatment. In order to do so they must have the legal capacity to take such a decision, the test being the same as required of any adult. The refusal of legally competent parents will be accorded respect by the law, but their power to act in this way is not absolute and may be overridden by the court. In practice the court will not allow a parental refusal – however much it is well informed and made in good faith – get in the way of what is perceived to be in the child's best interests. The child's interests must always be paramount[1]. The weight to be given to the parents' views will vary according to the circumstances – in *Re T (a minor) (wardship: medical treatment)* it was stated[2]:

> 'All these cases depend on their own facts and render generalisations tempting though they may be to the legal or social analyst wholly out of place. It can only be said safely that there is a scale, at one end of which lies the clear case where parental opposition to medical intervention is prompted by scruple or dogma of a kind which is patently irreconcilable with principles of child health and welfare widely accepted by the generality of mankind; and that at the other end lie highly problematic cases where there is genuine scope for a difference of view between parent and judge. In both situations it is the duty of the judge to allow the court's own opinion to prevail in the perceived paramount interests of the child concerned, but in cases at the latter end of the scale, there must be a likelihood (though never of course a certainty) that the greater the scope for genuine debate between one view and another the stronger will be the inclination of the court to be influenced by a reflection that in the last analysis the best interests of every child include an expectation that difficult decisions affecting the length and quality of its life will be taken for it by the parent to whom its care has been entrusted by nature.'[3]

Thus, there may be a form of rebuttable presumption that the parents' views should be respected, particularly when their rights to a family life under Art 8 of the European Convention on Human Rights are taken into account[4].

Nonetheless, where a parent's views place the child's life in danger or are otherwise detrimental to his or her interests, the courts will override the refusal. As stated in *Prince v Massachusetts*[5]:

> 'Parents may be free to become martyrs themselves, but it does not follow that they are free in identical circumstances to make martyrs of their children before they have reached the age of full and legal discretion when they can make choices for themselves.'

They will even do so where the parents' views on an issue – upon which there is no general social consensus – are supported by a significant proportion of the community, as in the case where the court authorised the separation of conjoined twins against the parents' opposition, although the operation was bound to result in the death of the weaker twin[6]. In practice the court's view will almost invariably prevail. As a Master of the Rolls put it[7]:

> 'I would for my part accept without reservation that the decision of a devoted and responsible parent should be treated with respect. It should certainly not be disregarded or lightly set aside. But the role of the court is to exercise an independent and objective judgment. If that judgment is in accord with that of the devoted and responsible parent, well and good. If it is not, then it is the duty of the court, after giving due weight to the view of the devoted and responsible parent, to give effect to its own judgment. That is what it is there for. Its judgment may of course be wrong. So may that of the parent. But once the jurisdiction of the court is invoked its clear duty is to reach and express the best judgment it can.'

Nonetheless there are limits to the power of the court. Even where it disagrees with the parental views, it may have the child Claimant accept them where treatment cannot be accomplished successfully without the parents' co-operation and they are either unwilling or unable to give it. Orders will not be made which cannot be enforced. Thus a court declined to order a mother to desist from breast-feeding her baby in spite of the risks to the baby's health caused thereby[8].

In *Re T* three doctors had concluded that T – who had been lawfully taken out of the jurisdiction by his mother – was suitable for a liver transplant and that, even though the surgery was major and complicated, it had a good chance of success. Without surgery T would die within 12 to 18 months: with surgery T had a good chance of living a normal life for many years. T's mother objected to the treatment. Connell J at first instance gave consent for the treatment to be performed. The Court of Appeal overturned that decision, holding that the first instance judge had failed to take sufficient account of T's mother's views. Permitting the treatment would have the effect of coercing T's mother into playing the 'crucial and irreplaceable' role in the aftermath of major invasive surgery which would be essential to the success or otherwise of the treatment. The reasonableness of the mother was not the primary issue (although the Court of Appeal doubted Connell J's conclusion that she was unreasonable): what mattered in this case was the dependence of the child on the mother:

> 'This mother and this child are one for the purpose of this unusual case and the decision of the court to consent to the operation jointly affects the mother and son and it also affects the father. The welfare of this child depends upon his mother. The practical considerations of her ability to cope with supporting the child in the face of her belief that this course is not right for him, the requirement to return probably for a long period to this country, either to leave the father behind and lose his support or to require him to give up his present job and seek one in England were not put by the judge into the balance when he made his decision.
>
> ... I would stress that, on the most unusual facts of this case with the enormous significance of the close attachment between the mother and baby, the court is not concerned with the reasonableness of the mother's refusal to consent but with the consequences of that refusal and whether it is in the best interests of C for this court in effect to direct the mother to take on this total commitment where she does not agree with the course proposed. The effect of the evidence of Dr P respecting the mother's decision and the prospect of forcing the devoted mother of this young baby to the consequences of this major invasive surgery lead me to the conclusion, after much anxious deliberation, that it is not in the best interests of this child to give consent and require him to return to England for the purpose of undergoing liver transplantation. I believe that the best interests of this child require that his future treatment should be left in the hands of his devoted parents.'[9]

A further limit on a parent's power of refusal is that it is will only be effective if both parents agree. As the consent of any parent will validate treatment, the refusal of one will not override the consent of the other. The remedy of the parent who wishes to stop treatment being provided is to apply to the court for an order prohibiting it.

Article 8(1) of the European Convention on Human Rights states that:

> 'Everyone has the right to respect for his private and family life.'

It is likely that this article will be relied upon by parents in order to assert that their views about their child should be respected, regardless of the prevailing medical opinion. ECHR jurisprudence has applied Art 8 in support of a parents' right to control their children[10]. However, the right is not absolute: legitimate and proportionate restrictions can be placed on parental rights and parental control when the child's health or morals are at stake or when conflicting rights come into play. As stated by the European Court of Rights[11]:

> 'a fair balance has to be struck between the interests of the child in remaining in public care and those of the parent in being reunited with the child ... In carrying out this balancing exercise, the Court will attach particular importance to the best interests of the child,

which, depending on their nature and seriousness, may override those of the parent.'

In assessing whether there has been a breach of a parent's right to family life it also necessary to consider other potentially conflicting rights, for example, the child's own right to autonomy. Article 8 protects the moral and bodily integrity of a person from unjustified assault[12]: thus, it protects patients' right to self-determination. In order to give meaning to a child's right to autonomy the court may have to make decisions on the child's behalf which are against the wishes of parents.

In practice it is suggested that the Strasbourg approach mirrors that of the United Kingdom: the ultimate test is what is in the best interests of the child. Whilst a parent's Art 8 rights must be respected and placed in the balance when the courts take decisions concerning a child, the overriding interest is that of the child[13]. Thus, the European jurisprudence supports a view that the Art 8 right of parent to control his or her child exists not for the benefit of the parent but for the benefit of the child.

The European Court of Human Rights has allowed Member States a wide margin of appreciation in their approach to child care matters:

> 'In determining whether ... measures were "necessary in a democratic society" ... the Court will have regard to the fact that perceptions as to the appropriateness of intervention by public authorities in the care of children vary from one Contracting State to another, depending on such factors as traditions relating to the role of the family and to State intervention in family affairs and the availability of resources for public measures in this particular area.'[14]

1 Children Act 1989, s 1(1).
2 *Re T (a minor) (wardship: medical treatment)* [1997] 1 WLR 242 at 254 per Waite LJ.
3 Fortin, *Children's Rights and the Developing Law* (Butterworths, 1998: Update 3, Chap 11), contrasts the respect given to the views of the parents in *Re T* with the perfunctory dismissal of the parents' views in *Re C* and comments that 'one is left with the uneasy feeling that the judiciary's attitude to parents' strong convictions about their children's health care is influenced by the way in which parents are perceived, in terms of societal orthodoxy and background.'
4 See the hint to this effect by Wall J in *Re C (a child) (HIV testing)* [2000] 2 WLR 270 at 280.
5 (1944) 321 US Reports 158: quoted by Ward J in *Re E (a minor)* [1993] 1 FLR 386 at 394D, and as stated by Ward J at 394E the court 'should be very slow to allow an infant to martyr himself.'
6 *Re A (children) (conjoined twins: surgical separation)* [2000] 4 All ER 961, [2000] 3 FCR 577, [2000] 1 FLR 1, [2001] Fam Law 18, CA.
7 *Re Z (a minor) (identification: restrictions on publications)* [1997] Fam 1 at 32–33.
8 As was suggested in *Re T* (n 2 above); see also *Re C (a child) (HIV testing)* [2000] 2 WLR 270 at 280.
9 *Re T (a minor) (wardship: medical treatment)* [1997] 1 WLR 242 per Butler-Sloss LJ.
10 For example, *Nielsen v Denmark* (1988) 11 EHRR 175.
11 *Johannsen v Norway* 23 EHRR 33, para 64.
12 See above and cases cited of *X and Y v The Netherlands* (1985) 8 EHRR 235 and *Peters v Netherlands* 77A DR 75 (1994).
13 Article 3(1) of the UN Convention on the Rights of the Child states: 'In all actions concerning children, whether undertaken by public or private social welfare institutions, courts of law, administrative authorities or legislative bodies, the best interests of the child shall be a primary consideration.' And see, for example, *Hoffman v Austria* (1993) 17 EHRR 293; *Bronda v Italy* [1998] EHRLR 756; and note in *Garcia v Switzerland*,

Application No 10148/82 (DR 42, p 98) the Commission stated: '... having regard to Article 8 para 2, when as in the instant case there is a serious conflict between the interests of the child and those of one of his parents which can only be resolved to the detriment of one of these parties the interests of the child must prevail.'
14 *Johannsen v Norway* 23 EHRR 33, para 64.

The court

[3.22] A judge exercising the inherent jurisdiction of the court or making a specific issue or prohibited steps[1] order under the Children Act 1989 has the ultimate power to prevent treatment being given whatever the views of the child, his or her parents, and the treating doctors. The court will intervene where it perceives it to be in the interests of the child's welfare to do so. Thus a proposed sterilisation of a disabled 11 year old girl was prevented[2] on the ground that:

> 'A review of the whole of the evidence leads me to the conclusion that in a case of a child of 11 years of age, where the evidence shows that her mental and physical condition and attainments have already improved, and where her future prospects are as yet unpredictable, where the evidence also shows that she is unable as yet to understand and appreciate the implications of this operation and could not give a valid or informed consent, but the likelihood is that in later years she will be able to make her own choice, where, I believe, the frustration and resentment of realising (as she would one day) what had happened, could be devastating, an operation of this nature is, in my view, contraindicated.'

In determining the best interests the court will consider the views of both the child and the parents, but ultimately the decision is the court's alone. For example, in *Re E (a minor)*[3] Ward J in assessing the child's and his father's view that life-saving blood transfusions should not be permitted stated[4]:

> '... is this choice of death one which a judge ... can find to be consistent with the welfare of the child? ... life is precious ... When therefore I have to balance the wishes of father and son against the need for the chance to live a precious life, then I have to conclude that their decision is inimical to his well-being.'

The court will therefore act to preserve life even when parents feel that the point has been reached when no more life-saving efforts should be made[5]. Conversely when it is no longer in a child's best interests that his or her life be preserved at all costs, the court will authorise doctors either to take no further active treatment steps or even to withdraw treatment which is being provided[6]. It can be in a child's best interests to cease life-saving treatment even when he or she is not terminally ill[7].

In the most extreme circumstances the court has been prepared to approve an operation on one conjoined twin to give the stronger twin a good chance of a relatively normal life even though the operation would result in the immediate death of the weaker twin. It was held that where there was a conflict between the duty owed to one twin and that owed to the other, a balancing exercise had to be performed. While the operation was against the interests of one twin[8] the doctrine of necessity permitted the operation to be lawful in the interests of the stronger twin.

It is too early for the full ramifications of this controversial case to have become apparent, but it is unlikely that procedures at the expense of one child for the benefit of another will often be permitted. Indeed it is an established principle that organ and tissue donation for the benefit of a sibling will not be permitted unless it is in the interests of the donor child[9].

Where applications are made to the court in the context of a family dispute it will be necessary to consider the appropriate method of getting the matter before the court by reference to the requirements of the Children Act 1989. Where it is those who are proposing to provide treatment who wish to apply it is desirable and more practicable to make application under the court's inherent jurisdiction. This provides the court with as much flexibility as possible in dealing with the issues raised, and avoids unnecessary technicality in circumstances which are often urgent.

1 A prohibited steps order is 'an order that no step which could be taken by a parent in meeting his parental responsibility for a child, and which is of a kind specified in the order, shall be taken by any person without the consent of the court; . . .' (CA 1989, s 8). It may be made against a person who is not a party to the proceedings before the court; *Re H (minors)* [1995] 1 WLR 667.
2 *Re D (a minor) (wardship: sterilisation)* [1976] Fam 185.
3 [1993] 1 FLR 386 (Ward J).
4 [1993] 1 FLR 386 at 393 per Ward J.
5 *Re B (a minor) (wardship: medical treatment)* [1981] 1 WLR 1421, CA (A Down's syndrome child required a life-saving operation. The parents refused to consent. It was held that because it had not been demonstrated that the child should be condemned to die, the court would make an order that the operation should be performed).
6 *Re C (a minor)* [1990] Fam 26, CA (The court approved recommendations designed to ease the suffering rather than prolong the life of a terminally-ill hydrocephalic baby); *Re J (a minor) (wardship: medical treatment)* [1991] Fam 33, [1991] 2 WLR 140, [1990] 3 All ER 930, [1990] 2 Med. LR 67, CA (The curtailment of treatment of a severely brain damaged baby was in the baby's best interests; an 'absolutist test' should not be applied; the sole question was what is in the child's best interests); *Re C (a minor) (medical treatment)* [1998] 1 FCR 1, [1998] 1 FLR 384, [1998] Lloyd's Rep Med. 1, [1998] Fam Law 135 (C had a fatal disease. Treatment only prolonged her life and did not alleviate her suffering. The court supported the doctors' view that it was in C's best interests for ventilation to be withdrawn and for it not to be restored should C suffer a further relapse). See also *R v Portsmouth Hospitals NHS Trust, ex p Glass* [1999] 3 FCR 145, [1999] 2 FLR 905 (inappropriate to direct a medical team to take active steps to prolong the life of a boy with severe disabilities and a limited life span).
7 *Re J (a minor) (wardship: medical treatment)* [1991] Fam 33, CA (J was a profoundly handicapped baby who suffered intermittent convulsions. J was not terminally-ill. Nonetheless the court held that consent to life-saving treatment could be withheld in the child's best interests).
8 Although this was not free from doubt: the first instance judge and a minority in the Court of Appeal considered the operation was also in the weaker twin's interests.
9 *Re Y (mental patient: bone marrow donation)* [1997] Fam 110, [1997] 2 WLR 556, [1996] 2 FLR 787, [1997] 2 FCR 172 (An operation to transplant bone marrow from Y, a mentally and physically handicapped adult, into her terminally-ill sister was in Y's best interests because this they would tend to prolong the life of both her sister and her mother, and Y would thereby receive emotional, psychological and social benefit with minimal detriment to Y).

Carers

If both the parents and, where competent, the child refuse to authorise **[3.23]** treatment it will normally be unlawful to perform it without the authority of the court or another person with parental responsibility, such as a local authority which has acquired the relevant powers. In such circumstances any treatment provided contrary to the refusal may amount to an assault and render the carer liable to criminal and civil proceedings. Where, however, doctors consider that treatment is necessary in order to save the life of child or prevent a risk of serious harm, *and* there is no time to approach the court, it is suggested that they may proceed despite the parental refusal.

In *Re A (children) (conjoined twins: surgical separation)*[1] part of the court's justification for authorising a procedure which would result in the death of one conjoined twin to enable the other to survive was that the doctors owed a duty of care to the stronger twin to save her life. If this is so, then the doctrine of necessity can probably be relied on to justify the intervention in accordance with the principles established in *Re F (mental patient: sterilisation)*[2].

It should be borne in mind, however, that the court can be approached very quickly in appropriately urgent cases and it will invariably be prudent to do so where there is active opposition to treatment from all those having parental responsibility, if this can be done without endangering the life or health of the child. Where available, palliative measures should be taken as opposed to definitive and irreversible treatment, if by doing so sufficient time to make an application to the court can be obtained.

1 [2000] 4 All ER 961, [2000] 3 FCR 577, [2000] 1 FLR 1, [2001] Fam Law 18, CA.
2 [1990] 2 AC 1.

D PROCEDURES AND REMEDIES

General
[3.24] In most cases mentally incompetent patients can be provided with necessary treatment without the need for an application to the court. There are certain categories of case where it is either advisable, or in practice mandatory, for an application to be made for a declaration that it would be lawful to give the treatment without the patient's consent:

- Cases where there is doubt or a dispute concerning the patient's competence;
- Procedures primarily intended for irreversible sterilisation;
- Organ or human tissue donation;
- Caesarean section or any surgical obstetric delivery; and
- Withdrawal of life sustaining treatment from patients in a permanent vegetative state or similar condition.

The nature of a declaration
[3.25] The purpose of a declaration is to provide a degree of protection to the doctors where there would otherwise be doubt about the legality of what they propose to do[1]. Without such a procedure there might be understandable hesitation on their part in providing necessary but possibly controversial treatment to a person unable to make a decision for himself. A declaration obtained after a hearing at which the interested parties are represented or have had the opportunity to be represented operates solely by creating a judgment estoppel[2] between the parties[3]. In other words, the patient who is the subject of a declaration cannot be heard afterwards to argue that the treatment concerned was unlawful by

reason of a lack of consent. It could be argued that this will be the case even if it subsequently emerges that the court was given misleading information. Nevertheless, as the declaration can only apply to the factual circumstances as they were presented to the court it is arguable that the declaration has no effect where the relevant treatment was given in different factual circumstances.

A declaration can only be obtained as a final order. This means that there is no jurisdiction in the court to grant an interim declaration[4]. It is now established that the court will not – even if there is jurisdiction to do so, which is doubtful – make an ex parte 'final' declaration, as it can be of no effect, not being binding on the party not represented[5]. This jurisdiction is the best the common law has been able to devise, in the absence of any more general power, to protect the interests of adults who are vulnerable by reason of mental incapacity in relation to their physical well-being. There have been several judicial calls for Parliament to give judges wider powers. Hale J has said[6]:

> 'It is clear from, however, the troubling circumstances of this case that there exists no wholly appropriate legal mechanism for examining whether or not W should be free to make her own decisions in the vital matter of her relationship with her family and if she should not what decisions should be made on her behalf. I share the view expressed by Eastham J in *Re C (Mental Patient: Contact)* [1993] 1 FLR 940, 946 that it is a sad state of affairs that the law is unable to provide suitable protections in such a situation. The 1959 Act was thought to have placed all the necessary features of the ancient prerogative jurisdiction on a statutory footing. Cases such as this have proved that judgement wrong and it is to be hoped that Parliament will before too long turn its attention to the matter once more.'

Thorpe LJ has recently said[7]:

> 'We would only say that we would wish to see the Family Division judge given wider powers to deal with the welfare of adult patients where that cannot be fully achieved under the provisions of the Mental Health Act 1983.'

To date these calls have been unheeded.

1 *Re F (mental patient: sterilisation)* [1990] 2 AC 1 at 56.
2 Estoppel per rem judicatum.
3 *St George's Healthcare NHS Trust v S* [1999] Fam 26, CA.
4 *F v Riverside Mental Health NHS Trust* [1994] 1 FLR 614.
5 *St George's Healthcare NHS Trust v S* [1999] Fam 26, CA.
6 *Cambridgeshire County Council v R (An Adult)* [1995] 1 FLR 50.
7 *Re F (Mental Health Act: guardianship* [2000] 1 FLR 192 at 200.

Cases not requiring a court application

Assessment of capacity

In all cases where it is proposed to embark on surgical or other invasive **[3.26]** treatment, and there is a possibility that the patient lacks capacity, it is important that a proper assessment of mental competence is performed and recorded. This question must be investigated at the earliest opportunity. Acting erroneously on the purported consent of a mentally incompetent patient leaves those treating the patient potentially without any justification for treatment. On the other hand it must be borne in mind that every adult is presumed to be competent unless there is evidence to the contrary and that the irrationality, or even immorality, of the decision is not a basis for finding incapacity.

If possible the assessment of capacity should be carried out by a consultant psychiatrist. The assessment should be in accordance with the criteria set out in *Re C* and *Re MB*[1] and should also determine whether the patient is capable of managing his own property and affairs within the meaning of the Mental Health Act 1983.

If a patient is mentally incompetent it is important to establish whether the incapacity is permanent or temporary. If the latter, an assessment of the likely duration of the incapacity is required.

1 See App 6.1: *Re MB.*

Action if patient is mentally incompetent
[3.27] If practicable the patient's family should be consulted for information about his likely wishes, and any factor relevant to the assessment of his best interests.

Inquiries should be made to establish whether there is a valid advance directive. Assuming there is none, it must be decided whether the proposed treatment is in the patient's best interests.

If there is a dispute about the patient's competence or about whether the proposed treatment is in his best interests, consideration should be given to an application to the court.

If the case is not one where an application is required the treatment or care may be provided.

Cases requiring a court application
It must be remembered at all times that this is not conventional adversarial litigation, but a process of seeking to ensure that the rights of the patient are determined, and, if necessary, that the patient is treated in his or her best interests if unable to make a decision personally.

Obtaining instructions
[3.28] Direct contact must be established with those responsible for treating the patient to establish:

(1) the degree of urgency and gravity of the case;
(2) whether there is sufficient evidence of the patient's mental state to judge; whether or not he or she is incompetent; and
(3) the history of the case, and the reasons for the present situation.

Obviously steps which prejudice the life or health of the patient should be avoided if at all possible.

Contact with the patient
[3.29] Contact must be made with the patient to warn him or her of the intention to make an application. All necessary assistance must be offered to find legal assistance if the patient wishes this to be done. It is

obviously not the hospital solicitor's function to assess the patient's competence, but any relevant information in that respect ought to be passed to the doctors.

How the contact should be made will depend on the circumstances, but it may on occasions be better, and less threatening for this to be effected via an intermediary, such as a local hospital social worker, or even a member of the patient's family.

A full record of what the patient has to say must be kept with a view to the court being informed of it.

Assessment of capacity

It is important that the status of the patient is established as soon as **[3.30]** possible, in the same way as indicated above. Hospitals and their staff will be vulnerable to criticism if there is delay in appreciating that there is or may a problem relating to consent, thereby rendering the application to court an urgent one.

Action if the patient is incompetent

If the patient is found to be incapable of managing his own affairs a **[3.31]** guardian ad litem will have to be appointed to represent his interests in the court proceedings.

If the patient has already instructed solicitors they should be informed of any decision with regard to treatment and of the need for an application to court as soon as possible. Where no solicitors have been instructed, steps must be taken to ensure that the patient is represented. In appropriate cases assistance can be obtained from the Official Solicitor who can act as litigation friend for patients incapable of managing their own affairs.

Where there is real doubt as to capacity, or there are foreseeable significant issues to be resolved it is important to make the application to the court as far in advance of the need for treatment as possible to avoid the unsatisfactory nature of an emergency application.

The patient's family must be consulted as suggested above in relation to what the patient might have wanted, and as to his interests.

An assessment of the patient's interests must be made, to include the non-medical interests.

In appropriate cases independent experts will have to be retained to confirm the treating doctor's diagnosis of capacity, condition and required treatment.

Proceedings should be started for an appropriate declaration as soon as possible[1].

There is no jurisdiction for the court to make an ex parte declaration, and in practice the court will not now make a declaration without an inter partes hearing. Without such a hearing any declaration obtained will not be binding on the party not represented.

The court must be provided accurately with all relevant information including the reasons why the patient has been found to lack capacity, the reasons why he needs the proposed treatment, and, if relevant, why the patient is refusing it. The judge must be made aware of any opposing views, whether or relatives or others, and of all information thought relevant to the determination of the patient's interests.

Any order of the court must be recorded and approved by the judge before transmission to the hospital or doctors concerned.

Where proceedings have been commenced in circumstances of urgency without the formal issue of proceedings these must be issued as soon as possible[2], and any assertions of fact communicated to the judge confirmed by affidavit. Evidence supporting the urgency of the application should also be filed.

1 Precedents for such applications are to be found in the Appendices, eg Draft claim form for claim for declaration that sterilisation of an adult patient be lawful; Incompetent Pregnant woman: Application for determination of capacity and declaration of best interests; Draft order in PVS case.
2 And an undertaking given that they will be issued.

Procedure

Form

[3.32] As a matter of practice treatment decision cases are generally heard in the Family Division of the High Court. Family proceedings as defined by the Matrimonial and Family Proceedings Act 1984, s 40 are excluded from the ambit of the Civil Procedure Rules 1998[1], and thus cases concerning children brought under the inherent jurisdiction or the Children Act 1989 continue to subject to the existing Family Division procedures. However, proceedings for a declaration in relation to adults are not family proceedings as defined by the MFPA 1984 and are, therefore, subject to the Civil Procedure Rules 1998[2]. Non-family treatment cases have not as yet been the subject of any specific practice direction in relation to the application of the Civil Procedure Rules 1998. However, *Practice Direction 8B*[3] specifies that any proceedings not otherwise dealt with which would have been brought by originating summons before 26 April 1999 shall be brought by means of a Part 8 claim form. Therefore, in so far as adult cases are concerned, that form should be used[4]. In cases concerning children the appropriate procedure under the inherent jurisdiction or the Children Act 1989 should be used.

1 CPR 1998, r 2.1(2).
2 CPR 1998, r 2.1.
3 Paras A.1.3 and A.3.
4 The Part 8 form is appropriate in any event where there is unlikely to be a substantial dispute of fact: CPR 1998, r 8.1(2). Otherwise, the Part 7 form must be used: CPR 1998, Pt 7 – *Practice Direction*, para 3. It is not thought that this requirement overrides *Practice Direction 8B*.

Remedies

[3.33] The remedy sought from the court will depend on whether the aim is to have the proposed treatment sanctioned or stopped.

- The doctor or authority seeking support for the treatment of a mentally incompetent adult patient will seek a declaration to the effect that the patient is incapable of consenting to it, that the proposed treatment is lawful and that it is in the best interests of the patient.
- If those acting on behalf of the patient seek to prevent the treatment they may apply for an injunction restraining those treating the patient from proceeding, and a declaration that the patient is capable of

consenting to or refusing treatment, and that the proposed treatment is not in the patients best interests, as appropriate to the case.

For the purposes of considering procedure, the same steps apply to each of these.

Commencement

Parties– In an application for a declaration that treatment is lawful, the **[3.34]** normal claimant will be the hospital authority whose doctor will be responsible for the treatment: this task should not be left to the patient, or his representatives, still less his family, even if the patient is being cared for at home[1]. Where the patient is being cared for in a private hospital it might be thought that the hospital, or the consultant responsible for the treatment should bring the application on the same principle. In any case in which the hospital authority or the doctor fail to bring the proceedings, they ought to be brought in the name of the patient, where necessary by a Litigation Friend. This will usually be a close relative or the Official Solicitor. The normal defendant in an 'approval' case will be the patient, represented where necessary by a Litigation Friend who will usually be either a close relative or the Official Solicitor. It is for the claimant bringing proceedings against a person incapable of managing their own affairs to ensure that such a representative is appointed: without this the proceedings and any order obtained will be of no effect.

If a close relative or other legitimately interested person objects to the order sought, it is occasionally appropriate for them to be joined as interested parties to enable their point of view to be represented at the final hearing. This is not always appropriate, however, particularly if an opposing view can be presented by the Litigation Friend or amicus, and may cause unnecessary delay. It has to be remembered that relatives and others have no legal right to be consulted in relation to the treatment of an adult, competent or incompetent, whatever may happen as a matter of good practice.

1 *Swindon v Marlborough NHS Trust v S* [1995] 3 Med LR 84.

Originating process – All proceeding for a declaration in relation to an **[3.35]** adult patient must be issued by a Part 8 claim form in the Family Division[1]. In relation to a child an originating summons should be used, again in the Family Division[2]. The process must be supported by an affidavit setting out the facts and grounds relied on for the relief which is sought.

1 For adult precedents see Appendices: eg, Draft claim form for claim for declaration that sterilisation of an adult patient be lawful; Incompetent Pregnant woman: Application for determination of capacity and declaration of best interests; Draft order in PVS case; Forcefeeding Particulars of Claim.
2 For child precedent see, App 6.5: *Draft declaration permitting Caesarean section.*

Non-publicity orders – In most treatment cases it will be appropriate to **[3.36]** apply for an order prohibiting publicity which identifies or is capable of identifying the patient or his family. It is established that the court has jurisdiction to make such an order[1] and will exercise its discretion to do so when it is necessary in the interests of the patient. Generally, the court will allow all the relevant facts to be published apart from those which would lead to the disclosure of the identity of the patient, thus balancing the public interest in open justice with the right of the patient to treatment without interference from the media and, less forcefully, medical confidentiality[2].

In *R v Westminster City Council, ex p Castelli*[3] anonymity was not granted to HIV positive applicants on the grounds that the court's discretion was not to be used merely to protect publicity or to avoid embarrassment. However, under the Human Rights Act 1998 it is arguable that such publicity would infringe the right to a private life under Art 8[4].

It should be emphasised that such orders are not intended to be for the benefit of the hospital, or its staff, and their identity will only be withheld where this is necessary to protect the identity of the patient from disclosure.

The effect of a non-publicity order survives the death of the patient, but any interested person may apply to the court for it to be lifted. There is no presumption that the order will be lifted in such circumstances. Indeed, if the case is of a sensitive type the order may be kept in force on the ground that staff might be deterred from treating such a patient if aware that publicity might follow his death.

The legal justification for such orders has not been considered fully at appellate level, and may be open to challenge.

Such an order will not be made where it will be of no effect, such as where the identity of the patient and his condition has been well publicised before proceedings are started[5]. There are some cases where publicity will be in the interests of the patient, such as where it might lead to the provision of important treatment[6].

1 *Re G (adult patient: publicity)* [1995] 2 FLR 528.
2 For an example of an order restricting publication of the identity of the patient and the hospital's staff see App 9.3: *Draft order in PVS case.*
3 [1996] 1 FLR 534.
4 Article 8 of the ECHR provides: '(1) Everyone has the right to respect for his private ... life, ... (2) There shall be no interference by a public authority with the exercise of this right except such as is in accordance with the law and is necessary in a democratic society in the interests of national security, public safety or the economic well-being of the country, for the prevention of disorder or crime, for the protection of health or morals, or for the protection of the rights and freedoms of others.' In *Botta v Italy* (1998) 26 EHRR 241 ECtHR, para 32 it was stated: 'the guarantee afforded by article 8 is primarily intended to ensure the development without outside interference of the personality of each individual in his relations with other human beings.'
5 As occurred in *Airedale NHS Trust v Bland* [1993] AC 789.
6 See *R v Cambridge DHA, ex p B (No 2)* [1996] 1 FLR 375.

[3.37] *Directions* – In all non-urgent cases an application should be made for directions. These will be given by a judge at a hearing in private and will usually address the following matters:

- Affidavit (or Statement of Truth) evidence;
- Attendance of expert and factual witnesses for cross-examination;
- Service of expert reports;
- Representation of patient;
- Leave for interested parties to be represented;
- Appointment of amicus curiae, if necessary;

- Leave to amicus to call evidence;
- Publicity; and
- Date of hearing.

Evidence – As a general rule evidence is adduced in the first instance in **[3.38]** affidavit (or Statement of Truth) form, but it is common for witnesses to be required to attend for cross-examination. In urgent cases formality has often been dispensed with, with expert reports being accepted without being formally verified, and even information being relayed to the court via counsel who has spoken to witnesses by telephone. This form of proceeding has been disapproved of by the Court of Appeal[1] and should be avoided if at all possible. It is likely to lead at best to a declaration which is ineffective, and at worst to the court being inadvertently misled and an order being made which, if acted on, exposes the doctors involved to criminal and civil liability.

Where informal evidence has been allowed, steps should always be taken as soon as possible after the hearing to obtain verification of it on affidavit of statement of truth and lodge this with the court. If it transpires that the court has been misled inadvertently the matter should be drawn to the attention of all parties to the proceedings and to the court.

1 *St George's Healthcare NHS Trust v S* [1999] Fam 26, CA.

Hearing – The hearing will, following *St George's Healthcare NHS Trust* **[3.39]** *v S*[1], invariably be inter partes, however urgent the matter may be. Hearings are possible at any hour of the day or night[2], but in most cases, if proper attention has been paid to the consent process, the need for a declaration will be perceived in good time for a hearing to be arranged on proper notice during normal court hours. If an urgent application is required, clear evidence explaining why the case is urgent and the degree of urgency should be obtained.

The hearing will proceed in the normal manner for a contested hearing. If possible skeleton arguments including the relevant points of law and authority for them should be prepared, as should a draft order.

1 [1999] Fam 26, CA.
2 The first instance hearing in *Re MB (an adult: medical treatment)* [1997] 2 FLR 426, [1997] FCR 541, [1997] 8 Med LR 217, took place between about 8 am and 9 pm, and the Court of Appeal sat between about 11 pm and 1 am.

Privacy – Hearings concerning treatment are often conducted in private, **[3.40]** and, in the case of children, invariably so. In relation to adult cases, hearings may be in private when the proceedings relate to confidential information and the confidentiality may be damaged by a public hearing and where a private hearing is necessary to protect the interests of any child or patient[1]. Where privacy is desired, it would be prudent to seek an order to this effect at the directions hearing to ensure that the case is listed appropriately.

1 CPR 1998, r 39.2(4).

Costs – There is no general rule with regard to costs in treatment cases. **[3.41]** Costs certainly do not normally follow the event as in other forms of litigation. In cases in which the Official Solicitor appears, either as Litigation Friend or as amicus it has been his policy to apply for an order for half his costs from the hospital authority. This is allowed on some occasions but not on others, without any general principle emerging from the decisions. The Court of Appeal has confirmed that there is a general discretion in these cases[1].

1 *LB v Croydon Health Authority (No 2)* [1995] 3 FCR 44, [1996] 1 FLR 253, [1996] Fam Law 141, CA (the Court of Appeal held that the judge had acted within his discretion in ordering the respondent to pay half of the Official Solicitor's costs).

[3.42]   *Appeals* – Appeal from a final order for a declaration to the Court of Appeal can only be made with permission of the first instance court or the Court of Appeal[1] and is subject to the usual rules for an appeal from the High Court. As with courts at first instance the Court of Appeal is able to act swiftly in cases of urgency.

1 CPR 1998, Pt 52.3.

E   OFFICIAL SOLICITOR

[3.43]   The Official Solicitor is an officer of the Supreme Court appointed by the Lord Chancellor[1]. He performs such duties as are provided for by statute or by, and in accordance with, any direction given by the Lord Chancellor[2]. The functions relevant to the subject-matter of this book are set out below.

1 Supreme Court Act 1981, s 90.
2 For details of the history of the office and its other functions, see the Official Solicitor's web site: **www.offsol.demon.co.uk**

Adviser to the judges of the High Court

[3.44]   The Official Solicitor may be called on at any time by a High Court judge for advice whether on a confidential basis or by appearing in cases as amicus curiae, in which role he will often instruct counsel, but may also appear by a solicitor from his office.

Investigation and report in any case at the request of the judge[1]

[3.45]   In cases involving treatment decisions in relation to an incapacitated adult the Official Solicitor will often be asked to report to the court on the issues in the case.

1 See *Harbin v Masterman* [1896] 1 Ch 351.

Representation of persons under a disability

[3.46]   The Official Solicitor will act for children or incapacitated adults if there is no-one else to do so. In such capacity he will act as guardian or litigation friend of the patient or child. The circumstances in which the Official Solicitor will act for a child are limited as there are a number of alternatives usually available. Further, by virtue of the Criminal Justice and Courts Services Act 2000 a new combined service will take over responsibility for acting as guardian ad litem for children. It is to be called the Children and Family Court Advisory and Support Service. By virtue of s 12 of the CJCSA 2000, the function of the Service (CAFCASS) will be to:

'(*a*) safeguard and promote the welfare of the children,

(*b*) give advice to any court about any application made to it in such proceedings,

(*c*) make provision for the children to be represented in such proceedings,

(*d*) provide information, advice and other support for the children and their families.'

At the time of writing it is intended that CAFCASS should assume responsibility for these functions on 1 April 2001. Thus, following the introduction of the Service, any references in this book to the Official Solicitor in relation to the conduct of proceedings concerning children should read as references to CAFCASS.

Intervention as party to prosecute an appeal

The Official Solicitor may prosecute an appeal to the Court of Appeal as a party in any case involving a person under a disability within the meaning of CPR 1998, Pt 21, r 1 which has been heard and determined by the High Court or county court where: **[3.47]**

(*a*) the Official Solicitor deems it in the patient's interest that the case should be considered by the Court of Appeal;

(*b*) the case may not otherwise be considered by the Court of Appeal; and

(*c*) the Court of Appeal gives leave[1].

This power will be required very rarely, as usually either the Official Solicitor or some other guardian will be acting for the party in whose interests an appeal should be launched.

1 *Practice Direction (Mental Health Appeal)* [1989] 1 WLR 133. This direction was given by the Lord Chancellor during and for the purpose of the appeal of *Re F (mental patient: sterilisation)* [1990] 2 AC 1.

Consultation

In cases concerning sterilisation of mentally incapacitated adults or withdrawal of artificial nutrition and hydration the Official Solicitor should always be consulted by anyone intending to make an application for a declaration[1]. His office will be prepared to give advice about procedure and an indication as to whether it is a case in which his office will wish to be interested[2]. **[3.48]**

In other treatment cases it is prudent to alert the Official Solicitor's office to the case and establish whether he will wish to intervene. It should always be remembered that this type of case should not be conducted in the same way as conventional litigation between parties solely pursuing their own interests, but in recognition that there is a difficult problem for the parties and the court to solve. Therefore openness and a sharing of all relevant information with the Official Solicitor will assist in the resolution of the difficulties which have resulted in a case being referred to the court in the first place.

In cases of extreme urgency it is possible to contact the staff of the Official Solicitor outside normal office hours.

1 See Chaps 4 and 9 for the procedures described.
2 Contact details can be found at **www.offsol.demon.co.uk** and the current legal enquiries number is (020) 7911 7127.

CONTENTS

A   GENERAL

Sterilisation is one of the most fundamental forms of medical treatment   **[4.1]**
that can be provided. It removes, often permanently, the ability to
reproduce. Medically it is now relatively simply achieved, and therefore

the temptation to solve perceived social problems by this route may be increased. While the procedure is performed on men and women who consent to it as a matter of routine, this will always be a socially sensitive area requiring meticulous attention to counselling and consent protocols if the anxieties provoked by history are to be allayed.

Sterilisation of people unable to make their own decisions is an emotive and sensitive subject and any case involving it must be treated with considerable care and caution. The reasons are perhaps obvious, but are worth stating clearly.

First, the twentieth century has seen horrific policies implemented for this purpose of promoting ethnic purity. The Nazis embarked on widespread sterilisation of those groups, including the mentally disabled, as part of their overall plan of Aryanization. Less well remembered is the policy followed by many states in the USA encouraging the compulsory sterilisation of mental patients, a policy found to be constitutional by the Supreme Court in 1927 where Holmes J was able to say with impunity[1]:

'Three generations of imbeciles is enough.'

Such attitudes have now largely disappeared by reason of the emphasis placed on human rights which are recognised now in domestic law to include a right to a private and family life, and the right to found a family[2]. Therefore a proposal to sterilise someone without their consent or even understanding can at first sight seem to be a denial of these rights and a harking back to old attitudes.

However, the second factor sometimes counter-balances the first. Paternalistic attitudes towards the care of those with learning disabilities have to some extent been replaced with a desire to enable such people to live as independent and fulfilled lives as possible. A potential partner who lacks capacity to consent may be prevented from having sexual intercourse because of the disadvantages – both psychological and physical – of producing children. However, sterilisation may allow a sexual relationship to develop unhindered. Thus sterilisation, rather than being a restriction on a person's liberties, can be a means of freeing a person with learning disabilities from the constraints that would otherwise be necessary.

The third factor adds a constraint on sterilisation to the first. The last two decades of the twentieth century have seen an increasing awareness of and concern about the sexual abuse of those who cannot look after themselves, both children and adults. Therefore the supervision of those who care for vulnerable people has become increasingly strict.

For these reasons, and doubtless many others, the sterilisation of a patient, whether child or adult, should not currently be undertaken without an appropriate application to the court being made. As with any other invasive procedure sterilisation cannot be performed without the consent of the competent patient. With regard to the competent patient the normal requirements for obtaining consent apply[3]. However, particular attention needs to be paid to the need to explain to the patient the risks of the procedure.

1 *Buck v Bell* 247 US 200 at 207 (1927).

2 See the Human Rights Act 1998; and the European Convention on Human Rights, Arts 8 and 12.
3 See Chap 1, *Consent – General.*

B THE COMPETENT PATIENT

General rule
No sterilisation should be performed on a competent patient without his   **[4.2]**
or her consent. There are likely to be very few, if any, exceptions to this rule. Where in the course of some other operation, for example a Caesarean section, it is considered necessary to perform some further operation the result of which would be to sterilise the patient, it would be most unwise to proceed without consent unless it can definitely be demonstrated that the preservation of the life or health of the patient requires immediate intervention before a consent can be obtained. It should not be presumed that a patient would have consented to such a step.

Informed consent
While the transatlantic doctrine of informed consent forms no part of   **[4.3]**
English law[1] there will be a duty to abide by the practice of a body of responsible and competent professional opinion in relation to warning patients of the potential consequences and risks of the proposed procedure.

It is now general professional practice, and therefore a requirement of the duty of care, for patients to be counselled as to the risks of the sterilisation not being effective, and as to any interim precautions that ought to be taken until confirmatory tests or examinations have been performed. Failure to comply with such a practice will render the medical practitioner liable in an action for negligence should the patient consent to what turns out to be an ineffective sterilisation in reliance on defective counselling. Damages awarded may include compensation for the pregnancy and birth but in general will not now include damages for the maintenance of the child[2]. In such an action it is necessary for the patient to prove that he or she would not have consented to the procedure but for the defective counselling[3].

The NHS now uses a standard form of consent for sterilisation[4], but practitioners need to be aware that the completion of a form does not necessarily amount to proof that the duty in relation to counselling has been fulfilled.

1 *Sidaway v Board of Governors of the Bethlem Royal Hospital and the Maudsley Hospital* [1985] AC 871, [1985] 2 WLR 480, [1985] All ER 643; see further Chap 1, *Consent – General.*
2 *MacFarlane v Tayside Health Board* [2000] 2 AC 59, [1999] 3 WLR 1301 restricted the right to recovery of maintenance of a child. Note the subsequent decision in *Rand v East Dorset Health Authority* (2000) 56 BMLR 39.
3 *Rance v Mid-Downs Health Authority* [1991] 1 QB 587, [1991] 2 WLR 159, [1991] 1 All ER 801.
4 See App 4.1: *Consent form (sterilisation or vasectomy).*

The role of partner/spouse
As in other areas of patient care there is no duty in law to obtain the   **[4.4]**
consent of the spouse or partner of the patient who is to be sterilised.

Further, the consent of the partner or spouse does not amount to legal authority for the procedure, even if the patient is unconscious or otherwise unable to give consent at the time. However, where the patient is accompanied by the partner or spouse to consultations and the patient wishes him or her to be included in the counselling and to participate in the decision, then the medical practitioner is likely to be found to owe a duty of care to the partner or spouse as well as the patient. Family planning is, after all, a family matter with consequences for persons other than the patient, and is an area where many patients will wish to share the decision-making process.

On the other hand, there is no duty on the part of the medical practitioner to include the spouse or partner in the decision-making process, unless the patient wishes this to happen. A third party has no right to prevent a sterilisation procedure taking place, any more than a termination of pregnancy[1].

1 *Paton v British Pregnancy Advisory Service Trustees* [1979] QB 276, [1978] 3 WLR 687, [1978] 2 All ER 987; *Paton v United Kingdom* [1980] 3 EHRR 408.

Procedure

[4.5] While in principle there is no legal distinction between the requirements for obtaining consent to a sterilisation to any other form of medical treatment it would be prudent in the interests of both the patient and the medical practitioner to ensure that not only has a proper counselling process taken place, but that there is proof available of this, in a form which also provides a reminder to the patient of the advice. Therefore the following steps should be considered:

- Adequate time – well in advance of the proposed procedure – should be allowed for counselling.
- The counselling should be performed by the medical practitioner who is to perform the procedure or a practitioner who is in possession of adequate knowledge of the available techniques, the proposed method, the general outcome figures for that procedure as compared with all others, and the outcome rates of the practitioner who is to perform the operation, where this is known.
- While much information may be provided in written form, it is unwise to rely solely on printed leaflets, without ensuring by discussion that the patient understands the information provided.
- The patient may be encouraged to involve the spouse or partner in the discussion, but the decision whether to do so is the patient's, not the medical practitioner's.
- If possible the patient should be provided with a written summary of the information provided in counselling. While general information might be in the form of a leaflet, information specific to the patient will need to be in a letter or similar form.
- The medical practitioner should keep a record of the advice given. While the record of routine information might be reduced to a common printed form, it is more convincing proof of what has been said if it is recorded at the time of the consultation and is specific to the patient.

C CHILDREN

General principle – children with no learning disabilities

It will obviously be rare for anyone to wish to sterilise a child who is   [4.6]
expected to grow up into a mentally competent adult for non-therapeutic
or 'social' reasons. It is difficult to think of circumstances in which any
competent medical practitioner would wish to carry out such an operation or in which a person with parental responsibility would be willing to
consent to it. If such a thing were contemplated the procedures referred
to in the next section would have to be considered.

On occasion it will be necessary to consider treatment required for
compelling therapeutic reasons which will have the side effect of sterilis-
ing the patient. Radiotherapy or surgery in the area of the uterus for
cancer are examples. Obviously the effects of such treatment must be
discussed very carefully with those having parental responsibility, and, to
the extent that is appropriate having regard to the age and maturity of the
child, with the patient. However, if the treatment is consented to in
accordance with the general principles governing authority for treating a
child[1], it may be performed without reference to the courts.

General principle – children with learning disabilities

Where children with learning disabilities require treatment for ther-   [4.7]
apeutic reasons which will have sterilisation as a side effect, it may be
authorised in the same way as for children without such disabilities.

Occasionally it has been thought necessary to propose sterilisation of a
child with mental disabilities for the sole purpose of preventing the child
becoming pregnant. In the first such case to come before the English
courts[1], concerning an 11 year old girl suffering from Sotos syndrome,
whose mother was anxious, with the support of a surgeon, that she should
be prevented from having children, the proposal received short shrift. As
the case has conditioned much of the approach by the courts to this class
of case, it is worth setting out part of the judgment in full[2]:

> 'Dr Gordon, however, maintained that provided the parent or
> parents consented the decision was one made pursuant to the
> exercise of his clinical judgement and that no interference could be
> tolerated in his clinical freedom. The other consultants did not
> agree. Their opinion was that a decision to sterilise a child was not
> entirely within a doctor's clinical judgment, save only when
> sterilisation was the treatment of choice for some disease, as for
> instance, when in order to treat a child and to ensure her direct
> physical well-being, it might be necessary to perform a
> hysterectomy to remove a malignant uterus. Whilst the side effect
> of such an operation would be to sterilise, the operation would be
> solely performed for therapeutic purposes.
>
> I entirely accept their opinions. I cannot believe, and the
> evidence does not warrant the view, that a decision to carry out an
> operation of this nature performed for non-therapeutic purposes
> on a minor can be held to be within the doctor's sole clinical
> judgement.
>
> It is quite clear that once a child is a ward of court no important
> step in the life of that child can be taken without the consent of the

court, and I cannot conceive of a more important step than that which was proposed in this case.

A review of the whole of the evidence leads me to the conclusion that in a case of a child of 11 years of age, where the evidence shows that her mental and physical condition and attainments have already improved, and where her future prospects are as yet unpredictable, where the evidence also shows that she is unable as yet to understand and appreciate the implications of this operation and could not give a valid or informed consent, but the likelihood is that in later years she will be able to make her own choice, where, I believe, the frustration and resentment of realising (as she would one day) what had happened could be devastating, an operation of this nature is, in my view, contraindicated.

For these, and for the other reasons, to which I have adverted, I have come to the conclusion that this operation is neither medically indicated nor necessary, and that it would not be in D's best interests for it to be performed.'

It should be noted that the support of a responsible medical practitioner and of a caring mother advocating the procedure was insufficient to persuade the court to allow it. The sole test was whether the procedure was then and there in the best interests of the child. To the judge the answer was that the procedure was clearly not in the child's best interests.

In contrast the House of Lords[3] permitted the sterilisation of a 17 year old suffering from a moderate degree of mental handicap and very limited intellectual development determining that it was in her best interests. The evidence was that she was showing signs of sexual awareness and that pregnancy would have been highly detrimental to her well-being. However, *Re D* has influenced judges in later cases to place a heavy restriction on how decisions in such cases should be taken. In a speech which was not expressly supported by the other Law Lords Lord Templeman expressed the view that[4]:

'sterilisation of a girl under 18 should only be carried out with the leave of a High Court judge. A doctor performing a sterilisation operation with the consent of the parents might still be liable in criminal, civil or professional proceedings. A court exercising the wardship jurisdiction emanating from the Crown is the only authority which is empowered to authorise such a drastic step as sterilisation after a full and informed investigation.'

This statement cannot be taken literally. It has been since pointed out by Lord Donaldson of Lymington that an operation performed with the consent of the parents on a girl who was not a ward of court would not necessarily be unlawful. However, it laid down a practice which ought to be followed:

'I think he was combining two propositions. First, he was saying that no such operation ought ever to be undertaken without the court's approval even if the parents or the child consented and that if such an operation was contemplated the child should be made a ward of court and the leave of the court sought[5]. Second, he was saying that, where this was done, the decision was of such difficulty and delicacy that it should be undertaken not only by a High Court judge, but one having special experience.'[6]

In the same case Lord Griffiths said of *Re D (a minor) (wardship: sterilisation* that[7]:

'it stands as a stark warning of the danger of leaving the decision to sterilise in the hands of those having the immediate care of the woman, even when they genuinely believe that they are acting in her best interests.'

The position in relation to children is, therefore, that, although a sterilisation operation for non-therapeutic reasons *might* be lawful if performed with the consent of a person having parental responsibility, or, if *Gillick* competent, of the child herself, no prudent practitioner or hospital would be well advised to proceed without ensuring that the permission of a Family Division judge had been obtained. Where the operation is for therapeutic reasons no application to the court is required[8].

1 *Re D (a minor) (wardship: sterilisation)* [1976] Fam 185, Helibron J.
2 [1976] Fam 185 at 196.
3 *Re B (a minor) (wardship: sterilisation)* [1988] AC 199.
4 [1988] AC 199 at 206–207.
5 It may be that it is unnecessary to make the child a ward of court. As with other treatment decisions what is required is that the court exercises its inherent jurisdiction: it is not necessarily a wardship jurisdiction and unless there is a need for on-going wardship supervision a simple application under the inherent jurisdiction should be made.
6 *Re F (mental patient: sterilisation)* [1990] 2 AC 1 at 20.
7 [1990] 2 AC 1 at 69. See also Butler-Sloss LJ at page 41–42, Lord Brandon at page 54 and 56, Lord Goff at page 79.
8 *Re E (a minor) (medical treatment)* [1991] 2 FLR 585; and *Re GF* [1992] 1 FLR 293.

Best interests

A sterilisation procedure for non-therapeutic reasons, like any other **[4.8]** form of treatment, should only be carried out if it is in the best interests of the child. Clearly such interests cannot be assessed by exclusive reference to medical factors, and, indeed, many doctors may feel that they are not well equipped to make the assessment, given the social issues involved.

The factors which are taken into account in assessing the best interests of a child are much the same as those for an adult[1].

1 As to which see para **[4.11]** below. For a short-list of factors see *Practice Note (Official Solicitor: Sterilisation)* [1996] 2 FLR 111, reproduced at App 4.2 below; and see also *Re M (Wardship: Sterilisation)* [1988] 2 FLR 497, [1988] Fam Law 434; *Re P (A Minor) (Wardship: Sterilisation)* [1989] 1 FLR 182, [1989] Fam Law 102.

Procedure

Where a proposal to sterilise a child irreversibly is being considered the **[4.9]** following steps need to be taken.

It must be determined whether the procedure is merely the side effect of treatment required for therapeutic reasons, eg to treat cancer. If it is, then the normal procedures for obtaining authority to treat a child may be adopted. It is suggested that proposals justified on the ground of the treatment of dysmenorrhoea should be examined carefully to ensure that there is no less radical treatment available pending the child's attainment of majority.

If the prime purpose of the procedure is sterilisation, and the child is not mentally disabled, it is highly unlikely that the procedure could be found to be in the best interests of the patient and careful consideration would need to be given to whether the decision should not be deferred until the child has achieved adulthood. If the child is *Gillick* competent and desires the operation, given the sensitivities described above, an application to the court should be seriously considered before proceeding.

If the child is mentally disabled and the proposed procedure is 'non-therapeutic' there should be a full discussion with those having parental responsibility. Relevant information should be obtained from social workers and others who may have views on the child's best interests.

Consideration should be given to the possibility of alternative contraceptive measures particularly where there is a prospect of the child gaining in maturity and understanding, and to whether even with sterilisation, sexual encounters are likely to occur or be permitted, or be in the child's interests.

If it is decided after discussions that an operation in childhood for permanent sterilisation would be in the child's best interests, and that it would not be reasonable to wait until adulthood, an application should be made to the Family Division under the inherent jurisdiction for leave to perform the operation, rather than under s 8 of the Children Act 1989 for a specific issue order[1]. The application should be made either by the person having parental responsibility, or by the hospital[2]. The patient must always be a party and will require a guardian; the Official Solicitor will often act in this role. Where the Official Solicitor is not the litigation friend of the patient, he should be joined as a defendant or respondent[3]. There may be some doubt as to the effect of any order made when the Official Solicitor is the defendant to proceedings brought in the name of the patient. Any order made in such a case will not bind non-parties, such as the doctor or hospital proposing to perform the treatment, and may not prevent a later action by the patient against them. This is, however, likely to be a matter of academic interest only where the operation performed is one which the court has approved. An action then brought in the patient's name would be liable to be struck out. However, to avoid this theoretical problem it would be desirable for the hospital managers to be made a party to the application.

The application will need to be supported by evidence from carers and others to explain why an irreversible operation is necessary in the best interests of the child, and to describe the consideration and consultation that led to the decision. Medical evidence will be required about the risks to the patient of not being sterilised, and of the operation itself[4].

The Official Solicitor will carry out his own investigations and obtain expert evidence as appropriate. He will require the patient to be interviewed in private by his representative[5].

Hospitals may be required to pay at least a contribution towards the costs of the Official Solicitor where he is involved in the case.

1 See *Practice Note (Official Solicitor: Sterilisation)*, para 2, reproduced in App 4.2 below.
2 See n 1, para 4.
3 See n 2 above.
4 See below for the factors likely to be taken into account and para 8 of *Practice Note (Official Solicitor: Sterilisation)*, reproduced in App 4.2 below.
5 See *Practice Note (Official Solicitor: Sterilisation)*, para 7, reproduced in App 4.2 below.

D ADULTS

Competent adults

The general principles are dealt with above.   **[4.10]**

Adults lacking capacity to consent

Capacity

The mental capacity of an adult to consent to a sterilisation procedure is   **[4.11]**
no different from that applicable to any other form of medical treatment[1].
As, however, the procedure is intended to be irreversible, and involves
the fundamental right to reproduce and found family, the capacity must
be commensurate with the gravity of the decision to be taken[2]. Therefore,
although there is a presumption that patients have capacity, unless the
contrary is shown, it is incumbent on those proposing to perform a
sterilisation procedure to ensure that the patient has the requisite degree
of capacity. Doctors who proceed on an assumption of capacity risk a
subsequent, retrospective finding that their patient lacked the relevant
capacity. If a finding of incapacity is made it must be considered whether
this is likely to be permanent, or whether there is some prospect of it
being regained. Sterilisation is unlikely to be an appropriate step in the
interests of the patient, if capacity may be regained in the foreseeable
future.

1 See Chap 2, *Consent – Adults* and *Re C (adult: refusal of medical treatment)* [1994] 1 WLR 290.
2 *Re T (adult: refusal of treatment)* [1993] Fam 95 at 113.

Best interests

Where an adult lacks the mental capacity to consent to sterilisation, it will   **[4.12]**
be lawful for the operation to be performed if it is in the patient's best
interests that it be performed[1]. Where the procedure is 'non-therapeutic',
ie for contraceptive purposes and not ancillary to the treatment of some
physical condition, a declaration of the court should be sought that the
procedure is lawful before embarking on it: it falls into the special
category of cases where such a step is required. In *Re GF* it was stated
that it was not necessary to apply to court where two medical practitioners are satisfied that a procedure which will sterilise the patient is:

> '(1) necessary for therapeutic purposes, (2) in the best interests of
> the patient, and (3) that there is no practicable, less intrusive means
> of treating the condition.'[2]

In *Re S*[3] the Court of Appeal stressed that parties should err on the side
of bringing sterilisation cases before the court: the President noted that
the *Re GF* criteria should be 'cautiously interpreted and applied'[4]:

'if a particular case lies anywhere near the [*Re GF*] boundary line it should be referred to the court by way of application for a declaration of lawfulness.'[5]

Thus, even in 'therapeutic' sterilisation cases, the court will examine critically whether the sterilisation is in the patient's best interests[6].

The potential for confusion about how the patient's best interests are to be judged is discussed in Chapter 2 above. In sterilisation cases, as in others, in practice the court will judge for itself where the best interests of the patient lie, paying all due regard to medical opinion.

Best interests encompasses medical, emotional and all other welfare issues. The court will examine the proportionality of the proposed treatment as against the problem to be solved. Although a doctor must assess the patient's best interests in accordance with a professional standard of care, the court will not be bound by a medical opinion, but will seek the best answer from the alternatives available. In the words of Thorpe LJ[4]:

'In practice the dispute will generally require the court to choose between two or more possible treatments both or all of which comfortably pass the Bolam test. As most of us know from experience a patient contemplating treatment for a physical condition or illness is often offered a range of alternatives with counter-balancing advantages and disadvantages. One of the most important services provided by a consultant is to explain the available alternatives to the patient, particularly concentrating on those features of advantage and disadvantage most relevant to his needs and circumstances. In a developing relationship of confidence the consultant then guides the patient to make the choice that best suits his circumstances and personality. It is precisely because the patient is prevented by disability from that exchange that the judge must in certain circumstances either exercise the choice between alternative available treatments or perhaps refuse any form of treatment. In deciding what is best for the disabled patient the judge must have regard to the patient's welfare as the paramount consideration. That embraces issues far wider than the medical. Indeed it would be undesirable and probably impossible to set bounds to what is relevant to a welfare determination.'

1 *Re F (mental patient: sterilisation)* [1990] 2 AC 1.
2 *Re GF* [1992] 1 FLR 293 per Butler-Sloss P at 294; and see also *Re E (a minor) (medical treatment)* [1991] 2 FLR 585.
3 *Re S (Sterilisation)* [2000] 2 FLR 389, [2000] 2 FCR 452, [2000] Fam Law 711.
4 *Re S (Sterilisation)* [2000] 2 FLR 389 at 401 per Butler-Sloss P.
5 *Re S (Sterilisation)* [2000] 2 FLR 389 at 405 per Thorpe LJ.
6 *Re S (Sterilisation)* [2000] 2 FLR 389, [2000] 2 FCR 452, [2000] Fam Law 711; and see *Re Z (medical treatment: hysterectomy)* [2000] 1 FLR 523, [2000] 1 FCR 274, (2000) 53 BMLR 53, [2000] Fam Law 321.

General application of best interests principle in sterilisation cases

[4.13]   While every case will obviously turn on its own facts reference should be made to the cases that have been before the courts for guidance on the considerations that will be taken into account in deciding on the patient's best interests[1].

1 *Re F (mental patient: sterilisation)* [1990] 2 AC 1; *Re W* [1993] 1 FLR 381; *Re LC (medical treatment: sterilisation)* [1997] 2 FLR 258; *Re S (adult sterilisation)* [1998] 1 FLR 944; *Re X (adult sterilisation)* [1998] 2 FLR 1124; and *Re A (medical treatment: male sterilisation)* [2000] 1 FLR 549, CA sub nom *Re A (male: sterilisation)*.

It is suggested that the following factors are among those which need to be considered:

The capacity of the patient – While patients may lack the capacity to consent to sterilisation, they may be able to take decisions about their sexual life, perhaps guided by skilled counselling. The disability of others may not be permanent. If there is a prospect of improvement, certainly if there is a chance that a patient will regain the capacity to consent to treatment, or to marriage, then it would be highly unlikely that the court would find sterilisation in his or her best interests[1]. **[4.14]**

1 *Re D (a minor) (wardship: sterilisation)* [1976] Fam 185 at 195. While this case concerned a child, there is no reason why the factors considered would not be relevant in the case of an adult.

The risk of sexual contact – Many disabled people will be sheltered from the chance of sexual contact for their own protection and that of other disabled people they may meet in residential homes, and day centres, whether or not they are capable of reproduction. Others will have evinced no or little interest in such contact. Thus one of the reasons in *Re D (a minor) (wardship: sterilisation)* for the declaration being refused was that the patient: **[4.15]**

> 'had as yet shown no interest in the opposite sex, and … her opportunities for promiscuity, if she were so minded, were virtually non-existent, as her mother never leaves her side and she is never allowed out alone.'[1]

In *Re B (a minor) (wardship: sterilisation)*, on the other hand, the patient was showing signs of sexual awareness and drive, and her carers' philosophy was to allow her as much freedom as was consistent with her disability[2]. Similarly, in *Re F (mental patient: sterilisation)* the patient had benefited from being given a greater degree of freedom of movement within the hospital grounds, and had already formed an attachment with a fellow patient which was not thought to be harmful[3]. In *Re W*[4] the presence of such a risk influenced the court in favour of the declaration. In contrast the possibility of a risk arising in the future may not be sufficient[5]. The risk may need to be 'identifiable' as opposed to 'speculative'[6].

1 [1976] Fam 185 at 194.
2 [1988] AC 199 at 208.
3 [1990] 2 AC 1 at 9.
4 [1993] 1 FLR 381.
5 *Re LC (medical treatment: sterilisation)* [1997] 2 FLR 258; *Re S (adult sterilisation)* [1998] 1 FLR 944 at 949D-E, cf *Re X (adult sterilisation)* [1998] 2 FLR 1124 at 1126G–1127A.
6 *Re S (adult sterilisation)* [1998] 1 FLR 944 at 949D-E.

[4.16] *The availability of other methods of contraception* – The sensitivity concerning sterilisation is because of its irreversibility. Therefore other methods should be considered before opting for it. In *Re D* the judge found that other methods could be used, if contraception was necessary[1]. In *Re B* and in *Re F*, by contrast, an oral contraceptive had been found to produce undesirable side effects[2].

In *Re ZM and OS*[3] the court considered the case of Z, a 19 year old with Down's syndrome. She had menstrual periods that were heavy, painful and irregular. There was medical disagreement about what was in Z's best interests. Bennett J determined that a 'Mirena' contraceptive coil was not sufficient to achieve the aim of stopping Z's troubling periods and that it was in her best interests to undergo a laparoscopic subtotal hysterectomy.

In contrast, in *Re S*[4] the Court of Appeal over-turned the first instance judge's determination that a subtotal hysterectomy should be performed on a 29 year old woman with severe learning disabilities. The Court of Appeal decided that the judge had failed to give sufficient weight to the unanimous medical opinion which favoured using the less invasive 'Mirena' coil. Whilst S's mother favoured hysterectomy, the Court of Appeal held – applying a true best interests test[5] – that it was appropriate first to undertake the less invasive coil procedure and only if it failed would it be appropriate for the matter to be returned to court to consider whether hysterectomy should be undertaken[6].

Where a patient is developing a relationship of significance, consideration should be given to the capacity and maturity of his/her partner. Thus even if it is felt that the patient does not have the ability adequately to ensure birth control, if their partner can adequately ensure that contraception is used then there is no current need for sterilisation.

1 [1976] Fam 185 at 195.
2 [1988] AC 199 at 207; [1990] 2 AC 1 at 10.
3 *Re Z (medical treatment: hysterectomy)* [2000] 1 FLR 523, [2000] 1 FCR 274.
4 *Re S (Sterilisation)* [2000] 2 FLR 389.
5 Discussed above in Chap 3, *Deciding for Others*, para **[3.7]**.
6 See *Re S (Sterilisation)* [2000] 2 FLR 389 at 401F per Butler-Sloss P.

[4.17] *The need for counselling and preparation* – Expert evidence was adduced in *Re A*[1] to the effect that sterilisation on its own was not a solution to the problems involved in allowing a patient with learning disabilities to enjoy sexual relations and that there was a need for counselling and education which it was the duty of local services to provide. The Court of Appeal commented that to expect such facilities to be available might be unrealistic. Nonetheless it might be thought that it would be a denial of the right of the patient with learning disabilities to lead as full and rewarding a life as possible, to claim that sterlisation on its own is likely to be a solution to the problems involved.

1 *Re A (medical treatment: male sterilisation)* [2000] 1 FLR 549, CA, sub nom *Re A (male sterlisation)*.

[4.18] *The risks of pregnancy* – In some patients with mental disabilities, the experience of pregnancy would be disastrous because of a lack of understanding of the process or its consequences, inability to care for a child, with the consequent adverse effects on the patient's mental and physical condition[1].

1 For example, see *T v T* [1988] Fam 52, where the patient had already become pregnant
and required a termination as well as sterilisation; *Re B (a minor) (wardship: sterilisation)*
[1988] AC 199 at 208–209. *Re F (mental patient: sterilisation)*, where it was said ([1990] 2
AC 1 at 10): 'For F to become pregnant would be a disaster ... She has a much
diminished ability to cope with the problems of pregnancy and would not be able to cope
with labour or looking after the child once born. Professor B...used the word "catastrophic" to describe the psychiatric consequences of her having a child'.

Freedom of association – In some cases the patient can be given more   [4.19]
freedom to associate with others and form friendships which might be
dangerous if there was a risk of pregnancy. The patient in *Re F* was
clearly enjoying her relationship with a man with whom she could not be
safely left on their own because the encounters risked a catastrophic
pregnancy.

The effect on the standard of care – It is sometimes argued that the   [4.20]
knowledge that a patient is incapable of reproduction will cause the
regime of supervision and care to be slackened, even when his interests
would still require a high level of protection from exploitation, and other
dangers.

Male patients – To date there has only been one application to the court   [4.21]
seeking a declaration for the sterilisation of a male[1]. This was refused as
not being in his best interests, although there was evidence that he was
sexually aware and might proceed to sexual intercourse if not prevented
from doing so[2]. However, there was no immediate risk of his being
allowed to have casual intercourse, and he enjoyed no stable relationship
in which this was likely to be permitted. The risks that a disabled partner
might become impregnated were not taken into account as being relevant.

1 *Re A (medical treatment: male sterilisation)* [2000] 1 FLR 549, CA.
2 Mr James Munby QC comments in his chapter in *Principles of Medical Law* (Kennedy &
Grubb eds, OUP (1998)), p 260 that this scarcity of cases is: 'A revealing insight into
societal attitudes to gender, sexuality and contraception'.
  It may also be due to the greater difficulty in identifying the advantages of sterilisation
to the male patient, as opposed to his carers and associates.

The immediacy of the risks

The court will be slow to grant an order approving of a non-therapeutic   [4.22]
sterilisation unless the risks identified as justifying the operation are
present risks and not theoretical future risks. The Official Solicitor
emphasises this in his guidance[1]:

> '... the Official Solicitor anticipates that the judge will normally
> require evidence clearly establishing ...
>   That the condition which it is sought to avoid will in fact occur,
> eg, in the case of a contraceptive sterilisation that there is a need for
> contraception because: (*a*) the patient is physically capable of
> procreation, and (*b*) the patient is likely to engage in sexual activity,
> at the present or in the near future, under circumstances where
> there is a real danger as opposed to mere chance that pregnancy is
> likely to result.'

The cases at first instance now establish that there must be a clearly
identifiable[2] risk against which sterilisation is the only practicable means

of protecting the patient. Thus, in three recent cases declarations have been refused because there is no immediate realistic chance of the patient being allowed to have sexual contact whether or not there was a sterilisation. These cases emphasise that a desire to prevent a mentally disabled person procreating is no reason of itself to permit a sterilisation to be performed.

1 *Practice Note (Official Solicitor: Sterilisation)* [1996] 2 FLR 111 reproduced at App 4.2 below.
2 See *Re LC (medical treatment: sterilisation)* [1997] 2 FLR 258, Thorpe J; *Re S (adult sterilisation)* [1998] 1 FLR 944 at 944D-E, Johnson J; *Re A (medical treatment: male sterilisation)* [2000] 1 FLR 549, CA; cf *Re X (adult sterilisation)* [1998] 2 FLR 1124 at 1126G–1127A, Holman J.

Procedure

[4.23] Where it is proposed to perform a non-therapeutic sterilisation operation on a patient incapable of consenting to the procedure, there should be the fullest consultation with the carers, and any close relatives who have a caring role, about the need for the procedure, the circumstances in which the patient lives, and the benefits and disadvantages of proceeding.

If it is apparent that a court application will have to be made in order to sanction the performance of the procedure[1], it would be prudent for those making the application to have available the favourable opinion of an independent surgical expert, and of a psychiatrist specialising in the rehabilitation and care of patients with learning difficulties.

The application should be started by issue of a claim form under CPR 1998, Pt 8[2]. The proceedings should be issued in the Family Division. This should be accompanied by the claimant's evidence in writing. All such cases will be treated as multi-track, and therefore subject to case management under CPR 1998, Pt 29. Provision will have to be made for:

- the hearing to be in private, in accordance with the usual practice in sterilisation cases, and for an order that the identity of the parties, and such witnesses and others who may lead to the identification of the patient should not be disclosed[3];
- evidence to be admitted in writing;
- a timetable for the service of evidence in reply;
- the identification of the witnesses of fact who will be required to attend for cross-examination;
- the discipline and identity of expert witnesses, whether their evidence is to be admitted only in writing, and whether they are to attend for cross-examination. While the court will have the power to order there to be a single expert[4], this is unlikely to be desirable in any other than the most clear and undisputed case in this field. The whole purpose of the matter coming before the court is to ensure that the issues are properly examined in the interests of the patient and the public; there will be a danger of the public perceiving the court as merely rubber-stamping the opinion of the appointed expert if this sort of restriction were to gain currency;
- the joinder of any further parties thought necessary, such as the medical practitioner or hospital it is proposed should perform the operation, or any relative strongly opposing the application;

● a timetable for progress towards and during the hearing.

1 See para **[4.12]** above: no application is needed when the procedure is necessary for therapeutic purposes, in the best interests of the patient, and *importantly* (3) that there is no practicable, less intrusive means of treating the condition. If there is any doubt whether all these factors are satisfied an application should be made: see *Re S (Sterilisation)* [2000] 2 FLR 389.
2 See App 4.3: *Draft Order for Claim Form for declaration that sterilisation of adult lawful.*
3 See Chap 3, para **[3.22]** above.
4 CPR 1998, Pt 37, r 37.2.

CHAPTER 5

Abortion

CONTENTS

The termination of pregnancy is largely governed by statute law. While **[5.1]** this book is primarily concerned with decision-making in medicine, in this field it is necessary to be aware of the legal framework within which the decision must be taken. Any practitioner in this area must be aware of the fact that any termination of pregnancy is likely to be unlawful and a serious criminal offence unless there is a legal justification for it. By the same token the patient's freedom of choice and decision is circumscribed by the law.

Offences Against the Person Act 1861

The procuring of a miscarriage of a foetus is a criminal offence unless **[5.2]** some legal justification can be identified[1]:

> 'Every woman, being with child, who, with intent to procure her own miscarriage, shall unlawfully administer to herself any poison or other noxious thing, or shall unlawfully use any instrument or other means whatsoever with the like intent, and whosoever, with intent to procure the miscarriage of any woman, whether she be or not with child, shall unlawfully administer to her or cause to be taken by her any poison or other noxious thing, or shall unlawfully use any instrument or other means whatsoever with the like intent shall be guilty ... '

This offence is not committed by the termination of the life of a child in the course of delivery[2]. It is a lawful justification for procuring a miscarriage that it was done for the purpose of saving the life of the mother[3].

1 Offences Against the Person Act 1861, s 58.
2 But see below for the offence of child destruction.
3 *R v Bourne* [1939] 1 KB 687.

Infant Life (Preservation) Act 1929

If a foetus is capable of being born alive, ending its life unlawfully **[5.3]** whether in utero or during delivery amounts to the offence of child destruction[1]:

> 'Subject as hereinafter in this subsection provided, any person who, with intent to destroy the life of a child capable of being born alive, by any wilful act causes a child to die before it has an existence independent of its mother, shall be guilty ... Provided that no person shall be found guilty of an offence under this section unless it is proved that the act which caused the death of the child was not done in good faith for the purpose only of preserving the life of the mother.'

Under the statute a foetus is presumed to be capable of being born alive at the gestational age of 28 weeks[2]:

> 'For the purposes of this Act, evidence that a woman had at any material time been pregnant for a period of 28 weeks or more shall

be prima facie proof that she was at that time pregnant of a child capable of being born alive.'

Clearly the presumption is rebuttable by evidence that a particular child was not capable of being born alive. A foetus is capable of being born alive if it is capable of:

'breathing and living by reason of its breathing through its own lungs alone, without deriving any of its living or power of living by or through any connection with its mother.'[3]

The statute does not mean that a foetus of a lower gestational age cannot be proved to be capable of being born alive, and the performance of an abortion of a foetus capable of these functions, whatever its age, would be an offence of child destruction[4].

1 Infant Life (Preservation) Act 1929, s 1(1).
2 Infant Life (Preservation) Act 1929, s 1(2).
3 *Rance v Mid-Downs Health Authority* [1991] QB 587, [1991] 2 WLR 159 at 188; see also *R v McDonald* [1999] N I 150 (It was not necessary for the prosecution to prove that the child would have lived for any particular period of time, provided it proved that the child would have lived, even for a short period of time).
4 See *Rance*, n 3 above.

Abortion Act 1967

[5.4] The Act makes lawful what would otherwise be unlawful under the 1861 and 1929 Acts if certain conditions are met[1]:

'Subject to the provisions of this section, a person shall not be guilty of an offence under the law relating to abortion when a pregnancy is terminated by a registered medical practitioner if two registered medical practitioners are of the opinion, formed in good faith:
> (*a*) that the pregnancy has not exceeded twenty four weeks and that the continuance of the pregnancy would involve risk, greater than if the pregnancy were terminated, of injury to the physical or mental health of the pregnant woman or any existing children of her family; or
> (*b*) that the termination is necessary to prevent grave permanent injury to the physical or mental health of the pregnant woman; or
> (*c*) that the continuance of the pregnancy would involve risk to the life of the pregnant woman, greater than if the pregnancy were terminated; or
> (*d*) that there is a substantial risk that if the child were born it would suffer from such physical or mental abnormalities as to be seriously handicapped.'

1 Abortion Act, s 1(1), as amended by the Human Fertilisation and Embryology Act 1990, s 37.

Human Fertilisation and Embryology Act 1990

[5.5] The 1967 Act was amended to the form quoted above to achieve a number of objectives:

- A time limit of 24 weeks was imposed on abortions performed on the 'social' ground[1];

- The time limit that was imposed by the 1929 Act was removed from terminations on other grounds. In particular this means that a termination of a pregnancy on the grounds that it is feared the child will be seriously handicapped may be performed at any gestational age, even if the foetus is capable of being born alive;
- Compliance with the 1967 Act legalises what was previously an offence under the 1929 Act.

1 Abortion Act 1967, s 1(1)(*a*).

B   PARTICULAR ISSUES OF COMPLIANCE WITH THE ABORTION ACT 1967
CONDITIONS

Conscientious objection

The general rule that a patient is not entitled to force a doctor to provide treatment he is unwilling to give[1] is, in the case of abortions reinforced by a statutory exemption for those who have a conscientious objection to participation: **[5.6]**

> 'No person shall be under any duty, whether by contract or by any statutory or other legal requirement, to participate in any treatment authorised by this Act to which he has a conscientious objection[2].'

The exemption does not, however, cover treatment needed to save life or prevent permanent injury to the physical or mental health of the pregnant woman[3]. Therefore a doctor, or nurse[4], faced with circumstances in which a termination is required under s 1(1)(*b*), could be obliged to undertake the treatment[5] or face the relevant legal consequences, however strong his or her conscientious objection. The exemption does not cover activities which do not amount to participation in the procedure of termination, such as the typing of a referral letter by a secretary[6]. It is unclear whether the act of certification of grounds for a termination amounts to participation in the treatment[7]. It can be argued that it does, as the certification is a legal step which initiates the process of treatment and without which it cannot take place lawfully, and in that sense is participation in it. In other contexts[8] the concept of treatment includes the ancillary care made necessary by it. There is no reason why that should not be the position in relation to certification[9].

The entitlement of a practitioner to take advantage of the exemption does not relieve him or her of all duties towards the pregnant woman who has come for advice and assistance. Unless the practitioner is able to decline to assume any duty towards the patient, a duty of care will almost inevitably arise under which the doctor's conscientious objection should be explained and advice offered about how to seek advice and treatment elsewhere[10]. A conscientious objection does not entitle a practitioner to seek to impose his or her own views on patients. The practical solution for a practitioner with a conscientious objection is to make a standing arrangement with a colleague to accept referrals.

1 *Re J (a minor) (wardship: medical treatment)* [1991] Fam 33.
2 Abortion Act 1967, s 4(1).
3 Abortion Act 1967, s 4(2).
4 It is not only doctors and paramedical professionals who are entitled to the exemption, but anyone who participates in the termination of a pregnancy.

5 If otherwise under a relevant duty of care for the woman.

6 *Janaway v Salford Area Health Authority* [1989] AC 537.

7 The point was noted in *Janaway* but no opinion expressed on it.

8 See, for example the Mental Health Act 1983, s 145(1) and *B v Croydon Health Authority* [1995] Fam 133.

9 For a contrary view see Kennedy & Grubb's *Principles of Medical Law* (OUP, 1998), p 639.

10 See *Barr v Matthews* 52 BMLR 217 for an example of a claim – albeit unsuccessful – against a practitioner (who was opposed to abortion on ethical and religious grounds) on the ground that he had prevented an abortion in breach of his duty to the patient.

Multiple foetuses

[5.7]   It is on occasion necessary or desired to destroy one of multiple foetuses being carried by a pregnant woman. It might have been argued that to leave one or more foetuses to be delivered alive would not amount to a termination of pregnancy for the purposes of acquiring the protection of the 1967 Act. Now the Act provides[1] that, where, in the case of one of the foetuses, there is a substantial risk that, if born, the child would be seriously handicapped[2], the Act applies to anything done with intent to procure the miscarriage of that foetus, and, in the case of any other ground applying to the pregnancy, the Act applies to anything done with intent to procure the miscarriage of any foetus.

1 Abortion Act 1967, s 5(2), as amended by the Human Fertilisation and Embryology Act 1990, s 37(4).

2 Ie the ground specified in s 1(1)(*d*) of the Act.

Does the procedure have to be successful to be lawful?

[5.8]   The 1967 might appear to require the actual termination to be completed for the Act to provide a defence in relation to the 1861 and 1929 Acts by use of the words:

'when a pregnancy is terminated.'

Where a termination procedure fails and the foetus is born alive, certainly the Act provides no defence to an act of killing or attempting to kill it. Any such act will be subject to the full rigour of the law against homicide. However, it is unlikely that the mere failure of the termination procedure to achieve its intended goal would render the procedure unlawful. Both the 1861 and 1929 Acts require a specific intent to perform an act which would amount to the offence described. That intent must be absent if the practitioner honestly believes that he is performing a procedure which will end the pregnancy in compliance with the 1967 Act. The point is not free from controversy. One Law Lord has expressed the view that the Act is not intended to cover failed terminations[1]. The better view, expressed in the same case[2], is that the Act legitimises the whole treatment for the termination of the pregnancy and that it cannot have been the intention of Parliament to limit the legal protection to cases where the procedure was successful.

1 Per Lord Wilberforce in *Royal College of Nursing of the United Kindgom v Dept of Health and Social Security* [1981] AC 800 at 823, [1981] 2 WLR 279 at 295.

2 Per Lord Diplock at [1981] AC 800 at 823, [1981] 2 WLR 279 at 299, with whom on this point, Lord Edmund-Davies agreed: [1981] AC 800 at 823, [1981] 2 WLR 279 at 303.

Does the procedure have to be performed by a medical practitioner?

The Abortion Act 1967 requires the procedure to be carried out by a **[5.9]** registered medical practitioner, that is, one who is registered by the General Medical Council under the Medical Act 1983. This does not mean that the doctor has to perform every part of the procedure personally, and a procedure will be lawful if it is prescribed and initiated by a medical practitioner who remains in charge of it[1]. It has been suggested[2] that the protection covers nurses in relation to a late termination which would otherwise be an offence under the 1929 Act. However, the requirement in that Act for a 'wilful act' may well import the requirement of an intent to act in circumstances which would be unlawful, rather than knowledge of the illegality of those circumstances. An act – albeit in accordance with a doctor's instructions and under his supervision – in circumstances where the doctor is acting unlawfully could be said to have been a wilful act for these purposes. It is unfortunate that there is a lack of clarity in relation to conduct which could have criminal consequences.

1 *Royal College of Nursing of the United Kingdom v Dept of Health and Social Security* [1981] AC 800.
2 Kennedy & Grubb (eds), *Principles of Medical Law* (OUP, 1998), p 618.

Certification of medical opinion

The doctors must give their opinion in the prescribed form[1] before **[5.10]** treatment is begun, except in an emergency. Even then, the doctors must still have formed their opinion before the treatment is begun. There is no express requirement that the doctors should have examined the patient personally, or that either of them is the practitioner who actually performs the procedure. It might be envisaged there would be difficulties in establishing good faith without some form of examination or at least personal knowledge of the case. Therefore, medical practitioners would be well advised to examine the patient for themselves[2].

It has been suggested that the two doctors need not agree on the ground on which termination is justified[3]. This may be an over liberal construction of the Act. While the section contemplates more than one ground being present in any one case, there would seem to be a requirement that the ground relied on should, in the opinion of at least two doctors, be present. If only one doctor considers a particular ground is present, the wording of the section would not appear to be satisfied.

There is no requirement that the ground chosen by the medical practitioners is in fact correct. All that is required is that the doctors are of the opinion, formed in good faith, that the ground exists. As was said in a rare criminal prosecution under the Act[4]:

'Thus a great social responsibility is firmly placed by the law upon the shoulders of the medical profession.'

1 Abortion Regulations 1991 (SI 1991/499), reg 3(1); see App 5.2 to 5.4 below.
2 Note that the determination of whether particular actions were done in good faith are to be determined in criminal trials by the jury, albeit guided by appropriate evidence concerning accepted medical practice: *R v Smith* [1973] 1 WLR 1510, [1974] 1 All ER 376.
3 Kennedy & Grubb (eds), *Principles of Medical Law* (OUP, 1998), p 620.

4 *R v Smith* [1973] 1 WLR 1510 at 1512 per Scarman LJ.

The grounds

Risk of injury to the mother greater than if pregnancy terminated

[5.11]   The doctors must be of the opinion that:

[5.12]   *The pregnancy has not exceeded 24 weeks* – The Act does not specify the precise starting date of the pregnancy for this purpose, and there is no authoritative guidance from the courts. While arguably this could mean the date of implantation, rather than the more conventional date of the last menstrual period[1], it might be prudent for practitioners to adhere to the earlier date, bearing in mind the potentially serious consequences that might follow.

1 Kennedy & Grubb (eds), *Principles of Medical Law* (OUP, 1998), p 624.

[5.13]   *There is a risk to the mental or physical health of the woman or any existing children of her family* – The Act does not quantify or describe what degree or type of risk must be present. There is no requirement that the doctors be satisfied that there will actually be physical harm or mental illness. Essentially 'health' is likely to encompass whatever a doctor acting with professional competence and in good faith considers is a matter of health. There is no definition of 'children of her family' but is presumably not intended to be limited to children born to her, but could include not only adopted children but any accepted by her as children of her family, by comparison with the similar concept in the matrimonial law. It is the lack of definition which permits abortion on so-called 'social' grounds. This is further reinforced by the liberty given for the doctor to take into account the:

'pregnant woman's actual and foreseeable environment.'[1]

1 Abortion Act 1967, s 1(2).

[5.14]   *The risk identified must be thought to be greater if the pregnancy were allowed to continue than if it were terminated* – How that comparison is to be undertaken is clearly a matter for the medical practitioners acting in good faith.

Termination is necessary to prevent grave permanent injury

[5.15]   This condition has no time attached to it, so that a termination may be carried out at any stage of the pregnancy before the baby is delivered, if the condition is satisfied. The condition requires more than a risk of injury: the procedure must be necessary to prevent the injury occurring. Thus, the doctors must be of the opinion that such injury will actually occur unless the pregnancy is terminated and that there is no alternative means of preventing the injury. Of course, as this can only be matter of opinion, the doctors do not subsequently have to prove that they were indubitably correct, only that they held the opinion in good faith. The injury sought to be prevented must be both grave and permanent, and may be to mental or physical health or both. This is to be contrasted to the injury contemplated in s 1(1)(*a*) and (*b*) where any injury will suffice, if there is a greater risk of it occurring than if the pregnancy were terminated. What is or is not 'grave' may be a matter on which there can be different opinions, and may vary from case to case. Again, therefore, it is suggested that the doctor's opinion, so long as it is formed in good faith must be conclusive.

Risk to life of pregnant woman greater than if the pregnancy were terminated

Again no time limit is placed on the deployment of this condition. Life in the context of this subsection must be taken literally, and will not include injuries which will affect the quality of life, which might be included in other conditions. The degree of risk is not quantified in the statute; therefore any level of risk will suffice to satisfy this condition, so long as the risk is greater than that which would exist if the pregnancy were terminated. **[5.16]**

Substantial risk of the child being seriously handicapped from physical or mental abnormalities

There is no gestational time limit in relation to this condition. The risk involved must be 'substantial' and the handicap envisaged must be 'serious'. Neither of these adjectives is defined in the Act. Professor Grubb has argued that whether or not a risk is 'substantial' is a matter of law, and that it will not be defined by the opinion of medical practitioners, however compliant they are with accepted medical practice and however much they form the opinion in good faith[1]. If this is correct then medical practitioners run a risk: if they are found to have formed an opinion contrary to the view taken by a court as to what is properly described as substantial, they may be prosecuted for participating in an unlawful abortion because they would not, as a matter of law, have formed the requisite opinion. There is, however, a contrary argument. It must be remembered that this is a criminal statute and should be construed narrowly. It is suggested that if more were required than an honest doctor's opinion that the risk was substantial (whether or not others would agree with that opinion) then Parliament would have said so clearly. The same consideration ought to apply to the meaning of 'seriously'. **[5.17]**

1 Kennedy & Grubb (eds), *Principles of Medical Law* (OUP, 1998), p 628.

The place of treatment

Termination of pregnancy may only be performed in a National Health Service facility or a place approved by the Secretary of State, unless a medical practitioner forms the opinion in good faith that the termination is[1]: **[5.18]**

> 'immediately necessary to save the life or to prevent grave permanent injury to the physical or mental health of the pregnant woman.'

1 Abortion Act 1967, s 1(4). The Secretary of State now has the power to approve of a class of places in relation to medicinal abortions: see s 1(3A).

C THE PATIENT'S CONSENT

[5.19] It goes without saying that the normal requirements for obtaining authority to treat a patient apply to a termination of pregnancy, and nothing in the legislation is intended to derogate from them. The following particular points should be noted.

Competent adults

[5.20] No termination of pregnancy should be proceeded with unless the patient has been fully advised of the alternatives to termination, the relative risks of proceeding with the pregnancy and having the termination. In the case of an adult possessing the legal capacity to consent to the procedure, her refusal to have a termination is determinative, and it cannot lawfully be performed. No other person has any entitlement either to consent on her behalf or to prevent the procedure taking place. Therefore, the father of the foetus has no right to be consulted or to have his consent sought[1].

1 *Paton v British Pregnancy Advisory Service Trustees* [1979] QB 276; *C v S* [1988] QB 135, [1987] 2 WLR 1108, [1987] 1 All ER 1230, [1987] 2 FLR 505, [1987] Fam Law 269.

Children

[5.21] A child, who has attained 16 years of age[1] or who is sufficiently mature in understanding[2] may consent to a termination of pregnancy. Such a consent will be sufficient authority even if the child's parents are unaware of the proposed treatment or actively oppose it. However, the consent of the parent will provide the doctor with legal justification, even where the child refuses[3]. Where there is a dispute between parents and the child, or between child and the doctor, the latter would be well advised to seek the guidance of the court exercising its parental jurisdiction before proceeding to a termination of pregnancy, but there is no obligation to do so, unless the child is already a ward of court[4]. While theoretically it would be possible for an abortion to be imposed on an unwilling child, it is suggested that most practitioners and the courts will be very reluctant to proceed in this way, unless the pregnancy caused a serious risk to her life or health which she refused or was unable to recognise.

1 Family Law Reform Act 1969, s 8.
2 *Gillick v West Norfolk and Wisbech Area Health Authority* [1986] AC 112. See also *JS C and CH C v Wren* [1987] 2 WWR 669 (An Albertan court refused parents' application seeking to prevent their daughter from having an abortion: the 16 year old girl had sufficient intelligence and understanding to make up her own mind).
3 *Re R (a minor) (wardship: consent to treatment)* [1992] Fam 11.
4 *Re G-U (a minor) (wardship)* [1984] FLR 811.

Incompetent adults

[5.22] It might be thought that there would be an obligation to seek a declaration of the court similar to that required in sterilisation cases[1]. However abortion has not been included in that category of cases, and, in so far as applications have been attempted they have been rejected on the ground that there is no need for court review given the statutory framework already in place[2]. In *Re SG (a patient)* the President decided that, in a case where a pregnant woman clearly lacked capacity, the provisions of the Abortion Act 1967 provided adequate safeguards which made a declaration as to best interests unnecessary[3]. Nonetheless where the question of capacity is not clear, it would be prudent to seek a declaration before embarking on a termination and the High Court, whilst refusing an application for determination of 'best interests', has granted a declaration in relation to the capacity of a woman to consent to termination[4].

1 See Chap 4, *Sterilisation.*
2 *Re SG (a patient)* [1991] 2 FLR 329, [1993] 4 Med LR 75.
3 See also *Re X* (1987) Times, 4 June (an abortion would not be unlawful merely because the patient lacked the capacity to give informed consent).
4 Unreported decision in chambers in 1998.

Determining competence: termination of pregnancy

Very difficult and interesting questions arise when consideration is given to capacity in the context of a refusal to undergo a termination of pregnancy. The question to be addressed in the context of a refusal of termination is:

[5.23]

> '*How much information* must the patient be able to comprehend, retain, believe and weigh in the balance in order to be able to arrive at a clear choice?'

This question involves considering whether the patient must be able to understand only that she now is carrying a foetus which is likely to be born alive if there is no termination, and that she will not have this baby if she has a termination of pregnancy, or whether she must be capable of understanding the wider psychological, physiological, social and economic consequences of her decision. It will be apparent that if there is a requirement of an ability fully to understand the latter, then a far wider range of patients will lack the relevant capacity to consent to this sort of decision.

Re F (mental patient: sterilisation)[1] and *Re B (a minor) (wardship: sterilisation)*[2] provide some guidance on the nature of the issues to be considered in assessing the best interests of the patient. It might be argued that to be found to be competent to make the decision for herself the patient should be capable of understanding these issues and coming to a balanced judgment on them. However, it may be doubted how many patients can prove the intellectual ability to understand these complex issues in relation to a wide range of important treatments. It must be remembered that there is a presumption in favour of capacity. Therefore, it is suggested that a patient seeking a termination of pregnancy – or indeed refusing one – should be regarded as having the capacity to make the decision for herself unless she is incapable of understanding any of the following:

- the nature of her condition, ie that she is carrying a foetus which is likely to be born alive unless the pregnancy is terminated by the procedure under consideration;
- the physical consequences of the procedure, namely that the foetus she is now carrying will not be born alive;
- the nature of the procedure to be performed, eg suction, or induction of labour;
- a general understanding of such information concerning the subsequent consequences of her decision which would be drawn to her attention by any competent medical practitioner.

It might be thought that any higher level of requirement than this would impose undue restrictions on a patient's autonomy.

In considering the 'best interests' test the interests of persons other than the patient (even the baby[3], certainly society as a whole) are irrelevant. Nonetheless it might be argued that the patient's ability to consider the interests of others *is* relevant to the assessment of her capacity.

1 [1990] 2 AC 1.
2 [1988] AC 199 at 202 per Lord Hailsham.
3 See Chap 6, *Caesarean Sections*, para **[6.12]** below. Also note that it may in the future be argued that Art 2 of the European Convention on Human Rights applies to the unborn child and that as such the unborn child's interests should also be considered when addressing the best interests tests. However, it is unlikely – given the approach adopted in *Paton v United Kingdom* (1980) 3 EHRR 408 – that this argument will succeed. See also *Christian Lawyers Association of South Africa v Minister of Health* (1998) 50 BMLR 241 (reference to 'everyone' or 'every person' in South Africa's written Constitution was not reference to an unborn child). Note the preamble to the UN Convention on the Rights of the Child which states: 'Bearing in mind that, as indicated in the Declaration of the Rights of the Child, the child, by reason of his physical and mental immaturity, needs special safeguards and care, including appropriate legal protection, before as well as after birth'. Note also that the United Kingdom declared that: 'The United Kingdom interprets the Convention as applicable only following a live birth'.

Best interests: termination of pregnancy

[5.24] As discussed above, the authority of *Re SG (a patient)*[1] means that questions of 'best interests' will not usually arise for consideration by a court. However, where an issue is before the court in relation to capacity, it may be appropriate also to seek a order:

> 'That the Respondent's best interests in relation to the termination or continuation of her current pregnancy be determined.'

This will particularly apply if there has been no certification prior to the hearing of grounds for lawful termination.

The courts have applied the 'best interests' test in favour of allowing children to undergo abortions. For example, in *Re B*[2] a mother opposed her 12 year old undergoing an abortion. The child, her putative father and her maternal grandparents supported the procedure. The courts agreed with the local authority's view that it was in her best interests to have the abortion: continuation of the pregnancy involved greater risks to her mental and physical health than having an abortion.

1 [1991] 2 FLR 329.
2 *Re B (child: termination of pregnancy)* [1991] 2 FLR 426.

Use of force: Non-consensual incompetent patients

[5.25] If an incompetent patient is reluctant to undergo a termination, it may be that it will have to be performed under sedation or restraint. In both *Tameside and Glossop Acute Services Trust v CH*[1] and *Norfolk & Norwich Healthcare (NHS) Trust v W*[2] it was held that the mothers lacked capacity. The obstetricians wished to bring delivery forward in time by, if necessary, Caesarean section. It was held that it would be lawful to use reasonable force to achieve this in the best interests of the patient. This principle was affirmed in *Re MB (an adult: medical treatment)*[3]. The court held that it followed from the determination that treatment was in her best interests that treatment could be given forcibly despite the patient's objections, although difficult questions arose as to how to strike the balance between continuing treatment which is *forcibly* opposed and deciding not to continue with it. The same principle would apply in the case of the termination of the pregnancy of a patient lacking the capacity to refuse such a procedure, but who was resisting it. In all such cases, the doctors will have to decide whether it is ethically acceptable to impose a termination on a resisting woman, even if she does not have the relevant mental capacity.

1 [1996] 1 FLR 762 at 773H–774B.
2 [1996] 2 FLR 613.
3 [1997] 2 FLR 426, (1997) 8 Med LR 217.

Procedure and Evidence

A report preferably from two Consultant Psychiatrists that the patient lacks capacity to form or withhold consent should be obtained. Care must be taken to ensure that the psychiatrists consider the test as set out in *Re MB*[1]. **[5.26]**

Important particular considerations for the court will be as follows:

1 See App 6.1: *Re MB Guidelines.*

Statutory position

The views of any treating doctors and in particular their opinion about the existence of grounds for a termination under the Abortion Act 1967 and whether such a procedure was appropriate for the patient. **[5.27]**

Capacity

- The basis on which it is asserted that the patient lacks the ability to weigh treatment information in the balance. (For example, the mere fact that a patient is unwilling to discuss the pregnancy with psychiatric staff and is frightened cannot in itself be sufficient to show lack of capacity for this particular decision.) **[5.28]**
- The information which has been put to the patient about the advantages and disadvantages of pregnancy/termination and her response to it.
- The patient's comprehension of:
  (i) the consequence of sexual intercourse in leading to pregnancy;
  (ii) the nature and extent of the physical and emotional stress associated with childbirth and responsibilities of having a child;
  (iii) (if relevant, say because of extensive drug treatment of the patient) the risk of her child being mentally impaired.
- Whether the possibility of foetal abnormality has been put to the patient, and, if so, the manner in which this was done and her response.
- Any evidence from a Speech and Language Therapist may assist, where there are issues concerning the patient's ability to comprehend. His/her view on the patient's understanding of everyday vocabulary and complex adult language may assist. A view as to her ability to understand is crucial to a determination under the *Re MB* test.

Best Interests

[5.29] A report from the relevant Care Manager, if Social Services have been involved.

- The ability of the patient to care for the baby after the birth, with or without support.
- The availability of such support, if it is needed.
- The likelihood of the baby being taken into care immediately after birth and the impact this would have on the patient.
- The risk of the baby being born disabled.
- Any difficulties foreseen in getting the patient to hospital, and persuading her to stay there. Evidence should be sought on this from any Community Nurses involved in the patient's care.
- If the patient is undergoing other forms of treatment, the impact the termination will have on her relationship with her treating physicians and the risk of permanent damage to this relationship.
- The likely difference between termination and continuing to full term on the patient's future (1) mental state; (2) relationship with therapeutic staff.
- The physical risks of the patient continuing with the pregnancy, as assessed by the gynaecology team.
- If the patient is young, the attitude of her parents or close family to the pregnancy.
- If the patient is attending a school or college the views of any tutor with detailed knowledge of her abilities, personality and needs.
- If the patient is likely to abscond, the available supervision options.
- The nature of the relationship with the father of the unborn child, and, where this is continuing, his attitude to the pregnancy, and likely affect on the relationship of a termination.
- The maturity of the pregnancy and any associated urgency.
- If an application is being considered, the Official Solicitor should be informed of the case immediately. If there are issues concerning what would happen to the baby after delivery it would be important to consider adding Social Services as a party.
- It is suggested that a declaration should be sought[1] in the terms:

  > '(*a*) The Respondent [patient] lacks the capacity to consent to [or refuse] a termination of her current pregnancy
  > (*b*) It is in her best interests that it should be terminated.
  > (*c*) In the present circumstances it is lawful for the Defendant's current pregnancy to be terminated in spite of her inability to consent to this procedure.'[2]

1 By way of Originating Summons for a child and (currently) by way of Part 8 procedure for an adult.
2 In relation to a child, an order (rather than declaration) should be sought.

CHAPTER 6

Caesarean Sections

CONTENTS

A INTRODUCTION

The use of surgical deliveries has long been a controversial and sensitive   [6.1]
subject. Concerns have been raised about a perceived increase in the
incidence of such procedures and suggestions made that this is due to
excessively 'defensive' medical practice as opposed to a proper consideration of the interests of the patient[1]. On the other hand, some
medical opinion has viewed the movement in favour of natural birth with
scepticism, doubting whether it is in the true interests of mother and
child. Given that background it is not surprising that in recent years
controversy has been caused by a small number of instances in which
patients have been subjected to non-consensual surgical delivery. In most

85

cases this has occurred in the cases of women who were, or were at least perceived to be, lacking in the mental capacity to decide whether or not to undergo such a procedure. In at least two cases, however, women who did not lack capacity were forced to have their babies surgically. Following the appearance of this type of case in the United States courts, it was not surprising that the English courts were drawn into the search for a legal sanction for non-consensual surgical deliveries. The development of legal thinking in this class of case is worth recounting as an object lesson of what can happen when the courts are placed under the pressure of demands to take urgent action to save life, and to demonstrate the dangers of assuming that the conclusions of previous cases can always be relied upon. The cases concerning Caesarean section provide a useful guide to many of the principles involved in the application of the declaratory jurisdiction to medical treatment decisions and are therefore considered in some detail.

1 But see Baldwin, 'Defensive medicine and obstetrics' ((1995) November 22/29 *Journal of the American Medical Association* 274(20), pp 1606–1610) which indicated that obstetricians who had been more exposed to US medical malpractice suits did not in fact have higher caesarean section rates.

B THE LEGAL BACKGROUND[1]

Patient and foetal rights in obstetrics

[6.2] An obstetrician continually faces the dilemma caused by the perception of an ethical duty to both the mother and her foetus as separate entities. The Royal College of Obstetricians' own guidelines state that:

> 'The aim of those who care for pregnant women must be to foster the greatest benefit to both the mother and foetus, and inform and advise the family, utilising their training and experience in the best interests of both parties.
>
> Obstetricians must recognise the dual claims of the mother and her embryo or foetus and inform and advise the family, utilising their training and experience in the best interests of both parties.'[2]

The common law has not in general recognised this dual obligation. On several occasions the courts have refused to recognise the foetus as having any legal personality giving the court jurisdiction to intervene. Thus, a husband may not apply for an injunction to restrain the abortion of a foetus of which he is the father[3]. It has been made clear that in such a case the foetus has no rights:

> 'The first question is whether this plaintiff has a right at all. The foetus cannot, in English law, in my view, have a right of its own at least until it is born and has a separate existence from its mother. That permeates the whole of the civil law of this country (I except the criminal law, which is now irrelevant), and is, indeed, the basis of the decisions in those countries where law is founded on the common law ... there can be no doubt, in my view, that in England and Wales the foetus has no right of action, no right at all, until birth.'[4]

An action cannot be brought on behalf of an unborn child to prevent an abortion[5]:

> 'The authorities, it seems to me, show that a child, after it has been born, and only then, in certain circumstances, based on he or she having a legal right, may be a party to an action brought with regard to such matters as the right to take, on a will or intestacy, or for damages for injuries suffered before birth. In other words, the claim crystallises upon the birth, at which date, but not before, the child attains the status of a legal persona, and thereupon can then exercise that legal right.'[6]

There is no jurisdiction to make an unborn child a ward of court even to protect it from damage likely to be caused by its mother[7].

This is not to say that acts and omissions before birth may not have consequences after birth. Thus the common law recognises that an action in negligence may be brought by a child once born alive in respect of injuries inflicted as a result of ante natal acts or omissions[8]. A charge of homicide will lie in respect of an assault on a pregnant woman resulting in the death of the child, if initially born alive[9]:

> 'Murder or manslaughter can be committed where unlawful injury is deliberately inflicted either to a child in utero or to a mother carrying a child in utero in the circumstances postulated in the question. The requisite intent to be proved in the case of murder is an intention to kill or cause really serious bodily injury to the mother, the foetus before birth being viewed as an integral part of the mother. Such intention is appropriately modified in the case of manslaughter ...
>
> The fact that the death of the child is caused solely in consequence of injury to the mother rather than as a consequence of injury to the foetus does not negative any liability for murder and manslaughter provided that the jury are satisfied that causation is proved.'

A similarly ambivalent view is taken by the English legislature. On the one hand the Abortion Act 1967 authorises terminations of pregnancy in a wide range of cases. On the other, the Infant Life (Preservation) Act 1929 prohibits the destruction of any child capable of being born alive[10]. The Congenital Disabilities (Civil Liability) Act 1976 clarifies the common law position in relation to liability to the child born alive in respect of injuries in utero.

Turning to the mother, the law has to resolve the conflict between the principle that a competent adult patient cannot be forced to submit to medical treatment, however well intentioned, and however necessary to preserve life or health[11], and the principle[12] that treatment could be given to a patient incapable of consenting if it was in their best interests. As will be seen, the perceived imperative to save life, foetal and maternal, resulted in what may be considered surprising developments in the definition of mental capacity and of patients' best interests.

---

1 This section is based on an article by one of the authors published in the Catholic University of America's *Journal of Public Health Law*.

2 *A Consideration of the Law and Ethics in relation to Court-Authorised Obstetric Intervention* (Royal College of Obstetricians and Gynaecologists, 1996), paras 4.3.1 and 4.3.2.

3 *Paton v British Pregnancy Advisory Service* [1979] QB 276; *Paton v United Kingdom* (1980) 3 EHRR 408.

4 *Paton v British Pregnancy Advisory Service* [1979] QB 276 at 279 per Sir George Baker P.

5 *C v S* [1988] QB 135.

6 *C v S* [1988] QB 135 per Heilbron J at 140, citing Canadian authorities *Medhurst v Medhurst* (1984) 46 OR (2d) 263; *Dehler v Ottawa Civic Hospital* (1979) 25 OR (2d) 748, (1980) 29 OR (2d) 677.

7 *Re F (in utero)* [1988] Fam 122.

8 *Burton v Islington Health Authority* [1993] QB 204, CA.

9 *A-G's Reference (No 3 of 1994)* [1998] AC 245.

10 This is subject to an exception under the Abortion Act 1967 in relation to a fetus of 24 weeks or more likely to be seriously handicapped on birth: Abortion Act 1967, s 1 (as amended by the Human Fertilisation and Embryology Act 1990); and see Chap 5, *Abortion* at para **[5.3]** above.

11 *Sidaway v Board of Governors of the Bethlem Royal Hospital and the Maudsley Hospital* [1985] AC 871.

12 *Re F (mental patient: sterilisation)* [1990] 2 AC 1.

Compulsory obstetrics

[6.3] Until 1988 no case appears to have been brought before the English courts in which an attempt was made to authorise the imposition obstetric management on a woman without a lawful consent. The extension of the declaratory jurisdiction[1] by the cases of *T v T*[2] and *Re F (mental patient: sterilisation)*[3] to include issues of mental capacity and best interests – combined with a practical requirement for 'sensitive' cases to be referred to court – inevitably set the scene for obstetric cases to be the subject of applications.

1 Part of which has been described as 'one of the most remarkable developments of modern British administrative law' (Zamir & Woolf, *The Declaratory Judgement* (2nd ed, Sweet & Maxwell, 1993, p 8).

2 [1988] Fam 52.

3 [1990] 2 AC 1; see the judgments of Lord Brandon at 56-57, 62–65; Lord Griffiths at 70–71; Lord Goff at 79–80, 83. The practise is now followed in sterilisation cases (see Chap 4, *Sterilisation* and App 4.2: *Practice Note (Official Solicitor: Sterilisation)* and for the withdrawal of life sustaining nutrition and hydration (see Chap 9, *Permanent Vegetative State* and App 9.1: *Practice Note (Official Solicitor: Vegetative State)*.

The Caesarean section cases

[6.4] While they have provoked considerable controversy, there have in fact been very few cases in which courts in this country have been asked to consider a proposal to deliver a baby by Caesarean section against the will of the mother. It might be presumed that before the advent of the declaratory jurisdiction referred to above doctors did not consider it necessary to seek such a safeguard relying on some form of medical paternalism to justify their actions. In the case of competent patients it is more likely that it did not occur to doctors to perform such procedures if their persuasive powers failed to convince the patient of the need for it. In any event, as will be seen from the cases that have come before the courts, such problems usually arise in circumstances of great urgency and it may not have been thought practicable to involve the machinery of justice in addressing the issues. It may be possible that the ever increasing threat of litigation arising out of obstetric accidents has been a powerful motivating force behind the modest flow of cases in this area.

The mentally competent adult patient: *Re S*

Re S (adult: refusal of treatment)[1] was the first case brought before the **[6.5]**
courts for a declaration that it would be lawful to perform a Caesarean
section delivery on a woman in labour. The circumstances in which the
case was brought were extraordinary and unlikely to produce reasoned
jurisprudence. A 30 year old woman was in labour with her third
pregnancy, being six days overdue with the foetus in a transverse lie and
a foetal elbow projecting through the cervix. For deeply held religious
reasons the mother refused to consent to delivery by Caesarean section
although she had been advised and understood that without such a
procedure she and the baby were in mortal danger. An application was
made to the court by the hospital for a declaration that surgical delivery
would be lawful. The mother was not represented, but the court was
assisted by an amicus curiae. The judge, Sir Stephen Brown P, has
described what occurred in a lecture[2]:

> 'During the luncheon adjournment ... my clerk came to me and
> said "I think there is an application which somebody wishes to
> make about a caesarean section operation. I don't know anything
> about it ... It was 1.20pm or just after by the time I got in touch with
> [the Official Solicitor] and by 2.10pm he had briefed counsel, a QC,
> in court. I had nothing except the form of summons, which had been
> issued by the health authority ... seeking a declaration that it would
> be lawful for the doctors to carry out a caesarean section operation
> on a 30 year old woman who was in the last stages of labour with her
> third pregnancy. The consultant gynaecologist gave oral evidence
> before me ... this lady had a genuine religious objection to a
> caesarean section being carried out; this was a desperate situation,
> the foetus was lying in a position where it was nearly emerging, and
> if there was no intervention – and there was no doubt about it – the
> mother would die and also the child ... The question was, should
> that be allowed? ... It was very clear – this was minutes, not hours
> – both would die. I heard very helpful submissions by counsel for
> the Official Solicitor and I made the ... declaration, telling the
> consultant "please go to my clerk's room and use the telephone": it
> was as vital as that.'

The report of the case discloses that judgment was delivered at 2.18pm.
The judge noted that there was no English authority on the point
although it had been said that it might be possible to override the will of
a competent woman to save a viable foetus[3]. However, he considered
there was American authority[4] suggesting that in a case like this the
American courts would be likely to favour the grant of a declaration. He
then granted a declaration in the following terms[5]:

> 'It is declared that the operation of caesarean section and necessary
> consequential treatment which the Plaintiff, by its servants or
> agents proposes to perform on the Defendant at [hospital] is in the
> vital interests of the Defendant and the unborn child she is carrying
> and can lawfully be performed despite the Defendant's refusal to
> give her consent.'

The aftermath of the case was described by an obstetrician who had been on duty in the labour ward[6]:

> 'Well, of course there was chaos. I think it was understood that the wording [of the declaration] was to save the life of the mother and the baby ... but what happened was that the baby died during the court hearing ... [T]hey got the phone call saying "It's been agreed", which was completely startling, because everyone was saying, "There is no law on which you can bet", and the woman was wheeled down the corridor, with the husband saying, "What's happening?", and they said "Oh, we've got the agreement of the court", and they said "Well, what about human rights?", and they said "Oh, don't know about that". They were completely dazed ... they are African and not aware of the system, not aware of their rights, unrepresented in the court when the decision was made ...
> If this hadn't happened, the baby would have died and we would have renegotiated with the woman: "Now, look, the baby has died and it's not going to come out. Can we now do a caesarean section?", and she would still have refused; and she would have died without [the] court order, I am sure of that.'

It appears from this account that the non-consensual procedure was persisted in although it was known that the fetus had died in utero and that one justification on which the declaration was based, 'the vital interests of the unborn child' was no longer applicable. The only interests remaining were those of the mother, who was at all times considered to be mentally competent and was unwilling to submit to the procedure. Doubtless it was thought there was no time to consult lawyers, let alone the court, again, but it must have been open to debate whether the judicial instinct in favour of a declaration would have remained as strong in the absence of a foetus capable of being born alive.

The same doctor described the subsequent reaction to these events of the participants:

> 'A long time later people who were working in the hospital had not recovered from the incident, the staff, let alone the lady in question ... [T]he mother felt that God was acting through the agency of the gynaecologist, and that is how she has forgiven him for this incident, and how she has ended up explaining it. That is how she has interpreted it now and that is why no appeal has come through. As far as the obstetricians are concerned, I think we are deeply divided about this. Having understood that our duty is to the baby through the mother, we don't quite like this idea of maternal/foetal conflict, because the vast majority of our work is done with the mothers and through the mothers, and the idea we can breach confidentiality and then go to make applications to divide mothers and children legally, when we can't divide them physically, is actually an anathema to many.'

The human reaction of the judge faced with minutes to decide an unprecedented case was wholly understandable: he acted to save the lives of mother and baby. Yet, partly for the reasons expressed by the doctor quoted above, the case had many unsatisfactory features. It was found to be lawful for doctors to override the clearly expressed will of a mentally competent woman and to perform invasive surgery on her. While time did not permit a reasoned judgment, it is clear that the justification cannot have been any perceived irrationality of the decision: there was and remains binding House of Lords authority that a competent adult has an absolute right to choose whether or not to undergo medical treatment:

> 'If the doctor making a balanced judgment advises the patient to submit to the operation, the patient is entitled to reject that advice for reasons which are rational, or irrational, or for no reason.'[7]

The President relied on the American case of *Re AC*[8] as authority for the proposition that the American courts would have granted a declaration in similar circumstances. Unfortunately a more leisurely study of this case suggests the precise opposite: the court very strongly suggested that the will of a mentally competent woman should never be overridden. They held that it would have been improper to presume that a patient is incompetent[9]. They supported two further arguments against overriding the patient's objections: first that it destroyed the necessary trust between patient and doctor, and might drive high risk mothers out of the health care system, and, secondly, in this type of case the urgency rendered justice almost impossible to achieve (for reasons which applied even more cogently in *Re S* itself). The reasoning of the court is worth quoting because it applies in all such cases wherever they arise:

> ' ... any judicial proceeding in a case such as this will ordinarily take place – like the one before us here – under time constraints so pressing that it is difficult or impossible for the mother to communicate adequately with counsel, or for counsel to organize an effective factual and legal presentation in defense of her liberty and privacy interests and bodily integrity. Any intrusion implicating such basic values ought not to be lightly undertaken when the mother is not only precluded from conducting pre-trial discovery ... but is in no position to prepare meaningfully for trial. As one commentator has noted:
>
> The procedural shortcomings rampant in these cases are not mere technical deficiencies. They undermine the authority of the decisions themselves, posing serious questions as to whether judges can, in the absence of genuine notice, adequate representation, explicit standards of proof, and right of appeal, realistically frame principled and useful legal responses to the dilemma with which they are confronted.'[10]

The court also stated:

> 'We emphasize, nevertheless, that it would be an extraordinary case indeed in which a court might ever be justified in overriding the patient's wishes and authorizing a major surgical procedure such as a caesarean section. Throughout this opinion we have stressed that the patient's wishes, once ascertained, must be followed "in

virtually all cases" ... unless there are "truly extraordinary or compelling reasons to override them" ... *Indeed some may doubt that there could ever be a situation extraordinary or compelling enough to justify a massive intrusion into a person's body, such as a caesarean section against that person's will.* Whether such a situation may someday present itself is a question we need not strive to answer here.'[11]

Therefore, the decision was hardly a ringing endorsement of compulsory Caesarean sections[12].

Re S was the subject of considerable academic[13] and feminist[14] criticism. A competent adult's refusal of invasive surgery had been overridden in part in the interests of her foetus, but, the foetus having died, in favour of her interests as determined by others. This momentous step was taken without any representation on her behalf, and with only the most rudimentary evidence. In so far as the decision was taken to protect the interests of the foetus it would seem to have conflicted with the powerful obiter dictum of Balcombe LJ in *Re F (in utero)*[15]:

'If the law is to be extended in this manner, so as to impose control over the mother of an unborn child, where such control may be necessary for the benefit of that child, then under our system of parliamentary democracy it is for Parliament to decide whether such controls can be imposed and, if so, subject to what limitations or conditions ... If Parliament were to think it appropriate that a pregnant woman should be subject to controls for the benefit of her unborn child, then doubtless it would stipulate the circumstances in which such controls may be applied and the safeguards appropriate for the mother's protection. In such a sensitive field, affecting as it does the liberty of the individual, it is not for the judiciary to extend the law.'

Following this case the Royal College of Obstetricians issued guidelines[16] which concluded by suggesting a practice of respecting the competent mother's wishes in these circumstances:

'A doctor must respect the competent pregnant woman's right to choose or refuse any particular recommended course of action whilst optimising care for both mother and foetus to the best of his or her ability. A doctor would not then be culpable if these endeavours were unsuccessful.

We conclude that it is inappropriate, and unlikely to be helpful or necessary, to invoke judicial intervention to overrule an informed and competent woman's refusal of proposed medical treatment, even though her refusal might place her life and that of her foetus at risk.'[17]

It was considered that resort to law to overturn the presumption in favour of patient autonomy:

'raised more difficulties than it solves.'[18]

1 [1993] Fam 123.

2 *Matters of Life and Death* (Lecture to the Medico-Legal Society, 14 October 1993) (1994) 6 Med Leg J 52.
3 *Re T (adult: refusal of treatment)* [1993] Fam 95.
4 *Re AC* (1990) 573 A.2d 1235, 1240, 1246–1248, 1252.
5 The text is taken from the official transcript as it does not appear in the report.
6 (1994) 62 Med Leg J 65.
7 *Sidaway v Board of Governors of the Bethlem Royal Hospital and the Maudsley Hospital* [1985] AC 871 at 904–905 per Lord Templeman.
8 *Re AC* (1990) 573 A.2d 1235, 1240, 1246–1248, 1252.
9 *Re AC* (1990) 573 A.2d 1235 at 1247.
10 *Re AC* (1990) 573 A.2d 1235 at 1248.
11 *Re AC* (1990) 573 A.2d 1235 at 1252, a page actually cited by Sir Stephen Brown P; emphasis added.
12 There was in fact some US authority in favour of non-consensual deliveries, some of which was cited in *Re AC: Jefferson v Griffin Spalding County Hospital Authority* (1981) 274 S.E.2d 457; *Re Madyun* (1986) 573 A.2d 1259. However, following the final decision in *Re AC*, the family of AC sued for malpractice in a suit settled on terms which included a statement endorsed by the AMA and ACOG, including the following: 'A judicial proceeding is the least desirable manner to obtain authorization for treatment and should be utilized only in the absence of other surrogates ... Judicial authorization to override a patient's competent decision is virtually never justified' (1992) 142 NLJ 1638.
13 See commentary by Professor Grubb at (1993) 1 Med L Rev 92.
14 (1992) 142 NLJ 1638.
15 [1988] Fam 122 at 144.
16 See App 6.7: *A Consideration of the Law and Ethics in relation to Court-Authorised Obstetric Intervention* (Royal College of Obstetricians and Gynaecologists, 1996).
17 See n 16 above at paras 5.11–5.12.
18 See App 6.7: *A Consideration of the Law and Ethics in relation to Court-Authorised Obstetric Intervention* (Royal College of Obstetricians and Gynaecologists, 1996), para 4.5.8.

The mentally ill patient: *Tameside & Glossop Acute Services NHS Trust v CH*[1]

After an interval of over three years the Family Division was called upon in circumstances of slightly less urgency to consider the case of a female paranoid schizophrenic who was compulsorily detained in a mental hospital under s 3 of the Mental Health Act 1983. Such detention does not carry any necessary implication that the patient has lost the mental capacity to consent to or refuse medical treatment[2]. The patient wanted to have her baby and care for it, but suffered from a delusional belief that the doctors caring for her were evil and wished to harm the baby. She had a history of resisting treatment. The treating doctors became concerned at intra-uterine growth retardation and concluded that delivery by caesarean section was necessary to safeguard the baby. They feared that the patient, whom they considered incapable of understanding the advice she received, would resist. They sought a declaration that it would be lawful to provide such treatment and to use reasonable restraint to the extent necessary for that purpose. [6.6]

A hearing took place with the patient represented by counsel instructed by the Official Solicitor acting as guardian ad litem for the patient. Oral evidence was heard from the responsible psychiatrist and obstetrician. It was common ground that the evidence proved the patient to be mentally incompetent in accordance with the test formulated for medical cases in *Re C (adult: refusal of medical treatment)*[3] in which Thorpe J defined the necessary ingredients of competence for this purpose to be the ability to:

(1) comprehend and retain treatment information;

(2) believe that information;

(3) weigh the information in the balance and arrive at a choice.

The judge would have been prepared to declare that it was lawful at common law to provide the appropriate treatment to this incompetent patient as being in her best interests. He hesitated to do that because of an uncertainty about whether the common law permitted the use of restraint for this purpose, given that the legislature had made detailed provision for the detention of mental patients and for the protection of civil liberty in this context[4]. He therefore turned to consider whether the legislation permitted such treatment to be given without the patient's consent. He concluded that s 63 of the Mental Health Act 1983[5] permitted a caesarean section to be imposed on the patient without her consent on the grounds that it was treatment for the mental disorder from which she was suffering. The evidence before him was that without surgical delivery, the foetus would die, but there would be no physical harm to the mother. However, the birth of a stillborn baby would have had a profound deleterious effect on her mental health and would have impeded recovery.

This interpretation of the statute is controversial[6], but there would seem to be a pragmatic argument in favour of it in this type of case. On the evidence the mother wished to protect her baby, but, by reason of her serious mental disorder, believed that the very act which would save it was intended to do it harm. If such a patient cannot be protected from such serious consequences of her illness, it might be thought that the mental health legislation was deficient. In any event, as we shall see[7], it was confirmed in subsequent cases that the procedure and restraint to facilitate it would have been lawful at common law on the facts of this case.

1 [1996] 1 FCR 753.

2 See *B v Croydon Health Authority* [1995] Fam 133, [1995] 2 WLR 294, [1995] 1 All ER 683, CA and see Chap 7, *Feeding.*

3 [1994] 1 FLR 31 at 36.

4 This uncertainty was subsequently resolved in *Re MB (an adult: medical treatment)* [1997] 2 FLR 425, (1997) 8 Med LR 217.

5 'The consent of a patient shall not be required for any medical treatment given to him for the mental disorder from which he is suffering . . . if the treatment is given by or under the direction of the responsible medical officer'.

   It had previously been established that this section could justify the force feeding of an anorexic patient or one suffering from a self-harming personality disorder as being treatment for the disorder: *B v Croydon Health Authority* (n 2 above).

6 Professor Grubb (1996) 4 Med L Rev 194–198 argues that it is 'incredible'. Barbara Hewson wrote: 'A cynic's response might be: women (at any rate whilst pregnant or in labour) are a species of inferior being, who are not the same as, and are therefore not entitled to claim the same fundamental rights as men' (1996) 146 NLJ 1385.

7 See paras **[6.7]** and **[6.11]** below.

An attack on the competence of pregnant women?

[6.7] On 21 June 1996 two cases were heard by the same judge urgently, one so much so that the hearing of the other was interrupted for the purpose[1]. The more urgent case, *Rochdale Healthcare NHS Trust v C*[2] received the most rudimentary of hearings. The proceedings have been graphically described by the lawyer for the hospital:

'At 4.30pm a call was made to our Manchester office indicating that

Mrs C was in labour in a trial of scar. Matters had not gone well and in the opinion of the Consultant, her uterus at the time was rupturing. He believed that he could deliver an intact baby within an hour, but if the matter were delayed further the child would die and shortly after so would the mother.

The call was relayed to our London office and after taking direct instructions from the obstetrician we alerted the Official Solicitor who told us that another case raising similar issues was at that time in progress before Mr Justice Johnson. We attended court and ascertained that the other case was slightly less urgent in the opinion of the attending consultants and the Court kindly broke off to take our case and made an Order some 35 minutes after the first contact with our Manchester office.'

The patient was not represented, and there was no amicus curiae. It is unclear from the transcript of the judgment whether the patient had any notice of the application. No formal evidence was before the court. The solicitor merely reported what he had been told by telephone from the hospital. This was to the effect that the patient objected to a Caesarean section because she had suffered backache and pain after a previous similar procedure. She said she would rather die than have a Caesarean section again. There had insufficient time to obtain a psychiatric opinion on the patient's competence, but the consultant obstetrician believed her to be fully competent. In an understandably short judgment the judge said he was acutely aware that the time for performing the operation had almost elapsed and that he had only the scantiest information on which to act. However, he felt able to conclude that the patient lacked the mental competence to make the relevant decision:

'I accepted that view of the consultant obstetrician in relation to the first two elements in the analysis of Wall J in *Tameside* (supra) as to the capacity of the patient in the sense of her ability to comprehend and retain information and retain information and to believe such information. However I concluded that the patient was in the throes of labour with all that is involved in terms of pain and emotional stress. I concluded that a patient who could, in those circumstances, speak in terms which seemed to accept the inevitability of her own death, was not a patient who was able properly to weigh up the considerations that arose so as to make any valid decision, about anything of even the most trivial kind, surely still less one which involved her own life.'

Accordingly he found it was in the patient's best interests to undergo the operation and made a declaration that such a procedure would be lawful. In his judgment, delivered some days later, the judge recorded that he had been informed that in fact by the time news of the declaration had been transmitted to the hospital, the patient had changed her mind and consented to the operation which was performed successfully.

Despite the happy outcome, the judgment was the cause of some concern. Not only had an order been made on an ex parte basis, but the judge appeared to suggest in the passage quoted above that a woman 'in the throes of labour' was incapable by reason of that fact of making any decision, however trivial. Such a view is unlikely to appeal to labouring mothers or, indeed, women in general. Indeed, there appeared to be no evidence, of even an informal kind, to justify the finding. The judge seems to have been influenced by a perceived irrationality in refusing a Caesarean section to save a baby's life because of pain experienced previously. Such a decision may well be thought to be irrational, but, the general principle set out in *Sidaway*[3] precludes deciding competence on the basis of the absence of good reasons for a decision.

The other case decided on the same day, *Norfolk & Norwich Healthcare NHS Trust v W*[4], was arguably only slightly less controversial. While the patient was not represented, the Official Solicitor provided leading counsel to act as amicus. However there was no formal written evidence, information being supplied to the court by counsel for the hospital and a representative of the Official Solicitor, both having spoken to the responsible consultants by telephone. It appeared that, although the woman was in the second stage of labour which had arrested, she denied she was pregnant. She had a history of psychiatric treatment. The consultant wished to effect delivery by forceps, but wanted authority to deliver by Caesarean section in the event that this failed. He considered that the foetus would die if not delivered within $1\frac{1}{4}$ hours of the time the application began. The attending consultant psychiatrist considered that, although the patient was not suffering from a mental disorder warranting detention under the Mental Health Act 1983 she was incapable of balancing treatment information given to her so to make a choice. The judge could have found her incompetent on that ground alone, but he chose to go further:

> 'I held that although she was not suffering from a mental disorder within the meaning of the statute, she lacked the mental competence to make a decision about the treatment that was proposed because she was incapable of weighing up the considerations that were involved. *She was called upon to make that decision at a time of acute emotional stress and physical pain in the ordinary course of labour* made even more difficult for her because of her own particular mental history.'[5]

He went on to find that the proposed method of delivery would be in her best interests to prevent damage to her uterus, and because the death of the foetus would have detrimental psychological effects on her. He also ruled that at common law reasonable force could be used as a necessary incident of treatment, thus deciding the point left open in *Tameside*, on the ground that it was in accordance with the doctrine of necessity enunciated in *Re F (mental patient: sterilisation)*[6].

A hint at the reality of such decisions was given at the conclusion of the judgment:

> 'Throughout this judgement I have referred to "the foetus" because I wish to emphasise that the focus of my judicial attention was upon the interests of the patient herself and not upon the interests of the foetus which she bore. However, the reality was that the foetus was a fully formed child, capable of normal life if only it could be delivered from the mother.'[7]

Many would agree that a patient who for reasons of mental disorder[8] was incapable of believing she was pregnant in the circumstances of this case should in some way be protected from danger. However, the judge in this case seems to have been influenced once again by a particular view of the abilities of labouring women, and by the dangers posed to a viable foetus. Furthermore, the court was prepared to make an order which effectively authorised compulsory invasive surgery and restraint at a hearing of which the patient appears to have had no notice and at which she was unrepresented, without any formal evidence.

Barbara Hewson suggested[9]:

> 'The assumption in the most recent cases seems to be that pregnant women are not really autonomous individuals entitled to equal protection, but merely a subdivision of what the courts once called infants and lunatics, incapable of making decisions for themselves, for whom doctors and courts should be surrogate decision-makers.'

1 See [1997] 1 FCR 274, [1996] Hempson's Lawyer 505.
2 See n 1 above.
3 *Sidaway v Board of Governors of the Bethlem Royal Hospital and the Maudsley Hospital* [1985] AC 871.
4 [1996] 2 FLR 613.
5 [1996] 2 FLR 613 at 616 (emphasis added).
6 *Re F (mental patient: sterilisation)* [1990] 2 AC 1.
7 [1996] 2 FLR 613 at 616.
8 As Professor Grubb stated at (1996) 4 Med L Rev 197: 'it is difficult to believe that her denial of the obvious was based upon a difference of opinion or values rather than having a psychiatric history.'
  It was clearly important for the court to be satisfied that the inability is due to mental disorder rather than: 'the tendency most people have when undergoing medical treatment to self-assess and then puzzle over the divergence between medical and self-assessment'. See *B v Croydon Health Authority* (1994) 22 BMLR 13 at 25 per Thorpe J.
9 (1996) 146 NLJ 1385 at 1386 – *Women's rights and legal wrongs*.

Needle phobias: *Re L*[1]

On 5 December 1996 the Family Division heard an application for a declaration that it would be lawful to insert needles for the purpose of anaesthesia and to perform an emergency Caesarean section operation on a patient in labour. The hearing took 24 minutes and was attended by counsel for the hospital, and a representative of the Official Solicitor. Again there was no formal evidence before the court, but only information relayed by counsel and the Official Solicitor who had obtained it from the consultant by telephone. The patient, in her 20s, was in labour at full term, but progress was obstructed. The consultant considered that without intervention, deterioration in foetal health and eventual death were inevitable. The patient wanted to have her child safely, but suffered from an extreme needle phobia and would not consent to any injection such as would be necessary for an anaesthetic. The alternative of inducing anesthesia by gas inhalation carried a 60% chance of causing the patient's death, and the anaesthetist considered this unacceptable.

It was reported that the consultant obstetrician considered the patient to be incapable of weighing treatment information to make a choice. The

[6.8]

judge ruled that the patient lacked the capacity to make treatment decisions on the ground that:

> 'her extreme needle phobia amounted to an involuntary compulsion that disabled L from weighing treatment information in the balance to make a choice. Indeed it was an affliction of a psychological nature that compelled L against medical advice with such force that her own life would be in serious peril.'[2]

The judge was willing to make such a finding despite the absence of any psychiatric evidence or even reported opinion. However, where an urgent situation arises, it might be argued that it is better for the matter to receive some form of judicial review than for doctors to proceed without any external reference.

1 *Re L (an adult: non-consensual treatment)* [1997] 1 FCR 609.
2 [1997] 1 FCR 609 at 612E.

A solution? – *Re MB*[1]

[6.9]   The concerns raised by the previous cases were to some extent resolved in *Re MB*. The case was heard in circumstances of considerable urgency: an application was made by telephone to a Family Division judge, Hollis J between 9.25 and 9.55pm, when he granted a declaration in the following terms:

> 'It shall be lawful for 2 days from the date of this order, notwithstanding the inability of [the patient] to consent thereto:
> (i)   for the [hospital's] responsible doctors to carry out such treatment as may in their opinion be necessary for the purposes of the [patient's] present labour, including, if necessary, caesarean section, including the insertion of needles for the purposes of intravenous infusions and anaesthesia;
> (ii) for reasonable force to be used in the course of such treatment;
> (iii) generally to furnish such treatment and nursing care as may be appropriate to ensure that the [patient] suffers the least distress and retains the greatest dignity.'[2]

The patient was represented by counsel who had had some opportunity to take instructions from her, if only by telephone. The Official Solicitor's representative was present as amicus. No formal evidence was available, and as in previous cases information gleaned by counsel for both parties by telephone was relayed to the judge.

The case concerned a woman with a 33 week pregnancy with a footling breech presentation and an extreme needle phobia. If normal labour was allowed to proceed there was a considerable risk of harm to the foetus, but little danger to the mother herself. She did not oppose a Caesarean section as such but adamantly refused to allow the insertion of a needle for any purpose. In this case the anaesthetist was prepared to take the risks involved in the gas inhalation technique, but the patient continually changed her mind as to whether she would consent to this. Her consultant psychiatrist's opinion was:

'Away from the need to undergo the procedure, I had no doubt at all that she fully understood the need for a caesarean section and consented to it. However in the final phase she got into a panic and said she could not go on. If she were calmed down I thought she would consent to the procedure. At the moment of panic, however, her fear dominated all.'[3]

Hollis J found that she lacked the mental capacity to make treatment decisions and made the declaration set out above. An appeal was immediately launched against the decision and the Court of Appeal convened to hear it in open court at 11.00pm. The hearing concluded at 1.00am with the dismissal of the appeal. As this was the first occasion on which a case of this type had been before the Court of Appeal they reserved judgment, which should be read in full by anyone proposing to undertake a non-consensual operation or apply to the court in connection with one[4]. Many of the problems seen above were addressed. In summary, the court made the following rulings.

1 *Re MB (an adult: medical treatment)* [1997] 2 FLR 426.
2 [1997] 2 FLR 426 at 432.
3 [1997] 2 FLR 426 at 431.
4 See App 6.1: *Re MB Guidelines.*

Capacity

It was emphasised that every adult is presumed to have the capacity to make decisions about treatment unless and until that presumption is rebutted, and that a competent person is entitled to make a decision: **[6.10]**

'for religious reasons, other reasons, for rational or irrational reasons or for no reason at all ... [to] choose not to have medical intervention, even though the consequences may be the death or serious handicap of the child she bears, or her own death. In that event the courts do not have the jurisdiction to declare medical intervention lawful and the question of her own best interests objectively considered does not arise.'

The irrationality which the competent patient was entitled to indulge in was defined in very wide ranging terms:

'a decision so outrageous in its defiance of logic or of accepted moral standards that no sensible person who had applied his mind to the question to be decided could have arrived at it.'

However, it was suggested that:

'Although it might be thought that irrationality sits uneasily with competence to decide, panic, indecisiveness and irrationality in themselves do not as such amount to incompetence, but they may be symptoms or evidence of incompetence. The graver the consequences of the decision, the commensurately greater the level of competence required to take the decision.'

They approved of the *Re C* test[1], but added the gloss that temporary factors, such as confusion, shock, fatigue, pain or drugs, or panic induced by fear might destroy or erode capacity. It was emphasised that careful examination of the evidence was required to determine whether fear had destroyed capacity as opposed to being a rational reason for refusal. Applying these principles to the facts[2] the court held that the patient had lost her capacity by reason of her needle phobia dominating her thinking.

1 See para **[6.7]** above.
2 By the time the Court of Appeal delivered their reserved judgment affidavit evidence verifying the information given at the hearing had been filed.

Reasonable force
[6.11] The court affirmed the previous decisions on this point and held that reasonable force could be used where necessary in the best interests of the patient. It was accepted that the issue may need to be examined in greater depth on a future occasion.

Interests of foetus
[6.12] After a thorough consideration of statute and case law, including human rights cases and US authorities[1] it was held emphatically that there was no jurisdiction at common law to declare non-consensual medical intervention to be lawful to protect the interests of the unborn child:

> 'The law is, in our judgment, clear that a competent woman who has the capacity to decide may, for religious reasons, other reasons, or no reasons at all, choose not to have medical intervention, even though ... the consequence may be the death or serious handicap of the child she bears or her own death. She may refuse to consent to the anaesthesia injection in the full knowledge that her decision may significantly reduce the chance of her unborn child being born alive. The foetus up to the moment of birth does not have any separate interests capable of being taken into account when a court has to consider an application for a declaration in respect of a caesarean section operation.'[2]

Thus the court dealt a mortal blow to the validity of *Re S* as an authority and emphatically restored the primacy of the competent adult woman's autonomy, while seeking to maintain a level of protection for those who are incapable of making a decision for themselves.

1 *Re T (adult: refusal of treatment)* [1993] Fam 95; *Paton v British Pregnancy Advisory Service Trustees* [1979] QB 276; *C v S* [1989] QB 135; *Burton v Islington Health Authority* [1993] QB 204; *A-G's Reference (No 3 of 1994)* [1998] AC 245, HL; *Villar v Sir Walter Gilbey* [1907] AC 139; Offences Against the Person Act 1861, s 58; Abortion Act 1967; Congenital Disabilities Act 1976; *Bruggemann and Scheuten v Federal Republic of Germany* (1978) 10 DR E Com HR 100; *Paton v United Kingdom* (1980) 3 EHRR 408; *H v Norway* (1992) 73 DR 155, E ComHR); *Open Door and Dublin Well Woman v Ireland* (1992) 15 EHRR 244; *Jefferson v Griffin Spalding County Hospital Authority* (1981) 274 SE 2d 457; *Crouse Irving Memorial Hospital v Paddock* (1985) 485 NYS 2d 443; *Re Madyun* (1986) 573 A 2d 1259; *Re AC* (1987) 533 A 2d 611; *Re Baby Boy Doe* (1994) 632 NE 2d 32.
2 Transcript p 28.

Procedure
[6.13] Procedural guidelines were offered. While it was said that the court was unlikely to entertain an application for a declaration of this type unless

capacity was in issue, it was suggested that 'for the time being at least' doctors ought to seek a ruling on the issue of competence. It was unclear whether this related only to cases where there was a dispute on that issue. It was made clear that it was highly desirable for this type of case to be brought as soon as a potential problem was identified rather than at the last, desperate minute, and that the hearing should be inter partes with the mother being represented in all cases if she wished to be. It was preferable for evidence on competence to be given by a psychiatrist.

The solution imposed – *St George's Healthcare NHS Trust v S*[1]

This case brought together the most unfortunate features of the cases which preceded *Re MB* and resulted in firm guidelines being laid down by the Court of Appeal. A young adult woman of full mental capacity, who was 36 weeks pregnant with pre-eclampsia rejected medical advice that she needed urgent attention and an induced delivery in the interests of the health of herself and her baby. She refused, insisting on a natural delivery. A social worker and two doctors approved her detention in hospital under s 2 of the Mental Health Act 1983 for assessment. A few hours later an ex parte application was made to a Family Division judge sitting in chambers. No evidence was presented, but erroneous information was given to the court. The judge granted a declaration which purported to dispense with the patient's consent to treatment. Later the same day she was subjected to delivery of her baby by caesarean section without her consent. No judicial consideration was given to the issue of the patient's capacity. In combined actions for judicial review and damages the Court of Appeal held:

[6.14]

- An adult of full mental capacity cannot be ordered to undergo surgery or any form of medical treatment against his or her wishes.
- An unborn child is not a separate person from its mother and its need for medical assistance does not prevail over the mother's right to refuse treatment.
- No person may be detained under the Mental Health Act 1983 unless the patient falls within the conditions prescribed by the Act: detention for the purpose of providing non-consensual obstetric treatment, as opposed to assessment or treatment of a mental disorder, does not come within the Act.
- A person detained under the Act still possessing full mental capacity cannot have medical treatment imposed on him or her unless it is permitted by the Act. Treatment other than for the mental disorder for which the patient is detained can only be administered with the consent of the patient.
- An inter partes declaratory order has effect as a conclusive definition of the legal rights of those parties and should therefore only be made as a final order: it should not be made on an interim or ex parte basis or without adequate investigation of the evidence. A declaration made on an ex parte application which the defendant could not oppose and of which he or she knew nothing has no effect and, in particular, is no defence to an action by the patient for damages for trespass to the person, once set aside on appeal.

1 [1999] Fam 26, [1998] 3 WLR 936, [1998] 3 All ER 673.

C THE COURT OF APPEAL GUIDELINES

[6.15] In the *St George's Healthcare* case the Court of Appeal issued guidelines[1] after consultation with the President of the Family Division, the Official Solicitor and further submissions by the parties, who had themselves taken soundings from a wide range of professional bodies. These replaced guidelines given at the time of their original judgment. Although principally aimed at obstetric cases, they apply to all instances of proposed invasive treatment of a patient lacking the capacity to consent to or refuse treatment. These are set out in full in the Appendix below[2]. In summary these provide that:

- It is pointless making an application to the court if the patient has full mental capacity.
- Refusals should be recorded and authenticated in writing wherever possible.
- A patient lacking the relevant mental capacity should be treated and cared for according to the hospital authority's judgement of his or her best interests.
- A competently made advance directive should be respected; if there was doubt about its validity an application should be made to the court.
- Any problem about mental capacity to consent to treatment should be identified as soon as possible and assessed as a priority. While assessment by a general practitioner or other non-specialist might suffice, in serious or difficult cases it should ideally be performed by a consultant psychiatrist approved under the Mental Health Act 1983.
- If on assessment there was a serious doubt about competence, the patient's capacity to manage his or her own property or affairs should also be considered. If this is in doubt legal advice should be sought as soon as possible, as a guardian ad litem may need to be appointed and the Official Solicitor notified.
- The patient's solicitors must be informed immediately of any intention to make an application for a declaration, and an opportunity given to take instructions and obtain legal aid.
- Potential witnesses for the health authority must be made aware of the guidance in *Re MB*[3], *St George's Healthcare NHS Trust v S*[4], and any guidance issued by the DoH and the BMA.
- Any application for a declaration should be inter partes, as any other form of proceeding will not bind the patient.
- Although the Official Solicitor will not act for a patient capable of instructing a solicitor, he can be called upon by the court to act as amicus curiae.
- On any such application the court must be supplied with all accurate and relevant information, including the reasons for the treatment, any alternatives, and any ascertainable reason why the patient is refusing the treatment.
- The terms of the order must be recorded and approved by the judge before they are communicated to the health authority. The patient must be informed of the precise terms.
- Applicants for emergency orders made without issuing and lodging the relevant documents have a duty to comply with proper procedure and

pay the relevant court fees.

• There might be cases which are so urgent that it is impracticable to apply to the court at all: where delay might damage the patient's health rigid adherence to the guidelines may be inappropriate.

The practical problem for all practitioners and authorities left by this guidance is to know in what type of case it is desirable or obligatory to make an application to the court for a declaration, and in what cases it is acceptable to provide treatment without such an application in what is assessed to be the best interests of the patient. The original case was concerned with a caesarean section, as was *Re MB*. The guidance, however, is deliberately designed to cover any form of surgical or invasive treatment. It would appear that it is not every case which ought to be referred to court, but that a judgment must be made. It is suggested that consideration must be given to making an application in *every* case where it is considered that the patient lacks capacity to consent to or refuse treatment and is actively refusing the proposed treatment. The guidance should not be read as meaning that such consideration should only be given when there is a serious doubt about competence in the sense that there is a professional disagreement between practitioners on the issue. In every case where the patient refuses or claims the right to refuse treatment he or she is asserting the right, and prima facie claiming the capacity, to do so. In that important sense the question of competence is in dispute and a serious doubt is raised where a properly qualified practitioner seeks to override that refusal. It is suggested that it would be prudent, at least for the time being, to make an application in the case of any such patient on whom it is proposed to perform a Caesarean section or other form of surgical or assisted delivery. The cases demonstrate that such circumstances are almost inevitably serious and complex[5].

1 [1998] 3 WLR 936 at 968, [1998] 3 All ER 673 at 702.
2 See App 6.1: *St George's Healthcare v S Guidelines*.
3 [1997] 2 FLR 426, [1997] 8 Med LR 217; see also App 6.1: *Re MB Guidelines*.
4 [1998] 3 WLR 936, [1998] 3 All ER 673.
5 In other forms of treatment it must be a matter of degree whether an application should be made. It is suggested that the court should be involved in any case of invasive treatment carrying significant risk to the patient, or involving serious irreversible consequences, where the patient is thought by an appropriately qualified medical practitioner to lack the relevant capacity, or in any case where there is a dispute between practitioners, or practitioners and the patient's family or partner about capacity, or where for any other reason the treating doctor reasonably considers he requires the protection of a declaration before proceeding.

D A SUGGESTED PROCEDURE FOR OBSTETRIC UNITS

While it is impossible to legislate for all circumstances it would be **[6.16]** prudent for all obstetric units to develop a practice for detecting and dealing with cases where a problem of capacity may arise. A simple and properly applied practice is likely to alleviate many of the problems which are illustrated in the cases described above, including the stress and distress on patients and their families, unnecessary prejudice to the health of mothers and their babies, and exposure of doctors and other to litigation.

Assessment of capacity

[6.17] On first referral or admission the responsible consultant should ensure that an assessment is made of the patient's capacity to make decisions on obstetric issues. All examiners should be aware of the three stage test of capacity set out in *Rochdale Healthcare NHS Trust v C*[1] and approved in *Re MB*[2] and the *St George's* case[3]. Such an initial assessment can probably be made from the patient's reaction to a careful explanation of the likely course of the pregnancy and requirements for management of labour. It must always be remembered that patients will be presumed in law to have the relevant capacity until the contrary is shown.

1 See para **[6.7]** above; [1997] 1 FCR 274.
2 [1997] 2 FLR 426, [1997] 8 Med LR 217; see also App 6.1: *Re MB Guidelines*.
3 [1998] 3 WLR 936, [1998] 3 All ER 673; see also App 6.1: *St George's Healthcare v S Guidelines*.

Advice to patients about nature of possible treatment

[6.18] In the light of the experience of the courts, it would be prudent to ensure that patients are made aware as soon as is practicable of any possible need to administer injections, intravenous fluids or to insert needles for other purposes to establish whether she suffers from any form of needle phobia.

Discussion with patient about possible loss of capacity

[6.19] If there is a real possibility of a transient loss of capacity occurring in the future due to a phobia or pain, or panic, this should be discussed with the patient well before the event arises, in order to agree with her, while she retains capacity, what should be done in that eventuality.

Psychiatric referral and assessment where capacity in doubt

[6.20] If on initial assessment or at any subsequent time a real doubt emerges about the patient's competence, she should be referred to a consultant psychiatrist for an opinion on her capacity.

Contingency planning for court application

[6.21] If it is established that the patient lacks or is likely to lack the relevant capacity, is likely to refuse invasive treatment required for the health of herself or her baby, and there is a reasonable possibility of such treatment being required, legal advice should be sought at the earliest opportunity. This should enable a decision to be made as to whether a court application should be made, and, if so, when and in what circumstances that ought to be done[1].

1 See App 6.5: *Draft declaration permitting Caesarean section.*

Compliance with Court of Appeal guidelines

[6.22] If an application is to be made the Court of Appeal's guidance must be followed.

Continual advice to patient

[6.23] At all stages the patient should be advised of what is being done and of her rights to obtain her own advice and representation. To this end hospital authorities and their legal advisers should be in a position to assist patients to contact a lawyer when this is required.

E PROCEDURE FOR PATIENTS

Where a patient fears that doctors are likely to try to impose an unwanted **[6.24]**
surgical delivery on her she has the right to seek an injunction restraining
them from doing so. If she retains the capacity to make her own decisions,
or has made her wishes clear when in possession of her full capacity, or
such an operation is not in her best interests, the court is likely to grant an
injunction or a declaration that the proposed treatment would be unlawful, whichever remedy is appropriate. A declaration is appropriate where
the hospital is prepared to give an undertaking to abide by the decision of
the court, and that appears to give sufficient protection to the patient in
the circumstances of the case.

The evidence on which those seeking to impose treatment rely should
be obtained at the earliest opportunity. A request by a solicitor on behalf
of the patient for disclosure of such information should be acceded to by
any reasonable hospital authority.

For the best prospect of mounting a successful application those
advising the patient should seek evidence on the following matters:

- her mental capacity to make decisions for herself – generally this will
  have to be given by a psychiatrist. In theory the patient could rely on
  the presumption of capacity, but it is likely that the hospital authority
  will adduce some evidence of incapacity which will require rebuttal;
- any evidence of previously declared wishes in relation to the mode of
  delivery;
- the intentions of the attending hospital staff;
- the patient's reasons for refusing the proposed mode of delivery; and
- any reasons why it is not in her interests to undergo the proposed mode
  of delivery – generally this should be supported by independent
  medical opinion.

Proceedings for an injunction should be started in the Family Division. It
is suggested that a Part 8 claim form is used, accompanied by a statement
of truth from the patient, and any other evidence available. The form of
relief sought will depend on the precise circumstances, but general
precedents are contained in Appendix 6 below.

Usually time will be short and the court must be notified immediately
of the need for an urgent hearing.

CHAPTER 7

Feeding

CONTENTS

A INTRODUCTION

[7.1] An unfortunate group of patients suffer from a compulsion to deny themselves nutrition. The compulsion not to eat or drink can in some cases be so severe as to be life-threatening. These cases must be distinguished from those who through conscience, protest or other conscious reasons deliberately refuse to take food or drink, such as the rational prisoner who wishes to go on hunger strike in protest at his conviction or someone who wishes to end their life in the face of the onset of a devastating illness.

Disorders of eating fall into two principal diagnostic categories: anorexia nervosa and bulimia nervosa. It is the former which is more likely to cause challenges in relation to the justification of treatment, as it is more likely to give rise to life threatening complications for which the patient is likely to refuse treatment. There are also cases of borderline personality disorder in which the patient becomes compelled to harm him or herself: this may on occasions take the form of deprivation of food.

Disorders of eating tend to be suffered more by women than men, and the onset is generally in the teenage years. The dividing line between an irrational decision taken by a competent mind, and such a decision taken by an incompetent mind will always be difficult, never more so than in this particular field. The prevalence of the disorder among those who are just on the point of attaining their majority and releasing themselves from even the theoretical control of parents adds to the challenges of ensuring that treatment given is legally justified.

This section principally addresses the problems posed by patients who do not wish to receive nutrition or other treatment for their self-inflicted condition, and inevitably concentrates on cases of involuntary feeding[1]. Obviously a book written by lawyers cannot purport to pass an opinion on when such treatment might be medically or ethically justified. It must be recognised that in a controversial field such as this medical and professional practice will be constantly under review, and it should not, therefore, be assumed in any case that involuntary treatment is necessarily the appropriate solution.

1 Those opposing such treatment will often use the phrase 'force-feeding'. This is avoided here as it carries connotations which do not necessarily correspond to the reality of what is actually done.

B CHILDREN

General principles

Children under the age of 16

The treatment of children under the age of 16 may be authorised by a person having parental responsibility, or by the court in proceedings under the inherent jurisdiction, even if the child is *Gillick* competent, and refuses the treatment[1].

[7.2]

1 *Re R (a minor) (wardship: consent to treatment)* [1992] Fam 11; *Re W (a minor) (medical treatment: court's jurisdiction)* [1993] Fam 64.

Children aged 16 and 17

While statute[1] creates a presumption that a competent consent given by a 16 or 17 year old is as valid as if given by an adult, it does not follow that a refusal by such a patient is a bar to treatment. A refusal by the patient does not amount to a veto of treatment if someone with parental responsibility has consented[2].

[7.3]

1 Family Law Reform Act 1969, s 8:
(1) The consent of a minor who has attained the age of 16 years to any surgical, medical or dental treatment which, in the absence of consent, would constitute a trespass to his person, shall be as effective as it would be if he were of full age; and where a minor has by virtue of this section given an effective consent to any treatment it shall not be necessary to obtain any consent for it from his parent or guardian.
(2) In this section 'surgical, medical or dental treatment' includes any procedure undertaken for the purposes of diagnosis, and this section applies to any procedure (including, in particular, the administration of an anaesthetic) which is ancillary to any treatment as it applies to that treatment.
(3) Nothing in this section shall be construed as making ineffective any consent which would have been effective if this section had not been enacted.
2 As is made clear by s 8(3) of the Family Law Reform Act 1969: see above.

Effect of disorder on Gillick competence

The views of the child are an important fact to be taken into account by parents and doctors in deciding whether treatment should be proceeded with. However, it has been pointed out that in this condition these views may be of less significance[1]:

[7.4]

'I have no doubt that the wishes of a 16 or 17 year old or indeed a younger child who is "*Gillick* competent" are of the greatest importance both legally and clinically ... I personally consider that religious or other beliefs which bar any medical treatment or treatment of particular kinds are irrational, but that does not make minors who hold those beliefs any the less "*Gillick* competent." They may well have sufficient intelligence and understanding fully to appreciate the treatment proposed and the consequences of their refusal to accept that treatment. What distinguishes W from them, ... is that it is a feature of anorexia nervosa that it is capable of destroying the ability to make an informed choice. It creates a compulsion to refuse treatment or only to accept treatment which is likely to be ineffective. This attitude is part and parcel of the disease, and the more advanced the illness, the more compelling it may become. Where the wishes of the minor are themselves something which the doctors reasonably consider need to treated in the minor's own best interests, those wishes will clearly have a much reduced significance.'

In other words the disorder itself may deprive the patient of the capacity to make decision for him or herself.

1 *Re W (a minor) (medical treatment: court's jurisdiction)* [1993] Fam 64 at 80 per Lord Donaldson of Lymington MR.

Exercise of court's jurisdiction

[7.5] In practical terms, if the court's jurisdiction is invoked, and there is evidence before it that a continued refusal of treatment will probably lead to death or serious injury, the refusal of a child, however, near majority, is likely to be overruled:

'It will normally be in the best interests of a child of sufficient age and understanding to make an informed decision that the court should respect its integrity as a human being and not lightly override its decision on such a personal matter as medical treatment, all the more so if that treatment is invasive. In my judgment, therefore, the court exercising the inherent jurisdiction in relation to a 16 or 17 year old child who is not mentally incompetent will, as a matter of course, ascertain the wishes of the child, and will approach its decision with a strong predilection to give effect to the child's wishes. (The case of a mentally incompetent child will present different considerations, although even there the child's wishes, if known, must be a very material factor.) Nevertheless, if the court's powers are to be meaningful, there must come a point at which the court, while not disregarding the child's wishes, can override them in the child's own best interests, objectively considered. Clearly such a point will have come if the child is seeking to refuse treatment in circumstances which will in all probability lead to the death of the child or to severe permanent injury.'[1]

The jurisdiction of the court extends to authorising the detention of the child patient in a place where treatment can be provided, so long as the court's jurisdiction is not ousted by the accommodation being secure accommodation under the Children Act 1989[2]. The court has power to direct that reasonable force be used if necessary. However it is important that careful attention should be paid to the safeguards under the Act, and any order is likely to be made of limited duration and subject to review[3].

1 Section 25: *Re W (a minor) (medical treatment: court's jurisdiction)* [1993] Fam 64 at 88 per Balcombe LJ.
2 *Re C (a minor) (detention for medical treatment)* [1997] 2 FLR 180; see also *Re B (a minor) (treatment and secure accommodation)* [1997] 1 FCR 618, sub nom *A Metropolitan Borough Council v DB* [1997] 1 FLR 767, Cazalet J.
3 *Re C (a minor) (detention: medical treatment)* [1997] 2 FLR 180. It must be doubtful whether doctors, acting on the authority of parents, can detain a *Gillick* competent child against his or her will without the authority of the court. Such a step might well contravene the requirement of Art 5 of the ECHR that any deprivation of liberty must be in accordance with a procedure prescribed by law. However, see *Nielsen v Denmark* (1988) 11 EHRR 175, where the Court of Human Rights held (by 9 votes to 7) that detention of a child in a psychiatric ward on his mother's authorisation did not bring in to play Art 5 because the deprivation of liberty was not by the authorities of the State. It may be doubted whether the court would adopt the same stance today and it is suggested that unless such action is authoritatively established to be lawful it is suggested that a court application should invariably be made if involuntary detention is thought to be necessary. See for example: *R v Kirklees Metropolitan Borough Council, ex p C (a minor)* [1992] 2 FLR 117, where it was held that a 12 year old child had been validly detained in a mental hospital even though not under the Mental Health Act 1983, on the authority of those having parental responsibility, but the court made it clear that the child was not *Gillick* competent.

Procedure

Where is it is desired to obtain approval for treatment for which the child is unwilling or unable to give, the following steps need to be taken: **[7.6]**

- Unless the child is '*Gillick* competent' and refuses to allow his or her parents to be involved in the decision-making process – and even then if it is in the child's best interests – the parents or those having parental responsibility should be consulted about the proposed treatment and, if possible, their consent obtained. If such consent is obtained, that is sufficient legal authority to proceed with treatment despite the child's refusal. The position will obviously have to be explained carefully to the child whose co-operation should be sought if at all possible.
- If no parental consent can be obtained, or the doctors are met with a parental refusal, and it is considered that it remains in the child's best interests that the treatment should be given – unless the case is of such extreme urgency that there is no time to do so – an application should be made to the Family Division of the High Court under the inherent jurisdiction of the court for an order giving leave for the treatment in question to be given. If the child is already a ward of court then the application should be made in the wardship proceedings.
- In preparing for such an application those seeking the order should be prepared with evidence of the medical history, the present condition and prognosis of the patient, the need for treatment, the capacity and views of the patient, the views of the parents or those having parental responsibility, the risks and benefits of the treatment, and the possible results if treatment is not given. Independent expert opinion is always helpful, and should be obtained if at all possible.
- It is always important that the most up-to-date information be available to the court. Therefore applicants should not merely rely on

evidence even a few weeks old, but must be prepared to inform the court of the current position.

C ADULTS

Competent adults – general rule

[7.7] As in any other sphere of medical activity, the general rule is that a competent adult has the absolute right to refuse any form of treatment. Competent adults are fully entitled to refuse to take food or drink for any reason, or for no reason at all. Therefore, a mentally competent adult prisoner who chooses to go on hunger strike and to refuse any form of life saving care must be allowed to do so[1].

> 'The right of the defendant to determine his future is plain. That right is not diminished by his status as a detained prisoner ... against the specific right of self determination held by the defendant throughout his sentence there seems to me in this case to be no countervailing state interest to be set in the balance[2].
>
> Even if the refusal to eat is tantamount to suicide, as in the case of a hunger strike, he cannot be compelled to eat or be forcibly fed'[3].

1 *Secretary of State for the Home Department v Robb* [1995] Fam 127; but note *R v Dr Collins and Ashworth Hospital Authority, ex p Brady* (10 March 2000, unreported), QBD (discussed in Chap 10, *Treatment of Suicidal Patients* at para **[10.11]** below).
2 *Secretary of State for the Home Department v Robb* [1995] Fam 127, [1995] 2 WLR 722 at 727.
3 *B v Croydon Health Authority* [1995] Fam 133 at 137 per Hoffman LJ: for a patient to allow himself to die by declining food has been said not to amount to suicide: see Robb above, Lord Goff in *Airedale NHS Trust v Bland* [1993] AC 789 at 864.

Competent adults detained under the Mental Health Act 1983

[7.8] Adults will often retain their legal capacity to consent to or refuse medical treatment despite being lawfully detained under the Mental Health Act 1983. Such adults who suffer from anorexia nervosa, and who require involuntary feeding to remain alive may be fed by virtue of s 63 of the Mental Health Act 1983[1]. Feeding of this type will be lawful, in spite of the patient's refusal of treatment if:

- The steps to be taken are properly described as medical treatment. Naso-gastric feeding is medical treatment[2].
- The treatment must be for the mental disorder for which the patient is being detained. So far as anorexia is concerned it has been held that naso-gastric feeding is treatment for the mental disorder for the following reasons:

> 'it is pointed out that the mental disorder from which she is suffering is anorexia nervosa which is an eating disorder and relieving symptoms is just as much a part of treatment as relieving the underlying cause. If the symptoms are exacerbated by the patient's refusal to eat and drink, the mental disorder becomes progressively more and more difficult to treat and so the treatment by naso-gastric tube is an integral part of the treatment of the mental disorder itself. It is also said that the treatment is

necessary in order to make psychiatric treatment possible at all.

> This argument, in my judgment, is correct and makes it clear that feeding by naso-gastric tube in the circumstances of this type of case is treatment envisaged under s 63 and does not require the consent of the patient.'[3]

Therefore, if the patient is lawfully detained under the mental health legislation for treatment for an eating disorder, it will be possible, under s 63 of the Mental Health Act 1983, to impose life-saving treatment on the patient. It will be a matter of medical judgement whether this is appropriate or not, even where the patient has the mental capacity to consent to or refuse treatment. While there have been a number of cases in which declarations have been sought from the court to sanction treatment in such circumstances[4], this is not a category of case where court proceedings are necessary in every case. It is suggested that they are only required where there is likely to be controversy, such as where friends or family of the patient support his or her opposition to treatment.

1 'The consent of a patient shall not be required for any medical treatment given to him for the mental disorder from which he is suffering, not being treatment falling within section 57 or 58 above, if the treatment is given by or under the direction of the responsible medical officer.'
2 *Airedale NHS Trust v Bland* [1993] AC 789.
3 *South West Hertfordshire Health Authority v KB* [1994] FCR 1051 at 1053 per Ewbank J.
4 *F v Riverside Mental Health NHS Trust* [1994] 2 FCR 577; *South West Hertfordshire Health Authority v KB* [1994] FCR 1051, sub nom *Re KB (Adult) (Mental Patient: Medical Treatment)* (1994) 19 BMLR 144; *B v Croydon Health Authority* [1995] Fam 133.

Adults lacking the capacity to consent

It is perhaps surprising to contemplate the possibility that a patient who [7.9] is compelled by a mental disorder to deprive him- or her-self of food to the point of death might have the mental capacity to refuse treatment designed to alleviate the consequences, but there is no necessary connection between such a disorder and incapacity. In one case of a woman who had a borderline personality disorder as a result of which she had starved herself to a near lethal extent and was refusing treatment, she was found to have the mental capacity to entitle her at common law to refuse the treatment designed to save her life, although treatment was permitted under s 63 of the Mental Health Act 1983[1]. Had she not been detained under the Act, there would have been no means of requiring her to have treatment. However, careful consideration of the facts will be required in every case to establish whether the patient does have the relevant capacity, as there may sometimes be more than one possible view. It was said by an appeal judge in that case[2]:

> 'I am bound to say that I have some difficulty with the judge's conclusion ... I am as impressed as the judge was by her intelligence and self-awareness. It is, however, this very self-awareness and acute self-analysis which leads me to doubt whether at the critical time, she could be said to have made a true choice in refusing to eat

> ... I find it hard to accept that someone who acknowledges that in refusing food at the critical time she did not appreciate the extent to which she was hazarding her life, was crying inside for help but unable to break out of the routine of punishing herself, could be said to be capable of making a true choice as to whether or not to eat.'

Further, the principles established in the Caesarean section cases indicate that incapacity can be temporary[3]. Therefore, it would seem that an eating disorder which provokes an unwillingness to accept treatment at the very moment that it is most needed might well lead to an incapacity.

Where an adult patient suffering from an eating disorder lacks the capacity to consent to treatment, and it is not possible to provide that treatment under the Mental Health Act 1983, such treatment as it is necessary in the patient's best interests may be given.

1 *B v Croydon Health Authority* [1995] Fam 133.
2 *B v Croydon Health Authority* [1995] Fam 133 at 140–141 per Hoffmann LJ.
3 *Re MB (an adult: medical treatment)* [1997] 2 FLR 426, [1997] 8 Med LR 217; see also Chap 6, *Caesarean Sections* at para **[6.9]** above.

Procedure – declaration

[7.10] Where a patient lacks the capacity to consent to or refuse life-saving treatment rendered necessary by an eating disorder, it may be given without reference to the court unless there is a dispute among those wishing to provide the treatment, and others who seek to represent the interests of the patient. If there is a dispute of substance, those proposing to treat the patient against his or her will need to consider whether to apply to the court for a declaration that it is lawful to give proposed treatment. An application should only be made if it thought necessary to protect those providing the treatment from later criticism or litigation. Generally, the professionals should, having taken care to ensure that their views are in accordance with the best contemporary practice, proceed on their own judgment, just as they would in any other case. Where, however, it is thought likely that proceedings will be taken against those providing the treatment, or there is a genuine and substantial dispute about capacity or what the interests of the patient require, an application for a declaration can be made.

The steps that should then be taken are as follows:

- Given the predictability of a refusal of treatment during a crisis, preparatory steps should be taken as long before a crisis develops as possible. These include:
- Full discussion with the patient, where this is practicable, to consider the options which will confront the patient and the carers if and when there is a crisis.
- An assessment at as early a stage as possible of the patient's capacity to consent to or refuse medical treatment. The patient may have capacity to make advance decisions about treatment for a crisis before that event occurs, even if capacity is likely to be lost then. If possible patients should be encouraged to decide for themselves when capable of doing so what should happen. Full records of any such decision must

be made and if possible approved by the patient. If these steps are taken many legal difficulties will be avoided.

- If the point comes when treatment considered to be necessary to save life is being refused and no prior advance consent or refusal is available, an assessment must be made as to the urgency of the case. This should be realistic. It helps no-one for a false alarm to be raised, but on the other hand, delay should not be allowed where the patient's life is at risk.
- A decision should be made whether the case is suitable for treatment under the Mental Health Act 1983. If this is appropriate the necessary steps to detain the patient and provide treatment should be undertaken. No court application will in general then be needed to be made by those treating the patient.
- If Mental Health Act treatment is inappropriate, consideration must be given to the patient's capacity to refuse the proposed treatment. If the patient is found to possess legal capacity, then his or her wishes must be respected. If there is a substantial dispute about capacity it will be appropriate to make an application to the court for a declaration as to capacity, but in general doctors should proceed on their clinical judgement.
- If the patient lacks capacity, but treatment under the Mental Health Act 1983 is not available, an assessment should be made of whether the treatment is nonetheless in the patient's best interests. Factors taken into account will include: the wishes and views of the patient expressed during interludes when he or she had the relevant capacity, the views currently expressed by the patient, the views of close family or partners on what they perceive the patient would have wanted, the likely effectiveness of the treatment, the availability of alternatives, the risks and benefits of the treatment proposed.
- If it is agreed by those responsible for the care of the incapacitated patient that treatment is required, generally no court application will be required, but if physical detention or force is required it would be prudent to seek the approval of the court.
- If an application is to be made, however urgent the case, evidence of the need for treatment, the patient's incapacity, and the reasons why the treatment is in the patient's best interests will be required. Therefore, appropriate statements should be prepared of the relevant evidence.
- If it is decided to make an application to the court, as much notice as possible should be given to the patient and practical assistance given to enable him or her to obtain legal advice and assistance. The Official Solicitor should be notified and, unless there is an obvious alternative, invited to become the patient's litigation friend.
- As interim declarations cannot be granted[1], the applicant must be prepared to proceed with a substantive hearing, however urgent the case. Hearings can be conducted by telephone where appropriate, and at any time of day or night. However it should be borne in mind that a final declaration can be sought to cover a limited period of time or defined circumstances. Obviously this means that if the time provided for expires or the circumstances change a new application has to be made.

1 *F v Riverside Mental Health NHS Trust* [1994] 2 FCR 577.

Procedure – injunction

[7.11]   Where the carers intend to proceed with treatment without first applying to the court, the patient may wish to contest that decision either because he or she does not accept that there is a lack of capacity or that the treatment is necessary or in his or her best interests. In such circumstances the patient, or a litigation friend acting on his or her behalf, are likely to need to apply to the court for an injunction. The following procedure may be followed:

- Unlike the lack of jurisdiction to grant an interim declaration, the court can grant an interim injunction, and in an urgent case will frequently do so, in order to preserve the status quo until the full merits of a case have been able to be considered. Obviously where there is an urgent need to decide whether or not life saving treatment should be given, the court will be more likely to make a substantive decision at the first hearing on the best evidence available. The first step, however, on behalf of a patient, should be to commence proceedings and ask for an interim injunction restraining the carers from proceeding with the proposed treatment under CPR 1998, Pt 25[1]. This may be brought before the commencement of an action, but generally a claim form should be issued if this is possible.
- Evidence in the form of affidavits or statements of truth should be obtained to support any assertion that the patient has the capacity to refuse treatment, and from expert witnesses that it is not in the patient's interests to have the treatment imposed against his or her will.
- Urgent steps should be taken to have the interim application heard in private as soon as possible.
- Because of the nature of the case it will rarely be necessary to proceed to a substantive trial, as the issues will have been sufficiently resolved by the interim hearing.

1 See CPR 1998, PD 25, para 4 for the procedure for urgent interim applications by telephone etc.

CHAPTER 8

Religious Objections to Treatment

CONTENTS

A INTRODUCTION

On occasions patients will object to proposed medical treatment on **[8.1]** religious grounds. The circumstance in which this has arisen most frequently has been in relation to the administration of blood transfusions. The best known religious objectors to the use of blood in treatment are the Jehovah's witnesses. They believe that the use of blood and some blood products is prohibited by laws laid down in the Bible such as:

'You shall not partake of the blood of any flesh, for the life of all

115

flesh is its blood. Anyone who partakes of it shall be cut off.'[1]

Where the refusal of treatment involves, in the view of the medical attendants, the inevitability of death, very difficult choices and decisions face all concerned, whether the patient is a young child whose parents are seeking to limit medical treatment or a competent adult with a settled and principled view.

This chapter seeks to set out the considerations which will apply in such cases. While the emphasis is on the administration of blood transfusions, the same principles will obviously apply to any refusal of potentially life-saving medical treatment on religious grounds. It is essential in any well run medical institution, where treatment which might be objected to on religious grounds is offered, for the practitioners and management to have considered the problem in advance, to ensure that the staff are informed of the issues, and to have developed a general policy for the handling of such cases. Often problems in this field can be foreseen and managed with sensitive counselling, discussion and consideration of alternative approaches to treatment. Nothing can be more destructive of the necessary confidence between doctor and patient than a hurried decision to impose treatment on a patient against his or her will or the demands of the parents of a child.

1 Leviticus 17:10. This is not the place for study of the grounds for this belief or the controversy that surrounds it, but it is suggested that practitioners who may have to confront the very real problems thrown up by it need to acquaint themselves with the arguments for and against it. It should not be assumed that even all Jehovah's witnesses adhere to the same beliefs.

B COMPETENT ADULTS

General principle

[8.2] As considered in detail elsewhere[1], the competent adult has the absolute right to refuse invasive treatment for any reason, good or bad, or for no reason at all, even where that refusal may lead to serious injury, deterioration in health or death. Clearly a refusal based on religious grounds is a reason that must be respected, however much others may disagree with it. The right to freedom or religious belief is regarded as a fundamental human right, as is the right to privacy and physical inviolability[2]. The imposition of invasive treatment on a mentally competent adult patient without his or her consent will render those doing so liable to civil and criminal proceedings for assault and trespass to the person[3]. Therefore, any decision to override a choice apparently made by a mentally competent adult must be taken with great care and not a little hesitation for full consideration of the issues.

1 See Chap 2 above.
2 See the European Convention on Human Rights and Fundamental Freedoms:
  Article 8 – Right to respect for private and family life
  (1) Everyone has the right to respect for his private and family life, his home and his correspondence.
  (2) There shall be no interference by a public authority with the exercise of this right except such as is in accordance with the law and is necessary in a democratic society in the interests of national security, public safety or the economic well-being of the country, for the prevention of disorder or crime, for the protection of health or morals, or for the protection of the rights and freedoms of others.

Article 9 – Freedom of thought, conscience and religion

(1) Everyone has the right to freedom of thought, conscience and religion; this right includes freedom to change his religion or belief and freedom, either alone or in community with others and in public or private, to manifest his religion or belief, in worship, teaching, practice and observance.

(2) Freedom to manifest one's religion or beliefs shall be subject only to such limitations as are prescribed by law and are necessary in a democratic society in the interests of public safety, for the protection of public order, health or morals, or for the protection of the rights and freedoms of others.

3 In *Malette v Shulman* (1990) 67 DLR 321 at 336, [1991] 2 Med LR 162 Robins JA said in a blood transfusion case in the Ontario Court of Appeal: 'The right to determine what shall be done with one's own body is a fundamental right in our society. The concepts inherent in this right are the bedrock upon which the principles of self-determination and individual autonomy are based. Free individual choice in matters affecting this right should, in my opinion, be accorded very high priority.'

Steps to be taken

The will of the competent adult patient refusing a blood transfusion must be respected, even where the result is likely to be fatal. The following steps need to be taken in the interests of both the patient and those providing medical care.   **[8.3]**

Confirmation that the patient is mentally competent

The attending practitioners must satisfy themselves that the patient is competent to make the very serious decision of refusing life-saving medical treatment by reference to the *Re C/MB* test[1]. In the context of a refusal of treatment for religious reasons, various points require emphasis: **[8.4]**

1 *Re C (adult: refusal of medical treatment)* [1994] 1 WLR 290, see Chap 2 and App 6.1: *Re MB*.

Ability to take in information – In order to assess whether the patient can 'take in and retain' treatment information, it will have been necessary to ensure that the patient has been given all the relevant information. As the patient may believe, from information given by other adherents of his church, for example, that there are other equally effective forms of treatment to those being proposed, it is necessary to ensure that the patient is able to take in and retain information on the effectiveness of alternatives as well as of the treatment being advocated.   **[8.5]**

Ability to believe information – The requirement that the patient is able to believe the information should not be taken as an excuse to define as incompetent those who reject treatment advice on religious grounds. It could be argued that a patient who believes that he will die spiritually if he submits to the proposed treatment is incapable of believing that it will save his life. The temptation to do so should be resisted. A patient can be quite capable of believing that a doctor is genuinely of the opinion that the treatment is life saving while disagreeing that it is in his interests to submit to it. A competent woman who has the capacity to decide may for religious reasons, other reasons, for rational or irrational reasons or for no reason at all, choose not to have medical intervention, even though the consequence may be the death or serious handicap of the child she bears, or her own death[1].   **[8.6]**

1 See App 6.1: *Re MB*.

Counselling

[8.7] There is an obvious need both in the interests of the patient and those offering treatment that the options and their risks are clearly and calmly laid out for the patient to enable a balanced and informed judgment to be made, if that is the patient's wish. This requires anticipation of the particular problems likely to be thrown up by the patient's condition and the proposed treatment in the light of his or her known beliefs and discussion of these by all concerned. A doctor or other carer is clearly entitled where appropriate to give advice in strong and clear terms, but should not act in a way which might be interpreted as bringing undue influence to bear on the patient. Any decision taken by a patient whose will has been dominated by a doctor will be as invalid as if the undue influence had been imposed by a relative or friend. It is always important to ensure that the decision is that which the patient intends of his or her own free will to take.

Undue influence

[8.8] Religious and similar beliefs are held with differing strength of conviction by different people. Some, faced with the prospect of death, will retreat from the apparent consequences and change their views; others will find their stand strengthened. Whatever the position is in the individual case, it is important that those attending the patient are satisfied that the patient's own views and wishes are being communicated, not those of relatives or other interested individuals or groups such as church representatives. A patient's decision arrived at under duress or undue influence is not a valid decision and need not be followed by the attending doctors[1]:

> 'A special problem may arise if at the time the decision is made the patient has been subjected to the influence of some third party. This is by no means to say that the patient is not entitled to receive and indeed invite advice and assistance from others in reaching a decision, particularly members of the family. But the doctors have to consider whether the decision is really that of the patient. It is wholly acceptable that the patient should have been persuaded by others of the merits of such a decision and have decided accordingly. It matters not how strong the persuasion was, so long as it did not overbear the independence of the patient's decision. The real question in each such case is "Does the patient really mean what he says or is he merely saying it for a quiet life, to satisfy someone else or because the advice and persuasion to which he has been subjected is such that he can no longer think and decide for himself?" In other words, "Is it a decision expressed in form only, not in reality?"
>
> When considering the effect of outside influences, two aspects can be of crucial importance. First, the strength of will of the patient. One who is very tired, in pain, or depressed will be much less able to resist having his will overborne than one who is rested, free from pain, and cheerful. Second, the relationship of the 'persuader' to the patient may be of crucial importance. The influence of parents on their children or of one spouse on the other can be, but is by no means necessarily, much stronger than would be

the case in other relationships. Persuasion based upon religious belief can also be much more compelling and the fact that some arguments based upon religious beliefs are being deployed by someone in a very close relationship with the patient will give them added force and should alert the doctors to the possibility – no more – that the patient's capacity or will to decide has been overborne. In other words the patient should really mean what he says.'

It will be seen from the above passage that the attending carers must ask themselves the following questions:

- Has the patient's expressed decision been influenced by some third party or parties?
- If so, who are these parties and what form did their influence take?
- Whatever the nature of the influence, did it overbear the independence of the patient or his or her own will? Factors to take into account in deciding this will include, but not be limited to the nature of the relationship, ie whether the relationship was one in which the third party might be expected to be dominant, such as parent and child, or priest and church member, and the physical and mental fitness of the patient to withstand pressure.
- Does the patient really mean what he or she is saying?

These are unlikely to be easy matters to consider, particularly in the case of urgently needed treatment where there may be little time in which to undertake a detailed social inquiry. The issue requires difficult value judgments to be made about the nature of relationships, the effect of behaviour which may not have been witnessed or be part of a background history of which the carers have little or no knowledge. It is impossible to give more than general guidance about what to do without considering the facts of an individual case. Inevitably there will be many cases where more than one view of the facts could reasonably be taken[2]. Where the patient's refusal appears to have been influenced unduly by others, it would, therefore, generally be prudent to seek the sanction of the court before proceeding wherever that is possible. If a patient's life may be lost even in the time it might take to make an urgent court application, and the attending doctors are of the view after whatever inquiry is possible that the patient's will has been overborne by undue influence, then they should proceed to give whatever treatment they consider necessary to save the patient's life.

1 *Re T (adult: refusal of treatment)* [1993] Fam 95 at 113 per Lord Donaldson of Lymington MR.
2 See *Re C (adult: refusal of treatment)* [1994] 1 WLR 290, where the Court of Appeal took a different view to the first instance judge on whether there had been a vitiating influence.

Scope of the decision

The attending doctors will have to decide precisely what circumstances **[8.9]** the refusal of a blood transfusion is intended by the patient to cover. Where the patient is still conscious and apparently competent the matter can obviously be discussed with him or her. Where the patient has become unconscious when the need for a transfusion actually arises the position is more difficult. The Jehovah's Witness of many years' standing who has calmly and carefully listened to the potential consequences of refusing this treatment and has maintained a refusal to contemplate a transfusion in any circumstances may well be entitled to have his or her refusal respected. A doctor is not entitled to assume once a particular need for a transfusion is perceived that the patient would not have maintained a refusal on those particular circumstances, if the advance refusal was clear and universal[1]. On the other hand, a refusal reported to the doctor by members of the family, apparently based on some unspecified will of God might more easily be interpreted as not necessarily covering the situation actually facing the doctor.

1 *Re T (adult: refusal of treatment)* [1993] Fam 95 at 114 per Lord Donaldson of Lymington MR.

The role of relatives and close friends

[8.10] It is well established that family members, spouses and friends have no power to authorise or veto treatment on behalf of an adult patient who has been rendered incapable of making his or her own decision[1]. Nonetheless, anyone who has knowledge of the patient and his or her beliefs and wishes may have a role to play in providing information to the medical attendants and carers of the patient and thereby in assisting them to come to an informed decision. Where a patient is suspected to have been subjected to undue influence, or where the intended scope of the decision under debate is uncertain, those with personal knowledge of the patient may be able to give information which will clarify the position. Doctors and others are then faced with the invidious task of assessing the reliability of the information they are given. They will face the challenge of deciding the extent to which their informant's views have been coloured by his or her own personal convictions, rather than those of the patient, while ensuring that their own strong desire to provide life saving treatment does not interfere in their own objective assessment of the situation. These are difficulties which it might be doubted many doctors have been trained to face. Therefore in cases likely to provoke dispute it would be prudent to seek legal advice. However undesirable it will be felt in many circumstances to introduce lawyers to treatment decisions, at least they have the training to define the issues and help in the objective assessment of evidence supplied by lay witnesses.

1 See Chap 3, *Deciding for others.*

Recording of decision against medical advice

[8.11] The validity of a patient's decision will not depend as a matter of law on whether or not it is recorded in writing. However, it will always be desirable for any decision of a patient not to accept the treatment advised by doctors to prevent death or a serious deterioration in health to be entered in the patient's medical records, together with a statement, preferably signed by the patient, acknowledging that the decision is against the medical advice received and may be prejudicial to health. If the patient refuses to sign such a statement, the refusal to accept the recommended treatment and a record of the potential consequences should be confirmed in writing by the responsible doctor, and by some other professional, such as the ward sister, who has witnessed or participated in the advice given. A draft form is contained in the Appendices[1]. In the past some forms used by hospitals have contained a disclaimer of liability. It may be thought that it is inappropriate to seek the patient's agreement to a legal position at what is likely to be a stressful time in any event, and when he or she will probably not have access to legal or independent medical advice. If the patient has been advised and treated in accordance with good medical practice, and his or her refusal to accept advice is properly recorded it is unlikely that any liability will arise, whether or not a disclaimer has been signed. If a disclaimer is to be asked for, it should be visibly separated:

> 'from what really matters namely the declaration by the patient of his decision with a full appreciation of the possible consequences, the latter being expressed in the simplest possible terms and emphasised by a different and larger type face, by underlining, the employment of coloured print or otherwise.'[2]

1 See App 8.1: *Draft Form for refusal of treatment to be signed by the patient.*
2 Per Lord Donaldson of Lymington MR in *Re T (adult: refusal of treatment)* [1993] Fam 95 at 115.

C INCAPACITATED ADULTS

General principle

As with every other field of medical treatment, if a blood transfusion is thought to be required by an adult who currently lacks the capacity to consent to or refuse the treatment, it may be administered if the treatment is in the patient's best interests. However, it may sometimes be easier to determine the patient's lack of capacity than to decide where a patient's best interests lie when a close relative or friend claims either that the patient has made it very clear previously that he or she would never be willing to accept this form of treatment.   **[8.12]**

Advance decisions

A practitioner faced with a suggestion that an incapacitated patient in a life threatening condition has previously expressed a determination not to have the one form of treatment he believes can save his life has an awesome responsibility. If he disregards the suggestion and proceeds to save the life of the patient he may find he has condemned him or her to spiritual exile or even damnation and a fate far worse, in the patient's eyes, than physical death. On the other hand, if he complies with a purported advance refusal of treatment and allows the patient to die, subsequent information may indicate that the information was incorrect or that the patient's decision had been the result of undue pressure from others. Inevitably decisions about the validity of advance treatment decisions will arise in cases thought to require urgent treatment when there is little or no time for leisurely and thorough inquiries into the history of the decision that has been communicated. While it has been suggested that doctors who have made honest mistakes in this field will be liable to actions for damages[1], in reality a court is unlikely to find against a doctor who has acted honestly and in accordance with good medical practice or if it does, only for nominal damages. Nonetheless, wherever possible, the most careful consideration will be required to be   **[8.13]** given to the question of whether the patient has actually made an advance statement binding on attending doctors and carers.

1 Per Staughton LJ in *Re T (adult: refusal of treatment)* [1993] Fam 95 at 122.

Reported oral advance decisions

[8.14] It must be recognised that a patient who is an established member of a religion which is known to oppose certain forms of treatment, such as blood transfusions, may, but will not necessarily, have expressed an advance decision about that form of treatment. It would be erroneous without further inquiry to conclude from a simple report of a person belonging to a particular religion that he or she would adhere to all the tenets of that religion as expressed by the informant. After all there is fierce debate within most religions about matters of doctrine, and many give considerable scope for personal variations[1]. In assessing the available evidence the following points should be borne in mind:

- Careful inquiry into the views expressed by the patient must be undertaken, where this is possible. An advance refusal to accept a transfusion should not be rejected merely because it is not evidenced in writing, but it may be difficult to determine the extent to which the patient merely expressed a general view, or made a statement intended to be complied with in the future.
- Reliable evidence should be required of a firm and clearly expressed intention to decline the proposed type of treatment in the type of circumstances now prevailing. A general reluctance would not be sufficient.
- There should be evidence of an understanding of the potential consequences of declining the treatment in question before it is accepted that the patient had expressed a binding advance refusal of treatment. The doctors may need to be aware of the general teaching of a particular religion about the efficacy of alternative methods of treatment. Such beliefs cannot be disregarded by doctors merely because they believe them to be wrong, but they should consider whether the patient made the advance statement in the knowledge that the medical profession might disagree with the church's view[2].
- Those making the assessment on this issue should also seek assurance that at the time the statement relied on was made the patient had the capacity to make it and was not subjected to undue influence.

1 For example Christian Scientists, although advocating prayer rather than medical treatment as a means of curing illness, do not condemn members who choose medical treatment.
2 Jehovah's Witnesses advocate a range of alternative therapies in the place of blood transfusions. In an appropriate case the attending doctors might wish to consider whether the patient had access to knowledge of the relative risks of the various treatments advocated.

The effect of uncertainty

[8.15] What does the doctor do if left uncertain about any of these matters, or simply has no information at all?

- If there is no evidence that an advance statement was made, then the doctor should proceed as if there had been none.

- If, on the other hand, it is clear that such a statement was made, compliance with it cannot be excused on the ground that there is no information one way or the other about the existence of undue influence. To assume that there had been such a vitiating factor in the absence of evidence to the contrary would potentially open the practitioner to the charge of discriminating against an individual on the grounds of his religion. Before being entitled to rely on undue influence as a vitiating factor, the practitioner would have to be able to show evidence that it existed. Such evidence might exist where, for example, the statement was reported to the doctor by a parent or spouse who was a devout adherent of the religion in question after a long and private meeting with a patient in a weak condition[1].

- Where there is no evidence that the patient made the statement in the knowledge of opinions contrary to those expressed by the church the practitioner might be entitled to ignore the statement on the grounds that he or she could not be satisfied that the patient understood the nature and effect of the decision. It should be emphasised that there is no authority on this issue, but this would seem to follow from the requirement that medical decisions should be taken by competent patients who are able to understand in at least general terms the nature and effect of the treatment they are considering. Where there is more than one relevant view of the efficacy of the treatment and any alternative advocated, then it would seem reasonable to require evidence that the patient had some knowledge of that fact.

1 See, for example the facts of *Re T (adult: refusal of treatment)* [1993] Fam 95, where it was remarked (at 111): '(*g*) The matrimonial history ... suggests that Miss T's mother is a deeply committed Jehovah's Witness, who would regard her daughter's eternal salvation as more important and more in her daughter's best interests, than lengthening her terrestrial life span. (*h*) We do not know what the mother said to Miss T, because she has not chosen to tell the court, but it appears to be the fact that on the two occasions when Miss T raised the issue of blood transfusions, she did so suddenly and 'out of the blue' without inquiry from the hospital staff and immediately following occasions when she had been alone with her mother.'

Written declarations

These issues may be easier to resolve if the patient has made a written **[8.16]** declaration. The focus of the investigation can than be on the circumstances in which that statement came to be made. The same questions which are relevant in the case of an alleged oral advance decision are to be considered[1]. Ideally the document will have been made after the patient has participated in a full discussion of the issues with the attending doctors so that the latter can be fully aware of the patient's wishes, and have had the opportunity to give the patient the benefit of their advice[2]. If a written declaration is produced by someone other than the patient, the doctors will need to be satisfied of its authenticity. A copy should be kept in the patient's records. Those who have made advance directives complain sometimes that the copies given to medical practitioners are frequently not kept in the records and are thus not made accessible to all who might need to know that an advance directive has been made.

1 See paras **[8.14]** et seq above.
2 A form similar to that in the App 8.1: *Draft Form for refusal of treatment to be signed by*

the patient can be used, if the specific treatment for a specific condition is contemplated, or otherwise an advance directive form such as the precedent in App 2.1: *Draft Advanced Directive*.

D CHILDREN

General principle

[8.17] Generally the consent of one parent (or whoever has parental responsibility) will be sufficient authority for treatment, even if the other objects, whether on religious or other grounds. In the case of proposed circumcision or sterilisation, however, such a disagreement will mean that the dispute should be referred to the court before treatment is given[1]. The courts have frequently been faced with cases of conflict between parents with strong religious convictions against blood transfusions and doctors and other carers who wish to administer what they regard to be life saving treatment[2]. The almost invariable outcome has been that the court will authorise the treatment as being in the best interests of the child. In effect the court will do so where there is clear evidence that the child's condition requires a blood transfusion without which treatment will be unsuccessful and harm will be suffered by the child as a result, whatever the parent's views might be. However, consultation with the parents will be encouraged, as will consideration of reasonable alternatives to blood transfusions[3].

In any decision to override the views of one or both parents adequate account must be taken of their rights to family life, and to manifest their religion under Arts 8 and 9 of the European Convention[4]. These rights have to be balanced against the welfare of the child and the equivalent rights of the other parent[5].

1 *Re J (child's religious upbringing and circumcision)* [2000] 1 FLR 571 at 577. It is unclear what other cases fall within this category, but they may include any 'non-therapeutic' treatment which could cause important irreversible changes to the child's physical abilities.
2 See *Re E (a minor)* [1992] 2 FCR 219; *Re O (a minor) (medical treatment)* [1993] 2 FLR 149; *Re R (a minor) (medical treatment)* [1993] 2 FLR 757; *Re S (a minor) (refusal of medical treatment)* [1995] 1 FCR 604.
3 See the form of order taken from *Re R (a minor) (medical treatment)* [1993] 2 FLR 757 in App 8.3: *Draft Specific Issue Order for Administration of Blood Products to Child*.
4 See para **[8.2]** above.
5 See *Re J* (n 1) above.

Best interests

[8.18] Doctors faced with a refusal of parents to consent to a blood transfusion to save a child patient's life should act in the child's best interests. If it is possible to apply to a court for an order approving the treatment, then this should be done. Judges of the family courts have immense experience and far greater powers than doctors to assess the best interests of children. The doctor faced with the immediacy of the need for a course of medical treatment is not always in the best position to obtain, let alone assess, all the relevant information. For example, if the child might be ostracised by its parents and community if given blood, and there might be some chance of recovery with an alternative form of treatment, then a difficult judgment has to be made. Similarly, if only a very poor quality of life is likely to be enjoyed by the child even with the proposed treatment, then there might be arguments for withholding it. Parental refusals seen as unreasonable by doctors will not always be rejected by the court[1]. The consequences of overriding the parents' views will be taken into account. Where there is some medical opinion supporting doubts expressed by the parents as to the efficacy or risks of proposed treatment, greater weight may be given to the parental view than where medical opinion is unanimous. Therefore, it should not be automatically assumed that the medical view is the correct one.

1 See in a different treatment context *Re T (a minor) (wardship: medical treatment)* [1997] 1 WLR 242.

The 'Gillick competent' child

Where the child is old and mature enough to understand the nature and effect of the treatment and the consequences of refusing it, it may be competent in law to make treatment decisions for itself, but both the parents and the court will still retain the power to override such a decision where to do so is in the best interests of the child[1]. In such a case it would be unwise of the doctors to proceed to treatment without the consent of either the parents or the court exercising its inherent jurisdiction. **[8.19]**

1 *Re R (a minor) (wardship: consent to treatment)* [1992] Fam 11.

E   Procedure

Anticipation

In any case of potential conflict between medical and parental opinion, it is obviously important that the issue is addressed as far ahead of the actual time when a decision becomes vital as is possible. Therefore practitioners should be constantly alert to the possibility that parents may hold particular views about certain types of treatment such as blood transfusions. Such issues should become apparent during careful history taking and discussion of the child's condition with the parents. **[8.20]**

Notice and consultation

Were there is a potential serious difference of opinion as to the correct course of action between the attending doctors and the parents, consideration must be given to whether an application should be made to the court for advice. The fact that such a step may be taken should normally be shared with the parents unless it is clearly not in the child's interests that they should be informed. They are entitled to the opportunity to obtain advice of their own, second medical opinions and so on. It must constantly be borne in mind that whatever the outcome, they will remain the parents of the child, and, in most cases, will retain responsibility for its care. Therefore to alienate them from the therapeutic process unnecessarily is to be avoided if at all possible. **[8.21]**

Evidence

Where it is decided that a court application is necessary, the relevant evidence must be prepared. At minimum this will include medical evidence of the child's condition, the reasons why the disputed treatment is needed, in addition to a full account of the parental or other objections, and any other information thought to be relevant to an assessment of the **[8.22]** child's interests. It must be remembered that *all* relevant information should be put forward, whether or not it appears to assist the case to be advanced. These should not be regarded as adversarial proceedings, but an engagement of the court in the process of caring for a vulnerable child. If not already involved the local social services should be consulted and invited to become involved in the case. They may wish to arrange for the child to be represented.

Relevant jurisdiction

[8.23] There has been some debate whether applications to the court should be made under its inherent jurisdiction or under s 8 of the Children Act 1989[1]. While this issue may be important to family practitioners it is of little significance to doctors or parents, and an application brought by one route can easily be converted to one by the other. A meritorious case is unlikely to fail on such a technicality. However, it is probably prudent to ensure that the application is brought under both jurisdictions where possible.

1 See *Re O (a minor) (medical treatment)* [1993] 2 FLR 149, [1993] 4 Med LR 272; and *Re R (a minor) (medical treatment)* [1993] 2 FLR 757.

Change of circumstance

[8.24] Medical conditions frequently change unexpectedly. New medical techniques are regularly discovered or found to be more effective than previously thought. Therefore, the obtaining of authority from the court or parents to proceed with a particular form of treatment should not be taken as exempting the medical attendants from continuing to review the condition of the patient and whether the treatment chosen remains in his or her best interests. Should there be a change of circumstances and it becomes desirable to vary the treatment plan, whoever gave the prevailing authority to treat must be approached again for the matter to be reconsidered, unless the authority explicitly covers what it is now desired to do. The form of order suggested in the Appendices[1] would avoid the need to refer back to the court in many situations.

1 See App 8.3: *Draft Specific Issue Order for Administration of Blood Products to Child.*

CHAPTER 9

Permanent Vegetative State

CONTENTS

A INTRODUCTION

Permanent Vegetative State ('PVS') has been described as a 'twilight **[9.1]**
zone of suspended animation where death commences while life, in some
form, continues[1].' Patients with PVS are in a state lacking all consciousness with no prospect of recovery. It is estimated that there are over 1,000
patients who suffer from 'permanent vegetative state' in Britain today[2].
Whether cared for in hospital or at home there is an immense human cost
in caring for these patients. Family members are unable to mourn for a
loved one who has departed: instead they have the enduring pain of
watching a 'living death'. There is also the significant burden and strain
placed on those nursing such a patient. Further, there are substantial
economic costs in caring for patients who have, by definition, no prospect
of any meaningful human existence.

'Given that there are limited resources available for medical care, is it right to devote money to sustaining the lives of those who are, and always will be, unaware of their own existence rather than to treating those who, in a real sense, can be benefited, eg those deprived of dialysis for want of resources.'[3]

Family members cannot consent to treatment on behalf of an unconscious adult: under English law no-one has the power to consent for an incompetent adult patient. Thus, an unconscious patient must be treated in accordance with his 'best interests'. Once a patient has an established diagnosis of PVS, two major ethical problems face doctors and family members: the first is whether active treatment should be provided to save the patient in the event of an illness and the second is whether artificial feeding and hydration should be withdrawn thereby allowing the patient to die. In essence both issues raise the same fundamental question: whether the PVS patient's life is so devoid of value that it should be allowed to end without the medical intervention afforded to other patients. Nonetheless, it is the second issue, the withdrawal of feeding and hydration which has been the most controversial. As discussed elsewhere feeding and hydration are not viewed in the same way as other medical interventions.[4] Headlines such as 'Shock at court ruling which lets coma woman "starve"'[5] have followed hearings where it has been declared lawful to withdraw feeding and hydration. Pro-Life pressure groups have attacked attempts at withdrawal of feeding in strong terms. Mike Willis, chairman of the Pro-Life Alliance has stated:

'As for this idea of considering hydration as a treatment, it's a basic human need and you wouldn't deny it to a dog.'[6]

Janet Allen of 'SOS-NHS Patients in Danger' has stated:

'Giving water is not treatment – that's not a medicine, it's the stuff of life.'[7]

Lord Mustill in *Bland* noted that it was a 'striking fact' that in 20 out of the 39 American states which have legislated in favour of 'living wills' the legislation specifically excludes termination of life by the withdrawal of nourishment and hydration[8].

Opposition to withdrawal of treatment in these cases stems from the absolute view that all human life is sacred and that it is therefore morally wrong to allow a PVS patient to die no matter how meaningless his existence or how bleak the prospect of recovery. Doctors, it is argued, should not therefore be allowed to withdraw the basic necessities of life – food and water – from a person merely for the emotional convenience of others or in order to release resources to others. This position finds ostensible support in the wording of Art 2 of the European Convention on Human Rights.[9]

However, the British courts have rejected the absolutist position (and as discussed below this has withstood challenge under the Human Rights Act 1998[10]) and have determined that not all human life is worth saving at all costs. *Bland* establishes that if the diagnosis of permanent vegetative state[11] is established a court will declare withdrawal of feeding and/or hydration lawful. Thus, legal uncertainty is only found in those cases where the condition does not match the established and recognised criteria for PVS.

The substantial difficulty for clinicians is in determining whether the PVS diagnosis has been established to an adequate degree of certainty. It is in this area of diagnosis that the second ground for challenging withdrawal of treatment in PVS cases has arisen, namely that it cannot be satisfactorily determined either that the condition is 'permanent' or that the patient is truly in a 'vegetative' state. Significant concern in relation to misdiagnosis of PVS has emerged within the medical profession[12] and has intermittently received national publicity[13]. Thus, before proceeding to a court hearing it is essential that all rehabilitative measures have been exhausted and that the diagnosis has been confirmed by at least two neurologists experienced in diagnosing PVS.

1 *Rasmussen v Fleming* 154 Ariz 207, 211, 741 P.2d 674, 678 (1987).
2 In *Airedale NHS Trust v Bland* [1993] AC 789, [1993] 2 WLR 316, [1993] 1 FLR 1026, HL [hereafter simply '*Bland*'] decided in February 1993, Lord Browne-Wilkinson indicated at [1993] AC 879B that they had been informed that the number of PVS patients was between 1,000 and 1,500.
3 *Airedale NHS Trust v Bland* [1993] AC 789 at 879D.
4 Despite the acceptance in *Bland* that artificial feeding and hydration are forms of medical treatment, see [1993] AC 789 at 857, 870.
5 *Electronic Telegraph* (1997) 23 March.
6 *BBC News* (1999) 23 June.
7 *BBC News* (1999) 23 June.
8 *Airedale NHS Trust v Bland* [1993] AC 789 at 890F.
9 'Everyone's right to life shall be protected by law. No one shall be deprived of his life intentionally save in the execution of a sentence of a court following his conviction of a crime for which his penalty is provided by law.'
10 Discussed at para **[9.4]** below; see *An NHS Trust 'A' v Mrs 'M'* and *An NHS Trust 'B' v Mrs 'H'* (25 October 2000, unreported).
11 *Bland* in fact refers to 'persistent vegetative state': however, since the judgment new guidelines (discussed below) have been issued advocating the terminology 'permanent vegetative state' for patients such as Anthony Bland where there is no prospect of recovery from the vegetative state.
12 See for example, Andrews K, Murphy L, Munday R, Littlewood C, 'Misdiagnosis of the vegetative state: retrospective study in a rehabilitation unit' *British Medical Journal* 1996, p 313.
13 See for example, 'Patients diagnosed as 'vegetables' were alert and aware', *Electronic Telegraph* (1996) July 5, a report on Dr Andrews research showing 'four out of 10 patients diagnosed as being in persistent vegetative state were found on further examination by specialists to be aware of themselves and what was going on around them'.

B Legal Principles

The law does not consider PVS patients to be dead: death occurs when **[9.2]** there is no longer any brain stem function[1]. In PVS patients the brain stem still functions.

The legal duty of a doctor is to ensure that those in his care receive adequate care and nourishment. In usual circumstances a failure by a doctor to provide adequate feeding and hydration resulting in a patient's death would normally result in a manslaughter charge. Thus, what is the legal rationale for allowing withdrawal of feeding/hydration of PVS patients?

1 *Re A* [1992] 3 Med LR 303; see also *An NHS Trust 'A' v Mrs 'M'* and *An NHS Trust 'B' v Mrs 'H'* (25 October 2000, unreported: transcript, para 17).

The *Bland* decision

[9.3]   In short, the legal position following *Bland*[1] is that it is lawful to withdraw nutrition and hydration from a patient who is in a permanent/persistent vegetative state. If a court determines that the PVS diagnosis is correct, a declaration allowing the withdrawal of feeding/hydration is likely to be granted.

This simple statement belies the substantial ethical and legal debate behind the decision in *Bland*. Whilst in determining how to deal with vegetative patients the key is to determine and be satisfied of the PVS diagnosis, it is worthwhile exploring the reasoning behind the *Bland* decision because it casts light on how English law reconciles the withdrawal of life-saving treatment with its opposition to euthanasia. In particular it provides guidance in the approach to 'near-PVS' cases or those cases where the BMA or Royal College of Physicians guidelines for PVS are not met.

The House of Lords concluded that the sanctity of life is not absolute: there is no absolute duty to prolong life. The principle underlying that determination is the sound view that an unconscious or incompetent person should not have to be subjected to what a rational and conscious person would reject. Thus, a rational person, it is argued, would not wish to be kept alive in a vegetative state as 'a person who has no conscious being at all'[2].

However, in reaching this 'rational' conclusion it was necessary for the Law Lords to address how such action can be taken without being construed as euthanasia. The problem in this situation is simple: a PVS patient is not dead and has all the rights of other human beings; taking his life would be a homicide[3]. If a child is starved to death by his parents that would amount to a homicide. They are under a duty to feed the child. Their omission to feed the child renders them liable for the consequences. If a doctor administered a lethal injection to a PVS patient again that would be homicide. Thus the legal dilemma here is: why is the failure to continue to feed a PVS patient not a homicide?

The House of Lords in determining why withdrawal of feeding does not constitute homicide found it necessary to distinguish between an act and an omission:

> 'to act is to cross the Rubicon which runs between on the one hand the care of the living patient and on the other hand euthanasia'[4].

An omission to act cannot be an offence unless one is under a duty to act. Those caring for a patient are usually under a duty to act: they have a duty to give food and drink to those in their care. If they do not do so and the patient dies they have committed a homicide (usually manslaughter but if the requisite intent were proved, murder)[5].

However, a medical practitioner is no longer under a duty to feed or hydrate when it is established that no benefit at all would be conferred by continuance, that is, it is not in the patient's 'best interests'. This 'best interests' test is often formulated as 'acting towards the patient in accordance with a responsible body of medical opinion', the *Bolam* test:

' ... on an application to the court for a declaration that the discontinuance of medical care will be lawful, the courts only concern will be to be satisfied that the doctor's decision to discontinue is in accordance with a respectable body of medical opinion and that it is reasonable.'[6]

This would lead to the conclusion that it is not a question of what the court thinks is in the patient's best interest but whether the doctor's belief is reasonable and bona fide. Given this rationale, it could be argued that a more precise way of formulating the duty is: a medical practitioner is no longer under a duty to feed or hydrate when it is established that a responsible body of medical opinion (a *Bolam* responsible body) supports the determination that no benefit at all would be conferred by continuance.

It is suggested that this is not the intended result of *Bland*. The requirement that this type of case be considered by the court before treatment is withdrawn does not suggest that in – of all cases – those where the patient would die as a result, the judge's function is to be a mere rubber stamp for the medical profession. As stated by the then Master of the Rolls in *Frenchay*:

'It is, I think, important that there should not be a belief that what the doctor says is the patient's best interest is the patient's best interest. For my part I would certainly reserve to the court the ultimate power and duty to review the doctor's decision in the light of all the facts.'[7]

Further, not all the Law Lords approached 'best interests' on the *Bolam* basis: Lord Mustill, for example, approached 'best interests' not through assessing the question of whether objectively the doctor's determination is reasonable and bona fide but by assessing the question of what (objectively) was in Anthony Bland's best interests. Thus a 'real' best interests test was applied: Lord Mustill determined that the withdrawal of feeding was objectively the best option for Anthony Bland rather than merely being an option supported by a body of medical opinion[8]. This is akin to the position in child cases in which the Court determines what is the best option for the child rather than merely declaring that a given course of treatment is lawful because it is *Bolam* reasonable.

Thus, if there is no longer a duty to continue to feed or hydrate a patient then no criminal or civil liability results from the omission to continue feeding and hydrating. Applied to a PVS patient this produces the following results.

Initially, it is appropriate to treat a vegetative patient if only to determine that patient's condition and prognosis. The basis for treating such an unconscious patient who can neither give nor withhold consent is that the practitioner is acting in the patient's 'best interests'. At first 'best interests' usually requires that the patient be treated and kept alive by artificial feeding and hydration.

However, a vegetative patient's 'best interests' will change. Whilst there may be a potential benefit in initial treatment, once it is established that there is no prospect of recovery for the vegetative patient and that continuing treatment is futile, the position changes. Existence in a vegetative state with no prospect of recovery is not a benefit. Lord Mustill commented that:

> 'the continued treatment of Anthony Bland can no longer serve to maintain that combination of manifold characteristics which we call a personality'.

Lord Goff stated:

> 'it is the futility of the treatment which justifies its termination.'[9]

Further, if the diagnosis is correct there will be no detrimental consequences for the PVS patient in the withdrawal of feeding or hydration: he has no consciousness, is not sensate and is not losing any opportunity for recovery.

Such an analysis of the patient's 'best interests' dictates that there is no longer a duty to feed and hydrate the patient. Any subsequent failure to feed or hydrate legally is not an act, it is merely an omission. Once the diagnosis is determined, given that those caring are no longer under any duty to feed or hydrate the patient, that omission does not constitute homicide. The operative cause of the patient's death will be the original accident or condition that caused the vegetative state in the first place.

The underlying rationale is: why should artificial feeding and hydration be different from other forms of medical treatment? Lord Goff stated:

> 'Indeed, the function of artificial feeding in the case of Anthony, by means of a nasogastric tube, is to provide a form of life support analogous to that provided by a ventilator which artificially breathes air in and out of the lungs of a patient incapable of breathing normally, thereby enabling oxygen to reach the bloodstream.'[10]

Regardless of the criticisms, the law is now clear: where the court is satisfied that a justifiable and firm diagnosis of irreversible PVS has been made, feeding and hydration can be withdrawn.

1 *Airedale NHS Trust v Bland* [1993] AC 789, [1993] 2 WLR 316, [1993] 1 FLR 1026, HL.
2 Sir Thomas Bingham MR in *Frenchay Healthcare NHS Trust v S* [1994] 1 WLR 601, [1994] 2 All ER 403, [1994] 1 FLR 485, [1994] 3 FCR 121, [1994] Fam Law 320.
3 The term 'homicide' is used here to connote the unlawful killing of another whether in law it comprises 'murder' or 'manslaughter'.
4 Lord Goff at [1993] AC 865.
5 See *Rex v Gibbins and Proctor* (1918) 13 Cr App R 134, cited in *Airedale NHS Trust v Bland at* [1993] AC 881.
6 Per Lord Browne-Wilkinson at [1993] AC 883.
7 *Frenchay Healthcare NHS Trust v S* [1994] 1 WLR 601, [1994] 2 All ER 403.
8 And this is the approach followed in the Court of Appeal decision in *Re SL (adult patient) (medical treatment)* [2000] 3 WLR 1288, [2000] 2 FCR 452.
9 [1993] AC 789 per Lord Mustill at 899 and Lord Goff at 869.
10 [1993] AC 789 at 870.

The problem with 'act' and 'omission'

[9.4] The withdrawal of feeding is deemed legally not to be an act. The distinction has not been free from criticism. Hoffmann LJ considered that it[1]:

'leads to barren arguments over whether the withdrawal of equipment from the body is a positive act or an omission to keep it in place.'

Returning to the example given earlier: why is it an 'act' which hastens death if an outsider comes in and removes the patient's feeding tube? The removal of the feeding tube is an 'act' when done by an outsider but paradoxically is an 'omission' when done by someone who used to have a duty to the patient. The outsider has no duty. The doctor now has no duty. How then can the act of pulling the tube be an 'omission' in one person's hands and an 'act' in another's?

The explanation given by Lord Goff was that the outsider is actively stopping the medical treatment[2]:

'I also agree that the doctor's conduct is to be differentiated from that of, for example, an interloper who maliciously switches off a life support machine because, although the interloper may perform exactly the same act as the doctor who discontinues life support, his doing so constitutes interference with the life-prolonging treatment then being administered by the doctor. Accordingly, whereas the doctor, in discontinuing life support, is simply allowing his patient to die of his pre-existing condition, the interloper is actively intervening to stop the doctor from prolonging the patient's life, and such conduct cannot possibly be categorised as an omission.'

An alternative might be that the outsider would be under a duty not to interfere with the patient's medical treatment. Thus, the removal of the feeding tube by the outsider would comprise criminal homicide because he was under a duty not to intervene.

1 [1993] AC 789 at 831, CA.
2 [1993] AC 789 at 866, HL.

European Convention on Human Rights
Article 2 of the European Convention on Human Rights provides: **[9.5]**

'Everyone's right to life shall be protected by law. No one shall be deprived of his life intentionally save in the execution of a sentence of a court following his conviction of a crime for which this penalty is provided by law.'

The Human Rights Act 1998[1] establishes direct liability on public authorities for breach of the European Convention on Human Rights. The absolute terms of Art 2, protecting the right to life, led to the suggestion that the current law would have to change.

However, in *An NHS Trust 'A' v Mrs 'M'* and *An NHS Trust 'B' v Mrs 'H'*[2] the President rejected the view that the *Bland* approach was incompatible with Art 2. Both patients M and H fell within the Royal College of Physicians definition of the Permanent Vegetative State. The patients' family supported the Trusts' application to withdraw artificial feeding and the Official Solicitor acting for the patients themselves agreed that withdrawal was in their best interests and did not violate Art 2.

The President concluded, first, that both patients were 'alive' within the meaning of Art 2.

Secondly, the President rejected an argument by the Trusts that the intention in withdrawing artificial nutrition and hydration was not to bring about the patient's death and agreed with the Official Solicitor's position that the intention here would be to end life. The Trusts had argued that the *purpose* of the withdrawal of treatment would not be to kill, therefore the intention would not be to kill. The intention was simply to withdraw futile treatment. Reliance was placed on Brooke LJ in *Re A (children) (conjoined twins: surgical separation)*[3]:

'I do not consider that the *Woolin* extension[4] of the meaning of the word "intention" is appropriate when determining whether a doctor who performed a separation operation on conjoined twins in circumstances like these was intentionally killing the twin whose life was to be sacrificed. The doctor's purpose in performing the operation was to save life, even if the extinction of another life was a virtual certainty. Like Robert Walker LJ I do not consider that the adoption of an autonomous meaning of the word "intentionally" in Article 2(1) of the Convention need have any effect on the interpretation of the concept of "intention" in our national law, which has at long last been settled by the House of Lords in *Woollin*'.

Reliance was also placed on Walker LJ in *Re A (children) (conjoined twins: surgical separation)*[5]:

'The Convention is to be construed as an autonomous text, without regard to any special rules of English law, and the word "intentionally" in Article 2(1) must be given its natural and ordinary meaning. In my judgment the word, construed in that way, applies only to cases where the purpose of the prohibited action is to cause death. It does not import any prohibition of the proposed operation [on the conjoined twins] other than those which are to be found in the common law of England.'

Concern was expressed by the Trusts in argument that a ruling that the intention in the PVS situation was to kill would impact on the doctrine of double effect. This doctrine serves to relieve doctors of criminal responsibility in circumstances where pain-relieving medication is given which is for pain relief but also has the effect of causing a premature death[6]. The President however stressed that[7]:

'This judgment is dealing only with the situation where treatment is to be discontinued and is not concerned with nor relevant to acts by doctors or other members of the health service, such as the giving of palliative drugs to a terminally-ill patient, which might have the effect of shortening his life.'

Thirdly, the President determined that, whilst the intention in withdrawing hydration and nutrition was to cause death, such withdrawal did not amount to an 'intentional deprivation of life' within Art 2. The President noted the decision in *Widmer v Switzerland*[8] in which the Commission[9] had concluded that Art 2 does not require that 'passive euthanasia' – by which a person is allowed to die by not being given treatment – be a crime[10]. Further, in *Association X v United Kingdom*[11] the Commission determined that where a small number of children died as a result of a vaccination scheme whose aim was to protect the health of society, their deaths could not be considered to be as a result of an intentional deprivation of life within Art 2(1).

The President stressed the importance of the autonomy of the patient. Treatment contrary to a patient's best interests violates that right to autonomy. Article 8 of the Convention defends that right: the moral and bodily integrity of a person should be protected from unjustified assault[12]. Given that for M and H ceasing medical treatment was in their best interests, it cannot be said that their death following the discontinuance of such treatment amounts to an intentional deprivation of life. By analogy there cannot be a duty in every case 'to take steps indefinitely, until the patient's body could no longer sustain treatment, irrespective of the circumstances or the prognosis'. Thus, the President accepted that there was not an intentional deprivation of life here:

'Although the intention in withdrawing artificial nutrition and hydration in PVS cases is to hasten death, in my judgment the phrase "deprivation of life" must import a deliberate act, as opposed to an omission, by someone acting on behalf of the state, which results in death. *A responsible decision by a medical team not to provide treatment at the initial stage could not amount to intentional deprivation of life by the state.* Such a decision based on clinical judgment is an omission to act. The death of the patient is the result of the illness or injury from which he suffered and that cannot be described as a deprivation. It may be relevant to look at the reasons for the clinical decision in the light of the positive obligation of the state to safeguard life, but in my judgment, it cannot be regarded as falling within the negative obligation to refrain from taking life intentionally. I cannot see the difference between that situation and a decision to discontinue treatment which is no longer in the best interests of the patient and would therefore be a violation of his autonomy, even though that discontinuance will have the effect of shortening the life of the patient.'[13]

Fourthly, the President considered the positive obligation on the State to protect life[14]. In *Osman v United Kingdom*[15] it was stated[16]:

'The first sentence of Article 2(1) enjoins the State not only to refrain from the intentional and unlawful taking of life, but also to take appropriate steps to safeguard the lives of those within its jurisdiction.'

However, the obligation to prevent harm:

'must be interpreted in a way which does not impose an impossible or disproportionate burden on the authorities.'[17]

The President noted that the standard to be applied in assessing this positive obligation bore a 'close resemblance' to the English common law negligence standard. Thus, where a responsible clinical decision is made, on grounds of the patient's best interests, to withhold treatment which is in accordance with a respectable body of medical opinion, 'the state's positive obligation under Article 2 is, in my view, discharged'. In summary[18]:

> 'Article 2 therefore imposes a positive obligation to give life-sustaining treatment in circumstances where, according to responsible medical opinion, such treatment is in the best interests of the patient but does not impose an absolute obligation to treat if such treatment would be futile.'

Finally, the President did not consider that Art 3 of the Convention applied to M or H. Article 3 provides that:

> 'No one shall be subjected to torture or to inhuman or degrading treatment or punishment.'

This was considered in two areas. First, Alert[19] had argued that the withdrawal of treatment itself violated Art 3. The President determined that the withdrawal of futile medical treatment could not be seen as torture or as punishment. Further, given that the withdrawal is for a benign purpose in accordance with the best interests of the patient, it was not inhuman or degrading treatment[20].

Secondly, the Trusts had argued that, given the broad approach to the definition of 'degrading treatment' in *D v United Kingdom*[21], Art 3 should be invoked in order to ensure protection of a PVS patient's right to human dignity: enforcing the continuation of life as a biological machine with no cognition was inhuman; allowing a family to witness their loved one in such an abhorrent state was degrading. Cazalet J had determined (two months before) that[22]:

> 'In *D v UK* ... it was held that Article 3 of the Convention which requires that a person is not subjected to inhuman or degrading treatment includes the right to die with dignity. It is that right ... which is to be protected through the declaration that I propose to make in this case.'

The issue was also addressed by Lynch J in *The Matter of A Ward of Court*[23] who sought to reconcile withdrawal of feeding from a PVS patient with the Irish Constitution's requirement that the State[24]:

> 'respect, and as far as practicable, defend and vindicate the personal rights of the citizen ... [and] in particular, by its laws protect as best it may from unjust attack ... the life, person ... of every citizen.'

Lynch J stated that:

> 'The State undoubtedly has an interest in preserving life but this interest is not absolute in the sense that life must be preserved and prolonged at all costs and no matter what the circumstances. Death is a natural part of life. All humanity is mortal and death comes in

the ordinary course of nature and this aspect of nature must be respected as well as its life-giving aspect ... A person has a right to be allowed to die in accordance with nature ...'

Lynch J further noted that the right to life whilst ranking 'first in the hierarchy of personal rights' may nevertheless be 'subjected to the citizen's right of autonomy or self-determination or privacy or dignity'. Thus, the constitution did not preclude the court determining withdrawal of feeding was in the patient's best interests.

The President, however, rejected the applicability of Art 3 to the withdrawal of treatment from a PVS patient because a victim has to be aware of the purported inhuman or degrading treatment he or she is experiencing: an insensate PVS patient has no feelings and no comprehension and thus there can be no violation of Art 3. The President did, in accord with Lynch J, assess the appropriate scope of Art 2 by reference to Art 8, which protects patient autonomy[25].

In deciding that the *Bland* decision was in accord with the values of democratic societies, the President noted whilst 'the jurisdictional basis varies and thought processes differ' the ultimate conclusion in *Bland* that withdrawal of nutrition and hydration was lawful had been accepted in many parts of the world[26].

In *M & H* the family supported the Trust's approach. Thus the case does not determine to what extent the right to family life under Art 8 impacts on the decisions to be made in this area. However, it is suggested that ultimately the assessment to be made is the same: is the withdrawal in the patient's best interets? The President – whilst not deciding the question – doubted whether a family has rights in this area under Art 8 separate from the rights of the patient.

Thomas J in *Auckland Area HB v AG*[27] summed up the importance of balancing human rights in this area. It was important, he stated, to set against the right to life 'another set of values which are central to our concept of life; values of human dignity and personal privacy'[28]:

'Medical science and technology has advanced for a fundamental purpose; the purpose of benefiting the life and health of those who turn to medicine to be healed. It surely was never intended that it be used to prolong biological life in patients bereft of the prospect of returning to an even limited exercise of human life ... Nor, surely, was modern medical science ever developed to be used inhumanly. To do so is not consistent with its fundamental purpose.'

1 Came into force: 2 October 2000.
2 (25 October 2000, unreported, President): the first case to consider the impact on medical treatment jurisprudence of the implementation of the HRA 1998.
3 [2000] 4 All ER 961.
4 In English law murder occurs when a life is ended by the intentional act of another. Further, causing death in circumstances where the defendant appreciates that death or serious harm is a virtually certain consequence of his positive act is also murder. (The 'foresight' test in *R v Woollin* [1999] AC 82.)
5 [2000] 4 All ER 961.
6 *Re A (children) conjoined twins: surgical separation)* per Ward, Brooke and Robert Walker LJJ.
7 Transcript, para 31.
8 No 20527/92 (1993).

9   This does not therefore represent a decision and merely provides some guidance as to
     the likely approach in the European courts.
10   Also note *Dec of Verieraltungsgericht Bremmen* of 9 November 1959, cited in *Fawcett*
     No 1287/61 (p 36) a West German case in which it was held that a doctor did not infringe
     Art 2 by giving an overdose of drugs to the terminally-ill.
11   (1978) 14 DR 31.
12   *X and Y v Netherlands* (1985) 8 EHRR 235; see also *X v Austria* and the ECJ decision
     in the HIV case cited at nn 1 and 2 of Nys, 'Physician Involvement in a Patient's Death
     – a Continental European Perspective' (1999) Med L Rev 7(2) at p 209. See also *Peters
     v Netherlands* (1994) 77A DR 75 at 79, indicating that unwanted medical intervention
     (the taking of urine samples) is an infringement of Art 8.
13   Transcript, para 30 [emphasis added].
14   The positive obligation is: 'Everyone's right to life shall be protected by law'. The
     negative obligation is: 'No one shall be deprived of his life intentionally.'
15   (1998) 29 EHRR 245, para 115.
16   Harris, O'Boyle (et al), p 38: 'The first sentence of Article 2(1) ... establishes a positive
     obligation for states to make adequate provision in their law for the protection of human
     life.'
17   *Osman v United Kingdom* (1998) 29 EHRR 245, para 116.
18   Transcript, para 37.
19   A 'pro-life' organisation whose attempt to be heard at the hearing was rejected by the
     President.
20   Noting *V and T v United Kingdom* (1999) 30 EHRR 121; *Herczegfalvy v Austria* (1992)
     15 EHRR 437 ('as a general rule, a measure which is a therapeutic necessity, cannot be
     regarded as inhuman or degrading. The Court may nevertheless satisfy itself that the
     medical necessity has been convincingly shown to exist').
21   (1997) 24 EHRR 423 ('the Court must reserve to itself sufficient flexibility to address the
     application of that Article in other contexts which might arise. It is not therefore
     prevented from scrutinising an applicant's claim under Art 3 where the source of the risk
     of proscribed treatment in the receiving country stems from factors which cannot
     engage either directly or indirectly the responsibility of the public authorities of that
     country, or which, taken alone, do not in themselves infringe the standards of that
     Article. To limit the application of Art 3 in this manner would be to undermine the
     absolute character of its protections').
22   *A National Health Service Trust v D* [2000] 2 FCR 577.
23   (5 May 1995) High Court of the Republic of Ireland.
24   Article 40, s 3 of the Irish Constitution (Bunreacht Na hÉireann).
25   Transcript, para 41.
26   See Grubb (et al), 'Reporting on the Persistent Vegetative State' (1998) Med L Rev 6(2)
     at 161–210; Scotland: *Law Hospitals NHS Trust v Lord Advocate* [1996] 2 FLR 407;
     Republic of Ireland: *Re A Ward of Court* [1995] 2 IRLM 901; New Zealand: *Auckland
     Area HB v AG* [1993] 1 NZLR 235, Thomas J; South Africa: *Clark v Hurst* [1992] (4) SA
     630 cited in Grubb (et al) at p 185. Also note in Germany the Supreme Court
     determined that 'the withdrawal of treatment or care which leads to death may be done
     consistently with a patient's rights: indeed may be a vindication of them even where
     there is a constitutionally protected right to life'. Cited in Nys, 'Physician Involvement
     in a Patient's Death – a Continental European Perspective' (1999) Med L Rev 7(2) 209
     at 227.
27   [1993] I NZLR 235 per Thomas J.
28   [1993] I NZLR 235 at 245.

Continuing treatment is an Assault

[9.6]   Theoretical complications arise from the Law Lords' determination that
it is no longer in a PVS patient's best interests to continue feeding and
hydration. As a PVS patient is unconscious and incompetent the only
lawful basis on which treatment in any form can be provided is if it is in
his 'best interests'. Given that feeding and hydration have been determined to be no longer in the patient's best interests, then any continued
feeding and hydration is an assault[1].

This will largely be a theoretical problem: the PVS patient will not sue,
although it is not inconceivable that a concerned relative would seek to

mount an action in the patient's name. After his death it might be open to his estate to sue for the additional loss of amenity caused by the assault.

Given the medical debate concerning the nature of the PVS condition and the difficulties of diagnosis, the problem can partially be addressed by allowing that there must be a period of time when it is in the patient's best interests for his condition, prognosis and long-term interests to be subjected to the most rigorous assessment[2]. It might also be argued that there will be a period during which it would be *Bolam* reasonable either to continue feeding or to cease feeding a patient. In such a situation no liability can flow from feeding during that time. However, the problem will still arise if the vegetative state continues for so long that no body of responsible medical opinion would consider that it was reasonable to continue feeding/hydration. On the basis of the *Bland* analysis the continued feeding and hydration at that stage would amount to an assault on the patient.

1 [1993] AC 789 per Lord Browne-Wilkinson at 883: 'if there comes a stage where the responsible doctor comes to the reasonable conclusion (which accords with the views of a responsible body of medical opinion) that further continuance of an intrusive life support system is not in the best interests of the patient, he can no longer lawfully continue that life support system: to do so would constitute the crime of battery and the tort of trespass to the person.'
2 See para **[9.10]** below.

Extending *Bland* to other cases

Given the concerns expressed about the withdrawal of feeding being 'backdoor euthanasia', the Law Lords in *Bland* were keen to emphasise that Anthony Bland's was an exceptional case: for example, Lord Browne-Wilkinson noted that it was[1]:   **[9.7]**

'an extreme case where it can be overwhelmingly proved that the patient is and will remain insensate: he neither feels pain from treatment nor will feel pain in dying and has no prospect of any medical care improving his condition.'

Lord Mustill stressed that he was *not* saying that he would support discontinuance of feeding in a patient with 'glimmerings of awareness'[2].

Nonetheless it appears that some doctors and carers have erroneously relied on *Bland*[3] to withdraw normal oral feeding in patients who cannot be described as in PVS or even 'near-PVS'. *The Times* in January 1999 ran an exposé into allegations that doctors caring for elderly patients were 'giving nature a helping hand' by withholding intravenous drips from dehydrated patients and allowing them to die. It was reported that by January 1999 the number of known cases where this had occurred was 60[4].

Thus the *Bland* decision itself is attacked as having opened the door to euthanasia:

'[The reasoning in Bland was] sophistry. Bland wasn't dying. And feeding wasn't treatment, though it might require invasive procedures – after all, what is the illness being treated? Hunger? Living? And so now – surprise – patients being fed orally are also being refused food and water: inevitable once the *Bland* judges made it legal to starve patients to death.'[5]

The *Bland* decision expressly does not warrant or support 'mercy killing' of patients. Families, clinicians and Trusts must be alert to attempts by individuals to extend withdrawal of feeding and hydration to circumstances well beyond those of vegetative patients. No doctor should attempt to extend withdrawal of feeding and hydration beyond PVS patients without first seeking a definitive court ruling. To do otherwise, risks criminal sanctions for the individual and a substantial erosion of public faith in the profession as a whole.

1 [1993] AC 789 at 885.
2 [1993] AC 789 at 899.
3 *Airedale NHS Trust v Bland* [1993] AC 789, [1993] 2 WLR 316, [1993] 1 FLR 1026, HL.
4 Also note the investigation in the *Daily Telegraph* in November/December 1999.
5 See n 4 above.

Advanced Directives/Prior consent

[9.8]   Can a patient consent in advance to the withdrawal of feeding and hydration? Limits are placed by law on an individual's power to consent to actions which will injure him or which are otherwise morally unacceptable. Under English law a person does not have full autonomy to allow someone to assault his person: moral limits are set[1]. A doctor is not entitled to kill someone merely because he consents to be killed.

However, the principle that an unconscious or incompetent person should not have to be subjected to what a rational and conscious person would reject provides an answer. Just as with other forms of medical treatment, a competent adult is able to refuse consent to artificial hydration and feeding[2]. In *Secretary of State for the Home Department v Robb*[3] a prisoner of sound mind and understanding went on hunger strike. The Home Office, prison officials, physicians and nursing staff responsible for his care could lawfully observe and abide by his refusal to receive nutrition and could lawfully abstain from providing hydration and nutrition. The Home Secretary was not under any duty to prolong the respondent's life.

Thus, if in advance a mentally competent individual indicates by way of a validly made advanced directive that should they deteriorate to a vegetative state they do not consent to the continuation of artificial feeding or hydration, that wish should be given effect. The Law Commission has proposed that a patient should not be able to prohibit the provision of 'basic care, which includes direct oral nutrition and hydration'[4] by way of an advance directive. Whether this is consistent with the present state of the law as expressed in *Robb* would require consideration by the courts.

In these circumstances it is advisable to seek a declaration from the court in relation to the validity and application of any advance directive prior to discontinuance in order to ensure the legal validity of the patient's advanced expression.

1 *R v Brown* [1993] 2 WLR 556, considered whether consent by the victim could amount to a defence to a charge of assault in relation to certain sado-masochistic practices. It was held that it was not in the public interest that a person should wound or cause actual

bodily harm to another for no good reason and, in the absence of such a reason, the victim's consent afforded no defence to a charge.

2 Artificial feeding and hydration was considered in *Bland* to be medical treatment: see para **[9.1]**, fn 4 above.

3 [1995] Fam 127, [1995] 1 FLR 412, [1995] 1 All ER 677, Thorpe J.

4 *Mental Incapacity* (1995) Law Com No 231, para 5.34.

Summary

The legality of the withdrawal of feeding in *Bland* was resolved by analysing whether the doctor should or should not continue treatment and not by an assessment of whether the doctor should take a course which in fact causes or accelerates the patient's death[1].

[9.9]

Not continuing feeding is an omission not an act. Criminal liability for the consequence of an omission to act can only arise when there is a duty to act. Here because continuing treatment is no longer in the patient's bests interests, there is no continuing duty to act; that is, there is no duty on the doctors to continue feeding. Thus, if death follows a failure to feed that death is not the criminal (or civil) responsibility of the doctor: the cause of the death is legally the original disease or trauma which caused the vegetative state.

1 Lord Mustill felt it was not a question of whether the patient's 'best interests' are in terminating life: it has to be question of whether continued treatment is in the best interests of the patient.

C   MEDICAL ISSUES

The granting of a declaration by the court permitting withdrawal of life supporting treatment will turn on whether the court is satisfied that the diagnosis of PVS is correct. Once that determination is made, following *Bland* only one result will generally follow, namely that withdrawal of feeding is lawful[1].

[9.10]

There has been significant concern about whether the diagnosis of PVS is being accurately applied in British hospitals. Permanent Vegetative State by definition indicates that that there is no prospect of recovery. There was significant public concern expressed following the well-publicised recovery of Andrew Devine.

It was reported that Devine had begun communicating with his family eight years after being diagnosed as being in a persistent vegetative state. He suffered brain damage when he was crushed during the Hillsborough football stadium disaster. He could now respond to questions by pressing an electronic pad with his finger.

The case was reported as being 'likely to fuel the controversy about experts' ability to diagnose persistent vegetative state, and raise fresh doubts about right-to die cases'[2].

The press and public concerns about mis-diagnosis are not ill-founded. A retrospective study has been reported by Dr Keith Andrews (Medical Director, Royal Hospital for Neuro-disability, Putney, London and a neurologist at the forefront of rehabilitation of 'vegetative' patients) and others[3] of forty patients with a diagnosis of vegetative state who were admitted to the Putney Brain Injury Rehabilitation Unit. Of those a staggering 42% were found to be able to communicate and were therefore not vegetative. One patient who had been thought to be vegetative for seven years was in fact dictating letters to his wife within two weeks of admission. This paper provides a stark warning to clinicians, lawyers and judges about the necessity to ensure that the diagnosis is accurate. It is not within the scope of this book to give medical guidance on how to diagnose the condition. It will be instructive for clinicians to read *The Vegetative State: Persisting Problems, Putting the Vegetative State into Perspective* by Dr Keith Andrews. He stresses that the vegetative state is a:

> 'syndrome of clinical features not a pathological, anatomical or disease process diagnosis',

and that the major problem of diagnosis is that the only way for a patient to demonstrate conscious awareness is by a motor act but that the very severity of the patient's physical disabilities may prevent or mask any such demonstration of awareness.

In *Bland* great emphasis was laid on compliance with BMA guidelines for the diagnosis of PVS[4] which in particular emphasised that:

- every effort should be made at rehabilitation for at least six months after the injury;
- the diagnosis of irreversible PVS should not be considered confirmed until at least 12 months after the injury, with the effect that any decision to withhold life-prolonging treatment will be delayed for that period;
- the diagnosis should be agreed by two other independent doctors; and
- generally, the wishes of the patient's immediate family should be given great weight.

Since *Bland* the Royal College of Physicians have provided guidance on the diagnosis of Permanent Vegetative State[5] which indicates that a diagnosis of permanent vegetative state can reasonably be made:

- when a patient is in a state of 'unawareness of self and environment' in which he or she:

> 'breathes spontaneously, has a stable circulation and shows cycles of eye closure and eye opening which may stimulate sleep and waking.' ('vegetative state'); and

- when it can be determined to a 'high degree of clinical certainty' that this state is irreversible.

Certain signs and symptoms are often interpreted by family members as indicating suffering or awareness:

- occasional movements of the head towards a peripheral sound;
- movement of the trunks and limbs in a purposeless way;
- watering of the eyes;
- 'grimace' to painful stimuli;
- roving eye movements.

However, provided such motor activities are 'inconsistent, non-purposeful and explicable as a reflex response', the RCP guidance concludes that they do *not* preclude a diagnosis of PVS.

142

Nonetheless, the guidance does indicate that the PVS diagnosis is *excluded* in patients with:

- a nystagmus[6] response to ice water caloric testing;
- the ability to track moving objects with the eyes;
- a 'menace response'.

Also, reference should be made to the assessment criteria published by an international working party in a report on the vegetative state[7] which advances slightly different diagnostic criteria[8].

1 It is impossible to say that the contrary result will never occur. However, the courts have yet to consider a case where it is known that the patient held strong pro-life convictions before losing capacity.
2 National newspaper and television coverage on 27 March 1997; quotation from the *British Media Review*.
3 Andrews K, Murphy L, Munday R, Littlewood C, 'Misdiagnosis of the vegetative state: retrospective study in a rehabilitation unit' *British Medical Journal* 1996, p 313.
4 A *Discussion Paper on Treatment of Patients in Persistent Vegetative State* issued in September 1992 by the Medical Ethics Committee of the British Medical Association.
5 *The Permanent Vegetative State*, a review by a working group convened by the Royal College of Physicians, first published in *The Journal of the Royal College of Physicians* Vol 30, No 2, March/April 1996.
6 Involuntary rapid, rhythmic movement of the eyeball.
7 See, eg Andrews, 'International Working Party on the Management of the Vegetative State: Summary Report'. (1996) *Brain Injury* 10(11), 797–806; and see *Medical Aspects of the Persistent Vegetative State* [Multi-Society Taskforce] Part 1: *New England Journal of Medicine*, Vol 330, No 21, 1499; Part 2: *New England Journal of Medicine*, Vol 330, No 22 1572].
8 See, eg *Re H (adult: medical treatment)* [1998] 2 FLR 36, where tracking eye movements by the patient fell within the working party's definition of PVS but outside the RCP definition.

Imaging

Research published since the RCP guidance may challenge their deter-   **[9.11]**
mination that MRI cannot improve on the clinical diagnosis: see, for example, the research from the University Hospital Innsbruck which suggests that MRI can provide useful supportive information in diagnosing PVS after traumatic brain injury[1]. Thus, before seeking a court declaration, consideration should be given to whether imaging techniques should be undertaken to confirm the diagnosis.

1 'The persistent vegetative state after closed head injury: clinical and magnetic response imaging findings in 42 patients', (May 1998) *J Neruosurg* 88(5), 809–816; and Kampfl, Schmutzhard, Franz, Pfausler Haring, Ulmer, Felber, Golaszewski and Aichner, 'Prediction of recovery from post-traumatic vegetative state with cerebral magnetic-resonance imaging', (June 1998) *Lancet* 13, 351(9118): 1763–1767.

Rehabilitation and time to allow for a recovery

The RCP guidance states that irreversibility can reasonably be deter-   **[9.12]**
mined when the vegetative state has continued for 12 months following a head injury and for six months following other causes of brain damage[1]. It also states that there is no 'firm scientific evidence' that treatment, 'in terms of special medical, physiotherapeutic or rehabilitative activities' improves outcome of patients in a continuing vegetative state. Thus, the RCP provides no mandatory requirement that rehabilitative measures be undertaken.

However, the high level of misdiagnosis and recovery demonstrated at Putney Brain Injury Rehabilitation Unit demonstrates the need for stronger and clearer general guidance as to the appropriate treatment and rehabilitative action to be applied in relation to apparently vegetative patients.

Thus, despite the definitive timescales outlined in the RCP guidance, a court may look sceptically on a diagnosis of PVS even if made after a year when there has been little or no attempt at rehabilitation. Detailed evidence from clinicians and nursing staff of attempts at communication and rehabilitation should be obtained for any court application.

1 The evidence accepted in *Bland* was that 'if a PVS patient shows no signs of recovery after six months, or at most a year, then there is no prospect whatever of any recovery.'

Cases outside the RCP guidelines

[9.13] In cases falling within the RCP guidelines it is unlikely that clinicians seeking a court declaration authorising withdrawal will face difficulties, provided that the diagnosis has been clearly and unequivocally made and confirmed by experts of sufficient standing. Cases outside the RCP guidelines are more problematic.

The issue whether feeding and hydration could be withdrawn in a patient who failed to meet the RCP criteria was addressed in *Re D (adult: medical treatment)*[1]. The patient:

- had nystagmus[2] in response to ice water caloric testing;
- was able to track movements with the eyes;
- had a menace response.

Thus, these clinical features placed the patient outside the 'permanent vegetative state' condition defined by the RCP.

The evidence of Professor Jennett was that D was in a permanent vegetative state. The evidence of the two other neurologists was that the patient had no awareness but both were reluctant to diagnose PVS because the case did not match the guidelines. D's mother commented[3] that her daughter:

'was no longer the victim of a severe head injury; she is now the victim of medical technology.'

On behalf of the Official Solicitor it was submitted that because the Guideline requirements of the Royal College of Physicians were not satisfied, it could not be determined that keeping the patient alive was futile and thus 'best interests' did not mandate withdrawal of feeding.

The case reasserts the importance of detailed evidence being available to the court concerning the patient and in particular the importance of reports from the clinicians and nurses in day-to-day contact with the patient. The President noted that 'every single witness – medical and ... nursing – have all made it clear that this patient has no awareness whatsoever'. He determined that she was in 'a living death' and that she was in PVS. He felt that allowing her to die would *not* extend the range of cases in which a declaration ought to be considered:

'The court recognises that no declaration to permit or to sanction the taking of so extreme a step could possibly be granted where there was any real possibility of meaningful life continuing to exist'.

As there was no evidence that D had a meaningful life and there was no prospect of recovery, a declaration permitting the clinicians *not* to re-establish feeding by gastrotomy[4] was granted.

Following *Re D*, in *Re H (adult: medical treatment)*[5] the patient had 'visual tracking': this placed her outside the RCP definition. However, both neurologists concluded that she fell within the international working party's definition and both were satisfied she was a vegetative state patient with no hope of recovery. The President commented that:

'It may be that a precise label is not of significant importance. This is ... a developing field for medical analysis'.[6]

The President also emphasised two key elements: first that the patient was 'wholly unaware of herself or of her environment' and, secondly, that there was no possibility of change. Thus, notwithstanding that the RCP criteria precluded the formal PVS diagnosis, the President determined that it was appropriate to grant a declaration in support of the discontinuance of feeding.

1 [1988] 1 FCR 498.
2 Involuntary rapid, rhythmic movement of the eyeball.
3 [1988] 1 FCR 498 at 502.
4 The gastronomy tube had become detached.
5 [1998] 2 FLR 36.
6 [1998] 2 FLR 36 at 38.

D ROLE OF THE FAMILY

The courts indicate that the views of the family members should be **[9.14]** considered. Further, care should be taken to note any information they have concerning the PVS patient's previously expressed wishes concerning what he would want to happen should he be in a vegetative state. The Official Solicitor's representative will normally interview the family members and others close to the patient.[1]

Whilst it is 'good practice for the doctor to consult relatives', their views are not determinative: as stated by Lord Goff of Chieveley in *Bland*, their Lordships were:

'firmly of the opinion that the relatives' views cannot be determinative of the treatment'[2].

This view flows inevitably from the approach of English law to the incompetent adult: no- one has power to consent on behalf of an incompetent adult. All questions of the continuation or discontinuation must be assessed whether by doctors or finally by the courts on the basis of the 'best interests' test. No individual no matter how closely related can override that determination.

In *Re G (persistent vegetative state)*[3] the President granted a declaration that feeding and hydration should be withdrawn, notwithstanding that the application (in which the Trust and the patient's wife concurred) was not supported by the patient's mother.

1 See App 9.1: *Practice Note (Official Solicitor: Vegetative State)* [1996] 4 All ER 766, [1996] 2 FLR 375, [1996] 3 FCR 606, [1996] Fam Law 579.
2 [1993] AC 789 at 871.
3 [1995] 2 FCR 46.

E   IS AN APPLICATION TO COURT REQUIRED?

[9.15]   Before discontinuance of feeding or hydration in a PVS patient an application must be made to the court.

The view expressed by the House of Lords was that 'at least for the time being'[1] an application should be made in every case where discontinuance is proposed. The extent to which there should be a relaxation of this, in particular where there are no areas of potential dispute, it was suggested, should be kept under review by the President of the Family Division.[2] The submission on behalf of the respondent in *Bland* – which was rejected by the House of Lords – was that applications should be limited to cases where:

- there was a medical disagreement as to the diagnosis or prognosis;
- problems had arisen with the patient's relatives or there was disagreement by the next of kin with the medical recommendation;
- there was an actual or apparent conflict of interest between the next of kin and the patient;
- there was a dispute between members of the patient's family;
- there was no next of kin to express a view about the appropriateness of discontinuance.

The current BMA guidance is:

> 'In England, Wales and Northern Ireland, where it is proposed to withdraw artificial nutrition and hydration from a patient in persistent vegetative state or a state closely resembling PVS, legal advice should be sought and a Court declaration is likely to be required until such time as the Courts have stated otherwise'[3].

To date the President has not relaxed the requirement that all cases of discontinuance of feeding or hydration in PVS patients should be brought before the court. There is intense public interest and widely-held concerns about the medical profession undertaking 'back door euthanasia'[4]. This is likely to remain the case while the full implications of the near-PVS cases are worked out. Against this background the courts are likely to maintain the current practice of requiring prior court sanction for all withdrawal of feeding and hydration cases for the foreseeable future.

In *Re M* and *Re H* the President noted that[5]:

> 'In our use of the declaratory jurisdiction of the High Court in PVS cases we impose in our domestic law a higher test that the standard set by the European Court, since the High Court reviews the medical conclusion on best interests and may not necessarily accept the medical opinion'.

1 [1993] AC 789 per Lord Keith at 859G and Lord Goff at 874.
2 [1993] AC 789 per Lord Goff at 874.
3 Section 22.1 of the BMA's *Withholding and withdrawing life-prolonging medical treatment: Guidance for decision-making.*
4 At the annual meeting of the BMA in 1999, the Worcestershire division of the BMA put down a motion that nutrition and hydration should not be withheld from patients ((1999) *Times*, 24 June). There is now a pressure group called SOS-NHS group formed by relations of non-terminally ill patients who died after drips were withdrawn or withheld.
5 *An NHS Trust 'A' v Mrs 'M'* and *An NHS Trust 'B' v Mrs 'H'* (25 October 2000, unreported, President).

Consequences of withholding nutrition without court approval

In relation to an adult, a court can merely declare that a given course of treatment or withdrawal of treatment would be lawful. Thus, in the absence of a court order retrospective assessment of the withdrawal of feeding or hydration in a criminal or civil court after a patient dies will turn on whether the patients' 'best interests' mandated such withdrawal. Clinicians face the risk of professional[1] or even criminal censure[2] in the absence of a prior court declaration. Pro-life pressure groups and individuals are keen to challenge any perceived attacks on the sanctity of life.   **[9.16]**

Following the death of Anthony Bland, the Reverend James Morrow sought privately to prosecute the treating clinician for murder. Given the court's advance declaration that withdrawal was lawful, the magistrates refused to issue a summons on the information laid by the private individual. This decision was upheld by the Divisional Court. Staughton LJ indicated that the guidance in *Bland* should inhibit prosecution or if the matter went ahead the ruling of the House of Lords would be an answer to prosecution.

Thus, prudence dictates that a clinician should seek the determination of the court as to the validity of his intention to withhold nutrition from a patient to avoid the risk of being faced with a prosecution for murder or disciplinary proceedings.

Further, 'best interests' connotes acting in accordance with a *Bolam* responsible body of opinion. Given that the courts have required a prior application and doctors' professional bodies have supported that requirement, is a doctor who does not seek court approval *Bolam* reasonable? Unless there is an exceptionally rapid emergency (and it should be stressed that the Family Division can respond exceptionally promptly in medical treatment decision cases), a failure to apply is likely to be considered *not* in accordance with a *Bolam* body of opinion[3] thereby placing the clinician at risk of criminal censure and his/her hospital at risk of a civil suit.

It should be emphasised that this requirement relates to cases where it is intended to withhold or withdraw nutrition from a patient in a permanent vegetative state, or a similar condition. Doctors are constantly having to make decisions about the withdrawal or withholding of ventilation, and other life prolonging treatment from accident victims and other seriously ill patients. It has never been suggested that all such cases should be referred to the courts before such a decision is implemented.

1 For example, the suspension by the General Medical Council of GP Dr Ken Taylor for failing to listen to nurses and consult colleagues in relation to the withdrawal of nutrition from an elderly patient (March 1999).

2 For example, note the prosecution of Dr David Moor following the death of an elderly patient after pain-relieving morphine had been administered: he was acquitted.

3 It should be noted that establishing *Bolam* responsible conduct does not merely require proof that there is a body of opinion, but also proof that the body of opinion 'stands up to analysis' and is 'not unreasonable in the light of the state of medical knowledge at the time': *Joyce v Merton and Sutton and Wandsworth Health Authority* [1995] 6 Med LR 60.

F APPLICATION TO COURT

[9.17] The first stage before making any application to court for withdrawal of feeding and hydration is to consider whether the patient expressed any wishes about how he wished to be treated in this situation. Is there a living will or any form of advanced directive?

The next stage is to consult the family and determine their wishes. Timing of any court application should be made sensitively. Time should be given to the family to come to terms with the determination that the patient will not recover. If family consent to discontinuance is initially not forthcoming, it is suggested that a significant period of time is allowed before forcing the issue to a court hearing.

As to the nature of the application itself and the appropriate procedure, reference must be made to the Official Solicitor's *Practice Note*[1].

The *Practice Note* indicates that applications to court should be 'by originating summons issued in the Family Division of the High Court'[2] seeking a declaration in the form:

> 'It is declared that despite the inability of X to give a valid consent, the [claimant/applicant] and/or the responsible medical practitioners[3]:
> - may lawfully discontinue all life-sustaining treatment and medical support measures (including ventilation, nutrition and hydration by artificial means) designed to keep X alive in his existing permanent vegetative state; and
> - may lawfully furnish such treatment and nursing care whether at hospital or elsewhere under medical supervision as may be appropriate to ensure X suffers the least distress and retains the greatest dignity until such time as his life comes to an end.
>
> It is ordered that in the event of a material change in the existing circumstances occurring before such withdrawal of treatment any party shall have liberty to apply for such further or other declaration or order as may be just.'

However, in *Re M and Re H*[4] the Official Solicitor proposed a new form of order as follows:

> 'X lacks the capacity to make decisions as to further medical treatment;
>
> It is not in the existing circumstances in the best interests of X for continued artificial nutrition and hydration to be provided;
>
> The Claimant and/or the responsible attending medical practitioners, nurses and health care staff:

    (*a*) may lawfully discontinue and withhold all life-sustaining treatment and medical support measures (including ventilation, nutrition and hydration by artificial means) designed to keep X alive in the permanent vegetative state; and

    (*b*) may lawfully furnish such treatment and nursing care whether at hospital or elsewhere under medical supervision as may be appropriate to ensure X retains the greatest dignity until such time as his life comes to an end.'[5]

This latter form of wording is to be preferred[6].

The parties should be either the next-of-kin or other individual closely connected with the patient and must include the relevant health authority or NHS trust[7] and:

> 'The Official Solicitor should normally be invited to act as guardian ad litem of the patient, who will inevitably be a patient within the meaning of RSC Ord 80. In any case in which the Official Solicitor does not represent the patient, he should be joined as a defendant or respondent.'

Otherwise the application should follow the procedure laid down for sterilisation cases[8].

It is suggested that the Official Solicitor should be contacted as soon as it is known that an application to court is contemplated in order that steps can then be initiated as soon as possible to instruct an independent expert to examine the patient and enable the Official Solicitor's detailed report to be prepared. Such early notice may prove crucial should circumstances suddenly change as a result, for example, of an inability to maintain feeding and an urgent application to court is required.

1 See App 9.1: *Practice Note (Official Solicitor: Vegetative State)* [1996] 4 All ER 766, [1996] 2 FLR 375, [1996] 3 FCR 606, [1996] Fam Law 579.
2 Whilst the Civil Procedure Rules have preserved the procedure by way of 'originating summons' for applications in relation to children, it appears at time of writing that no provision has been made preserving the procedure in relation to adult declarations. Thus, it is suggested that the new Part 8 procedure be used pending new rules or *Practice Directions* dealing with the appropriate procedure for treatment decisions.
3 In *Re D (adult: medical treatment)* [1998] 1 FCR 498 the order also included direct reference to 'members of the family' because the care was to be provided at home.
4 *An NHS Trust 'A' v Mrs 'M'* and *An NHS Trust 'B' v Mrs 'H'* (25 October 2000, unreported, President).
5 The order then continues (as before) to allow for liberty to apply and also non-publicity.
6 For a precedent, see App 9.3: *Draft Order in PVS case.*
7 *Re S (hospital patient: court's jurisdiction)* [1996] Fam 1, CA.
8 As established by the House of Lords in *Re F (mental patient: sterilisation)* [1990] 2 AC 1, [1989] 2 FLR 376 and in *Practice Note (Official Solicitor: Sterilisation)* [1996] 2 FLR 111.

Confidentiality

Re G (adult patient: publicity)[1] considered the issue of publicity in PVS   **[9.18]** cases: it was held that:

- the hearing should be in open court but;
- the court has power to consider whether particular evidence should be given in private; and

- injunctions may be granted preserving the anonymity of the patient.

Thus:

- the court may preserve the anonymity of other parties to the litigation if necessary to avoid the risk of identification of the patient;
- orders preserving the anonymity of the patient are capable of extending beyond the death of the patient until any successful application to have them discharged[2].

The new Civil Procedure Rules do not change this position.

However, it must be stressed that any coroner's inquest will be conducted in open court without protection of the identity of the deceased and the family should be made aware of this when an application for a declaration is being made. Whether a hearing is in fact conducted is within the discretion of the coroner.

1 [1995] 2 FLR 528.
2 *Re C (Adult Patient: restriction of publicity after death)* [1996] 2 FLR 251. And see, for example, App 9.2: *Draft Direction in PVS case*; and App 9.3: *Draft Order in PVS case*.

Evidence

[9.19] In *Bland* itself the Law Lords emphasised that the patient's lack of consciousness and absence of any prospects of recovery had been '*overwhelmingly proved*'[1]. Convincing and detailed evidence must be produced to the court which demonstrates that there is no benefit to the patient in his continued existence.

Statements/reports should be obtained from the treating clinician and from those in the nursing staff with closest daily contact with the patient. The Official Solicitor will ensure that statements are obtained from material family members. The medical and nursing notes should be available and any entries which might be interpreted as indicating awareness must be explained.

It is important before embarking on any court application, that, wherever possible, the hospital obtains a supportive independent report from at least one expert of standing in this field. The court will require evidence from at least two independent experts, one of these will be commissioned by the Official Solicitor. If the case raises particular complications of diagnosis and in particular if it falls outside the RCP guidelines it would be worthwhile the hospital commissioning two independent expert opinions itself before seeking a declaration.

The expert neurological assessments should:

- be undertaken separately;
- involve consultation with clinical and nursing staff, relatives and carers;
- involve a formal neurological examination, preferably undertaken in the presence of nursing staff and relatives who have had the opportunity to observe the patient over a prolonged period[2].

Both factual and expert evidence should be obtained addressing the following issues:

- what is the history of the patient's condition?

- what is his/her current condition?
- what benefit is likely from any treatment?
- what rehabilitative steps have been taken and what impact would any such steps in the future have?
- what is the diagnosis?
- what are the views concerning the proposed discontinuance of –
  - the treating clinician?
  - the nursing staff?
  - the family?
- how is any discontinuance of feeding/hydration going to be effected?
- (if requested) why is a confidentiality order required in the terms requested?
- what steps are being taken to offer counselling to relatives and staff?

In particular, care should be taken to ensure that the experts address the following questions[3]:

- is there any evidence of awareness of self or environment?
- is there any prospect of improvement in the patient's condition?
- does the patient meet the criteria for diagnosis of permanent vegetative state set out by the Royal College of Physicians in the Review dated April 1996? [if he/she does not, specify why]
- into which category of the Appendix to the International Working Party Report does the patient fall?
- are there any comments concerning the patient's current medication (if any) and in particular is it possible that such medication may be (or may have been) masking or dampening signs of awareness? What are the risks/benefits of withdrawing any such medication?
- how long will the patient survive in his/her current state? How long will the patient survive were hydration and feeding to be withdrawn?
- is it – in the expert's clinical judgment – appropriate to discontinue artificial nutrition and hydration? Are there any recommendations concerning treatment and nursing care at such time?

All sources of information must be assessed before a final diagnosis of Permanent Vegetative State should be considered. Often family members can describe patients as appearing to 'suffer': for the hospital a clear response to this is required explaining why the signs and symptoms viewed as 'suffering' are not in fact indicative of any underlying awareness. As stated in the Official Solicitor's *Practice Note*:

> 'The most important role of the medical practitioner in making the diagnosis is to ensure that the patient is not sentient and, in this respect, the views of the nursing staff, relatives and carers are of considerable importance and help.'

Prior to the final determination of the application there will ordinarily be a directions hearing[4] at which:

- the involvement and precise role of the Official Solicitor will be determined;
- the nature of the necessary medical evidence will be established;

- any orders preserving confidentiality are likely to be made.

The scope of the evidence to be heard at the final hearing should be addressed at the directions appointment. The extent to which clinicians, nursing staff and family members will be required to give evidence will turn on the extent to which (*a*) there is evidence concerning the patient's previously expressed wishes (*b*) the diagnosis is open to debate and (*c*) there is a dispute between clinicians and family members about the proposed discontinuance.

At the final hearing, the court is likely to require as a minimum evidence from the independent experts instructed and the responsible clinician. If family members dispute the proposed discontinuance they should ensure – and they should be invited to ensure – that they have adequate representation at this hearing.

At the final hearing the judge will determine on the basis of the evidence and submissions by all interested parties whether or not to grant the declaration. As stated above, in cases where the diagnosis of PVS falls within RCP guidelines it is likely that a declaration will be granted. Outside those guidelines each case will turn on its own merits and will face detailed scrutiny by the judge.

1 [1993] AC 789 at 885 per Lord Browne-Wilkinson.
2 See App 9.1: *Practice Note: (Official Solicitor: Vegetative State)*.
3 Derived from the Official Solicitor's excellent instructions in *Re D* (9 November 2000, unreported, Johnson J).
4 See Apps 9.2 and 9.3 below.

G EMERGENCY CASES

[9.20] In *Frenchay Healthcare NHS Trust v S*[1] a vegetative patient's gastrotomy tube had become dislodged. An urgent application came before the court. Time had not permitted independent examinations to be performed to assess the patient's condition. The Court of Appeal held that it was appropriate to grant a declaration authorising the hospital not to replace the gastrotomy tube. The court rejected the Official Solicitor's argument that the tube should be reinserted to allow independent opinions to be commissioned.

1 [1994] 2 All ER 403.

Critique of Frenchay Approach

[9.21] In *Bland* Lord Goff commented[1]:

> 'Even so, where (for example) a patient is brought into hospital in such a condition that, without the benefit of a life support system, he will not continue to live, the decision has to be made whether or not to give him that benefit, if available. That decision can only be made in the best interests of the patient. No doubt, his best interests will ordinarily require that he should be placed on a life support system as soon as necessary, *if only to make an accurate assessment of his condition and a prognosis for the future.*'

Thus, the House of Lords envisaged a situation whereby it can be in a patient's 'best interests' to continue treatment which may subsequently be demonstrated to be futile in order to allow an assessment of the patient's condition. It is submitted that this principle should be applied in an emergency situation such as *Frenchay*. It must be in the patient's 'best interests' to ensure that his condition is assessed adequately in accordance with the accepted guidelines. Thus pending final determination of the diagnosis by independent examination, it cannot be determined that continued feeding is against the patient's 'best interests' and an assault.

Further, given that death by starvation is not instantaneous, a significant amount of information can in fact be placed before the court in a short space of time. In *Re D* the court had detailed expert reports and evidence from clinicians and nurses, even though the hearing was on a Friday and the patient's gastrotomy tube had become detached on Tuesday[2].

Thus, the court and the Official Solicitor can act at short notice. However, a Trust should gather careful evidence from clinicians and experts in order to establish the precise degree of urgency in each case.

1 [1993] AC 789 at 867F [emphasis added].
2 Also note the significant information obtained for the emergency hearing in *Re S* (30 November 1994, unreported), Ward J; and note the short period of time in which evidence was gathered in the case of *Re H (An NHS Trust 'A' v Mrs 'M' and An NHS Trust 'B' v Mrs 'H'* (25 October 2000, unreported, President)).

H CHILDREN

Is the substantive and procedural position different if the PVS patient is **[9.22]** a child? Usually a parent can provide valid consent for a child. If the child is unconscious a parent can provide consent for that child to undergo medical procedures. Nonetheless, even if a parent consents to discontinuance of feeding and hydration in a PVS child, an application should still be made to court in relation to this terminal step[1]. The court can then objectively assess the question of 'best interests'. Further, the court has power to consent for a child and can therefore, go further than merely declaring the legality of the proposed discontinuance, it can in fact order that leave be given for discontinuance. As indicated by the Official Solicitor's *Practice Note*:

> 'the applicant should seek the leave of the court for the termination of feeding and hydration, rather than a declaration. The form of relief [proposed for adults] should be amended accordingly.'

Whilst suggested by the *Practice Note*, an application for wardship is no longer required. If there is no other reason to invoke the wardship jurisdiction, then the application can simply be made within the inherent jurisdiction.

The procedure and evidence for such a hearing will be substantially the same as outlined above in relation to adults. The test for children is whether the proposed discontinuance is in the best interests of the child. As discussed above[2] this is the same test as applied for adults.

1 At least until further guidance is given on this question by the President of the Family Division.
2 See para **[9.3]** above.

I DOCTORS WHO DISAGREE IN PRINCIPLE

[9.23] What steps should be taken by a doctor treating a PVS patient who is in principle against withdrawal of feeding/hydration? A doctor cannot be forced to undertake treatment he does not agree with[1]. However, given that – as discussed above – continued treatment of a patient in PVS could comprise an assault, the family of a PVS patient may be able to obtain an injunction ordering the cessation of the assault and the withdrawal of tube-feeding. Thus, a doctor who disagrees in principle with allowing the patient to die may wish to transfer the care of that patient to another doctor.

1 *Re J (a minor) (child in care: medical treatment)* [1993] Fam 15.

CHAPTER 10

Treatment of Suicidal Patients

CONTENTS

A INTRODUCTION

This chapter addresses the issue of the relative entitlements of patients **[10.1]**
and medical attendants in relation to the control of suicidal behaviour in
hospital. Of all situations facing doctors and other hospital staff, this is
the one where they are most likely to have to make decisions without
recourse to advice, let alone the courts, although the latter may on
occasion be available and, indeed, play a necessary part in what occurs.
The law on the treatment of suicidal patients results in very difficult
dilemmas for clinicians in reconciling their duty to protect and treat
patients with their obligation to respect patients' autonomy.

B   BASIC DEFINITION

What is suicide?

[10.2]   It is an intentional act of self-destruction committed in the knowledge of the probable consequences of the act[1]. Therefore, it requires the following ingredients.

1 *Clift v Schwabe* (1846) 3 CB 437 at 464; *Re Davis (deceased)* [1968] 1 QB 72.

An act

[10.3]   The vexed question of the distinction between acts and omissions discussed in the chapter on the withholding or withdrawing of treatment from PVS patients. It appears that the distinction is relevant here[1].

1 Note discussion below in relation to *Robb.*

An intention to act

[10.4]   By definition suicide cannot be committed by a person who is, at the time of the act in question, incapable, either temporarily or permanently of forming an intention, or of appreciating the quality of his or her actions.

An understanding of the likely consequences

[10.5]   This and the previously mentioned requirements do not necessarily mean that the individual must have the mental capacity required for consenting to and refusing medical treatment[1]. A person who is suffering from a depression may understand the consequences, but still wish for them. Thus, coroner's inquests may return a verdict of suicide while the balance of his/her mind was disturbed.

1 See Chap 1, *Consent – General.*

C   STATUTE

[10.6]   Until the passing of the Suicide Act 1961 the act of committing suicide was a crime, as was an attempt. Section 1 of the Act abolished that rule. It remains an offence to aid and abet suicide[1]. Therefore, it is criminally unlawful for anyone to seek to render assistance to a person wishing to kill himself, however moving their plight might be. In the medical context it is therefore totally unlawful for a doctor knowingly to supply a patient with the means of committing suicide, intending thereby to help him do so.

1 Suicide Act 1961, s 2.

European Convention on Human Rights: the Suicide Act 1961 itself

[10.7]   The Suicide Act 1961 may itself be challenged as contravening the European Convention of Human Rights[1]. The validity of s 2 of the Suicide Act 1961 has been considered by the European Commission on Human Rights in *R v United Kingdom*[2]. This was a challenge by a member of the Voluntary Euthanasia Society who was convicted of conspiracy to aid and abet a suicide. He argued that the section violated the right to privacy (Art 8) and the right to freedom of expression (Art 10). The Commission's view was that s 2 did not violate the right to privacy (Art 8) because the notionally private act of suicide encroached on the legitimate public interest of protecting life. Further, there was not a breach of freedom of expression (Art 10) on the ground that[3]:

> 'the State's legitimate interest in this area in taking measures to protect, against criminal behaviour, the life of its citizens particularly those who belong to especially vulnerable categories by reason of their age or infirmity'.

A further question arises whether the right to life (Art 2) could be also used to challenge the section. In Canada the constitutional 'right to life' was the basis for a challenge (albeit unsuccessful) to the Criminal Code which prohibited assisting suicide[4]. However, as Michael Freeman[5] states:

> ' ... Article 2 is limited to protecting an individual's right to life, and whether it protects a person's right to decide how to live or how to die must be regarded as dubious'

given that the Convention separates the right to life (Art 2) from the right to security (Art 5).

It is unlikely that s 2 of the Suicide Act 1961 will be declared incompatible with the Convention. Also, a further challenge in the European Court of Human Rights will probably not succeed.

Further, a change in the current law would not appear likely. The Report of the House of Lords' Select Committee on Medical Ethics concluded that there were 'no circumstances in which assisted suicide should be permitted'[6]. The report was accepted by the Government who commented that a change in the law to allow assisted suicide 'would be open to abuse and put the lives of the weak and vulnerable at risk'[7].

1 It should be noted that any challenge to the Act could not be made other than by seeking a declaration of incompatibility in the High Court (or by challenge within criminal proceedings – see *DPP v Kebeline*): as primary legislation, the courts have no power to override its effect unless and until it is repealed or amended by Parliament.
2 (1983) 33 DR 270.
3 (1983) 33 DR 270 at 272.
4 *Rodriguez v British Columbia* (1994) 107 DLR (4th) 342.
5 'Death, Dying and the HRA', *Current Legal Problems* 1999.
6 *Report of the Select Committee on Medical Ethics*, Vol 1, (HL Paper 21-I).
7 *Government Response to the Report of the Select Committee on Medical Ethics* (Cmnd 2553).

D REFINING THE DEFINITION OF SUICIDE: FAILURE TO TREAT OR FEED

In *Airedale NHS Trust v Bland*[1] it was concluded that a competent **[10.8]** patient who refuses to consent to treatment which would have the effect of prolonging his life and who by reason of the refusal subsequently dies does *not* commit suicide. Thus, it was stated that any doctor who complied with a patient's wishes in those circumstances cannot be said to be aiding and abetting suicide.

This view was followed in *Secretary of State for the Home Department v Robb*[2] in which it was determined that a prison hunger striker who starved himself to death was not thereby committing suicide. Thus, in considering whether the 'countervailing State interest' in preventing suicide should be set against the 'individual's right of self- determination' Thorpe J held that the State interest was inapplicable in this setting because the prisoner's:

> 'refusal of nutrition and medical treatment in the exercise of the right of self-determination does *not* constitute an act of suicide.'

This seems a surprising conclusion. Just as someone who failed to feed a dependant child would be guilty of homicide, so it would seem to follow that someone who does not feed themselves is committing self-homicide. However, the determination in *Robb* that refusing nutrition is not an act of suicide follows from the decision in *Bland*[3] that providing food and drink comprises medical treatment. Nonetheless, this determination is an unnecessarily contrived answer to ensure the (necessary) result that doctors are not liable under s 2 of the Suicide Act 1961 in failing to provide treatment to patients who refuse consent. Further *Robb* could be misconstrued as implying that in circumstances where a patient's acts or omissions can be construed as 'an act of suicide' it is by that reason alone lawful to treat or prevent that patient's 'act of suicide' and a failure to treat must comprise aiding and abetting suicide.

The proposition in *Bland* would be better expressed on the basis that a doctor is not aiding or abetting suicide in circumstances where it is unlawful for him to act to prevent the suicide. If in treating a patient without his consent the doctor would be assaulting the patient he cannot be held to have 'aided and abetted' a death when the law itself prevents any treatment. To assess the culpability of the doctor's acts or omissions solely in terms of the definition to be applied to the patient's actions is to downplay the importance of an adult's autonomy. A doctor cannot violate an adult's autonomy over his body to prevent his death whether that death is the result of 'suicide' as defined by the courts or as a result of a refusal to be treated. It would be simpler to accept[4] that starving oneself to death is suicide but that, given a competent refusal of nutrition, no-one can lawfully act to prevent that suicide because to do so would be an assault. Thus, no-one can be guilty of aiding and abetting the patient's death.

1 [1993] AC 789, [1993] 2 WLR 316, [1993] 1 FLR 1026, HL.
2 [1995] 1 FLR 412.
3 Applied, for example, in *B v Croydon Health Authority* [1995] 2 WLR 294, [1995] Fam 133.
4 Contrary to *Robb*.

E GENERAL PRINCIPLES

[10.9] The general principles in approaching suicidal patients can be derived from our chapter on capacity and consent. A distinction must clearly be drawn between the mentally well adult in possession of full capacity to make medical treatment decisions of importance, and others who lack such capacity or who are suffering from some degree of mental illness or disorder, whether or not that deprives them of capacity.

In general the law does not now seek to interfere in the actions of an adult possessing full capacity intended to cause that individual's death.

Further, where it is clear that the suicidal actions are the result of a firm and irrevocable decision to end life, taken by an adult possessing the relevant degree of capacity, and that individual evinces a wish to be left to die, any attempt at resuscitation by a person knowing those facts may well be unlawful.

There is, however, nothing to prevent anyone doing all in their power to persuade a suicidally inclined person to change his or her mind, and to take steps to avoid the individual acquiring the means of self destruction. In some circumstances there may be a duty owed to the suicidally inclined individual to take reasonable care to prevent him or her obtaining the means to commit or attempt suicide.

In the case of children[1], or adults lacking the appropriate degree of capacity, the position is quite different. Those responsible for their care may, and almost certainly must, take all reasonable steps in their best interests to prevent acts of suicide. Further, in treating such patients their best interests will generally mandate that doctors act to preserve their lives despite any refusal of consent.

In relation to adults who have a mental illness or disorder, the law may allow treatment following a refusal of consent if the adult is detained under the Mental Health Act 1983 and the treatment is considered to be for the patient's mental illness or disorder. This is so even if the illness or disorder does not in fact deprive the adult of capacity.

In relation to an unconscious patient whose wishes are not known, in an emergency situation, life-saving treatment can lawfully be administered on the legal ground of necessity.

1 Theoretically, a child might possess the relevant capacity under the *Gillick* principles, but not only is such a possibility remote, but those having parental responsibility would in any event have a right to seek to prevent suicide by a child. Therefore, the position of children is considered here as being identical to others lacking legal capacity. The only practical difference worth mentioning is that a child might be made a ward of court to allow it to be properly protected in such circumstances.

F PRACTICAL PROBLEMS

About 100,000 people present at hospital each year following acts of deliberate self-harm. Casualty officers are in the front line of the treatment of those who have attempted suicide. Often little thought is given to the legal basis on which such patients are treated. **[10.10]**

Three particular illustrations of the legal and ethical dilemmas may assist:

- First, if an adult presents at the Accident and Emergency Department with bleeding wounds having attempted to kill himself and he says he does not want his wounds bound, would binding the wounds be unlawful?
- Second, if an adult patient who has been assessed as competent and is voluntarily in hospital, starts to run towards a window, would it be an unlawful assault for a doctor to rugby-tackle him to prevent him from jumping out the window?
- Third, given that it is presumed that adults have capacity, if following a drugs overdose an unconscious adult is taken by ambulance to the Accident and Emergency Department, has he not thereby indicated

that he does not want to receive any treatment and that he wants to die?

The last problem is the more easily addressed. Often attempted suicides are 'cries for help': the ultimate intention of the person is not in fact to die. How then is a casualty officer to distinguish which patients are 'genuine' suicides from those that are cries for help? Quite simply, he or she cannot and must therefore treat the patient on the basis of necessity: as discussed above, in treating an unconscious patient a doctor can provide such treatment as is necessary to save the patient's life[1].

As to the first problem – the conscious patient who refuses treatment for his bleeding wounds – the general principle outlined above appears to provide the simple answer that, unless the patient is known to be incompetent, treatment is prohibited. In *Bland* it was asserted that the principle of sanctity of life is not an absolute one

> 'It does not compel a medical practitioner on pain of criminal sanctions to treat a patient who will die if he does not, contrary to the express wishes of the patient.'

However, whilst it easy for House of Lords judges and legal authors to assert the paramountcy of autonomy, it is another for a doctor to watch someone die. As stated by J A Strauss[2]:

> 'What doctor will fail to render medical aid to a person who has cut his pulses in a suicide attempt and is bleeding to death?'

The solution might ostensibly be to argue that there is not adequate time to assess competence, and thus the doctrine of necessity comes into play thereby mandating the treatment of the bleeding patient's wounds. However, in assessing the legality of the act, this argument would appear to ignore the doctrine of presumed capacity: it is to be assumed that the person with bleeding wounds has capacity to refuse consent unless the opposite is established.

Nonetheless, as the recent case of *Reeves*[3] establishes one can be liable for a failure to protect even competent people from themselves. Thus, the casualty officer may feel that he/she is in the impossible situation that a failure to treat the patient may in fact render him/her liable to civil, disciplinary or even criminal sanctions. The doctor is placed between the rock of patient autonomy and the hard place of negligence litigation.

1 This approach is supported, for example, by research findings on 34 'self-poisoners' which determined that only around 40% of such patients themselves in fact expressed a wish to die. James and Hawton, 'Overdoses: Explanation and Attitudes in Self-Poisoners and Significant Others' *British Journal of Psychiatry* (1985) 146, 481–485.
2 Professor of Law, University of South Africa in *Legal Questions Surrounding Hunger Strikes by Detainees and Prisoners* (1991) Med Law 10: 211–218.
3 *Reeves v Metropolitan Police Comr* [2000] 1 AC 360.

G Autonomy v Liability for Failing to Act

[10.11] More often than not – whether in textbooks or judgments – the question of suicidal patients' competence to refuse treatment is considered in a vacuum. The authors however feel it is unrealistic to address the question of a doctor's duty to respect a suicidal patient's refusal of treatment without also considering that doctor's liability for failure to protect a suicidal patient.

Generally the law will not impose a duty on a person to prevent someone else from self-inflicted harm. As stated by Lord Hoffmann in *Reeves*:

> 'This argument is based upon the sound intuition that there is a difference between protecting people against harm caused to them by third parties and protecting them against harm which they inflict upon themselves. It reflects the individualist philosophy of the common law. People of full age and sound understanding must look after themselves and take responsibility for their actions. This philosophy expresses itself in the fact that duties to safeguard from harm deliberately caused by others are unusual and a duty to protect a person of full understanding from causing harm to himself is very rare indeed.'

However, as seen in *Reeves* the courts will impose a duty on the police to take reasonable care to prevent known suicide risks from harming or killing themselves[1]. Surprisingly capacity or soundness of mind do not appear to have any role in determining when liability will be imposed on a third party for a person's deliberate acts (albeit these concepts will have a role in determining the degree of contributory negligence of the deceased[2]).

If the duty of care is owed, courts will impose civil and may even impose criminal liability on doctors who fail to act to preserve life. In *Reeves* the police failed to relay vital information concerning the suicidal status of a prisoner in their charge. Civil liability ensued. In circumstances where the failure to provide appropriate or any care or protection is found to amount a gross failure, criminal liability will flow.

But doctors faced with the dilemma of whether to treat or not to treat a patient with bleeding wounds may feel that the law here is not fair or consistent. The decision in *Reeves* does not adequately address the query raised by Michael Jones that as 'suicide is the supreme act of individual self-assertion'[3]:

> 'How can the law respect the individual's claim to self-determination, while at the same time making someone else legally responsible for failing to prevent a suicide attempt?'

How can doctors successfully negotiate the line between autonomy and protection when the law appears to point in different directions depending on whether doctor's negligence or patient autonomy is the issue.

In *Reeves*[4] the line was drawn as follows:

- a doctor will not be liable for a death resultant from a failure to act which stems from a competent patient's refusal of consent to the doctor's act: autonomy means that the doctor could not act to prevent death;
- a doctor (and hospital or prison authorities) will be liable for a death

161

resultant from a failure adequately to control the patient's environment (provided any such intervention would not have invaded the patient's autonomy).

Hoffman LJ stated:

> 'Autonomy means that every individual is sovereign over himself and cannot be denied the right to certain kinds of behaviour, even if intended to cause his own death. On this principle, if [the deceased] had decided to go on hunger strike, the police would not have been entitled to administer forcible feeding. But autonomy does not mean that he would have been entitled to demand to be given poison, or that the police would not have been entitled to control his environment in non-invasive ways calculated to make suicide more difficult. If this would not infringe the principle of autonomy, it cannot be infringed by the police being under a duty to take such steps.'

And as stated by Jauncey LJ:

> 'If an individual can do to his own body what he wills, whether by positive act or neglect then there can be no duty on anyone else to prevent his so doing ... [T]he cases in which the principle has been recognised ... were cases in which prevention of injury to health or death would have involved an unlawful physical invasion of the individual's rights. In this case performance of the duty of care by closing the flap [on the cell door from which the Deceased hanged himself] would have involved no invasion of any rights of the deceased.'

However, their Lordships' formulation – which defines permissible steps as those which do not interfere with patient autonomy – in fact leaves the line for doctors blurred. Excessive interference with a patient's environment could constitute an infringement of that patient's autonomy. In *Keenan v UK*[5] the European Commission on Human Rights in considering the appropriate regime to safeguard prisoners' lives noted that:

> 'it would run counter to other fundamental rights guaranteed under the Convention – the right to respect for private life and potentially the prohibition against torture and inhuman and degrading treatment – to impose a regime with the rigorous controls necessary to render any self-injurious attempts impossible.'

The imposition of liability based on fine distinctions between acts and omissions troubled Kay J in *R v Dr Collins and Ashworth Hospital Authority, ex p Brady*[6]. The case concerned the 'Moors' Murderer' Ian Brady. In the course of argument, the question was raised as to whether a prisoner who was engaged in a hunger-strike could be force-fed even if he had capacity and was not capable of being lawfully force-fed under s 63 of the Mental Health Act 1983. It was argued for the Respondent that the right to self-determination was not absolute and that it had to be balanced against public interests[7] such as:

(1) the preservation of life,
(2) the prevention of suicide,
(3) the maintenance of the integrity of the medical profession,
(4) institutional discipline[8].

Whilst Kay J ultimately determined that it was not possible on the facts of the case to decide the point, his observations are of interest. Kay J felt that if *Secretary of State for the Home Department v Robb*[9] stood alone the Respondent's argument would be difficult to sustain. However, the judge determined that the *Reeves* decision had an important impact on the jurisprudence in this area particularly in considering whether in fact autonomy should prevail. He stated:

> 'It would be somewhat odd if there is a duty to prevent suicide by an act (for example, the use of a knife left in a cell) but not even a power to intervene to prevent self-destruction by starvation. I can see no moral justification for the law indulging its fascination with the difference between acts and omissions in a context such as this and no logical need for it to do so.
>
> 'It seems to me that if one were dealing with a physically fit man with capacity but who is detained in hospital for medical treatment for mental illness or disorder, there should be circumstances in which state or public interests . . . would properly prevail over a self-determined hunger strike so as to enable, even if not to require, intervention.'

Whilst stressing that he was not deciding the point, Kay J expressed the view that authority did not appear to require him to find that autonomy was paramount, stating:

> 'it would seem to me to be a matter for deep regret if the law has developed to a point in this area where the rights of a patient count for everything and other ethical values and institutional integrity count for nothing.'

1   Whether the duty goes further was recently tested in Leeds County Court in the case of *Orange v Chief Constable of West Yorkshire* (29 June, 2000, unreported, Finnerty J), where an argument that the specific duty to take reasonable steps to prevent harm extends to all prisoners was rejected. The case may be subject to appeal.
2   Or as more accurately phrased in US jurisprudence: in assessing the 'comparative negligence' of the defendant doctors it will be necessary to assess the capacity and sanity of the patient. Put shortly, the saner the patient, the lower the percentage damages the defendant will have to pay.
3   Michael A Jones, 'Saving the patient from himself', *Professional Negligence* (September 1990).
4   It should be stressed that this was in the context of patients/prisoners known to be a suicide risk.
5   Report (06/09/1999) application (00027229/95).
6   (10 March 2000, unreported, QBD), Kay J (discussed also in relation to the test under s 63 of the Mental Health Act 1983.
7   Note *Thor v Superior Court* (1993) 5 Cal. 4th 725, Supreme Court of California (Refusal of food by a quadriplegic prison inmate. Right of self-determination held to prevail. However, noted four potential countervailing state interests: 'preserving life, preventing suicide, maintaining the integrity of the medical profession and the protection of innocent third parties'.)

8 It was argued that institutional discipline would be undermined 'if detained persons had the right to self-harm, or to commit suicide or to protest against their circumstances by the use of hunger strikes and the refusal of medical treatment.'

9 [1995] 1 FLR 412.

European Convention on Human Rights: duty to preserve life

[10.12] Kay J's preferred approach is mirrored in the decisions under the European Convention. The Commission has held[1] that force-feeding a prisoner who was on hunger strike was not a breach of the right to freedom from inhuman and degrading treatment (Art 3). They concluded that, given that Art 2 (the right to life) imposes 'in certain circumstances' a duty to take positive action to preserve life, it was incumbent on the State in particular to take:

> 'active measure to save lives when the authorities have taken the person in question into their custody.'

This was reiterated in *Keenan v UK*[2] in which it was noted that Convention case-law establishes that Art 2 (the right to life) is not exclusively concerned with intentional killing by the use of force by agents of the State but also imposes a positive obligation on the State to take appropriate steps to safeguard lives. The European Commission on Human Rights determined that prison authorities had an obligation under Art 2 to take appropriate steps to safeguard the lives of the prisoners under their control:

> 'When depriving an individual of his liberty, the authorities thereby assume a responsibility for his welfare, the individual's autonomy to undertake that responsibility for himself having been largely removed.'

However, as set out above the commission did recognise that limits have to be placed on the obligation to interfere and intervene. No regime which respects prisoners or patients as human beings can ensure that no attempts are made to self-harm.

1 In *X v Germany* (1984) 7 EHRR 152 at 153.
2 Report (06/09/1999) Application 0027229/95.

H GENERAL GUIDANCE

[10.13] There is a tension in the law between the desire to ensure that vulnerable people are afforded the best possible care and the defence of the right of autonomy. If what is at issue is a course of treatment that a competent adult refuses, then that refusal will be seen as absolute (save in relation to prisoners or persons detained under the Mental Health Act 1983).

However, even in respect of competent adults, the law will impose a duty on doctors to ensure that a patient is not presented with the means of taking his/her life. Thus great care will need to be exercised by doctors in controlling the environment of patients who are apparently suicidal or who have refused to be treated for the consequences of an act of self-harm.

In emergency situations where it is not possible to determine a patient's views (whether because s/he is unconscious or incoherent), life-saving treatment can be given under the doctrine of necessity.

Where treatment or care relates to a child or an adult without capacity then 'best interests' will usually operate to render lawful treatment against the person's wishes. The only exception would relate to unusual circumstances in which it would be considered that saving the patient's life was not in his/her best interests. Whilst it is impossible to predict all the situations when this dilemma will occur, it is likely that in nearly all the guidance of the court should be sought.

Emergency situations: inadequate time to assess capacity

A particular difficulty arises on those occasions where there is no time adequately to assess capacity. The current state of the law implies that the doctrine of presumed capacity means that treatment of patient following a refusal to consent would be an assault. However, it could be argued that: **[10.14]**

- in circumstances where someone has presented having harmed himself the doctrine of presumed capacity should not apply: the person has engaged in an act which questions – although clearly does not negate – capacity;
- pending an assessment of capacity, the doctrine of necessity should therefore protect a doctor who takes the minimum steps necessary to preserve life.

It should be stressed that this is an argument only and has not been tested in the courts.

The first problem set out above was: if an adult presents at the Accident and Emergency Department with bleeding wounds having attempted to kill himself and he says he does not want his wounds bound, would binding the wounds be unlawful? Applying this argument to that problem will often result in treatment of the patient. This proposed approach runs counter to the general thrust of the academic literature in this area which strongly supports autonomy, although the view of SA Strauss[1] is noted[2]:

> 'Social disapproval of suicide is still strong in many societies. It is generally accepted that the conduct of a person such as a policeman – or any other person – who endeavours to prevent a prospective suicide from ending his life, is not only lawful but in fact praiseworthy. Such conduct would accordingly not constitute assault. Juridically the rescuer's act is justified on the basis of necessity.'

In any event, even if the courts hereafter accept this approach, it will not negate the responsibility to ensure that all doctors are versed in the component elements of capacity: only in situations of dire emergency where no sensible answer to the *Re C/Re MB* test can be provided by the doctor should resort be had to the doctrine of necessity.

1 Professor of Law, University of South Africa in *Legal Questions Surrounding Hunger Strikes by Detainees and Prisoners* (1991) Med Law 10: 211–218.
2 Strauss also notes the view of Van Der Westhizen that under South African law – there is an entitlement to save a person's life 'even if it is against the will of the person rescued . . .'

Emergency situations: preventing a jump from a window

[10.15] The second practical problem posed was: if an adult patient who has been assessed as competent and is voluntarily in hospital, starts to run towards a window, would it be an unlawful assault for a doctor to rugby-tackle him to prevent him from jumping out the window? It is likely that the law would answer that question by stating that the action of rugby-tackling the patient was lawful. Again, the wider doctrine of necessity comes into play: it is potentially dangerous to others for a patient to jump out of a window. Thus in acting to prevent *this* suicide attempt the doctor is of necessity 'assaulting' the patient to prevent potential harm to others and is therefore acting lawfully.

Further, even in a differing factual scenario in which the focus would solely be on protecting the patient from him or herself – for example, in restraining a patient from using a blade on his wrists – the protective public policies behind the decision in *Reeves* and discussed in *Brady* surely mandate physical intervention to prevent the act of suicide or self-harm. Given these public policy imperatives, justification again is found for the notional assault under the doctrine of necessity.

European Convention on Human Rights: the balance to be struck

[10.16] In assessing the approach of the law as to the difficult balance to be struck between individual self-determination and the need to protect the vulnerable, it should be noted that the Convention by Art 2 (the right to life) imposes a positive obligation on the State to protect and preserve life[1]. This would provide support for a doctrine of necessity in taking steps immediately to preserve life – whether by preventing someone from jumping out a window or binding up someone's bleeding wrists – even in circumstances which ostensibly do not accord with the general presumption of competence in English law. Thus, there is scope for using the Convention to argue for legitimate and limited departures from the otherwise immutable principle of autonomy. English law could be developed (or current law explained) in accordance with the reasoning of Justice Stevens in the US Supreme Court that[2]:

> ' ... the value to others of a person's life is far too precious to allow the individual to claim a constitutional entitlement to complete autonomy in making a decision to end that life.'

1 Eg *McCann v UK* (1995) 21 EHRR 97; Series A No 324 (Art 2(1) imposes a positive obligation on States both to refrain from taking life intentionally and to take appropriate steps to safeguard life); see also *Andronicou and Constantinou v Greece* (1998) 25 EHRR 491, [1998] Cr LT 823.
2 *Washington v Glucksberg* (1997) 138 L Ed 772: the US Supreme Court declared that a Washington law prohibiting physician-based suicide was *not* unconstitutional.

I COMPULSORILY DETAINED PATIENTS

[10.17] The extensive protections in place in relation to the treatment of patients compulsorily detained under the Mental Health Act 1983 is outside the scope of this book. However, no consideration of the issues concerning treating 'suicides' and those engaged in self-harm can be complete without reference to a doctor's power to treat those detained under the Act without their consent.

As detailed throughout this book the law presents hospitals and doctors with difficult ethical and practical problems as to issues of capacity and consent. The major ethical problem is the need, if a patient lacks capacity, to determine whether treatment is in the patient's best interests. The major practical problem is the requirement for the doctor to determine whether or not a patient in fact has capacity. In relation to patients compulsorily detained under s 3 of the Mental Health Act 1983, the law ostensibly relieves the doctor of the practical problem of weighing up the difficult questions concerning whether a patient has capacity to refuse treatment. By s 63 of the Act a doctor can provide such a patient with treatment[1] for 'the mental disorder from which he is suffering' even if the patient has capacity and refuses to consent to the treatment.

The Court of Appeal in *B v Croydon Health Authority*[2] considered the meaning of this section: is treatment within s 63 limited to the core treatment directed at the mental disorder (eg psychotherapy) or does it extend to treatment for the symptoms or consequences of a mental disorder?

B had a psychopathic disorder known as borderline personality disorder. She engaged in self harming behaviour. She was compulsorily detained under s 3. Other methods of self-harming having been removed by the hospital, Ms B resorted to starvation. As her physical condition deteriorated, her doctor informed her that he would consider force-feeding to prevent her death.

Through the MIND representative at the hospital, Ms B sought legal assistance. She was granted an ex parte injunction restraining the hospital from feeding without consent. Following a hearing, which included evidence from Ms B herself, Thorpe J determined that: (*a*) Ms B had capacity to refuse to eat; and (*b*) nonetheless by s 63 it was lawful for the hospital to feed her by means of naso-gastric tube without her consent.

The Court of Appeal considered whether such tube feeding was treatment for Ms B's mental disorder. The Act defines medical treatment as including 'nursing ... care, habilitation, rehabilitation under medical supervision'[3], thus indicating a significant range of acts ancillary to core treatment.

It was held that treatment within s 63 included nursing and care:

- concurrent with the core treatment, or
- as a necessary prerequisite to such treatment, or
- to prevent the patient from causing harm to himself, or
- to alleviate the consequences of the mental disorder.

As Ms B's self-harming behaviour and therefore her refusal to eat were products of her mental disorder, the proposed medical treatment, namely naso-gastric tube feeding, was treatment within s 63 and could be performed without the patient's consent.

The B decision was followed by *Re VS (Adult: Mental Disorder)*[4].

The patient had a history of trying to harm herself. She was formally admitted under s 3 of the Mental Health Act 1983. She refused liquid or food and there was a real risk that she could die from renal damage. The Trust sought a declaration declaring that forced tube feeding and/or intravenous hydration would be lawful.

The court held that such treatment would be lawful: it was clear that she was suffering from a major depressive illness and her refusal to eat or drink was a product of this disorder; thus, by virtue of s 63 of the Mental Health Act 1983 it would be permissible for the hospital to hydrate or feed the patient artificially.

Thus, a doctor can treat a detained patient who has capacity without his/her consent if the treatment is to alleviate the symptoms of a mental disorder. Relieving the symptoms of the mental disorder is just as much a part of treatment as relieving the underlying cause of the disorder and is treatment within s 63 of the Act.

Therefore, the suggestion in the BMJ by both Dalal and Sensky[5] that the Mental Health Act 1983 cannot authorise treatment for physical disorders is an over-simplification. Whilst it is correct that detention under the Act is only lawful for the treatment of 'mental disorder', if a physical disorder or condition is the product or symptom of the mental disorder for which the patient is detained then medical treatment for that physical disorder or condition is lawful. Thus bandaging the cut wrists of a suicidally depressed s 3 patient without consent is lawful by virtue of s 63.

The *B* decision however does not provide the doctor with carte blanche to override the patient's wishes. In *Re C (adult: refusal of medical treatment)*[6] a mental patient refused consent for his leg to be removed because of the presence of gangrene. The gangrene (and the patient's response to it) was wholly unconnected with his mental disorder. His refusal to consent to the proposed treatment could not therefore be overridden by the Act.

Further, whilst s 63 may seem to provide the doctor with an easy way out of the practical problems posed by consent and capacity issues, the reality is that for clinical and legal reasons these issues must be addressed even in relation to treatment authorised by s 63. The Mental Health Act *Code of Practice*[7] requires practitioners to consider whether the patient lacks capacity to consent in all cases. Further, in *all* cases 'sufficient information must be given to ensure that the patient understands the nature, likely effects and risks of ... treatment including the likelihood of its success and any alternatives to it' and there must be a compelling reason, in the patient's interest, for not disclosing relevant information.

Thus, s 63 and the *B* decision merely provide a last resort for the treating clinician: treatment without consent should only be considered once endeavours to achieve the patient's consent have failed and once the doctor is satisfied that proceeding with the treatment in the absence of consent is in the patient's best interests.

1 Treatments specified under ss 57 or 58 (eg treatments destroying brain tissue; long-term administration of medicine) are *not* included.
2 [1995] 1 All ER 683.
3 Mental Health Act 1983, s 145(1).
4 (1995) 3 Med L Rev 292.
5 *British Medical Journal* (8 July 1995), 115–118.
6 [1994] 1 WLR 290.
7 Chapter 15.

Legal test in criticising a doctor's determination under s 63 of the Mental Health Act 1983

In *R v Dr Collins and Ashworth Hospital Authority, ex p Brady*[1] Kay J   **[10.18]**
considered an application by the 'Moors Murderer' Ian Brady challenging:

> 'the continuing decision ... to force feed the Applicant, ...
> apparently made pursuant to section 63 of the Mental Health Act
> 1983'.

In approaching the test for assessing the doctors' determination that
force-feeding was appropriate under s 63, the Applicant submitted
that[2]:

> 'the role of the court is to satisfy itself that force feeding was and is
> being applied to the Applicant "for the mental disorder from which
> he is suffering" and not just that Dr. Collins and his colleagues had
> reasonable grounds for considering it to be such.'

The judge rejected this submission[3]: it was not for the judge to determine
whether as a 'precedent fact' the feeding was for the mental disorder
from which he is suffering; the judge simply had to determine whether or
not the doctor's determination that it was for the mental disorder
satisfied the *Wednesbury* reasonableness test, namely was it a determination that a reasonable doctor could make. However, given that the
feeding interfered with the Applicant's human rights, it was necessary for
the Respondent to satisfy a higher evidential threshold, described in the
case as the 'super-*Wednesbury* approach'. Kay J stated:

> ' ... it would be wholly undesirable if RMOs were challengeable in
> relation to section 63 on any basis other than the appropriate
> Wednesbury one ... Section 63 is about the clinical judgment of the
> RMO in relation to patients who, by definition, are being detained
> for medical treatment for their mental disorders. When a RMO is
> challenged by way of judicial review ... the test to be applied [under
> section 63] by this court is the appropriate Wednesbury one. That
> means, in the context of this and similar cases, what counsel
> referred to as the 'super-Wednesbury test' appropriate to human
> rights cases as set out in *Regina v Ministry of Defence, ex parte
> Smith*[4]:
>
> > "The court may not interfere with the exercise of an
> > administrative discretion on substantive grounds save where
> > the court is satisfied that the decision is unreasonable in the
> > sense that it is beyond the range of responses open to a
> > reasonable decision-maker. But in judging whether the
> > decision-maker has exceeded the margin of appreciation the
> > human rights context is important. The more substantial the
> > interference with human rights, the more the court will
> > require by way of justification before it is satisfied that the
> > decision is reasonable in the sense outlined above".'

On the facts of the case, Kay J noted the evidence from Brady's treating clinician that Brady's hunger strike was a product of his personality disorder and that, in response to being moved against his will, Brady:

> 'would feel the need to "do something" and "get his own back". He would also feel the need to re-establish his sense of control and address the wounds to his self-image and his narcissism – What better way to do this than through a hunger strike, which, as his past experience had shown him, allowed him to dictate the agenda for others, so taking control, and give him a "psychological boost"?'

The doctors felt that the hunger strike was 'a florid example of his psychopathology in action'. Thus, the judge concluded that the treating doctors were acting reasonably in accordance with the 'super-*Wednesbury* test' in force-feeding him pursuant to s 63:

> 'The hunger strike is a manifestation or symptom of the personality disorder. The fact (if such it be) that a person without mental disorder could reach the same decision on a rational basis in similar circumstances does not avail the Applicant because he reached and persists in his decision because of his personality disorder.'

1 (10 March 2000, unreported, QBD), Kay J.
2 Transcript, para 27.
3 He stated nonetheless that he would have found for the Respondent even applying the Applicant's proposed test.
4 Per Sir Thomas Bingham MR [1996] QB 517 at 554.

J GUIDANCE ON APPROACH TO TREATMENT

[10.19] In general[1], a doctor cannot force treatment on a competent patient who refuses that treatment. A doctor faced with such a refusal should ensure that he/she is satisfied that:

- the patient is competent to make the refusal (preferably with the assistance of a psychiatric assessment);
- the patient has received a detailed and explicit explanation of the consequences of any failure to consent;
- consideration has been given as to whether the patient should be detained under the Mental Health Act 1983;
- even if a patient is competently refusing treatment, if it is felt that he/she is at continuing risk of self-harm he/she should be placed in as safe an environment as possible.

If treatment is not given because of a competent adult's refusal to consent, great care should be taken to record the patient's determination. The patient should sign a record indicating that he/she has refused to consent. The refusal, and the information provided to the patient, should if possible be witnessed by others.

In considering each case, in addressing the ethical dilemma and weighing up the litigation risk[2], a doctor should err on the side of preserving life rather than allowing a patient to die.

The court's assistance should be sought if time permits[3] in relation to suicidal adults when capacity is in question or there is a difficult issue concerning 'best interests'.

The court's assistance should be sought in relation to 'suicidal' children when:

- parent/s have refused consent to life-saving treatment;
- a *Gillick* competent child[4] and his/her parent/s have refused consent to life-saving treatment;
- consideration is being given to not providing life-saving treatment following a suicide attempt under the doctrine of 'best interests'.

In the prison setting court authorisation for forced intervention which overrides consent may be permitted in exceptional circumstances on the basis of the factors outlined in the *Brady* case namely:

(1) the preservation of life;
(2) the prevention of suicide;
(3) the maintenance of the integrity of the medical profession; and
(4) institutional discipline.

1 Exceptional circumstances may arise in the treatment of prisoners or of patients detained under the Mental Health Act 1983.
2 *Malette v Shulman* [1991] 2 Med LR 162: an Ontario court found for a Jehovah's Witness plaintiff who claimed assault on the ground that she had been given a blood transfusion without her consent. The court awarded $20,000 damages. This is a rare example of litigation founded on an assault derived from treatment against a refusal of consent which, if respected, would have resulted in the death of the patient.
3 It should be stressed that the Family Division of the High Court can act at very short notice.
4 Or child aged 17.

PART III

APPENDICES

Contents

Appendix 1.1

Patient Consent to Examination or Treatment: General Consent Form (DoH)

For medical or dental investigation, treatment or operation

Health Authority . . . . .Patient's Surname
Hospital . . . . .Other Names
Unit Number . . . . .Date of Birth
                      Sex: *(please tick)* Male ☐   Female ☐

DOCTORS OR DENTISTS *(This part to be completed by doctor or dentist. See notes on the reverse)*

TYPE OF OPERATION INVESTIGATION OR TREATMENT

I confirm that I have explained the operation investigation or treatment, and such appropriate options as are available and the type of anaesthetic, if any (general/regional/sedation) proposed, to the patient in terms which in my judgement are suited to the understanding of the patient and/or to one of the parents or guardians of the patient

Signature . . . . .Date. . . ./. . . ./. . . .

Name of doctor or dentist. . . . .

PATIENT/PARENT/GUARDIAN

1. Please read this form and the notes overleaf very carefully.

2. If there is anything that you don't understand about the explanation, or if you want more information, you should ask the doctor or dentist.

3. Please check that all the information on the form is correct. If it is, and you understand the explanation, then sign the form.

I am the patient/parent/guardian *(delete as necessary)*

I agree	■ to what is proposed which has been explained to me by the doctor/dentist named on this form.
	■ to the use of the type of anaesthetic that I have been told about.
I understand	■ that the procedure may not be done by the doctor/dentist who has been treating me so far.
	■ that any procedure in addition to the investigation or treatment described on this form will only be carried out if it is necessary and in my best interests and can be justified for medical reasons.
I have told	■ the doctor or dentist about any additional procedures I would *not* wish to be carried out straightaway without my having the opportunity to consider them first.

Signature   . . . .

Name   . . . .

Address   . . . .

(if not the patient) . . . .

175

Appendix 1.1

NOTES TO:

Doctors, Dentists

A patient has a legal right to grant or
withhold consent prior to examination or treatment. Patients should be
given sufficient information, in a way they can understand, about
the proposed treatment and the possible alternatives. Patients must be
allowed to decide whether they will agree to the treatment
and they may refuse or withdraw consent to treatment at
any time. The patient's consent to treatment should be recorded
on this form (further guidance is given in HC(90)22 *(A
Guide to Consent for Examination or Treatment.)*

Patients

- The doctor or dentist is here to help you. He or she will explain the proposed treatment and what the alternatives are. You can ask any questions and seek further information. You can refuse the treatment.
- You may ask for a relative, or friend, or a nurse to be present.
- Training health professionals is essential to the continuation of the health service and improving the quality of care. Your treatment may provide an important opportunity for such training, where necessary under the careful supervision of a senior doctor or dentist. You may refuse any involvement in a formal training programme without this adversely affecting your care and treatment.

For treatment by a health professional other than doctors or dentists

Health Authority . . . . .Patient's Surname
Hospital . . . . .Other Names
Unit Number . . . . .Date of Birth
Sex: *(please tick)* Male ☐   Female ☐

DOCTORS OR DENTISTS *(This part to be completed by health professional. See notes on the reverse)*

TYPE OF TREATMENT PROPOSED

Complete this part of the form
I confirm that I have explained the treatment proposed and such appropriate options as are available to the patient in terms which in my judgement are suited to the understanding of the patient and/or to one of the parents or guardians of the patient.

Signature . . . . .Date. . . ./. . . ./. . . .

Name of health professional. . . . .
Job title of health professional. . . . .

PATIENT/PARENT/GUARDIAN

1. Please read this form and the notes overleaf very carefully.

2. If there is anything that you don't understand about the explanation, or if you want more information, you should ask the health professional who has explained the treatment proposed.

3. Please check that all the information on the form is correct. If it is, and you understand the treatment proposed, then sign the form.

I am the patient/parent/guardian *(delete as necessary)*

I agree   ■   to what is proposed which has been explained to me by the doctor/dentist named on this form.

Signature   . . . .

Name   . . . .

Address   . . . .

(if not the patient)   . . . .

NOTES TO:

Health Professionals, other than doctors or dentists

A patient has a legal right to grant or withhold consent prior to examination or treatment. Patients should be given sufficient information, in a way they can understand, about the proposed treatment and the possible alternatives. Patients must be allowed to decide whether they will agree to the treatment and they may refuse or withdraw consent to treatment at any time. The patient's consent to treatment should be recorded on this form (further guidance is given in HC(90)22 (A Guide to Consent for Examination or Treatment.)

Patients

■ The health professional named on this form is here to help you. He or she will explain the proposed treatment and what the alternatives are. You can ask any questions and seek further information. You can refuse the treatment.

■ You may ask for a relative, or friend, or another member of staff to be present.

■ Training health professionals is essential to the continuation of the health service and improving the quality of care. Your treatment may provide an important opportunity for such training, where necessary under the careful supervision of a fully qualified health professional. You may refuse any involvement in a formal training programme without this adversely affecting your care and treatment.

Appendix 1.2

A Guide to Consent for Examination or treatment (DoH 1990)

Chapter 1
A PATIENT'S RIGHTS IN ACCEPTING TREATMENT

1.   A patient has the right under common law to give or withhold consent prior to examination or treatment (except in special circumstances which are described in Chapter 2, paras 10 to 15, and Chapter 4). This is one of the basic principles of health care. Subject to certain exceptions the doctor or health professional and/or health authority may face an action for damages if a patient is examined or treated without consent.

2.   Patients are entitled to receive sufficient information in a way that they can understand about the proposed treatments, the possible alternatives and any substantial risks, so that they can make a balanced judgment. Patients must be allowed to decide whether they will agree to the treatment, and they may refuse treatment or withdraw consent to treatment at any time.

3.   Care should be taken to respect the patient's wishes. This is particularly important when patients may be involved in the training of professionals in various disciplines and students. An explanation should be given of the need for practical experience and agreement obtained before proceeding. It should be made clear that a patient may refuse to agree without this adversely affecting his or her care.

4.   When patients give information to health professionals they are entitled to assume that the information will be kept confidential and will not be disclosed to anyone without their consent other than for the provision of their health care. The only exceptions to this general rule are where disclosure is ordered by a Court; required by statute; or considered to be in the public interest et for some forms of research. Further information will be issued shortly in health circulars on 'Confidentiality, Use and Disclosure of NHS Information' and 'Guidance on Local Research Ethics Committees'. Where disclosure is made in the public interest appropriate safeguards must be applied.

Chapter 2
HEALTH PROFESSIONAL'S ROLE IN ADVISING THE PATIENT AND OBTAINING CONSENT TO TREATMENT

Advising the patient
1.   Where a choice of treatment might reasonably be offered the health pro-fessional may always advise the patient of his/her recommendations together with reasons for selecting a particular course of action. Enough information must normally be given to ensure that they understand the nature, consequences and any substantial risks of the treatment proposed so that they are able to take a decision based on that information. Though it should be assumed that most patients will wish to be well informed, account should be taken of those who may find this distressing.

2.   The patient's ability to appreciate the significance of the information should be assessed. For example with patients who:

179

(i)   may be shocked, distressed or in pain;
(ii) have difficulty in understanding English;
(iii) have impaired sight, or hearing or speech;
(iv) are suffering from mental disability but who nevertheless have the capacity to give consent to the proposed procedure (*see also Chapter 5 – Consent by patients suffering from mental disorder*).

3.   Occasionally and subject to the agreement of the patient, and where circumstances permit, it may help if a close family member or a friend can be present at the discussion when consent is sought. If this is not possible another member of the staff may be able to assist the patient in understanding. Where there are language problems, it is important an interpreter be sought whenever possible.

4.   A doctor will have to exercise his or her professional skill and judgment in deciding what risks the patient should be warned of and the terms in which the warning should be given. However, a doctor has a duty to warn patients of substantial or unusual risk inherent in any proposed treatment. This is especially so with surgery but may apply to other procedures including drug therapy and radiation treatment. Guidance on the amount of information and warnings of risk to be given to patients can be found in the judgment of the House of Lords in the case of *Sidaway v Governors of Bethlem Royal Hospital* [1985] AC 871 (*See also Chapter 6*).

Obtaining consent
5.   Consent to treatment may be implied or express. In many cases patients do not explicitly give express consent but their agreement may be implied by compliant actions, eg by offering an arm for the taking of a blood sample. Express consent is given when patients confirm their agreement to a procedure or treatment in clear and explicit terms, whether orally or in writing.

6.   Oral consent may be sufficient for the vast majority of contacts with patients by doctors and nurses and other health professionals. Written consent should be obtained for any procedure or treatment carrying any substantial risk or substantial side-effect. If the patient is capable, written consent should always be obtained for general anaesthesia, surgery, certain forms of drug therapy, eg cytotoxic therapy and therapy involving the use of ionising radiation. Oral or written consent should be recorded in the patient's notes with relevant details of the health professional's explanation. Where written consent is obtained it should be incorporated into the notes.

7.   **Standard consent form**. The main purpose of written consent is to provide documentary evidence that an explanation of the proposed procedure or treatment was given and that consent was sought and obtained. The model consent forms (*see Appendices*) set out the requirements for obtaining valid consent to treatment in terms which will be readily understood by the patient. In the majority of cases these forms will be used by registered medical or dental staff but there may be occasions when other health professionals will wish to record formally that consent has been obtained for a particular procedure. A separate form is available for their use.

8.   It should be noted that the purpose of obtaining a signature on the consent form is not an end in itself. The most important element of a consent procedure is the duty to ensure that patients understand the nature and purpose of the proposed treatment. Where a patient has not been given appropriate information then consent may not always have been obtained despite the signature on the form.

9.   Consent given for one procedure or episode of treatment does not give any automatic right to undertake any other procedure. A doctor may, however,

undertake further treatment if the circumstances are such that a patient's consent cannot reasonably be requested and provided the treatment is immediately necessary and the patient has not previously indicated that the further treatment would be unacceptable.

SPECIAL CIRCUMSTANCES

Treatment of Children and Young People
10.   *Children under the age of 16 years.* Where a child under the age of 16 achieves a sufficient understanding of what is proposed, that child may consent to a doctor or other health professional making an examination and giving treatment. The doctor or health professional must be satisfied that any such child has sufficient understanding of what is involved in the treatment which is proposed. A full note should be made of the factors taken into account by the doctor in making his or her assessment of the child's capacity to give a valid consent. In the majority of cases children will be accompanied by their parents during consultations. Where, exceptionally, a child is seen alone, efforts should be made to persuade the child that his or her parents should be informed except in circumstances where it is clearly not in the child's best interests to do so. Parental consent should be obtained where a child does not have sufficient understanding and is under age 16 save in an emergency where there is not time to obtain it.

11.   *Young people over the age of 16 years.* The effect of Section 8 of the Family Law Reform Act 1969 (*see Chapter 3*) is that the consent of a young person who has attained 16 years to any surgical, medical or dental treatment is sufficient in itself and it is not necessary to obtain a separate consent from the parent or guardian. In cases where a child is over age 16 but is not competent to give a valid consent, then the consent of a parent or guardian must be sought. However, such power only extends until that child is 18.

12.   *Refusal of parental consent to urgent or life-saving treatment.* Where time permits, court action may be taken so that consent may be obtained from a judge. Otherwise hospital authorities should rely on the clinical judgment of the doctors, normally the consultants, concerned after a full discussion between the doctor and the parents. In such a case the doctor should obtain a written supporting opinion from a medical colleague that the patient's life is in danger if the treatment is withheld and should discuss the need to treat with the parents or guardian in the presence of a witness. The doctor should record the discussion in the clinical notes and ask the witness to countersign the record. In these circumstances and where practicable the doctor may wish to consult his or her defence organisation. If he/she has followed the procedure set out above and has then acted in the best interests of the patient and with due professional competence and according to their own professional conscience, they are unlikely to be criticised by a court or by their professional body.

Adult or competent young person refusing treatment
13.   Some adult patients will wish to refuse some parts of their treatment. This will include those whose religious beliefs prevent them accepting a blood transfusion. Whatever the reason for the refusal such patients should receive a detailed explanation of the nature of their illness and the need for the treatment or transfusion proposed. They should also be warned in clear terms that the doctor may properly decline to modify the procedure and of the possible consequences if the procedure is not carried out. If the patient then refuses to agree, and he or she is competent, the refusal must be respected. The doctor should record this in the clinical notes and where possible have it witnessed.

Teaching on patients
14. Detailed guidance about medical students in hospitals is the subject of a separate circular to be issued shortly. It should not be assumed, especially in a teaching hospital, that a patient is available for teaching purposes or for practical experience by clinical medical or dental or other staff under training.

Examination or Treatment without the patient's consent
15. The following are examples of occasions when examination or treatment may proceed without obtaining the patient's consent:

(i)   For life-saving procedures where the patient is unconscious and cannot indicate his or her wishes.
(ii) Where there is a statutory power requiring the examination of a patient, for example, under the Public Health (Control of Disease) Act 1984. However an explanation should be offered and the patient's co-operation should nevertheless be sought.
(iii) In certain cases where a minor is a ward of court and the court decides that a specific treatment is in the child's best interests.
(iv) Treatment for mental disorder of a patient liable to be detained in hospital under the Mental Health Act 1983 (*see Chapter 5*).
(v)   Treatment for physical disorder where the patient is incapable of giving consent by reason of mental disorder, and the treatment is in the patient's best interest (*see Chapter 5*).

Chapter 3
FAMILY LAW REFORM ACT 1969, SECTION 8

Consent by person over 16 to surgical, medical and dental treatment
1. The consent of a minor who has attained the age of sixteen years to any surgical, medical or dental treatment which, in the absence of consent, would constitute a trespass to his person, shall be as effective as it would be if he were of full age; and where a minor has by virtue of this section given an effective consent to any treatment it shall not be necessary to obtain any consent for it from his parent or guardian.

2. In this section 'surgical, medical or dental treatment' includes any procedure undertaken for the purpose of diagnosis, and this section applies to any procedure (including, in particular, the administration of an anaesthetic) which is ancillary to any treatment as it applies to that treatment.

3. Nothing in this section shall be construed as making ineffective any consent which would have been effective if this section had not been enacted.

Chapter 4
EXAMPLES OF TREATMENTS WHICH HAVE RAISED CONCERN

Maternity Services
1. Principles of consent are the same in maternity services as in other areas of medicine. It is important that the proposed care is discussed with the woman, preferably in the early antenatal period, when any special wishes she expresses should be recorded in the notes, but of course the patient may change her mind about these issues at any stage, including during labour.

2. Decisions may have to be taken swiftly at a time when the woman's ability to give consent is impaired, eg as a result of medication, including analgesics. If the

safety of the woman or child is at stake the obstetrician or midwife should take any reasonable action that is necessary. If, in the judgment of the relevant health professional, the woman is temporarily unable to make a decision, it may be advisable for the position to be explained to her husband or partner if available, but his consent (or withholding of consent) cannot legally over-ride the clinical judgment of the health professional, as guided by the previously expressed wishes of the patient herself.

Breast Cancer
3.   The usual principles of explaining proposed treatment and obtaining the patient's consent should be followed in treating cases of breast cancer. Breast cancer does not normally require emergency treatment. The patient needs reassurance that a mastectomy will not be performed without her consent, and that unless she has indicated otherwise the need for any further surgery will be fully discussed with her in the light of biopsy and other results. This is a particular case of the principle, set out in para 9 of Chapter 2, that consent to an initial treatment or investigation does not imply consent to further treatment.

Tissue and Organ Donation: Risk of Transmitted Infection
4.   Where tissues or organs are to be transplanted, the recipient should be informed at the time when consent to operation is obtained of the small, but unavoidable risk of the transplant being infected. Further guidance is available in a CMO letter, 'HIV Infection, tissue banks and organ donation' (PL/CMO/92).

Chapter 5
CONSENT BY PATIENTS SUFFERING FROM MENTAL DISORDER*

1.   Consent to treatment must be given freely and without coercion and be based on information about the nature, purpose and likely effects of treatment presented in a way that it is understandable by the patient. The capacity of the person to understand the information given will depend on their intellectual state, the nature of their mental disorder, and any variability over time of their mental state. The ability of mentally disordered people to make and communicate decisions may similarly vary from time to time.

2.   The presence of mental disorder does not by itself imply incapacity, nor does detention under the Mental Health Act. Each patient's capability for giving consent, has to be judged individually in the light of the nature of the decision required and the mental state of the patient at the time.

Mental Health Legislation – treatment for mental disorders
3.   The Mental Health Act 1983 took a major step forward in providing for mentally disordered people, detained in hospital under the powers of the Act, to be given treatment for mental disorder, without their consent where they are incapable of giving consent. Certain procedures and safeguards are laid down in relation to specific groups of treatment, including the need for multidisciplinary discussion and the agreement of doctors appointed to give a second opinion.

Mental Incapacity and treatment for physical conditions
4.   The Mental Health Act 1983 does not contain provisions to enable treatment of **physical disorders** without consent either for detained patients or those people who may be suffering from mental disorder but who are not detained under the Mental Health Act.
   The administration of treatment for physical conditions to people incapable of giving consent and making their own treatment decisions is a matter of concern to

all involved in the care of such people, whether they are detained in hospital or in hospital but non-detained, in residential care or in the community.

The House of Lords' decision in Re F [1989] 2 WLR 1025, [1989] 2 All ER 545
5.   This decision helped to clarify the common law in relation to general medical and surgical treatment of people who lack the capacity to give consent. No-one may give consent on behalf of an adult but the substantive law is that a proposed operation or treatment is lawful if it is in the best interests of the patient and unlawful if it is not. Guidance given in that case is set out below.

(i)   In considering the lawfulness of medical and surgical treatment given to a patient who for any reason, temporary or permanent, lacks the capacity to give or to communicate consent to treatment, it was stated to be axiomatic that treatment which is necessary to preserve the life, health or well-being of the patient may lawfully be given without consent.

(ii)   The standard of care required of the doctor concerned in all cases is laid down in *Bolam v Friern Hospital Management Committee* [1957] 1 WLR 582, namely, that he or she must act in accordance with a responsible body of relevant professional opinion.

(iii)   In many cases, it will not only be lawful for doctors, on the ground of necessity to operate or give other medical treatment to adult patients disabled from giving their consent, it will also be their common law duty to do so.

(iv)   In the case of the mentally disordered, when the state is permanent or semi-permanent, action properly taken, may well transcend such matters as surgical operation or substantial medical treatment and may extend to include such (humdrum) matters as routine medical and dental treatment and even simple care such as dressing and undressing and putting to bed.

(v)   In practice, a decision may involve others besides the doctor. It must surely be good practice to consult relatives and others who are concerned with the care of the patient. Sometimes, of course, consultation with a specialist or specialists will be required; and in others, especially where the decision involves more than a purely medical opinion, an inter-disciplinary team will in practice participate in the decision.

Documentation
6.   Proposals for treatment should as a matter of good practice, be discussed with the multidisciplinary team and where necessary other doctors and, with the consent of the patient where this is possible, with their nearest relative or friend. The decisions taken should be documented in the clinical case notes. In cases involving anaesthesia, and surgery, or where the treatment carries substantial or unusual risk it would also be advisable for documentation to record that the patient is incapable of giving consent to treatment and that the doctor in charge of the patient's treatment is of the opinion that the treatment proposed should be given and that it is in the patient's best interests. A model form is suggested to register medical opinion – where a patient is incapable of giving consent (*Appendix B*).

Sterilisation
7.   In *Re F* it was said that special features applied in the case of an operation for sterilisation. Having regard to those matters, it was stated to be highly desirable as a matter of good practice to involve the court in the decision to operate. In practice an application should be made to a court whenever it is proposed to perform such an operation. The procedure to be used is to apply for a declaration that the proposed operation for sterilisation is lawful, and the following guidance was given as to the form to be followed in such proceedings:

(i) applications for a declaration that a proposed operation on or medical treatment for a patient can lawfully be carried out despite the inability of such patient to consent thereto should be by way of originating summons issuing out of the Family Division of the High Court;

(ii) the applicant should normally be those responsible for the care of the patient or those intending to carry out the proposed operation or other treatment, if it is declared to be lawful;

(iii) the patient must always be a party and should normally be a respondent. In cases in which the patient is a respondent the patient's guardian ad litem should normally be the Official Solicitor. In any cases in which the Official Solicitor is not either the next friend or the guardian ad litem of the patient or an applicant he shall be a respondent;

(iv) with a view to protecting the patient's privacy, but subject always to the judge's discretion, the hearing will be in chambers, but the decision and the reasons for that decision will be given in open court.

Mental disorder means mental illness, arrested or incomplete development of mind, psychopathic disorder and any other disorder or disability of mind and 'mentally disordered' shall be construed accordingly.

Chapter 6
THE SIDAWAY CASE

The question of how much information and warning of risk which should be given to a patient was considered by the House of Lords in the case of *Sidaway v Governors of Bethlem Royal Hospital* [1985] AC 871. Lord Bridge indicated that a decision on what degree of disclosure of risks is best calculated to assist a particular patient to make a rational choice as to whether or not to undergo a particular treatment must primarily be a matter of clinical judgment. He was of the further opinion that a judge might in certain circumstances come to the conclusion that the disclosure of a particular risk was so obviously necessary to an informed choice that no reasonably prudent medical man would fail to make it. The kind of case which Lord Bridge had in mind would be an operation involving a substantial risk of grave adverse consequences. Lord Templeman stated that there was no doubt that a doctor ought to draw the attention of a patient to a danger which may be special in kind or magnitude or special to the patient. He further stated that it was the obligation of the doctor to have regard to the best interests of the patient but at the same time to make available to the patient sufficient information to enable the patient to reach a balanced judgment if he chooses to do so.

Appendix 1.3

GMC Guidance on Duties of Doctor

The duties of a doctor registered with the General Medical Council
Patients must be able to trust doctors with their lives and well-being. To justify that trust, we as a profession have a duty to maintain a good standard of practice and care and to show respect for human life. In particular as a doctor you must:

- make the care of your patient your first concern;
- treat every patient politely and considerately;
- respect patients' dignity and privacy;
- listen to patients and respect their views;
- give patients information in a way they can understand;
- respect the rights of patients to be fully involved in decisions about their care;
- keep your professional knowledge and skills up to date;
- recognise the limits of your professional competence;
- be honest and trustworthy;
- respect and protect confidential information;
- make sure that your personal beliefs do not prejudice your patients' care;
- act quickly to protect patients from risk if you have good reason to believe that you or a colleague may not be fit to practise;
- avoid abusing your position as a doctor; and
- work with colleagues in the ways that best serve patients' interests.

In all these matters you must never discriminate unfairly against your patients or colleagues. An you must always be prepared to justify your actions to them.

Appendix 1.4

GMC: Seeking Patient's Consent – the Ethical Considerations

General Medical Council
(February 1999)

Guidance to doctors
Being registered with the General Medical Council gives you rights and privileges. In return, you must meet the standards of competence, care and conduct set by the GMC.

This booklet sets out the principles of good practice which all registered doctors are expected to follow when seeking patients' informed consent to investigations, treatment, screening or research. It enlarges on the general principles set out in paragraph 12 of our booklet Good Medical Practice.

Introduction
1. Successful relationships between doctors and patients depend on trust. To establish that trust you must respect patients' autonomy – their right to decide whether or not to undergo any medical intervention even where a refusal may result in harm to themselves or in their own death[1]. Patients must be given sufficient information, in a way that they can understand, to enable them to exercise their right to make informed decisions about their care.

2. This right is protected in law, and you are expected to be aware of the legal principles set by relevant case law in this area[2]. Existing case law gives a guide to what can be considered minimum requirements of good practice in seeking informed consent from patients.

3. Effective communication is the key to enabling patients to make informed decisions. You must take appropriate steps to find out what patients want to know and ought to know about their condition and its treatment. Open, helpful dialogue of this kind with patients leads to clarity of objectives and under-standing, and strengthens the quality of the doctor/patient relationship. It provides an agreed framework within which the doctor can respond effectively to the individual needs of the patient. Additionally, patients who have been able to make properly informed decisions are more likely to co-operate fully with the agreed management of their conditions.

Consent to investigation and treatment

Providing sufficient information
4. Patients have a right to information about their condition and the treatment options available to them. The amount of information you give each patient will vary, according to factors such as the nature of the condition, the complexity of the treatment, the risks associated with the treatment or procedure, and the patient's own wishes. For example, patients may need more information to make an informed decision about a procedure which carries a high risk of failure or adverse side effects; or about an investigation for a condition which, if present, could have serious implications for the patient's employment, social or personal life[3].

5. The information which patients want or ought to know, before deciding whether to consent to treatment or an investigation, may include:

- details of the diagnosis, and prognosis, and the likely prognosis if the condition is left untreated;
- uncertainties about the diagnosis including options for further investigation prior to treatment;
- options for treatment or management of the condition, including the option not to treat;
- the purpose of a proposed investigation or treatment; details of the procedures or therapies involved, including subsidiary treatment such as methods of pain relief; how the patient should prepare for the procedure; and details of what the patient might experience during or after the procedure including common and serious side effects;
- for each option, explanations of the likely benefits and the probabilities of success; and discussion of any serious or frequently occurring risks, and of any lifestyle changes which may be caused by, or necessitated by, the treatment;
- advice about whether a proposed treatment is experimental;
- how and when the patient's condition and any side effects will be monitored or re-assessed;
- the name of the doctor who will have overall responsibility for the treatment and, where appropriate, names of the senior members of his or her team;
- whether doctors in training will be involved, and the extent to which students may be involved in an investigation or treatment;
- a reminder that patients can change their minds about a decision at any time;
- a reminder that patients have a right to seek a second opinion;
- where applicable, details of costs or charges which the patient may have to meet.

6.   When providing information you must do your best to find out about patients' individual needs and priorities. For example, patients' beliefs, culture, occupation or other factors may have a bearing on the information they need in order to reach a decision. You should not make assumptions about patients' views, but discuss these matters with them, and ask them whether they have any concerns about the treatment or the risks it may involve. You should provide patients with appropriate information, which should include an explanation of any risks to which they may attach particular significance. Ask patients whether they have understood the information and whether they would like more before making a decision.

7.   You must not exceed the scope of the authority given by a patient, except in an emergency[4]. Therefore, if you are the doctor providing treatment or under-taking an investigation, you must give the patient a clear explanation of the scope of consent being sought. This will apply particularly where:

- treatment will be provided in stages with the possibility of later adjustments;
- different doctors (or other health care workers) provide particular elements of an investigation or treatment (for example anaesthesia in surgery);
- a number of different investigations or treatments are involved;
- uncertainty about the diagnosis, or about the appropriate range of options for treatment, may be resolved only in the light of findings once investigation or treatment is underway, and when the patient may be unable to participate in decision making.

In such cases, you should explain how decisions would be made about whether or when to move from one stage or one form of treatment to another. There should be a clear agreement about whether the patient consents to all or only parts of the proposed plan of investigation or treatment, and whether further consent will have to be sought at a later stage.

Appendix 1.4

8. You should raise with patients the possibility of additional problems coming to light during a procedure when the patient is unconscious or otherwise unable to make a decision. You should seek consent to treat any problems which you think may arise and ascertain whether there are any procedures to which the patient would object, or prefer to give further thought to before you proceed. You must abide by patients' decisions on these issues. If in exceptional circumstances you decide, while the patient is unconscious, to treat a condition which falls outside the scope of the patient's consent, your decision may be challenged in the courts, or be the subject of a complaint to your employing authority or the GMC. You should therefore seek the views of an experienced colleague, wherever possible, before providing the treatment. And you must be prepared to explain and justify your decision. You must tell the patient what you have done and why, as soon as the patient is sufficiently recovered to understand.

Responding to questions
9. You must respond honestly to any questions the patient raises and, as far as possible, answer as fully as the patient wishes. In some cases, a patient may ask about other treatments that are unproven or ineffective. Some patients may want to know whether any of the risks or benefits of treatment are affected by the choice of institution or doctor providing the care. You must answer such questions as fully, accurately and objectively as possible.

Withholding information
10. You should not withhold information necessary for decision making unless you judge that disclosure of some relevant information would cause the patient serious harm. In this context serious harm does not mean the patient would become upset, or decide to refuse treatment.

11. No-one may make decisions on behalf of a competent adult. If patients ask you to withhold information and make decisions on their behalf, or nominate a relative or third party to make decisions for them, you should explain the importance of them knowing the options open to them, and what the treatment they may receive will involve. If they insist they do not want to know in detail about their condition and its treatment, you should still provide basic information about the treatment. If a relative asks you to withhold information, you must seek the views of the patient. Again, you should not withhold relevant information unless you judge that this would cause the patient serious harm.

12. In any case where you withhold relevant information from the patient you must record this, and the reason for doing so, in the patient's medical records and you must be prepared to explain and justify your decision.

Presenting information to patients
13. Obtaining informed consent cannot be an isolated event. It involves a continuing dialogue between you and your patients which keeps them abreast of changes in their condition and the treatment or investigation you propose. Whenever possible, you should discuss treatment options at a time when the patient is best able to understand and retain the information. To be sure that your patient understands, you should give clear explanations and give the patient time to ask questions. In particular, you should:

- use up-to-date written material, visual and other aids to explain complex aspects of the investigation, diagnosis or treatment where appropriate and/or practicable;
- make arrangements, wherever possible, to meet particular language and communication needs, for example through translations, independent interpreters, signers, or the patient's representative;

- where appropriate, discuss with patients the possibility of bringing a relative or friend, or making a tape recording of the consultation;
- explain the probabilities of success, or the risk of failure of, or harm associated with options for treatment, using accurate data;
- ensure that information which patients may find distressing is given to them in a considerate way. Provide patients with information about counselling services and patient support groups, where appropriate;
- allow patients sufficient time to reflect, before and after making a decision, especially where the information is complex or the severity of the risks is great. Where patients have difficulty understanding information, or there is a lot of information to absorb, it may be appropriate to provide it in manageable amounts, with appropriate written or other back-up material, over a period of time, or to repeat it;
- involve nursing or other members of the health care team in discussions with the patient, where appropriate. They may have valuable knowledge of the patient's background or particular concerns, for example in identifying what risks the patient should be told about;
- ensure that, where treatment is not to start until some time after consent has been obtained, the patient is given a clear route for reviewing their decision with the person providing the treatment.

Who obtains consent

14. If you are the doctor providing treatment or undertaking an investigation, it is your responsibility to discuss it with the patient and obtain consent, as you will have a comprehensive understanding of the procedure or treatment, how it is carried out, and the risks attached to it. Where this is not practicable, you may delegate these tasks provided you ensure that the person to whom you delegate:

- is suitably trained and qualified;
- has sufficient knowledge of the proposed investigation or treatment, and understands the risks involved;
- acts in accordance with the guidance in this booklet.

You will remain responsible for ensuring that, before you start any treatment, the patient has been given sufficient time and information to make an informed decision, and has given consent to the procedure or investigation.

Ensuring voluntary decision making

15. It is for the patient, not the doctor, to determine what is in the patient's own best interests. Nonetheless, you may wish to recommend a treatment or a course of action to patients, but you must not put pressure on patients to accept your advice. In discussions with patients, you should:

- give a balanced view of the options;
- explain the need for informed consent.

You must declare any potential conflicts of interest, for example where you or your organisation benefit financially from use of a particular drug or treatment, or treatment at a particular institution.

16. Pressure may be put on patients by employers, insurance companies or others to undergo particular tests or accept treatment. You should do your best to ensure that patients have considered the options and reached their own decision. You should take appropriate action if you believe patients are being offered inappropriate or unlawful financial or other rewards.

17.   Patients who are detained by the police or immigration services, or are in prison, and those detained under the provisions of any mental health legislation may be particularly vulnerable. Where such patients have a right to decline treatment you should do your best to ensure that they know this, and are able to exercise this right.

Emergencies
18.   In an emergency, where consent cannot be obtained, you may provide medical treatment to anyone who needs it, provided the treatment is limited to what is immediately necessary to save life or avoid significant deterioration in the patient's health. However, you must still respect the terms of any valid advance refusal which you know about, or is drawn to your attention. You should tell the patient what has been done, and why, as soon as the patient is sufficiently recovered to understand.

Establishing capacity to make decisions
19.   You must work on the presumption that every adult has the capacity to decide whether to consent to, or refuse, proposed medical intervention, unless it is shown that they cannot understand information presented in a clear way[5]. If a patient's choice appears irrational, or does not accord with your view of what is in the patient's best interests, that is not evidence in itself that the patient lacks competence. In such circumstances it may be appropriate to review with the patient whether all reasonable steps have been taken to identify and meet their information needs (see paragraphs 5-17). Where you need to assess a patient's capacity to make a decision, you should consult the guidance issued by professional bodies[6].

Fluctuating capacity
20.   Where patients have difficulty retaining information, or are only intermittently competent to make a decision, you should provide any assistance they might need to reach an informed decision. You should record any decision made while the patients were competent, including the key elements of the consultation. You should review any decision made whilst they were competent, at appropriate intervals before treatment starts, to establish that their views are consistently held and can be relied on.

Mentally incapacitated patients
21.   No-one can give or withhold consent to treatment on behalf of a mentally incapacitated patient[7]. You must first assess the patient's capacity to make an informed decision about the treatment. If patients lack capacity to decide, provided they comply, you may carry out an investigation or treatment, which may include treatment for any mental disorder[8], that you judge to be in their best interests. However, if they do not comply, you may compulsorily treat them for any mental disorder only within the safeguards laid down by the Mental Health Act 1983[9], and any physical disorder arising from that mental disorder, in line with the guidance in the Code of Practice of the Mental Health Commission[10]. You should seek the courts' approval for any non-therapeutic or controversial treatments which are not directed at their mental disorder.

Advance statements
22.   If you are treating a patient who has lost capacity to consent to or refuse treatment, for example through onset or progress of a mental disorder or other disability, you should try to find out whether the patient has previously indicated preferences in an advance statement ('advance directives' or 'living wills'). You must respect any refusal of treatment given when the patient was competent, provided the decision in the advance statement is clearly applicable to the present circumstances, and there is no reason to believe that the patient has changed his/

her mind. Where an advance statement of this kind is not available, the patient's known wishes should be taken into account – see paragraph 25 on the 'best interests' principle.

Children

23.   You must assess a child's capacity to decide whether to consent to or refuse proposed investigation or treatment before you provide it. In general, a competent child will be able to understand the nature, purpose and possible consequences of the proposed investigation or treatment, as well as the consequences of non-treatment. Your assessment must take account of the relevant laws or legal precedents in this area[11]. You should bear in mind that:

- at age 16 a young person can be treated as an adult and can be presumed to have capacity to decide;
- under age 16 children may have capacity to decide, depending on their ability to understand what is involved[12];
- where a competent child refuses treatment, a person with parental responsibility or the court may authorise investigation or treatment which is in the child's best interests. The position is different in Scotland, where those with parental responsibility cannot authorise procedures a competent child has refused. Legal advice may be helpful on how to deal with such cases.

24.   Where a child under 16 years old is not competent to give or withhold their informed consent, a person with parental responsibility may authorise investigations or treatment which are in the child's best interests[13]. This person may also refuse any intervention, where they consider that refusal to be in the child's best interests, but you are not bound by such a refusal and may seek a ruling from the court. In an emergency where you consider that it is in the child's best interests to proceed, you may treat the child, provided it is limited to that treatment which is reasonably required in that emergency.

'Best interests' principle

25.   In deciding what options may be reasonably considered as being in the best interests of a patient who lacks capacity to decide, you should take into account:

- options for treatment or investigation which are clinically indicated;
- any evidence of the patient's previously expressed preferences, including an advance statement;
- your own and the health care team's knowledge of the patient's background, such as cultural, religious, or employment considerations;
- views about the patient's preferences given by a third party who may have other knowledge of the patient, for example the patient's partner, family, carer, tutor-dative (Scotland), or a person with parental responsibility;
- which option least restricts the patient's future choices, where more than one option (including non-treatment) seems reasonable in the patient's best interest.

Applying to the court

26.   Where a patient's capacity to consent is in doubt, or where differences of opinion about his or her best interests cannot be resolved satisfactorily, you should consult more experienced colleagues and, where appropriate, seek legal advice on whether it is necessary to apply to the court for a ruling. You should seek the court's approval where a patient lacks capacity to consent to a medical intervention which is non-therapeutic or controversial, for example contraceptive sterilisation, organ donation, withdrawal of life support from a patient in a persistent vegetative state. Where you decide to apply to a court you should, as

soon as possible, inform the patient and his or her representative of your decision and of his or her right to be represented at the hearing.

Forms of consent

27.   To determine whether patients have given informed consent to any proposed investigation or treatment, you must consider how well they have understood the details and implications of what is proposed, and not simply the form in which their consent has been expressed or recorded.

Express consent

28.   Patients can indicate their informed consent either orally or in writing. In some cases, the nature of the risks to which the patient might be exposed make it important that a written record is available of the patient's consent and other wishes in relation to the proposed investigation and treatment. This helps to ensure later understanding between you, the patient, and anyone else involved in carrying out the procedure or providing care. Except in an emergency, where the patient has capacity to give consent you should obtain written consent in cases where:

- the treatment or procedure is complex, or involves significant risks and/or side effects;
- providing clinical care is not the primary purpose of the investigation or examination;
- there may be significant consequences for the patient's employment, social or personal life;
- the treatment is part of a research programme.

29.   You must use the patient's case notes and/or a consent form to detail the key elements of the discussion with the patient, including the nature of information provided, specific requests by the patient, details of the scope of the consent given.

Statutory requirements

30.   Some statutes require written consent to be obtained for particular treatments (for example some fertility treatments). You must follow the law in these areas.

Implied consent

31.   You should be careful about relying on a patient's apparent compliance with a procedure as a form of consent. For example, the fact that a patient lies down on an examination couch does not in itself indicate that the patient has understood what you propose to do and why.

Reviewing consent

32.   A signed consent form is not sufficient evidence that a patient has given, or still gives, informed consent to the proposed treatment in all its aspects. You, or a member of the team, must review the patient's decision close to the time of treatment, and especially where:

- significant time has elapsed between obtaining consent and the start of treatment;
- there have been material changes in the patient's condition, or in any aspects of the proposed treatment plan, which might invalidate the patient's existing consent;
- new, potentially relevant information has become available, for example about the risks of the treatment, or about other treatment options.

Consent to screening

33.   Screening (which may involve testing) healthy or asymptomatic people to detect genetic predispositions or early signs of debilitating or life threatening conditions can be an important tool in providing effective care. But the uncertainties involved in screening may be great, for example the risk of false positive or false negative results. Some findings may potentially have serious medical, social or financial consequences not only for the individuals, but for their relatives. In some cases the fact of having been screened may itself have serious implications.

34.   You must ensure that anyone considering whether to consent to screening can make a properly informed decision. As far as possible, you should ensure that screening would not be contrary to the individual's interest. You must pay particular attention to ensuring that the information the person wants or ought to have is identified and provided. You should be careful to explain clearly:

• the purpose of the screening;
• the likelihood of positive/negative findings and possibility of false positive/ negative results;
• the uncertainties and risks attached to the screening process;
• any significant medical, social or financial implications of screening for the particular condition or predisposition;
• follow up plans, including availability of counselling and support services.

If you are considering the possibility of screening children, or adults who are not able to decide for themselves, you should refer to the guidance at paragraphs 19–25. In appropriate cases, you should take account of the guidance issued by bodies such as the Advisory Committee on Genetic Testing[14].

Consent to research

35.   Research involving clinical trials of drugs or treatments, and research into the causes of, or possible treatment for, a particular condition, is important in increasing doctors' ability to provide effective care for present and future patients. The benefits of the research may, however, be uncertain and may not be experienced by the person participating in the research. In addition, the risk involved for research participants may be difficult to identify or to assess in advance. If you carry out or participate in research involving patients or volunteers, it is particularly important that you ensure:

• as far as you are able, that the research is not contrary to the individual's interests;
• that participants understand that it is research and that the results are not predictable.

36.   You must take particular care to be sure that anyone you ask to consider taking part in research is given the fullest possible information, presented in terms and a form that they can understand. This must include any information about possible benefits and risks; evidence that a research ethics committee has given approval; and advice that they can withdraw at any time. You should ensure that participants have the opportunity to read and consider the research information leaflet. You must allow them sufficient time to reflect on the implications of participating in the study. You must not put pressure on anyone to take part in research. You must obtain the person's consent in writing. Before starting any research you must always obtain approval from a properly constituted research ethics committee.

37.   You should seek further advice where your research will involve adults who are not able to make decisions for themselves, or children. You should be aware

that in these cases the legal position is complex or unclear, and there is currently no general consensus on how to balance the possible risks and benefits to such vulnerable individuals against the public interest in conducting research. (A number of public consultation exercises are under way.) You should consult the guidance issued by bodies such as the Medical Research Council and the medical royal colleges[16] to keep up to date. You should also seek advice from the relevant research ethics committee where appropriate.

Notes

1. This right to decide applies equally to pregnant women as to other patients, and includes the right to refuse treatment where the treatment is intended to benefit the unborn child. See *St George's Healthcare NHS Trust v S* [1998] Fam Law 526 and 662, and *Re MB (an adult: medical treatment)* [1997] 2 FCR 541, CA
2. Advice can be obtained from medical defence bodies such as the Medical Defence Union, Medical Protection Society, the Medical and Dental Defence Union of Scotland, or professional associations such as the BMA, or your employing organisation.
3. Our booklet 'Serious Communicable Diseases' gives specific guidance on seeking consent to testing for conditions like HIV, Hepatitis B and C.
4. Guidance on treating patients in emergencies is included in paragraph 18.
5. A patient will be competent if he or she can: comprehend information, it having been presented to them in a clear way; believe it; and retain it long enough to weigh it up and make a decision. From *Re C (Adult: Refusal of Medical Treatment)* [1994] 1 All ER 819. But seek legal advice, in case of doubt.
6. For example the BMA/Law Society publication, 'Assessment of Mental Capacity: Guidance for Doctors and Lawyers' available from the BMA.
7. Except in Scotland where a 'tutor-dative' with appropriate authority may make medical decisions on behalf of the patient. Seek legal advice, in case of doubt.
8. Legal advice should be obtained in case of doubt. A relevant precedent is the case of *Regina v Bournewood Community and Mental Health NHS Trust ex parte L* [1998] 3 All ER, 289, HL.
9. And similar legislation in Scotland and Northern Ireland.
10. Code of Practice Dec 1998 Pursuant to s 118 of the Mental Health Act 1983.
11. You should consult your medical defence body or professional association for up to date advice. Appendix A lists some of the relevant key legislation.
12. Age of Legal Capacity (Scotland) Act 1991 (Section 2.4); *Gillick v West Norfolk and Wisbech AHA* [1985] 3 ALL ER 402.
13. This also applies to young people between 16 and 18 years old, except in Scotland.
14. ACGT can be contacted at: ACGT Secretariat, Department of Health, Room 401, Wellington House, 133–135 Waterloo Road, London, SE1 8UG. Telephone: 020 7972 4017
15. Consult your medical defence body, a professional association such as the BMA, or your employing organisation.
16. Appendix B gives an indicative list of published guidance. The GMC plans to publish further guidance on research.

APPENDIX A
Children and Consent to Treatment and Testing: Some Key Legislation

England & Wales
- Family Law Reform Act 1969
- Gillick v West Norfolk and Wisbech AHA [1985], 3 AER 402
- Children Act 1989

Scotland
- Age of Legal Capacity (Scotland) Act 1991
- Children Act (Scotland) 1995, Section 6, Part 1.

Northern Ireland
- Age of Majority Act 1969, s 4.

APPENDIX B
Other Guidance on Research: Indicative List of Relevant Publications

- 'Good Medical Practice', paragraphs 55–56. The General Medical Council, 178–202 Great Portland Street, London, W1W 5JE. 1998.
- 'The Ethical Conduct of Research on Children'. MRC Ethics Series. The Medical Research Council, 20 Park Crescent, London, W1N 4AL. 1991 and 1993.
- 'Responsibility in Investigations on Human Participants and Materials and on Personal Information'. MRC Ethics Series. The Medical Research Council. 1992.
- 'The Ethical Conduct of Research on the Mentally Incapacitated'. MRC Ethics series. The Medical Research Council. 1991 and 1993.
- 'Research Involving Patients'. The Royal College of Physicians of London, 11 St Andrew's Place, London, NW1 4LE. January 1990.
- 'Guidelines on the Practice of Ethics Committees in Medical Research Involving Human Subjects'. Second Edition. The Royal College of Physicians of London, 11 St Andrew's Place, London, NW1 4LE. January 1990.
- 'Local Research Ethics Committees' (HSG(91)5). Department of Health, Richmond House, 79 Whitehall, London, SW1A 2NS. 1991.
- 'Multi-Centre Research Committees' (HSG(97)23). Department of Health, Richmond House, 79 Whitehall, London SW1A 2NS. 1997.
- 'ABPI Guidance Note. Patient Information and Consents for Clinical Trials'. Association of British Pharmaceutical Industry, 12 Whitehall, London, SW1A 2DY. May 1997.
- 'International Ethical Guidelines for Biomedical Research Involving Human Subjects'. Council for International Organisations of Medical Sciences (CIOMS), c/o World Health Organisation, Avenue Appia, 1211 Geneva 27, Switzerland.
- 'Charter for Ethical Research in Maternity Care.'1997. National Childbirth Trust, Alexandra House, Oldham Terrace, Acton, London W3 6NH.
- 'Human Tissue: Ethical and Legal Issues 'Nuffield Council on Bioethics, 28 Bedord Square, London WC1B 3EG. April 1995.

Appendix 2.1

Draft Advanced Directive

I, *[Susan Patient]* of *[15 Mayday Avenue, Blankton, Blankshire]* hereby of my own free will declare that if I become incapable by reason of mental incapacity or unconsciousness of making an informed and competent decision regarding my health care, my wishes are as follows:

(1) In the following circumstances, namely:

  (*a*) If I should sustain an incurable and irreversible illness, disease or condition which is likely to result in my death in the near future;

  or

  (*b*) If I become permanently unconscious, and in the opinion of at least one independent practitioner of consultant status with the appropriate expertise I have totally and irreversibly lost consciousness and any awareness of myself, other people and my surroundings likely to be meaningful to me, whether or not I am diagnosed as being in a permanent vegetative state,

  or

  (*c*) If I suffer some form of incurable and irreversible illness, disease or condition which will, or is likely to, render me permanently incapable of making my own decisions and expressing competent wishes, or of leading an independent life:

  I desire that all life-sustaining treatment, including any form of artificial nutrition or hydration, be withheld or discontinued, and I hereby refuse my consent to any such treatment in such circumstances.

(2) For the avoidance of doubt, in the circumstances mentioned above, I do not wish to receive, or as the case may be, continue to receive, cardiopulmonary resuscitation, mechanical respiration, tube-feeding or hydration, or antibiotics.

(3) For the further avoidance of doubt I do consent in such circumstances and would wish to receive medical treatment for the purpose of relieving distress and preserving my comfort and dignity, and of allowing me to die in the greatest possible comfort, including pain relief, even if such treatment might have the incidental effect of shortening my life.

(4) I make this declaration having discussed it with *[Dr Goodwill]* and having read *Advance Statements about Medical Treatment – Code of Practice* [BMA 1996] I intend this to be legally binding on any medical practitioner attending me. I make it in particular contemplation of the surgery I am to undergo on or about *[10 April 2000]* but intend it to be of general application. In the event of any uncertainty whether my declaration applies in any particular case, or in the event of circumstances arising not expressly included in it, I request that if practicable *[my mother Janice Patient]* be consulted and regard had to his or her, as I have confidence that he/she would appreciate best what my wishes would be.

(5) I request that any medical practitioner in possession of a copy of this declaration being it to the attention of any medical or other practitioner for the

time being responsible for my care. In order to protect her from undue distress and anxiety I do not wish my spouse, *[Joseph Patient]* to be made aware of this document, unless it becomes necessary to consider its application to my treatment.

Date: *[1 April 2000]*

Signed: *[Susan Patient]*

I, *[Michael Neighbour]* declare that *[Susan Patient]* signed this document in my presence, and that he/she is personally known to me.

Signed: *[Michael Neighbour]*

Address: *[13 Mayday Avenue, Blankton, Blankshire]*

Telephone: *[01234 567 890]*

Appendix 3.1

Draft Originating Summons for Child Treatment Decision

Note that this is adapted from the originating summons and orders at first instance in Re A (children) (conjoined twins: surgical separation) [2000] 4 All ER 961, [2000] 3 FCR 577

IN THE HIGH COURT OF JUSTICE   **Case No**

FAMILY DIVISION

PRINCIPAL REGISTRY

IN THE MATTER OF:

XC

AND IN THE MATTER OF THE INHERENT JURISDICTION OF THE HIGH COURT
AND IN THE MATTER OF THE CHILDREN ACT 1989

B E T W E E N :

BLANKSHIRE HEALTHCARE NHS TRUST

Applicant

- and -

X Child

First Respondent

P Father

Second Respondent

R Mother

Third Respondent

ORIGINATING SUMMONS

Let all parties attend before Mr Justice Fairness at the Royal Courts of Justice, Strand, London on *[date]* at *[time]* for the hearing of the application of the Blankshire Healthcare NHS Trust for an Order:

1. That in the circumstances where the First Respondent cannot give her consent and where the Second and Third Respondents withhold their consent, it shall be lawful and in the First Respondent's best interests to carry out such operative and medical procedures on her as in the opinion of the consultant medical practitioners caring for the First Defendant are necessary for preserving her life and treating her leukaemia.

2. For the purpose of these proceedings and during the hearing:
    (*a*) The First Respondent be referred to as 'X';
    (*b*) The Second and Third Respondent be referred to as 'Mr P' and 'Mrs R' respectively.
    (*c*) The Applicant be referred to as 'the Y NHS Trust and the hospital at which the First Respondent is being cared for as 'the hospital'.

199

3. At the hearing of this application the following witnesses, namely the Second and Third Respondents and any witness other than an expert witness be permitted to give evidence without disclosing their name and address in open court.

4. An injunction be granted restraining until further order in the meantime any person (whether by himself or by his servants or agents or otherwise howsoever or in the case of a company whether by its directors or officers, servants or agents or otherwise howsoever)

   (*a*) from publishing in any newspaper or broadcasting in any sound or television broadcast or by means of any cable or satellite programme service or public computer network:

       (i) The name or address of:

           (1) The above-mentioned First Respondent as being the subject of these proceedings; or

           (2) Any natural person other than a parent having their day to day care; or

           (3) The above-mentioned Second and Third Respondents; or

           (4) Any witness who has given evidence in these proceedings;

       (ii) Any picture, whether photographic or otherwise of any of the persons mentioned in (*a*) above;

       (iii) Any other matter

   In each case in a manner calculated to lead to the identification of:

       (i) The First Respondent

       (ii) In the case of any establishment, of such establishment as being an establishment at or in which the First Respondent is residing or being treated;

       (iii) In the case of the Second and Third Respondents or any carers of the First Respondent, such persons as being the parents or carers of the First Respondent

   (*b*) Soliciting any information relating to the First Respondent (other than information already in the public domain);

       (i) From the staff or persons employed at the hospital

       (ii) From any carer;

       (iii) From the Second and Third Respondents

   (*c*) Notwithstanding the provisions of section 12(2) of the Administration of Justice Act 1960 without prejudice to paragraph 5 below including in any publication of the text or a summary of the whole or any part of any order made in these proceedings any of the matters referred to in paragraph 4(*a*)(i) above.

Provided that nothing in the order shall of itself prevent any person:

    (i) publishing any particulars or information relating to any part of the proceedings before any court other than a court sitting in private;

    (ii) publishing any information or picture already lawfully in the public domain;

    (iii) enquiring of another person as to whether that person is one referred to in paragraph 4(*b*) above;

    (iv) seeking or receiving information from any person who has previously approached the person seeking or receiving information with the purpose of volunteering information

    (v) soliciting information relating to the First Respondent in the course of or for the purpose of the exercise by the person seeking such information of any duty or function authorised by statute or by a court of competent jurisdiction.

Appendix 3.1

5.   Copies of the order mentioned in the preceding paragraph endorsed with a penal notice be served on such newspapers and sound and television broadcasting cable or satellite programme services as the Applicant may think fit in each case by facsimile transmission or pre-paid first class post addressed to the editor in the case of a broadcasting cable or satellite programme service and on such other persons as the Applicant may think fit in each case by personal service.

Appendix 4.1

Consent Form (Sterilisation or Vasectomy) (DoH)

For sterilisation or vasectomy

Health Authority . . . . .Patient's Surname . . . .
Hospital . . . . .Other Names . . . .
Unit Number . . . . .Date of Birth . . . .
Sex: *(please tick)* Male ☐   Female ☐

DOCTORS *(This part to be completed by doctor See notes on the reverse)*

TYPE OF OPERATION: STERILISATION OR VASECTOMY

Complete this part of the form
I confirm that I have explained the procedure and any anaesthetic
(general/regional) required, to the patient in terms which in my judgement
are suited to his/her understanding.

Signature . . . . .Date. . . ./. . . ./. . . .

Name of doctor. . . . .

PATIENT

1. Please read this form very carefully.

2. If there is anything that you don't understand about the explanation, or if you want more information, you should ask the doctor.

3. Please check that all the information on the form is correct. If it is, and you understand the explanation, then sign the form.

I am the patient

I agree	■ to have this operation, which has been explained to me by the doctor named on this form.
	■ to have the type of anaesthetic that I have been told about.
I understand	■ that the operation may not be done by the doctor who has been treating me so far.
	■ that the aim of the operation is to stop me having any children and it might not be possible to reverse the effects of the operation.
	■ that sterilisation/vasectomy can sometimes fail, and that there is a very small chance that I may become fertile again after some time.
	■ that any procedure in addition to the investigation or treatment described on this form will only be carried out if it is necessary and in my best interests and can be justified for medical reasons.
I have told	■ the doctor about any additional procedures I would *not* wish to be carried out straightaway without my having the opportunity to consider them first.
For vasectomy I understand	■ that I may remain fertile or become fertile again after some time.
	■ that I will have to use some other contraceptive method until 2 tests in a row show that I am not producing sperm, if I do not want to father any children.

Signature   . . . .

202

NOTES TO:

Doctors, Dentists

A patient has a legal right to grant or withhold consent prior to examination or treatment. Patients should be given sufficient information, in a way they can understand, about the proposed treatment and the possible alternatives. Patients must be allowed to decide whether they will agree to the treatment and they may refuse or withdraw consent to treatment at any time. The patient's consent to treatment should be recorded on this form (further guidance is given in HC(90)22 *(A Guide to Consent for Examination or Treatment.)*

Patients

■ The doctor is here to help you. He or she will explain the proposed procedure, which you are entitled to refuse. You can ask any questions and seek further information.
■ You may ask for a relative, or friend, or a nurse to be present.
■ Training health professionals is essential to the continuation of the health service and improving the quality of care. Your treatment may provide an important opportunity for such training, where necessary under the careful supervision of a senior doctor. You may refuse any involvement in a formal training programme without this adversely affecting your care and treatment.

Practice Note (Official Solicitor: Sterilisation) [1996] 2 FLR 111

Sterilisation of minor – Mentally incompetent adult – Procedure – Applications to court – Parties – Evidence – Mental capacity -Consultation

The need for the prior sanction of a High Court judge
1.   The sterilisation of a minor or a mentally incompetent adult ('the patient') will in virtually all cases require the prior sanction of a High Court judge: *Re B (A Minor) (Wardship: Sterilisation)* [1988] AC 199, [1987] 2 FLR 314; *Re F (Sterilisation: Mental Patient)* [1990] 2 AC 1, [1989] 2 FLR 376.

Applications to court
2.   Applications in respect of a minor should be made in the Family Division of the High Court, within proceedings either under the inherent jurisdiction or s 8(1) ('a specific issue order') of the Children Act 1989. In the Official Solicitor's view, the procedural and administrative difficulties attaching to applications under s 8 of the Children Act 1989 are such that the preferred course is to apply within the inherent jurisdiction.

3.   Within the inherent jurisdiction, applicants should seek an order in the following or a broadly similar form:

> 'It is ordered that there be leave to perform an operation of sterilisation on the minor [X] *[if it is desired to specify the precise method of carrying out the operation add, for example, by the occlusion of her fallopian tubes]* and to carry out such post-operative treatment and care as may be necessary in her best interests.'

4.   Applications in respect of an adult should be by way of originating summons in the Family Division of the High Court for an order in the following or a broadly similar form:

> 'It is declared that the operation of sterilisation proposed to be performed on [X] *[if it is desired to specify the precise method of carrying out the operation, add, for example, by the occlusion of her fallopian tubes]* being in the existing circumstances in her best interests can lawfully be performed on her despite her inability to consent to it.
>
>   It is ordered that in the event of a material change in the existing circumstances occurring before the said operation has been performed any party shall have liberty to apply for such further or other declaration or order as may be just.'

The parties
5.   The plaintiff or applicant should normally be a parent or one of those responsible for the care of the patient or those intending to carry out the proposed operation. The patient must always be a party and should normally be a defendant (or respondent). In cases in which the patient is a defendant the patient's guardian ad litem should normally be the Official Solicitor. In any case in which the Official Solicitor does not represent the patient he should be a defendant.

Procedure
6.   There will in every case be a hearing before a High Court judge fixed for directions on the first open date after the passage of 8 weeks from the issue of the originating summons.

7.   The case will normally be heard in chambers. If it is heard in open court, the court will usually take steps to preserve the anonymity of the patient and the patient's family by making appropriate orders under the Contempt of Court Act 1981: *Re G (Adult Patient: Publicity)* [1995] 2 FLR 528.

Evidence
8.   The purpose of the proceedings is to establish whether or not the proposed sterilisation is in the best interests of the patient. The judge will require to be satisfied that those proposing sterilisation are seeking it in good faith and that their paramount concern is for the best interests of the patient rather than their own or the public's convenience. The proceedings will normally involve a thorough adversarial investigation of all possible viewpoints and any possible alternatives to sterilisation. Nevertheless, straightforward cases proceeding without dissent may be disposed of at the hearing for directions without oral evidence.

9.   The Official Solicitor will in all cases, in whichever capacity he acts, carry out his own investigations, call his own witnesses and take whatever other steps appear to him to be necessary in order to ensure that all medical, psychological and social evaluations are conducted and that all relevant matters are properly canvassed before the court. Expert and other witnesses called in support of the proposed operation will be cross-examined and all reasonable arguments presented against sterilisation. The Official Solicitor will require to meet and interview the patient in private in all cases where he or she is able to express any views (however limited) about the case.

10.   The Official Solicitor anticipates that the court will particularly require evidence clearly establishing the following:

Mental capacity
(1)   That the patient is incapable of making her own decision about sterilisation and is unlikely to develop sufficiently to make an informed judgment about sterilisation in the foreseeable future, having regard to the most up-to-date medical knowledge in this field. In this connection it must be borne in mind that–

(i)   the fact that a person is legally incompetent for some purposes does not mean that she necessarily lacks the capacity to make a decision about sterilisation; and
(ii)   in the case of a minor her youth and potential for development may make it difficult or impossible to make the relevant finding of incapacity.

Risk of pregnancy
(2)   That there is a need for contraception because the patient is fertile and is sexually active or is likely to engage in sexual activity in the foreseeable future. *(Re W (Mental Patient: Sterilisation)* [1993] 1 FLR 381.)

Potential psychological damage
(3)   That the patient is likely if she becomes pregnant or gives birth to experience substantial trauma or psychological damage greater than that resulting from the sterilisation itself.

Alternative methods of contraception
(4) That there is no appropriate reversible method of contraception available having regard to the most up-to-date medical knowledge in this field.

Consultation
11. Members of the Official Solicitor's legal staff are prepared to discuss sterilisation cases before proceedings have been issued. Contact with the Official Solicitor may be made by telephoning 0171 911 7127 during office hours.

OFFICIAL SOLICITOR
June 1996

Appendix 4.3

Draft Order for Claim Form for Declaration that Sterilisation of Adult Lawful

'It is declared that in the existing circumstances the operation of sterilisation proposed to be performed on [*name of patient*], (namely by application of clips to her fallopian tubes) [*describe here the nature of the procedure*][2], being in the existing circumstances in her best interests, may be lawfully performed on her despite her inability to consent to it.

It is further ordered that in the event of a material change of circumstances occurring before the operation referred to above has been performed, any party (or the Official Solicitor)[3] may apply to the court for such further or other declaration as may be just.'

1 Based on the order suggested in *Practice Note (Official Solicitor: Sterilisation)* [1996] 2 FLR 111; set out in App 4.2 above.
2 See n 1 above.
3 The explicit reference to the Official Solicitor should be added where, unusually he has not previously been made a party to the proceedings.

Appendix 4.4

Draft Order under Inherent Jurisdiction for Sterilisation of Child[1]

'It is ordered that there be leave to perform an operation of sterilisation on the child [*name*] by application of clips to her fallopian tubes [*describe here the nature of the procedure*][2] and to carry out such post-operative treatment and care as may be in her best interests.'

1 Based on the order suggested in *Practice Note (Official Solicitor: Sterilisation)* [1996] 2 FLR 111; set out in App 4.2 above.
2 While the Official Solicitor's *Practice Note* suggests that the description of the operation is optional, it is suggested that it should always be inserted. Even if sterilisation is in the patient's best interests, and generally agreed to be so, there might still be controversy about the method used, such as hysterectomy.

Appendix 5.1

Abortion Act 1967

An Act to amend and clarify the law relating to termination of pregnancy by registered medical practitioners

[27th October 1967]

1 Medical termination of pregnancy

(1) Subject to the provisions of this section, a person shall not be guilty of an offence under the law relating to abortion when a pregnancy is terminated by a registered medical practitioner if two registered medical practitioners are of the opinion, formed in good faith–

[(*a*) that the pregnancy has not exceeded its twenty-fourth week and that the continuance of the pregnancy would involve risk, greater than if the pregnancy were terminated, of injury to the physical or mental health of the pregnant woman or any existing children of her family; or

(*b*) that the termination is necessary to prevent grave permanent injury to the physical or mental health of the pregnant woman; or

(*c*) that the continuance of the pregnancy would involve risk to the life of the pregnant woman, greater than if the pregnancy were terminated; or

(*d*) that there is a substantial risk that if the child were born it would suffer from such physical or mental abnormalities as to be seriously handicapped].

(2) In determining whether the continuance of a pregnancy would involve such risk of injury to health as is mentioned in paragraph (*a*) [or (*b*)] of subsection (1) of this section, account may be taken of the pregnant woman's actual or reasonably foreseeable environment.

(3) Except as provided by subsection (4) of this section, any treatment for the termination of pregnancy must be carried out in a hospital vested in [the Secretary of State for the purposes of his functions under the National Health Service Act 1977 or the National Health Service (Scotland) Act 1978 [or in a hospital vested in [a Primary Care Trust or] a National Health Service trust] or in a place approved for the purposes of this section by the Secretary of State].

[(3A) The power under subsection (3) of this section to approve a place includes power, in relation to treatment consisting primarily in the use of such medicines as may be specified in the approval and carried out in such manner as may be so specified, to approve a class of places.]

(4) Subsection (3) of this section, and so much of subsection (1) as relates to the opinion of two registered medical practitioners, shall not apply to the termination of a pregnancy by a registered medical practitioner in a case where he is of the opinion, formed in good faith, that the termination is immediately necessary to save the life or to prevent grave permanent injury to the physical or mental health of the pregnant woman.

Amendment

Sub-s (1): paras (*a*)–(*d*) substituted for paras (*a*), (*b*) as originally enacted by the Human Fertilisation and Embryology Act 1990, s 37(1).

Sub-s (2): words in square brackets inserted by the Human Fertilisation and Embryology Act 1990, s 37(2).

Sub-s (3): words from 'the Secretary of State' to 'the Secretary of State' in square brackets substituted by the Health Services Act 1980, Sch 1, para 17.

Sub-s (3): words 'or in a hospital vested in a National Health Service trust' in square brackets inserted by the National Health Service and Community Care Act 1990, s 66(1), Sch 9, para 8.

Sub-s (3): words 'a Primary Care Trust or' in square brackets inserted by SI 2000/90, art 3(1), Sch 1, para 6. Date in force: 8 February 2000: see SI 2000/90, art 1.
Sub-s (3A): inserted by the Human Fertilisation and Embryology Act 1990, s 37(3).

2 Notification

(1)   The Minister of Health in respect of England and Wales, and the Secretary of State in respect of Scotland, shall by statutory instrument make regulations to provide–

 (*a*)   for requiring any such opinion as is referred to in section 1 of this Act to be certified by the practitioners or practitioner concerned in such form and at such time as may be prescribed by the regulations, and for requiring the preservation and disposal of certificates made for the purposes of the regulations;

 (*b*)   for requiring any registered medical practitioner who terminates a pregnancy to give notice of the termination and such other information relating to the termination as may be so prescribed;

 (*c*)   for prohibiting the disclosure, except to such persons or for such purposes as may be so prescribed, of notices given or information furnished pursuant to the regulations.

(2)   The information furnished in pursuance of regulations made by virtue of paragraph (*b*) of subsection (1) of this section shall be notified solely to the [Chief Medical Officer of the [Department of Health], or of the Welsh Office, or of the [Scottish Administration]].

(3)   Any person who wilfully contravenes or wilfully fails to comply with the requirements of regulations under subsection (1) of this section shall be liable on summary conviction to a fine not exceeding [level 5 on the standard scale].

(4)   Any statutory instrument made by virtue of this section shall be subject to annulment in pursuance of a resolution of either House of Parliament.

Amendment

Sub-s (2): words in square brackets beginning with the words 'Chief Medical Officer' substituted by SI 1969/388, art 2, Sch 1.
Sub-s (2): words 'Department of Health' in square brackets substituted by SI 1988/1843, art 5(4), Sch 3, para 3(*a*).
Sub-s (2): words 'Scottish Administration' in square brackets substituted by SI 1999/1042, art 5, Sch 3, para 2. Date in force: 1 July 1999: see SI 1999/1042, art 1(2)(*c*).
Sub-s (3): maximum fine increased by the Criminal Law Act 1977, s 31, Sch 6, and converted to a level on the standard scale by the Criminal Justice Act 1982, ss 37, 46.

3   Application of Act to visiting forces etc

(1)   In relation to the termination of a pregnancy in a case where the following conditions are satisfied, that is to say–

 (*a*)   the treatment for termination of the pregnancy was carried out in a hospital controlled by the proper authorities of a body to which this section applies; and

 (*b*)   the pregnant woman had at the time of the treatment a relevant association with that body; and

 (*c*)   the treatment was carried out by a registered medical practitioner or a person who at the time of the treatment was a member of that body appointed as a medical practitioner for that body by the proper authorities of that body,

this Act shall have effect as if any reference in section 1 to a registered medical practitioner and to a hospital vested in [the Secretary of State] included respectively a reference to such a person as is mentioned in paragraph (*c*) of this subsection and to a hospital controlled as aforesaid, and as if section 2 were omitted.

(2)   The bodies to which this section applies are any force which is a visiting force within the meaning of any of the provisions of Part I of the Visiting Forces

Act 1952 and any headquarters within the meaning of the Schedule to the International Headquarters and Defence Organisations Act 1964; and for the purposes of this section–

   (*a*) a woman shall be treated as having a relevant association at any time with a body to which this section applies if at that time–

      (i) in the case of such a force as aforesaid, she had a relevant association within the meaning of the said Part I with the force; and

     (ii) in the case of such a headquarters as aforesaid, she was a member of the headquarters or a dependant within the meaning of the Schedule aforesaid of such a member; and

   (*b*) any reference to a member of a body to which this section applies shall be construed–

      (i) in the case of such a force as aforesaid, as a reference to a member of or of a civilian component of that force within the meaning of the said Part I; and

     (ii) in the case of such a headquarters as aforesaid, as a reference to a member of that headquarters within the meaning of the Schedule aforesaid.

Amendment
Sub-s (1): words in square brackets substituted by the Health Services Act 1980, s 1, Sch 1, para 17(2).

4 Conscientious objection to participation in treatment
(1) Subject to subsection (2) of this section, no person shall be under any duty, whether by contract or by any statutory or other legal requirement, to participate in any treatment authorised by this Act to which he has a conscientious objection:

Provided that in any legal proceedings the burden of proof of conscientious objection shall rest on the person claiming to rely on it.
(2) Nothing in subsection (1) of this section shall affect any duty to participate in treatment which is necessary to save the life or to prevent grave permanent injury to the physical or mental health of a pregnant woman.
(3) In any proceedings before a court in Scotland, a statement on oath by any person to the effect that he has a conscientious objection to participating in any treatment authorised by this Act shall be sufficient evidence for the purpose of discharging the burden of proof imposed upon him by subsection (1) of this section.

5 Supplementary provisions
[(1) No offence under the Infant Life (Preservation) Act 1929 shall be committed by a registered medical practitioner who terminates a pregnancy in accordance with the provisions of this Act.]
(2) For the purposes of the law relating to abortion, anything done with intent to procure [a woman's miscarriage (or, in the case of a woman carrying more than one foetus, her miscarriage of any foetus) is unlawfully done unless authorised by section 1 of this Act and, in the case of a woman carrying more than one foetus, anything done with intent to procure her miscarriage of any foetus is authorised by that section if–

   (*a*) the ground for termination of the pregnancy specified in subsection (1)(*d*) of that section applies in relation to any foetus and the thing is done for the purpose of procuring the miscarriage of that foetus, or

   (*b*) any of the other grounds for termination of the pregnancy specified in that section applies].

Amendment
Sub-s (1): substituted by the Human Fertilisation and Embryology Act 1990, s 37(4).
Sub-s (2): words in square brackets substituted by the Human Fertilisation and Embryology
Act 1990, s 37(5).

6 Interpretation
In this Act, the following expressions have meanings hereby assigned to them:–

> 'the law relating to abortion' means sections 58 and 59 of the Offences
> against the Person Act 1861, and any rule of law relating to the
> procurement of abortion;
> . . .

Amendment
Definition omitted repealed by the Health Services Act 1980, s 25(4), Sch 7.

7   Short title, commencement and extent
(1)   This Act may be cited as the Abortion Act 1967.
(2)   This Act shall come into force on the expiration of the period of six months
beginning with the date on which it is passed.
(3)   This Act does not extend to Northern Ireland.

Appendix 5.2

Abortion Regulations 1991, SI 1991/499

1 Citation and commencement

(1)   These Regulations may be cited as the Abortion Regulations 1991, and shall come into force on 1st April 1991.

(2)   These Regulations extend to England and Wales only.

2 Interpretation

In these Regulations 'the Act' means the Abortion Act 1967 and 'practitioner' means a registered medical practitioner.

3 Certificate of opinion

(1)   Any opinion to which section 1 of the Act refers shall be certified–

(*a*) in the case of a pregnancy terminated in accordance with section 1(1) of the Act, in the form set out in Part I of Schedule 1 to these Regulations, and

(*b*) in the case of a pregnancy terminated in accordance with section 1(4) of the Act, in the form set out in Part II of that Schedule.

(2)   Any certificate of an opinion referred to in section 1(1) of the Act shall be given before the commencement of the treatment for the termination of the pregnancy to which it relates.

(3)   Any certificate of an opinion referred to in section 1(4) of the Act shall be given before the commencement of the treatment for the termination of the pregnancy to which it relates or, if that is not reasonably practicable, not later than 24 hours after such termination.

(4)   Any such certificate as is referred to in paragraphs (2) and (3) of this regulation shall be preserved by the practitioner who terminated the pregnancy to which it relates for a period of not less than three years beginning with the date of the termination.

(5)   A certificate which is no longer to be preserved shall be destroyed by the person in whose custody it then is.

4 Notice of termination of pregnancy and information relating to the termination

(1)   Any practitioner who terminates a pregnancy in England or Wales shall give to the appropriate Chief Medical Officer–

(*a*) notice of the termination, and

(*b*) such other information relating to the termination as is specified in the form set out in Schedule 2 to these Regulations,

and shall do so by sending them to him in a sealed envelope within 7 days of the termination.

(2)   The appropriate Chief Medical Officer is–

(*a*) where the pregnancy was terminated in England, the Chief Medical Officer of the Department of Health, Richmond House, Whitehall, London, SW1A 2NS; or

(*b*) where the pregnancy was terminated in Wales, the Chief Medical Officer of the Welsh Office, Cathays Park, Cardiff, CF1 3NQ.

5 Restriction on disclosure of information

A notice given or any information furnished to a Chief Medical Officer in pursuance of these Regulations shall not be disclosed except that disclosure may be made–

(*a*) for the purposes of carrying out their duties–
  (i) to an officer of the Department of Health authorised by the Chief Medical Officer of that Department, or to an officer of the Welsh Office authorised by the Chief Medical Officer of that Office, as the case may be, or
  (ii) to the Registrar General or a member of his staff authorised by him; or

(*b*) for the purposes of carrying out his duties in relation to offences under the Act or the law relating to abortion, to the Director of Public Prosecutions or a member of his staff authorised by him; or

(*c*) for the purposes of investigating whether an offence has been committed under the Act or the law relating to abortion, to a police officer not below the rank of superintendent or a person authorised by him; or

(*d*) pursuant to a court order, for the purposes of proceedings which have begun; or

(*e*) for the purposes of bona fide scientific research; or

(*f*) to the practitioner who terminated the pregnancy; or

(*g*) to a practitioner, with the consent in writing of the woman whose pregnancy was terminated; or

(*h*) when requested by the President of the General Medical Council for the purpose of investigating whether there has been serious professional misconduct by a practitioner, to the President of the General Medical Council or a member of its staff authorised by him.

6 Revocations

The whole of the Regulations specified in Schedule 3 to these Regulations are revoked.

Appendix 5.3

Form of Certification under the Abortion Regulations 1991

Part I

IN CONFIDENCE

CERTIFICATE A

ABORTION ACT 1967

Not to be destroyed within three years of the date of operation

Certificate to be completed before an abortion is performed under Section 1(1) of the Act

I,............. (Name and qualifications of practitioner in block capitals) of ....
(Full address of practitioner)
Have/have not (delete as appropriate) seen/and examined (delete as appropriate) pregnant woman to whom this certificate relates at....................................
(full address of place at which patient was seen or examined) on ....and I ....
(Name and qualifications of practitioner in block capitals) of ....
(Full address of practitioner)..
Have/have not (delete as appropriate) seen/and examined (delete as appropriate) the pregnant woman to whom this certificate relates at ....
(Full address of place at which patient was seen or examined) on ....

We hereby certify that we are of the opinion, formed in good faith, that in the case of..................... (Full name of pregnant woman in block capitals) of ....
(Usual place of residence of pregnant woman in block capitals)

(Ring appropriate letter(s))

A the continuance of the pregnancy would involve risk to the life of the pregnant woman greater than if the pregnancy were terminated;

B the termination is necessary to prevent grave permanent injury to the physical or mental health of the pregnant woman;

C the pregnancy has NOT exceeded its 24th week and that the continuance of the pregnancy would involve risk, greater than if the pregnancy were terminated, of injury to the physical or mental health of the pregnant woman;

D the pregnancy has NOT exceeded its 24th week and that the continuance of the pregnancy would involve risk, greater than if the pregnancy were terminated, of injury to the physical or mental health of any existing child(ren) of the family of the pregnant woman;

E there is a substantial risk that if the child were born it would suffer from such physical or mental abnormalities as to be seriously handicapped.

This certificate of opinion is given before the commencement of the treatment for the termination of pregnancy to which it refers and relates to the circumstances of the pregnant woman's individual case.

Signed.................Date..................

Signed.................Date..................

Form HSA1 (revised 1991)

Form of Certification under the Abortion Regulations 1991: Emergency Case

---

Part II

IN CONFIDENCE

CERTIFICATE B

Not to be destroyed within three years of the date of operation

ABORTION ACT 1967

CERTIFICATE TO BE COMPLETED IN RELATION TO ABORTION PERFORMED IN EMERGENCY UNDER SECTION 1(4) OF THE ACT

I,...............(Name and qualifications of practitioner in block capitals) of..............
(Full address of practitioner) hereby certify that I am/was (delete as appropriate) of the opinion formed in good faith that it is/was (delete as appropriate) necessary immediately to terminate the pregnancy of..
(Full name of pregnant woman in block capitals) of ....
(Usual place of residence of pregnant woman in block capitals)

(Ring appropriate number)

in order

1 to save the life of the pregnant woman; or

2 to prevent grave permanent injury to the physical or mental health of the pregnant woman.

This certificate of opinion is given–

(Ring appropriate letter)

A before the commencement of the treatment for the termination of the pregnancy to which it relates; or,

if that is not reasonably practicable, then

B not later than 24 hours after such termination.

Signed ....

Date...

Appendix 5.5

Draft Application for Declaration that Court Determine Whether Termination in Adult's Best Interests

---

IN THE HIGH COURT OF JUSTICE   **No.**

FAMILY DIVISION

IN THE MATTER OF THE INHERENT JURISDICTION OF THE HIGH COURT

B E T W E E N :

NORTH EAST WESSEX HEALTHCARE NHS TRUST Claimant

– and –

EMILY BRONTE   **Defendant**

DRAFT / APPLICATION

The Defendant seeks:

1. a declaration that:

(*a*) the Defendant lacks the capacity to decide between termination and continuation of her current pregnancy;

(*b*) the best interests in relation to the termination or continuation of her current pregnancy be determined

2. an order that the costs of these proceedings be provided for.

Appendix 5.6

Draft Order that in Best Interests for Adult to Undergo Termination

---

IN THE HIGH COURT OF JUSTICE   **No.**

FAMILY DIVISION

IN THE MATTER OF THE INHERENT JURISDICTION OF THE HIGH COURT

Before Mr Justice Hardy

B E T W E E N :

           NORTH EAST WESSEX HEALTHCARE NHS TRUST Claimant

           – and –

           EMILY BRONTE   **Defendant**

           DRAFT / ORDER

UPON HEARING Mr Jude Obscure, Counsel for the Claimant, and Miss Jane Austen, Counsel for the Defendant

AND ON HEARING evidence from Mr Dickens and from the Defendant

and upon reading the evidence filed herein

IT IS DECLARED THAT:

(*a*) The Defendant lacks the capacity to consent to a termination of her current pregnancy.

(*b*) It is in her best interests that it should be terminated.

(*c*) In the present circumstances it is lawful for the Defendant's current pregnancy to be terminated in spite of her inability to consent to this procedure.

(*d*) The Claimant and/or the responsible attending medical practitioners, nurses and health care staff may lawfully furnish such treatment and nursing care whether at hospital or elsewhere under medical supervision as may be app. opriate to ensure that the pregnancy may be terminated and that the Defendant retains the greatest dignity possible.

AND IT IS ORDERED THAT:

(1) In the event of a material change in the existing circumstances occurring each party shall have liberty to apply for such further or other declaration or orders as may be just;

(2) No person shall disclose or publish in connection with these proceedings nor when publishing the text of the whole or any part of this order, save for the purpose of caring for the Defendant or for the purpose of communications with any person exercising a function authorised by statute or by any court of competent jurisdiction, the name, address or photograph of:

     (*a*) the Claimant or its hospital;

     (*b*) the Defendant or any family members;

     (*c*) the responsible treating medical practitioners, nursing staff and care assistants or workers;

     (*d*) any witness, other than an expert witness, who gives evidence in these proceedings whether by statement or otherwise in writing or orally; and

(3) BY CONSENT the Claimant shall pay one-half of the costs of the Official Solicitor.

Dated etc

Appendix 5.7

BMA: The Law and Ethics of Abortion

BMA
March 1997
Revised December 1999

Summary
Abortion is a very sensitive issue and one on which members of the BMA hold a wide diversity of views. As with all ethical dilemmas, decisions must be reached by weighing the benefits and harms. Doctors must act within the boundaries of the law and of their own conscience. The BMA recommends that doctors should not be encouraged to stretch practice to the boundaries of what is legally permissible.

Legal considerations

The Law on Abortion in England, Scotland and Wales
Abortion in England, Scotland and Wales is governed by the Abortion Act 1967 as amended by the Human Fertilisation and Embryology Act 1990. This states that a registered medical practitioner may lawfully terminate a pregnancy, in an NHS hospital or on premises approved for this purpose, if two registered medical practitioners are of the opinion, formed in good faith:

'(*a*) that the pregnancy has not exceeded its twenty-fourth week and that the continuance of the pregnancy would involve risk, greater than if the pregnancy were terminated, of injury to the physical or mental health of the pregnant woman or any existing children of her family; or
(*b*) that the termination is necessary to prevent grave permanent injury to the physical or mental health of the pregnant woman; or
(*c*) that the continuance of the pregnancy would involve risk to the life of the pregnant woman, greater that if the pregnancy were terminated; or
(*d*) that there is a substantial risk that if the child were born it would suffer from such physical or mental abnormalities as to be seriously handicapped.'

In addition, where a doctor 'is of the opinion, formed in good faith, that the termination is immediately necessary to save the life or to prevent grave permanent injury to the physical or mental health of the pregnant woman' the opinion of a second registered medical practitioner is not required. Nor, in these limited circumstances, are there restrictions on where the procedure may be carried out.

The 1990 amendments to the Act removed preexisting links with the Infant Life Preservation Act 1929 which had made it illegal to 'destroy the life of a child capable of being born alive' with an assumption that a child was capable of being born alive after 28 weeks gestation. Thus, terminations carried out under sections 1(1)(b) to 1(1)(d) of the Act may be performed at any gestational age.

The question of what constitutes a 'serious handicap' under section 1(1)(d) is not addressed in the legislation. It is a matter of clinical judgment and accepted practice. In assessing the seriousness of a handicap, the following criteria may be used:

219

- the probability of effective treatment, either in utero or after birth;
- the child's probable potential for self-awareness and potential ability to communicate with others; and
- the suffering that would be experienced by the child when born or by the people caring for the child.

The law on abortion in Northern Ireland

The Abortion Act 1967 does not extend to Northern Ireland. The law on abortion in Northern Ireland is different and is based on the Offences Against The Person Act 1861 which makes it an offence to 'procure a miscarriage ... unlawfully'. The *Bourne* judgement of 1939, in which a London gynaecologist was found not guilty of an offence under this Act for performing an abortion on a 14 year old who was pregnant as a result of rape, was based on an interpretation of the word unlawfullyin this Act. The defence argued, and the judge accepted, that in the particular circumstances of the case, the operation was not unlawful since continuation of the pregnancy would severely affect the young woman's mental health. In reaching this decision, the judge turned to the wording of the Infant Life (Preservation) Act 1929 which gave protection from prosecution if the act was carried out in good faith 'for the purpose only of preserving the life of the mother'. This formed the basis of the judgment and extended the grounds for a lawful abortion to include the mental and physical well-being of the woman. Whereas the law in England, Scotland and Wales is covered by the 1967 Act, Northern Ireland has been left with the task of interpreting this word 'unlawfully' in the 1861 Offences Against the Person Act using also the 1945 Criminal Justice Act (Northern Ireland) (under which the 1929 Infant Life (Preservation) Act was applied to Northern Ireland) with the precedent set in *Bourne*.

It is known that abortions are carried out in Northern Ireland and that abortion is lawful in some circumstances. The cases of *K* and *A* in 1993 and 1994 respectively confirm this but in the judgment in A the judge stated that:

> 'The doctor's act is lawful where the continuance of the pregnancy would adversely affect the mental or physical health of the mother ... The adverse effect must, however, be a real and serious one and it will always be a question of fact and degree whether the perceived effect of non termination is s: fficiently grave to warrant terminating the unborn child'.

This judgment further clarifies the circumstances in which abortion is lawful in Northern Ireland. Doctors in Northern Ireland wishing to discuss particular cases or to seek advice on the law may contact the local BMA office. The BMA has policy supporting the extension of the Abortion Act to Northern Ireland (Annual Representatives Meeting 1985).

Conscientious Objection Clause

Legal scope

The Abortion Act 1967 has a conscientious objection clause which permits doctors to refuse to participate in terminations but which obliges them to provide necessary treatment in an emergency when the woman's life may be jeopardised. The BMA supports the right of doctors to have a conscientious objection to termination of pregnancy and believes that such doctors should not be marginalised. Some doctors have complained of being harassed and discriminated against because of their conscientious objection to termination of pregnancy. There have also been reports of doctors, who carry out abortions, being subjected to harassment and abuse. The Association abhors all such behaviour and any BMA members who feel they are being pressured, abused or harassed because of their views about termination of pregnancy, should contact their regional office for advice and support.

Appendix 5.7

The scope of the conscientious objection clause, in the 1967 Act, was clarified by a Parliamentary answer in December 1991. This made clear that conscientious objection was only intended to be applied to participation in treatment, although hospital managers had been asked to apply the principle, at their discretion, to those ancillary staff who were involved in the handling of fetuses and fetal tissue.

The same view emerged from the House of Lords' decision in case of *Janaway v Salford Health Authority* in 1988 when a doctor's secretary (Janaway) refused to type the referral letter for an abortion and claimed a conscientious objection under the Act. The House of Lords, in interpreting the word 'participate' in this context, decided to give the word its ordinary and natural meaning - that is, that in order to claim conscientious exemption under section 4 of the Act, the objector had to be required to actually take part in administering treatment in a hospital or approved centre. In the same case the judge went on to say that: 'The regulations do not appear to contemplate that the signing of the certificate would form part of the treatment for the termination of pregnancy'. This would seem to support the view that general practitioners cannot claim exemption from giving advice or performing the preparatory steps to arrange an abortion if the request for abortion meets the legal requirements. Such steps include referral to another doctor as appropriate.

Doctors with a conscientious objection to abortion should make their views known to the patient and enable the patient to see another doctor without delay if that is the patient's wish. Although they may not impose their views on others who do not share them doctors with a conscientious objection may explain their views to the patient if invited to do so.

General practitioners with a conscientious objection, who are working in a group practice, may ask a partner to see patients seeking termination. The restrictions imposed by paragraph 4 of the Terms of Service for Doctors, however, may prevent single-handed general practitioners from referring patients to another general practitioner and oblige them to refer directly to a specialist.

The position of medical students was clarified in personal communication with the Department of Health which has been passed to the Association for information. This made clear that the conscientious objection clause can be used by students to opt out of witnessing abortions. The BMA's advice is that those who have a conscientious objection should disclose that fact to supervisors, managers or GP partners (whichever is appropriate) at as early a stage as possible so that this fact can be taken into account when planning provisions for patient care.

Distinction between legal and moral duties
In some cases a distinction can be made between the legal and ethical obligations. Whilst noting the legal view, the BMA considers that some things which arguably fall outside the legal scope of the conscience clause, such as completion of the form for abortion, are arguably an integral part of the abortion procedure. In this case, the BMA considers that completion of a form for abortion falls morally within the scope of the conscience clause. Other preliminary procedures, such as clerking in the patient, are incidental to the termination and are considered outwith the scope of the conscience clause both legally and morally. Generally it will not be beneficial for women undergoing termination to be cared for by health professionals who feel distressed or unhappy about their involvement. Nevertheless where such tasks are unavoidable, health professionals must pursue a non-judgmental approach to the women concerned.

Conscientious objection applied to contraceptive services
There has, in the past, been some uncertainty about whether certain types of contraceptives, such as hormonal emergency contraception and intra uterine devices should be classed as abortifacients which could be issued only under the

terms of the Abortion Act. This question was resolved by a Parliamentary answer in May 1983 in which it was clarified that the prevention of implantation does not constitute the 'procuring of a miscarriage' within the terms of the Offences Against the Persons Act 1861. This interpretation was tested and confirmed in the case of *R v HS Dhingra* in 1991.

Although, legally, the use of contraceptives designed to prevent implantation does not constitute an abortion, the BMA recognises that some doctors, believing that life begins at fertilisation, may have an ethical objection to their use. Doctors holding this view are not obliged to prescribe these forms of contraception but must refer the patient to another doctor who would be willing to comply with the request. Guidelines on the use of emergency contraception are available from the Royal College of Obstetricians & Gynaecologists.

Early medical abortion

Since 1991 mifepristone (formerly known as RU486) has been available in England, Scotland and Wales for early medical abortions. These can be performed up to nine weeks' gestation and must comply with the terms of the 1967 Act (as amended). A 1990 amendment to the Abortion Act specifies that the power to approve premises for termination of pregnancy includes the power to approve premises for the administration of medicinal terminations. Without this amendment, the administration of mifepristone would have been lawful only if carried out on premises approved for surgical terminations.

Late abortion for fetal abnormality

Under the law in England, Scotland and Wales, a pregnancy may be terminated at any gestation if there is a 'substantial risk that if the child were born it would suffer from such physical or mental abnormalities as to be seriously handicapped'. Practical guidelines for health professionals involved with terminations for fetal abnormality are available from the Royal College of Obstetricians & Gynaecologists.

Women need to be given time to understand the nature and severity of fetal abnormality and, with the help of specialised counselling where appropriate, to reach a decision about how to proceed. The purpose of antenatal screening is to extend the choice available to the pregnant woman and to allow her to make an informed decision about whether to continue with the pregnancy or seek a termination. Women should not be rushed into making these important decisions but, if a firm decision is made to terminate the pregnancy, this should proceed without undue delay. Health and other appropriate professionals should provide support before and after the termination.

Selective abortion of multiple pregnancy

Until 1990 the legality of selective reduction of multiple pregnancies was unclear. This was clarified by section 37(5) of the Human Fertilisation & Embryology Act which amended the Abortion Act to explicitly include 'in the case of a woman carrying more than one fetus, her miscarriage of any fetus'. Thus, selective reduction of pregnancy would be lawful provided the circumstances matched the criteria for termination of pregnancy set out in the 1967 Act (as amended) and the procedure was carried out in an NHS hospital or premises approved for terminations. The same ethical and legal considerations apply to termination of all or part of a multiple pregnancy as to the termination of a singleton pregnancy. Under the new section 5(2) of the Abortion Act selective reduction of a multiple pregnancy may lawfully be performed if:

> '(*a*) the ground for termination of the pregnancy specified in subsection (1)(*d*) of [section 1] applies in relation to any fetus and the thing is done for the purpose of procuring the miscarriage of that fetus; or

(*b*) any of the other grounds for termination of the pregnancy specified in that section applies'.

Thus it has been suggested that a general risk of serious handicap to the fetuses, if the multiple pregnancy is not reduced, would not be covered by the Act and the risk must be to a specific fetus. Alternately where there is an increased risk to the mother, as a result of the multiple pregnancy, the selective reduction may be lawful under section 1(1)(*a*), (*b*) or (*c*).

The BMA considers selective termination to be justifiable where the procedure is recommended for medical reasons. Women who have a multiple pregnancy should be carefully counselled where medical opinion is that continuation, without selective reduction, will result in the loss of all the fetuses but they cannot be compelled or pressured to accept selective abortion. The Association does not, however, consider it acceptable to choose which fetuses to abort on anything other than medical grounds. Where there are no medical indications for aborting particular fetuses, the choice should be a random one. The Association would not consider it acceptable, when making this decision, to accede to the parents' desire for a male or a female child.

Abortion on grounds of fetal sex
Fetal sex is not one of the criteria for abortion listed in the Abortion Act of 1967 and therefore termination on this ground alone has been challenged as outwith the law. There may be circumstances, however, in which termination of pregnancy on grounds of fetal sex would be lawful. It has been suggested that if two doctors, acting in good faith, formed the opinion that the pregnant woman's health or that of her existing children would be put at greater risk than if she terminated the pregnancy, the abortion would be arguably lawful under section 1(1)(a) of the Abortion Act. The Association believes that it is normally unethical to terminate a pregnancy on the grounds of fetal sex alone except in cases of severe x-linked disorders. The pregnant woman's views about the effect of the sex of the fetus on her situation and on her existing children should nevertheless be carefully considered. In some circumstances doctors may come to the conclusion that the effects are so severe as to provide ethical justification for a termination. They should be prepared to justify the decision if it were challenged.

Ethical Consideration

Moral arguments
People generally take one of three main stances on abortion: pro-abortion, anti-abortion and the middle ground that abortion is acceptable in some circumstances. The main arguments for each of these positions is set out below.

Arguments used in support of abortion
Those who support the wide availability of abortion consider that abortion is not wrong in itself and need not involve undesirable consequences. These arguments tend not to recognise fetal rights or to acknowledge the fetus to be a person. According to some, abortion is a matter of a woman's right to exercise control over her own body. Moralists who judge actions by their consequences alone could argue that abortion is equivalent to a deliberate failure to conceive a child and since contraception is widely available, abortion should be too. Some think that even if the fetus is a person, its rights are very limited and do not weigh significantly against the interests of people who have already been born, such as parents or existing children of the family. The interests of society at large might outweigh any right accorded to the fetus in some circumstances, such as if, for example, overpopulation or famine threatened that society. In such cases, abortion might be seen by some people as moving from a neutral act to one which should be encouraged. Similarly utilitarians who see a duty to promote the

greatest happiness and maximise the number of worthwhile lives, could argue that there should be as few as possible unwanted children in the world.

Most people who support this position do so on the basis that the overriding principle is the woman's right to choose what happens to her body. This use of the language of 'choice' conveys approval regardless of the type of pressures the individual faces and any constraints on her freedom to make a genuine choice.

Arguments used against abortion
Some people consider that abortion is wrong in any circumstances because it fails to recognise the rights of the fetus or because it challenges the notion of the sanctity of all human life. Some argue that permitting abortion diminishes the respect society feels for other vulnerable humans, possibly leading to their involuntary euthanasia. Those who consider that an embryo, from the moment of conception, is a human being with full moral status, see abortion as killing in the same sense as the murder of any other person. Those who take this view cannot accept that women should be allowed to obtain abortion without legal repercussions, however difficult the lives of those women or their existing families are made as a result.

Such views may be based on religious or moral convictions that each human life has unassailable intrinsic value, which is not diminished by any impairment or suffering that may be involved for the individual living that life. It is also argued that abortion treats humans merely as a means to an end in that abortion can be seen as a discarding of a fetus in which the pregnant woman no longer has any interest. Many worry that the availability of abortion on grounds of fetal abnormality encourages prejudice towards any person with a handicap and insidiously creates the impression that the only valuable people are those who conform to some ill-defined stereotype of 'normality'.

Some people who oppose abortion in general, concede that it may be justifiable in very exceptional cases such as where it is the result of rape or the consequence of exploitation of a young girl or a mentally incompetent woman. Risk to the mother's life may be another justifiable exception but only where abortion is the only option. It would thus not be seen as justifiable to abort a fetus if the life of both fetus and mother could be saved by any other solution.

Arguments used to support abortion in some circumstances
Many people argue that abortion may be justified in a greater number of circumstances than those conceded by anti-abortionists but that it would be undesirable to allow abortion on demand. To do so might incur undesirable effects, such as encouraging irresponsible attitudes to contraception. It could also lead to a devaluation of the lives of viable fetuses and trivialise the potential psychological effects of abortion on women and on health professionals.

These types of argument are based on the premise that the embryo starts off without rights, although having a special status from conception in view of its potential for development, and that it acquires rights and status throughout its development. The notion of developing fetal rights and practical factors, such as the possible distress to the pregnant woman, nurses, doctors or other children in the family, gives rise to the view that early abortion is more acceptable than late abortion.

Some people support this position on pragmatic grounds, believing that abortions will always be sought by women who are desperate and that it is better for society to provide abortion services which are safe and which can be monitored and regulated, rather than to allow 'back-street' practices.

The BMA's view on abortion
In the 1970s and 1980s the BMA approved policy statements supporting the 1967 Abortion Act as 'a practical and humane piece of legislation' and calling for its expansion to Northern Ireland. The BMA does not consider that abortion is

unethical but as with any act having profound moral implications, the justifica-tions must be commensurate with the consequences. The BMA's advice to its members is to act within the boundaries of the law and of their own conscience. Patients are, however, entitled to receive objective medical advice regardless of their doctor's personal views for or against abortion. Furthermore, a doctor could be sued for damages if, because of a failure to refer, a delay is caused which results in the woman being unable to obtain a termination.

Fetal pain
Whether, and at what stage, a fetus feels pain has been a matter of much recent debate and past practice has been partly influenced by Department of Health advice. Interpretation of the evidence on fetal pain is conflicting with some arguing that the fetus has the potential to feel pain at ten weeks' gestation, others arguing that it is unlikely to feel pain before 26 weeks gestation and still others arguing for some unspecified gestational period in between.

There is clearly a need for further research to provide more conclusive evidence about the experiences and sensations of the fetus in utero. In the meantime the BMA recommends that, when carrying out any surgical procedures (whether an abortion or a therapeutic intervention) on the fetus in utero, due consideration must be given to appropriate measures for minimising the risk of pain. This should include an assessment of the most recent evidence available. Even if there is no incontrovertible evidence that fetuses feel pain the use of pain relief, when carrying out invasive procedures, may help to relieve the anxiety of the parents and of health professionals.

Consent

The competent adult
With consent to termination of pregnancy as with consent for other medical procedures, there are certain criteria which must be met in order for the consent to be valid. The woman must have sufficient competence to understand the procedure and its alternatives in broad terms and to make a decision, the consent must be voluntary and the decision must be made on the basis of sufficient, accurate information.

In 1993 Mr Justice Thorpe outlined the three stages to the decision whether or not to accept medical treatment as (1) to take in and retain treatment information (2) to believe it and (3) to weigh that information, balancing risks and needs. This formulation has been adopted in subsequent cases and forms a good working test for assessing capacity to consent to or refuse medical treatment both in relation to adults and older children.

The incompetent adult
No one can consent to treatment on behalf of another adult (over the age of 18) regardless of that individual's level of capacity. Decisions about treatment, or medical procedures, for mentally incompetent adults must be made on the basis of an assessment of their best interests. Health professionals approached by a pregnant woman lacking the capacity to give a valid consent must use their professional judgment to assess the patient's best interests. From a legal per-spective, provided the terms of the Abortion Act are complied with, and a termination is considered to be the best option for the patient, a High Court declaration will not be required. From a moral perspective, the need for an abortion to be considered in respect of a mentally incompetent woman will usually raise questions about that patient's ability to consent to sexual intercourse and is likely to require investigation as to whether a criminal offence has occurred. The BMA and Law Society have jointly issued guidance on the law relating to mental capacity and sexual relationships (chapter 9 of *Assessment of Mental Capacity*). This recognises the right of mentally disordered people to

enter voluntarily into sexual relationships but also focuses on the obligation to protect vulnerable adults from abusive relationships. If there are grounds to believe that the pregnancy has resulted from unlawful sexual intercourse (rape of an unwilling woman or one who is unable to consent), immediate steps must be taken to protect the woman from further possible abuse and the occurrence must be investigated.

Competent minors

Any competent young person, regardless of age, can independently seek medical advice and give valid consent to medical treatment. This legal position was established in the 1985 House of Lords' ruling in the Gillick case. Thus people under 16 are legally able to consent on their own behalf to any surgical, medical or dental procedure or treatment if, in the doctor's opinion, they are capable of understanding the nature and possible consequences of the procedure. It is clearly desirable for young people to have their parents' support for important and potentially life-changing decisions. Sometimes, however, young patients do not wish their parents to be informed of a medical consultation or its outcome and the doctor generally should not override patients' views. Doctors have an obligation, however, to encourage the patient voluntarily to involve parents. Young patients are likely to need help and support if the treatment sought has serious implications, such as contraception, abortion, or treatment for sexually transmitted disease. In very exceptional cases where the doctor has reason to believe that the pregnancy is the result of child abuse, incest or exploitation, a breach of confidentiality may be necessary and justifiable. The patient should be told in advance that secrecy in such cases cannot be guaranteed and must be offered appropriate help, counselling and support.

The main exception to these general rules is if the young woman is a ward of court, in which case the courts will need to approve a termination or other serious medical intervention. It is thus particularly important that it is always clear from the medical records that the child is a ward of court. Similarly if a young woman seeking termination is in care she should be encouraged to involve the local social services. If she refuses to consent to information being shared, legal advice should be sought before proceeding with the termination.

When consulted by a young woman under 16 requesting abortion the doctor should consider in particular:

- Whether the young woman understands the potential risks and possible longer-term effects of the proposed termination.
- Whether the young woman has sufficient maturity ie '*Gillick* competence' to make this decision and give a valid consent.

Parental support. The value of parental support must be discussed with the patient. Doctors should encourage young people to discuss their situation with parents but must provide reassurance that their confidentiality will be maintained. If the young woman is unwilling to inform her parents of the consultation there may be another adult, perhaps an aunt or a friend of the family, in whom she would be prepared to confide. The importance of support during and after the termination should be discussed.

Appropriate communications with the patient's own GP. If the doctor consulted is not the patient's own general practitioner, the young woman should be encouraged to consent to information being provide to her GP. It should be explained that this is in her own medical interest and an assurance given that confidentiality will be maintained but that, if she refuses, her wishes will be respected.

Requests by young people for abortion and contraceptive services, without parental involvement, raise serious ethical dilemmas for doctors. The BMA takes the view that establishing a trusting relationship between the patient and doctor at this stage will do more to promote health than if doctors refuse to see young patients without parental consent. Further information is available in Confidentiality and Under 16s, available from the BMA Medical Ethics Department.

Incompetent minors

If a young woman is pregnant and is not considered to be *Gillick*-competent she should be encouraged to involve her parents in decision-making and the parents may, legally, consent on her behalf. The word 'parents' includes other holders of parental responsibility including, in relation to a child in care, the local authority. Relatives who are not holders of parental responsibility cannot consent to treatment for a minor. If the young woman refuses consent to parental involvement the Official Solicitor's office has advised that legal advice should be sought about whether the parents should be informed, against her wishes, and whether the termination can proceed. This may require an application to the courts.

Partners' views

The decision to terminate a pregnancy, within the broad framework accepted by society, rests with the woman and her doctors. Legally, the woman's spouse or partner has no right to demand or refuse a termination. It is, however, good practice to encourage women to discuss such decisions with their partners. Where a woman refuses to share information with her partner, confidentiality must be maintained unless there are exceptional reasons to justify a breach of confidentiality.

Confidentiality

Adults

Patients have a right to expect that doctors will not disclose any personal health information to a third party without consent. Women seeking termination of pregnancy are likely to be particularly concerned about the confidentiality of this information and doctors should be sensitive to this.

Sometimes doctors are asked to remove information about previous terminations from a patient's medical records. The BMA advises doctors to be very wary of removing relevant medical information from a patient's record, especially if further consultations or treatment have arisen on the basis of this information. To remove relevant medical information may make the doctor's later decisions appear unsupported and could also be detrimental to the future care of the patient.

If the doctor consulted is not the patient's own general practitioner, the woman should be encouraged to consent to information being provided to her GP. If, however, she refuses to consent to the sharing of this information her wishes should be respected. Where such consent is withheld and the patient's GP is a fundholder, the procedure will be chargeable to the Health Authority in order to ensure that confidentiality is maintained.

Minors

The duty of confidentiality owed to a person under 16 is as great as the duty owed to any other person. An explicit request by a patient that information should not be disclosed to particular people, or indeed to any third party, must be respected except in the most exceptional circumstances, for example, where the health, safety or welfare of some person would otherwise be at serious risk. The exceptions set out above, where the child is a ward of court, or is in care, should be noted.

Appendix 5.7

Summary
The Abortion Act requires doctors to make an assessment in the context of each case. They must balance a respect for human life with the potential impact of the pregnancy and birth on the woman's physical and mental health and the well-being of existing siblings. The Association supports this position. Blanket rules cannot be applied to such sensitive and difficult decisions, which require an understanding of the woman's individual needs. A decision to terminate a pregnancy is never an easy one. In making these decisions, patients and doctors should ensure that the decision is supported by appropriate information and counselling about the options and implications.

Requests for advice or further information should be directed to: Medical Ethics Department, British Medical Association, BMA House, Tavistock Square, London WC1H 9JP.

Appendix 6.1

Court of Appeal Guidelines: *RE MB* Guidelines and *St George's Healthcare v S* Guidelines

---

Re MB *(an adult: medical treatment)*
[1997] 2 FCR 541, [1997] 2 FLR 426, CA

'Conclusions on capacity to decide
All the decisions made in the caesarian section cases to which we have referred arose in circumstances of urgency or extreme urgency. The evidence was in general limited in scope and the mother was not always represented as a party. With the exception of *Re S* (supra), in all the cases the court decided that the mother did not have the capacity to make the decision. In these extremely worrying situations, it is important to keep in mind the basic principles we have outlined, and the court should approach the crucial question of competence bearing the following considerations in mind. They are not intended to be determinative in every case, for the decision must inevitably depend upon the particular facts before the court.

1.   Every person is presumed to have the capacity to consent to or to refine medical treatment unless and until the presumption is rebutted.

2.   A competent woman who has the capacity to decide may for religious reasons, other reasons, for rational or irrational reasons or for no reason at all, choose not to have medical intervention, even though the consequence may be the death or serious handicap of the child she bears, or her own death. In that event the courts do not have the jurisdiction to declare medical intervention lawful and the question of her own best interests objectively considered, does not arise.

3.   Irrationality is here used to connote a decision which is so outrageous in its defiance of logic or of accepted moral standards that no sensible person who had applied his mind to the question to be decided it could have arrived at it. As Kennedy and Grubb (*Medical Law* (2nd edn, 1994)) point out, it might be otherwise if a decision is based on a misperception of reality (eg the blood is poisoned because it is red). Such a misperception will be more readily accepted to be a disorder of the mind. Although it might be thought that irrationality sits uneasily with competence to decide, panic, indecisiveness and irrationality in themselves do not as such amount to incompetence, but they may be symptoms or evidence of incompetence. The graver the consequences of the decision, the commensurately greater the level of competence is required to take the decision: *Re T* (supra), *Sidaway* (supra) at page 904 and *Gillick v West Norfolk and Wisbech Area Health Authority* [1986] 1 AC 112, 169 and 186.

4.   A person lacks capacity if some impairment or disturbance of mental function- tioning renders the person unable to make a decision whether to consent to or to refuse treatment: That inability to make a decision will occur when:

   (*a*)   the patient is unable to comprehend and retain the information which is material to the decision, especially as to the likely consequences of having or not having the treatment in question.
   (*b*)   the patient is unable to use the information and weigh it in the balance as part of the process of arriving at the decision. If as Thorpe J observed in

Re C (supra), a compulsive disorder or phobia from which the patient suffers stifles belief in the information presented to her, then the decision may not be a true one. As Lord Cockburn CI put it in *Banks v Goodfellow* (1370) LB. 5 QB 549 at p 569:

'One object may be so forced upon the attention of the invalid as to shut out all others that might require consideration.'

5. The 'temporary factors' mentioned by Lord Donaldson MR in *Re T* (supra) (confusion, shock, fatigue, pain or drugs) may completely erode capacity but those concerned must be satisfied that such factors are operating to such a degree that the ability to decide is absent.

6. Another such influence may be panic induced by fear. Again careful scrutiny of the evidence is necessary because fear of an operation may be a rational reason for refusal to undergo it. Fear may be also, however, paralyse the will and thus destroy the capacity to make a decision.'

St George's Healthcare NHS Trust v S
[1999] Fam 26, [1998] 2 FCR 685, CA

30 July. The court handed down the following guidelines to replace those set out at the end of the judgment handed down on 7 May:

'We have now received written submissions from Mr Havers and Mr Gordon. We understand that MS's solicitor has taken soundings from the Royal College of Midwives, the Royal College of Nursing, the United Kingdom Central Council for Nursing, Midwifery and Health Visiting, the Law Society's mental health and disability subcommittee, MIND, the Association for Improvements in the Maternity Services, the National Childbirth Trust, the Maternity Alliance and the Association of Community Health Councils for England and Wales. We further understand that Mr Havers received comments from the British Medical Association, who in the available time have not had any practical opportunity to carry out a formal consultation process, and the Department of Health. We have also received a letter from the Head of Legal Services for Merton London Borough Council confirming that no submissions in relation to the proposed guidelines would be made 'as they do not appear to impact upon the role of an approved social worker.'

In the light of these written submissions we have considered the draft guidelines set out at the end of the judgment handed down on 7 May, which are now superseded.

The case highlighted some major problems which could arise for hospital authorities when a pregnant woman presented at hospital, the possible need for Caesarean surgery was diagnosed, and there was serious doubt about the patient's capacity to accept or decline treatment. To avoid any recurrence of the unsatisfactory events recorded in the judgment, and after consultations with the President of the Family Division and the Official Solicitor, and in the light of the written submissions from Mr Havers and Mr Gordon, we shall attempt to repeat and expand the advice given in *Re MB (an adult: medical treatment)* [1997] 2 FCR 541 [*see above*]. This advice also applies to any cases involving capacity when surgical or invasive treatment may be needed by a patient, whether female or male. References to 'she' and 'her' should be read accordingly. It also extends, where relevant, to medical practitioners and health professionals generally as well as to hospital authorities.

Appendix 6.1

The guidelines depend on basic legal principles which we summarise:

(i) They have no application where the patient is competent to accept or refuse treatment. In principle a patient may remain competent notwithstanding detention under the Mental Health Act 1983.

(ii) If the patient is competent and refuses consent to the treatment, an application to the High Court for a declaration would be pointless. In this situation the advice given to the patient should be recorded. For their own protection hospital authorities should seek unequivocal assurances from the patient (to be recorded in writing) that the refusal represents an informed decision, that is, that she understands the nature of and reasons for the proposed treatment, and the risks and likely prognosis involved in the decision to refuse or accept it. If the patient is unwilling to sign a written indication of this refusal, this too should be noted in writing. Such a written indication is merely a record for evidential purposes. It should not be confused with or regarded as a disclaimer.

(iii) If the patient is incapable of giving or refusing consent, either in the long term or temporarily (eg due to unconsciousness), the patient must be cared for according to the authority's judgment of the patient's best interests. Where the patient has given an advance directive, before becoming incapable, treatment and care should normally be subject to the advance directive. However, if there is reason to doubt the reliability of the advance directive (for example it may sensibly be thought not to apply to the circumstances which have arisen), then an application for a declaration may be made.

Concern over capacity

(iv) The authority should identify as soon as possible whether there is concern about a patient's competence to consent to or refuse treatment.

(v) If the capacity of the patient is seriously in doubt it should be assessed as a matter of priority. In many such cases the patient's general practitioner or other responsible doctor may be sufficiently qualified to make the necessary assessment, but in serious or complex cases involving difficult issues about the future health and well being or even the life of the patient, the issue of capacity should be examined by an independent psychiatrist, ideally one approved under section 12(2) of the Mental Health Act 1983. If following this assessment there remains a serious doubt about the patient's competence, and the seriousness or complexity of the issues in the particular case may require the involvement of the court, the psychiatrist should further consider whether the patient is incapable by reason of mental disorder of managing her property or affairs. If so the patient may be unable to instruct a solicitor and will require a guardian ad litem in any court proceedings. The authority should seek legal advice as quickly as possible. If a declaration is to be sought the patient's solicitors should be informed immediately and if practicable they should have a proper opportunity to take instructions and apply for legal aid where necessary. Potential witnesses for the authority should be made aware of the criteria laid down in *Re MB (an adult: medical treatment)* [1997] 2 FCR 541 [*see above*] and this case, together with any guidance issued by the Department of Health and the British Medical Association.

(vi) If the patient is unable to instruct solicitors, or is believed to be incapable of doing so, the authority or its legal advisers must notify the Official Solicitor and invite him to act as guardian ad litem. If the Official Solicitor agrees he will no doubt wish, if possible, to arrange for the patient to be interviewed to ascertain her wishes and to explore the reasons for any refusal of treatment. The Official Solicitor can be contacted through the Urgent Court Business Officer out of office hours on (0171) 936 6000.

The hearing

(vii) The hearing before the judge should be inter partes. As the order made in her absence will not be binding on the patient unless she is represented either by a guardian ad litem (if incapable of giving instructions) or (if capable) by counsel or solicitor, a declaration granted ex parte is of no assistance to the authority. Although the Official Solicitor will not act for a patient if she is capable of instructing a solicitor, the court may in any event call on the Official Solicitor (who has considerable expertise in these matters) to assist as an amicus curiae.

(viii) It is axiomatic that the judge must be provided with accurate and all the relevant information. This should include the reasons for the proposed treatment, the risks involved in the proposed treatment, and in not proceeding with it, whether any alternative treatment exists, and the reason, if ascertainable, why the patient is refusing the proposed treatment. The judge will need sufficient information to reach an informed conclusion about the patient's capacity, and, where it arises, the issue of best interest.

(ix) The precise terms of any order should be recorded and approved by the judge before its terms are transmitted to the authority. The patient should be accurately informed of the precise terms.

(x) Applicants for emergency orders from the High Court made without first issuing and serving the relevant applications and evidence in support have a duty to comply with the procedural requirements (and pay the court fees) as soon as possible after the urgency hearing.

Conclusion

There may be occasions when, assuming a serious question arises about the competence of the patient, the situation facing the authority may be so urgent and the consequences so desperate that it is impracticable to attempt to comply with these guidelines. The guidelines should be approached for what they are, that is, guidelines. Where delay may itself cause serious damage to the patient's health or put her life at risk then formulaic compliance with these guidelines would be inappropriate.'

Appendix 6.2

Draft Injunction Application Restraining Caesarean Section

DETAILS OF CLAIM

The claim is a declaration that the Claimant retains capacity to consent to or refuse medical treatment including treatment in connection with her current pregnancy and labour, alternatively that she had such capacity at the time she expressed an advance refusal to undergoing a Caesarean Section operation, and for an injunction to restrain the Defendants from forcibly performing a Caesarean Section on her against her will.

1. The Defendant is an NHS Trust responsible for the management of the Blankshire Hospital.

2. The Claimant is a patient at the said hospital and is receiving treatment in connection with her current pregnancy and labour.

3. In the course of her attendance at the Defendant's ante-natal clinic the Claimants informed Mr Deliverance, a consultant obstetrician, that she would not consent to any form of surgical delivery of her baby as such a procedure would be against her religious beliefs. At the time she made the said statement the Claimant fully understood the potential consequences of such a decision, including the risk that either she or her baby might die or be seriously injured.

4. The Claimant is now in labour and has been advised by the attending doctor that they intend to perform a Caesarean Section on her to deliver her baby, whether or not she consents to such a procedure. The Claimant has repeated to the said doctor her unwillingness to have such an operation on religious grounds, but he has ignored her.

5. In the circumstances the Claimant seeks a declaration that she is competent to make decisions for herself, alternatively was so competent at the time of the said attendance at the ante-natal clinic, and an injunction to restrain the Defendants, their servants or agents from performing any treatment to which she does not consent.

Appendix 6.3

Draft Order Preventing a Caesarean Section

IN THE HIGH COURT OF JUSTICE   **Case No**

FAMILY DIVISION

PRINCIPAL DISTRICT REGISTRY

THE HONOURABLE MR JUSTICE JONES

IN THE MATTER OF THE INHERENT JURISDICTION OF THE COURT

B E T W E E N :

WENDY PATIENT
Claimant

– and –

BLANKSHIRE NHS TRUST
Defendant

ORDER

UPON HEARING Ms Jane Smythe on behalf of the Claimant and Mr Alfred Jones on behalf of the Defendant

IT IS ORDERED THAT

1. The Claimant possesses the capacity to give or withhold her consent to medical treatment including treatment in connection with her current pregnancy and labour.

2. The Defendants, by their servants or agents are restrained from providing any treatment to the Claimant to which she does not give her consent.

3. Each parties to have liberty to apply for any further order on notice to the other party.

4. No order as to costs.

    DATED   1st April 2000

Appendix 6.4

Draft Application for Declaration Permitting Caesarean Section

DETAILS OF CLAIM

The claim is for an order and declaration that it shall be lawful notwithstanding her inability to consent thereto to provide the Defendant with such medical treatment in connection with her present labour, including, if necessary, Caesarean Section, the insertion of needles for intravenous infusions, and anaesthesia and such other treatment and care as may be necessary to cause her the least distress and to preserve for her the greatest dignity, and for reasonable force to be used for such purposes.

1. The Claimant is an NHS Trust responsible for the management of the Blankshire District Hospital and the provision of obstetric services there.

2. The Defendant is a patient at the said hospital and is in the course of labour in her first pregnancy.

3. The Defendant is incapable of making decisions about her care during the said labour by reason of a phobia against the insertion of needles in any part of her body. The phobia has deprived her of the ability to retain or use treatment information.

4. The medical practitioners attending the Defendant are of the opinion that her baby must be delivered by Caesarean Section within the next 6 hours, to avoid dangers to the health of both the Defendant and her baby, but the Defendant has refused to consent to such a procedure on the grounds that she will not allow doctors to administer the necessary anaesthetic by use of any needle inserted in her body.

5. It is in the Defendant's best interests that the treatment advised by the attending medical practitioners be provided and therefore the Claimant seeks a declaration that such treatment is lawful.

6. Full details of the evidence relied on are set out in the affidavits served herewith.

Appendix 6.5

Draft Declaration Permitting Caesarean Section

IN THE HIGH COURT OF JUSTICE   **Case No**

FAMILY DIVISION

PRINCIPAL DISTRICT REGISTRY

THE HONOURABLE MR JUSTICE JONES

IN THE MATTER OF THE INHERENT JURISDICTION OF THE COURT

B E T W E E N :

BLANKSHIRE NHS TRUST
Claimant

– and –

WENDY PATIENT
[by her Litigation Friend, the Official Solicitor]

Defendant

ORDER

UPON HEARING Mr Alfred Jones on behalf of the Claimant and Ms Jane Smythe on behalf of the Defendant

IT IS ORDERED AND DECLARED THAT:

1. The Official Solicitor, having consented, be appointed litigation friend of the Defendant.

2. It shall be lawful for 2 days from the date of this order notwithstanding the inability of the Defendant to consent thereto:

    (*a*) For the medical practitioners attending the Defendant to carry out such treatment as may in their opinion be necessary for the purposes of the Defendant's present labour, including, if in their professional opinion it is necessary in her best interests, delivery by Caesarean Section, the insertion of needles for the purposes of intravenous infusions, and anaesthesia;

    (*b*) For reasonable force to be used in the course of such treatment;

    (*c*) Generally to furnish such treatment and nursing care as may be appropriate to ensure that the Defendant suffers the least distress and retains the greatest dignity.

3. Each parties to have liberty to apply for any further order on notice to the other party.

4. No order as to costs.

    DATED

    [The form of words used has been taken from *Re MB* and *Re L*.]

Appendix 6.6

Draft Order Permitting Administration of Blood Products and Caesarean Section

IN THE HIGH COURT OF JUSTICE W141/96

FAMILY DIVISION

PRINCIPAL REGISTRY

Before

IN THE MATTER OF CHIGAGO HOPE (a minor)

AND IN THE MATTER OF THE INHERENT JURISDICTION OF THE HIGH COURT WITH RESPECT TO CHILDREN

B E T W E E N:

WEST WING NHS TRUST Claimant

– and –

CHICAGO HOPE
(A minor, by her Litigation Friend, the Official Solicitor) First Defendant

and

MARY HOPE Second Defendant

ORDER

UPON HEARING Counsel for the Claimant, First Defendant and Second Defendant,

AND UPON hearing the evidence of the Second Defendant and Dr Ross

and upon reading the evidence filed herein;

IT IS ORDERED THAT:

1. If it is the professional opinion of those medically responsible for the First Defendant that she is in need of the administration of blood or blood products, it shall be lawful for her to be given such blood or blood products and any necessary ancillary treatment without her consent or the consent of her parents in any life-threatening situation during (*a*) the First Defendant's current pregnancy, labour and delivery; and (*b*) care for the First Defendant after delivery;

2. If it is the professional opinion of those medically responsible for her care that it is necessary for the protection of the First Defendant that a caesaren section operation be performed, it shall be lawful to undertake such operation and any necessary ancillary treatment (including, in a life-threatening situation, the administration of blood or blood products) without the First Defendant's consent or the consent of her parents during the course of the First Defendant's current pregnancy, labour and delivery.

3. The Claimant to pay one-half of the Official Solicitor's costs. Save as aforesaid, no order as to costs.

Dated etc

RCOG: A Consideration of the Law and Ethics in Relation to Court-authorised Obstetric Intervention

Royal College of Obstetricians and Gynaecologists
(No 1 – April 1994)

1 INTRODUCTION

1.1   In October 1992, for the first time, a court in the United Kingdom ruled that a Caesarean section could be lawfully performed.

1.2   In spite of the diverse personalities of obstetricians and their patients the nature of the relationship between them is such that consideration of any court ordered intervention remains an extremely rare event. In fact, courts in the United Kingdom do not order medical treatment; they authorise it, if deemed in the patient's best interest.

1.3   Most pregnant women are concerned to do their utmost on behalf of their fetus. However, occasionally conflict can arise between a mother's personal wishes and the wellbeing of her fetus as perceived by her professional attendants. Potential areas of conflict between the interests of the mother and the fetus can occur either in medical intervention for diagnosis and treatment of the fetus (Brodner 1987; Walters 1986) or indeed in the mother's way of life which may be considered harmful to the embryo or the fetus.

1.4   The chances of any individual obstetrician encountering circumstances where the danger to the mother, to the fetus or to both is significant and where the remedy is refused are very small; but such incidents by their very nature require urgent resolution leaving little time for deliberation or for seeking advice.

1.5   The Ethics Committee of the Royal College of Obstetricians and Gynaecologists offers this description of related law and comment on the ethical position as a guideline to members of the College.

1.6   Our endeavour has been to clarify the position of the current law in relation to this particular problem and to identify the ethical principles involved. Others have suggested modification to the legal process for pragmatic or ethical reasons (4.5.5; 4.5.6) but such considerations are not within our purpose.

2 EXPERIENCE IN AMERICA

2.1   The major experience of court-ordered intervention has so far been found in America and Canada. There are concerns in America that courts are being asked at short notice to restrict the liberty of choice by pregnant women by requiring them to behave in a manner that obstetricians determine are in the better interest of the fetus (Johnson 1987; Nelson 1988; Annas 1987; Elkins 1989).

2.2   An American survey (Kolder 1987) indicated that court orders had been obtained in 11 different states in order to carry out Caesarean sections against the mothers' refusal of consent. In only a few cases (14%) had the application for the order been refused. Significantly, in many of these latter cases the obstetric outcome was favourable.

2.3   A disproportionate number of cases of forced obstetric intervention involved non-English-speaking patients and those from ethnic minorities, women whose cultures and circumstances were different from their medical and legal attendants. One woman underwent a court ordered Caesarean section despite her own and her husband's opposition. Her husband who was forcibly removed during the procedure committed suicide a few months later (Kolder 1987).

2.4   Obstetricians have stated that they might be legally liable if they did not try to save a fetus (Strong 1987). They may have been fearful of prosecution by the mother, or fetus, or a close relative, but there have been no reported cases of litigation where doctors have been accused of failing to obtain court orders.

2.5   In the majority of cases (88%) the court orders were obtained within six hours of application and it is presumed that the judgments leant heavily on the statement in *Roe v Wade* that 'any state may assert a compelling interest in potential fetal life by barring certain abortions after the fetus is viable' (*Roe v Wade* 1973)[1].

2.6   The increase in litigation in the United States of America for prenatal injury tends to support the claims for 'legal personhood' on behalf of the fetus – a concept not yet admitted in English or Scottish law.

2.7   The American College of Obstetricians and Gynecologists and the American Medical Association have now issued their own recommendations concerning legal intervention during pregnancy (ACOG 1987; Johnson 1987). The opinion of the Ethics Committee of the American College of Obstetricians and Gynecologists concluded that whilst every effort should be made to protect the fetus the pregnant woman's autonomy should be respected.

2.8   The Committee stated that the role of the obstetrician should be one of an informed counsellor, weighing the risks and benefits to both patients and realising that tests, judgments and decisions are fallible. Obstetricians should not perform procedures that are declined by a pregnant woman. The use of judicial authority to implement diagnosis or impose treatment violated the pregnant woman's autonomy.

2.9   Sources in North America have produced clinical guidelines aimed at preventing conflicts between pregnant women and their doctors (Chervenak 1 990).

3   UNITED KINGDOM LAW

3.1   As the legal framework is pivotal to our understanding in this area of clinical obstetrics we make no apology for looking at this in some detail. Initially we consider the position of the mother and then the relationship between mother and fetus.

3.2   All members of the Royal College of Obstetricians and Gynaecologists should practice within the law. It is therefore pertinent to examine the implications of current United Kingdom law in this respect.

3.3   We are concerned primarily with the law in the UK, but we will of necessity draw on authorities from other jurisdictions.

3.4   Although laws often consolidate ethical positions, it is quite possible to have unethical practice which is legal (and vice versa).

3.5   Consent
3.5.1   Generally speaking, the usual rules relating to consent apply to pregnant women in the same way as to other patients. Thus the NHS Management Executive's document *A Guide to Consent for Examination or Treatment* (1990) states at chapter 4: 'Principles of consent are the same in maternity services as in other areas of medicine. It is important that the proposed care is discussed with the woman, preferably in the early antenatal period when any wishes she expresses should be recorded in the notes, but of course the patient may change her mind about these issues at any stage, including during labour.'

3.6   Refusal of Consent
3.6.1   Axiomatic to the patient's right to consent to treatment is the right to refuse treatment. The Court of Appeal in the case of *Re T (Adult: refusal of treatment)*[2] affirmed that right.

3.6.2   T was a 20 year old woman who was injured in a road traffic accident when she was 34 weeks pregnant. On admission to hospital, her condition deteriorated. T, who had been brought up by her mother as a Jehovah's Witness, stated spontaneously to a nurse that she did not want a blood transfusion, having spent a period of time alone with her mother. T gave birth to a stillborn child. She reiterated her opposition to a blood transfusion. Her condition became critical and she was sedated and placed on a ventilator. Her father, supported by her boyfriend, applied to the court for a declaration that it would not be unlawful for the hospital to administer a transfusion to her in the absence of her consent.

3.6.3   The Court of Appeal held that an adult patient was entitled to refuse consent to treatment, irrespective of the wisdom of the decision. However, for such refusal to be effective, doctors had to be satisfied that at the time of the refusal the patient's capacity to decide had not been diminished by illness or medication or given on the basis of false assumptions or misinformation, or that the patient's will had not been overborne by another's influence, and that any refusal had been directed to the situation which had become relevant. Only where a patient's refusal was ineffective could doctors treat in accordance with their clinical judgment of the patient's best interests. In T's situation, it was held that the effect of her condition, together with misinformation, rendered her refusal of consent ineffective.

3.6.4   What is important about this case, notwithstanding the outcome for the individual patient, is the general affirmation of a patient's absolute right, properly exercised, to refuse medical treatment. Lord Donaldson said:

> 'An adult patient who suffers from no mental incapacity has an absolute right to choose whether to consent to medical treatment, to refuse it or to choose one rather than another of the treatments being offered.'

3.6.5   Lord Justice Butler Sloss said: 'A man or woman of full age and sound understanding may choose to reject medical advice and medical or surgical treatment either partially or in its entirety. A decision to refuse medical treatment by a patient capable of making the decision does not have to be sensible, rational or well considered: see *Sidaway v Board of Governors of the Bethlem Royal Hospital and the Maudsley Hospital*[3].'

3.6.6   Agreeing with the reasoning of the Court of Appeal in Ontario in *Malette v Shulman*[4], (in which a blood transfusion was given to an unconscious card-carrying Jehovah's Witness) she cited Robbins J A who said:

'At issue here is the freedom of the patient as an individual to exercise her right to refuse treatment and accept the consequences of her own decision. Competent adults ... are generally at liberty to refuse medical treatment even at the risk of death. The right to determine what shall be done with one's body is a fundamental right in our society. The concepts inherent in this right are the bedrock upon which the principles of self determination and individual autonomy are based. Free individual choice in matters affecting this right should, in my opinion, be accorded very high priority.'

3.6.7   Likewise, Lord Justice Staughton said: 'An adult whose mental capacity is unimpaired has the right to decide for herself whether she will or will not receive medical or surgical treatment, even in circumstances where she is likely or even certain to die in the absence of treatment.'

3.6.8   The right of a competent patient to refuse medical treatment was endorsed by Lord Keith in the House of Lords' decision of *Airedale NHS Trust v Bland*[5].

3.6.9   Usually children will be considered competent to make decisions on their own behalf when they are capable of understanding fully the nature of what is proposed. (*Gillick v West Norfolk and Wisbech AHA*)[6]. Despite recent authorities to the contrary, a competent child's refusal should not be overridden, save in exceptional circumstances.

3.6.10   In law, no-one, including the court, is capable of providing consent on behalf of a mentally incompetent adult. Where an adult patient is incapable of giving consent, doctors may lawfully treat provided the procedure is in the patient's best interest. In such cases doctors should usually apply to the High Court for a declaration that their proposed conduct is lawful. Treatment will be in the best interests only if it is carried out either to save the patient's life or to ensure improvement or prevent deterioration in her physical or mental health. (*Re F*)[7].

3.7   Possible Exception to Right to Refuse Consent

3.7.1   In *Re T* Lord Donaldson made one hypothetical exception in relation to pregnancy to the right of a competent patient to refuse medical treatment. He said:

> 'The only possible qualification is a case in which the choice may lead to the death of a viable fetus.'

He stressed however that that was not the case, and that when the situation arose, the court would be faced with a novel problem of considerable legal and ethical complexity.

3.7.2   Although this statement was an obiter dictum*, it formed the basis of Sir Stephen Brown's decision in October 1992 to authorise a non-consensual Caesarean section. Is Lord Donaldson's position an accurate statement of the common law?

* an incidental remark tangential to the judicial opinion being given.

3.7.3   Whilst the direct point may never have been tested, there is considerable judicial authority to the effect that the interests of the fetus are necessarily subordinated to the rights of the pregnant woman. In *Paton v BPAS*[8], Sir George Baker, President, said:

'The fetus cannot, in English law, in my view, have a right of its own at least until it is born and has a separate existence from its mother. That permeates the whole of the civil law of this country.'

3.7.4   More significant are the comments made in *Re F (in utero)*[9], when the court considered whether it had the jurisdiction to make an unborn child a ward of court. The case concerned a 36 year old pregnant woman who suffered from severe mental disturbance, accompanied by occasional drug use. Her first son had been the subject of a care order and was being adopted by foster parents. The woman had a nomadic life style, and the local authority became concerned when she disappeared from her flat and could not be located. Expressing concern for the welfare of her unborn child, the local authority sought to extend the wardship jurisdiction to the child in utero. The Court of Appeal was entirely opposed to this course of action. Lord Justice Balcombe said:

'Since an unborn child has, ex hypothesi, no existence independent of its mother, the only purpose of extending the jurisdiction to include a fetus is to enable the mother's actions to be controlled ... indeed, that is the purpose of the present application.'

He cited an academic article by Lowe, who gave examples of how such control might operate in practice[10]:

'It would mean, for example, that the mother would be unable to leave the jurisdiction without the court's consent, the court being charged to protect the fetus' welfare would surely have to order the mother to stop smoking, imbibing alcohol and indeed any activity which might be hazardous to the child. Taking it to the extreme, were the court to be faced with saving the baby's life or the mother's it would surely have to protect the baby's.'

Lord Justice Balcombe actually went on to consider that another possibility would be that the court might be asked to order that the baby be delivered by Caesarean section. He said:

'it would be intolerable to place a judge in the position of having to make such a decision without any guidance as to the principles on which his decision should be based. If the law is to be extended in this manner, so as to impose control over the mother of an unborn child, where such control may be necessary for the benefit of that child, then under our system of parliamentary democracy, it is for Parliament to decide whether such controls can be imposed and, if so, subject to what limitations or conditions'. (our emphasis).

He went on to observe that in such a sensitive field, affecting as it does the liberty of the individual, it was not for the judiciary to extend the law.

3.7.5   Additionally, Lord Justice May pointed to the 'insuperable difficulties' which would be caused if one sought to enforce any order in respect of an unborn child against its mother, if that mother failed to comply with the order. He said:

'I cannot contemplate the court ordering that this should be done by force, nor indeed is it possible to consider with any equanimity that the court should seek to enforce an order by committal.'

All three of their Lordships stressed that such a drastic extension of wardship jurisdiction to protect the fetus at the expense of the liberty of the mother would be a matter for Parliament. Whilst these dicta are obiter they are fairly persuasive.

3.8 Court-Authorised Caesarean Section – United Kingdom

3.8.1   In light of the above, it is with some surprise that the President of the Family Division, Sir Stephen Brown, felt able to grant the declaration that he did in the case of *Re S (Adult: refusal of medical treatment)*[11]. In that case, a declaration was given that a Caesarean section and any necessary consequential treatment which the hospital and its staff proposed to perform on the patient could be lawfully performed despite the patient's refusal to give her consent being vital in the interests of the patient and her unborn child.

3.8.2   The facts as set out briefly by Sir Stephen Brown merit repetition:

'Mrs S is 30 years of age, she is in labour with her third pregnancy. She was admitted to a hospital last Saturday with ruptured membranes and in spontaneous labour. She has continued in labour since. She is already six days overdue beyond the expected date of birth, and she has now refused, on religious grounds, to submit herself to a Caesarean section operation. She is supported in this by her husband. They are described as "born again Christians" and are clearly quite sincere in their belief. I have heard the evidence of P. a Fellow of the Royal College of Surgeons who is in charge of the patient at the hospital. He has given, succinctly and graphically, a description of the condition of this patient. Her situation is desperately serious, as is also the situation of the as yet unborn child. The child is in what is described as a position of "transverse lie" with the elbow projecting through the cervix and the head being on the right side. There is the gravest risk of a rupture of the uterus if the section is not carried out and the natural labour process is permitted to continue. The evidence of P is that we are concerned with "minutes rather than hours" and that this is a "life and death" situation. He has done his best, as have other surgeons and doctors at the hospital, to persuade the mother that the only means of saving her life, and also I emphasise the life of her unborn child, is to carry out a Caesarean section operation. P is emphatic. He says it is absolutely the case that the baby cannot be born alive if a Caesarean operation is not carried out. He has described the medical condition. I am not going to go into it in detail because of the pressure of time.'

3.8.3   After proceedings conducted ex parte* lasting for under two hours, the President granted a declaration authorising non-consensual treatment (Hewson 1992). He gave only two justifications for granting the declaration, namely:

'The fundamental question appears to have been left open by Lord Donaldson in *Re T (Adult: refusal of medical treatment)*[12] and . . . there is no English authority which is directly in point.'

He also referred to:

'Some American authority which suggests that if this case were being heard in the American courts the answer would be likely to be in favour of granting a declaration in these circumstances.'

and cited *Re AC*[13].

---

* a legal expression applied to a proceeding in which only one side of the case is presented and the opposing side is absent.

3.8.4   The reliance on the case of *Re AC* (Annas 1988, 1990) was both extraordinary, and, it has been submitted by a number of legal commentators, wrong. In the Columbia Court of Appeal's decision in *Re AC*, the majority departed from the court's earlier decision in the case[14], and ruled that a Caesarean section should not have been authorised on AC by the trial court to save her unborn child. It was held that a full hearing, not an ex parte hearing, was required before a court could contemplate authorising a procedure upon a pregnant woman who was refusing treatment. Rather, the correct approach was for the court to determine whether the woman was competent, and if so what were her wishes. If she was not competent, the court should apply a substituted judgment test to decide what she would have wanted in the circumstances. Judge Terry stated in *Re AC* that the woman's wishes would be determinative in virtually all cases. The court left open whether there might be 'truly extraordinary or compelling reasons' to override the woman's wishes. The only possible justification for Sir Stephen Brown's decision could be an assumption by him that the facts of *Re S*[11] involved the truly exceptional case.

3.8.5   This seems unlikely, since even in *Re AC*, where the carrying out of a Caesarean section was likely to affect the mother's health adversely (the pregnant woman had cancer and died two days after the Caesarean), Judge Terry stated:

> 'Some may doubt that there could ever be a situation extraordinary or compelling enough to justify a massive intrusion into a person's body, such as a Caesarean section, against the person's will.'

3.8.6   Martha Swartz points out in the Cambridge Quarterly of Health Care Ethics (Volume 1, No 1 Winter 1992), that the decision of the district of Columbia Court of Appeals which overturned the decision in *Re AC* only applied to Washington DC, and elsewhere the overwhelming trend has, worryingly, been to override the pregnant woman's objections to treatment. Certainly Sir Stephen Brown's reliance on *Re AC* has made the *Re S* judgment be regarded with considerable scepticism by legal commentators.

3.8.7   The *Re S* case is not being appealed, and as such the decision stands. There is no legal justification for overriding a competent patient's wishes purportedly in her best interests. Thus to the extent the declaration in *Re S* purports to be in the mother's vital interest, this must surely be wrong. The justification provided by the case of *Re F (Mental Patient: Sterilisation)*[15] applies only in the case of incompetent adults, and should certainly not be applied in the case of competent female patients. Indeed, even if the woman were unconscious, *Re F* would only justify treating her if such treatment were in her best interests, either to save her life or to ensure improvement or prevent deterioration in her physical (or mental) health. This would not necessarily justify a Caesarean unless it fulfilled the above criteria.

3.8.8   The Infant Life Preservation Act 1929
The effect of the Act, in relation to abortion, was amended by the section 37 (4) of the Human Fertilisation and Embryology Act 1990 (vide infra). Before the amendments were introduced by the new legislation, the Abortion Act 1967 said at Section 5 (1):

> 'Nothing in this Act shall affect the provisions of the Infant Life (Preservation) Act 1929 (protecting the life of the viable foetus).'

Section 1 (2) of the Infant Life Preservation Act stated:

> 'For the purpose of this Act, evidence that a woman had at any material time been pregnant for a period of 28 weeks or more shall be prima facie

proof that she was at that time pregnant of a child capable of being born alive.'

Thus arose the mistaken belief that the lawful definition of viability was 28 weeks and that there was an upper limit of 28 weeks for performing lawful terminations. In fact, the offence of child destruction created by the 1929 Act applied to any termination where the child was capable of being born alive. The recognition by the medical profession that a child may be capable of being born alive substantially earlier than at 28 weeks is reflected in the amendments to the Abortion Act which reduce the upper limit, in various circumstances, to 24 weeks.

Does the Act have any application in the case of a viable fetus which dies at or before birth because of the mother's refusal of treatment? The answer is no. The Infant Life (Preservation) Act 1929 is a criminal statute, carrying a maximum sentence of life imprisonment.

Its passing was intended to remedy the mischief of unwanted babies being killed as they were in the process of being delivered. The key point is that the offence of child destruction is only caused by a person who 'with intent to destroy the life of a child capable of being born alive' causes it to die by some 'willful act'. A mother refusing treatment, or the obstetrician treating her, would not come within this definition.

3.8.9   *Re S* is also out of step in elevating the status of the fetus in law to such an extent that its supposed rights become more important than its mother's. To do so is out of line with both previous case law, and the Congenital Disabilities (Civil Liabilities) Act 1976, which gives a child a right of action for damage caused in utero against everyone except its mother (with the exception of motor accidents, for which the mother is insured). Indeed, as Grubb points out[16], the Law Commission in its report[17] on Injuries to Unborn Children explicitly stated that a woman should not be liable for 'rash conduct during pregnancy' which causes harm to the unborn child. Rather, the intent of Parliament was to leave it up to the individual mother to decide how to act in the 'best interests' of her unborn child.

3.8.10   Moreover, there is no other precedent in law for forcing one person to use his or her body to save the life of another. In *McFall v Shimp*[18], a cousin was found to be the only person with compatible bone marrow to save his cousin's life. After some reflection the cousin declined to have the tissue removed, even in the knowledge that his cousin would probably die as a result. The issue went to court. The court, unsurprisingly, was unwilling to order the removal of the tissue, even though the cousin's moral culpability was criticised heavily. This is a critical distinction. Although a pregnant woman may well have an extremely strong ethical responsibility towards her unborn child, this does not mean that it is correct to use the law to enforce these responsibilities.

3.9   Reliance on Re S
There are a number of dangers in relying on the *Re S* decision to seek further court authorisation for obstetric intervention.

3.9.1   An emergency ex parte hearing is the least appropriate forum in which to make these decisions even if life and death situations are at stake and time is pressing. Decisions of this magnitude with longer-term repercussions might be considered unsafe without a woman having a full opportunity to be represented adequately and to make her wishes known.

3.9.2   Confirmation of the *Re S* decision in a future court intervention could do immeasureable harm to the doctor-patient relationship. Some doctors might be tempted to threaten to use it to obtain maternal compliance. The fear of such a court intervention might drive away some of the very women who are in greatest need of antenatal and intrapartum care.

3.9.3   As well as a common law duty of care towards an unborn child, recently confirmed by the Court of Appeal in *Burton v Islington HA: de Martell v Merton and Sutton HA*[19], since July 1976, a third party has a statutory duty of care towards an unborn child who is subsequently born disabled, under the Congenital Disabilities (Civil Liability) Act of that year.

A child's right of action under this Act is derivative only. In other words, a person is only liable towards a child, if he or she would, if sued in time, be liable in tort to one or both of the child's parents.

This raises the question of a child damaged in utero or in the course of delivery as a result of maternal non-compliance. An obstetrician has a duty of care to a mother to exercise reasonable care for her wellbeing. If, however, the mother rejects the obstetrician's advice and refuses to permit the obstetrician to act in such a way as to secure her interests, and those of her unborn child, and the child suffers damage, no tort has been committed, because the obstetrician's duty is to respect the mother's wishes. To do otherwise would be to commit a battery. An obstetrician who complied with a mother's refusal of consent to a Caesarean section would not incur legal liability towards the child, even if it suffered harm.

3.10   Summary of Legal Position
3.10.1   Although obligations to the fetus increase with its growth in utero, UK law does not grant it any legal status. This comes from the moment of birth.

3.10.2   The law does not limit a woman's freedom because she is pregnant. Her bodily integrity cannot be invaded on behalf of her fetus without her consent. The fetus has no remedy against injuries caused by her.

4   PROFESSIONAL ETHICS

4.1   The Unique Relationship

4.1.1   The maternal-fetal relationship is unique. There are two patients with access to one through the other. For the duration of the pregnancy the woman is the only person who can directly control what is done to her fetus. Others can advise and encourage but she alone takes direct responsibility during every minute of every day for some nine months.

4.1.2   The fetus is totally reliant on the mother so long as it remains in utero. The protection of the fetus stands on her performance of her moral obligations, not on any legal right of its own.

4.2   Maternal Obligations

4.2.1   Pregnancy need not be, and is not usually, an enforced state for a woman, but rather a matter of personal choice (given contraception and, within legal limits, induced abortion) and so carries with it the obligations arising from liberty of choice.

4.2.2   Pregnant women and their partners are now more aware of the state of early pregnancy through the help of accurate diagnosis. Ultrasound creates early appreciation of a live embryo and a developing fetus. This new, constantly improving view of the developing fetus brings an earlier recognition of the depth of responsibility towards the fetus as it progresses towards 'personhood'.

4.2.3   The unique relationship between a mother and her embryo or fetus places on her a responsibility which increases as the pregnancy advances. The welfare of the child may well be dependent on her commitment to this unique obligation.

4.2.4   The pregnant woman's actions and lifestyle may enhance or damage her fetus. There are many ways in which a mother can influence her fetus. Indirectly she can accept or reject advice regarding drugs, alcohol, smoking, diet and also maternal examination and investigation. More directly related to the fetus, she alone decides whether to accept prenatal diagnosis and treatment, eg chorion villus sampling, amniocentesis, fetoscopy, fetal monitoring and Caesarean section.

4.2.5   The pregnant woman may have a different perspective from her professional adviser towards a recognised problem (Murray 1987). By giving up smoking, for example, she may feel she would put on significant weight or become clinically depressed. Some may have religious or other convictions which prevent their accepting a particular course of action.

4.3   Relationship Between Obstetrician and Patient

4.3.1   The concern of parents for their offspring in utero is normally both deep and genuine, and indeed many pregnant women are willing to put their lives or health at risk for the sake of the fetus.

4.3.2   The aim of those who care for pregnant women must be to foster the greatest benefit to both the mother and fetus with the least risk to both.

4.3.3   Obstetricians must recognise the dual claims of the mother and her embryo or fetus, and inform and advise the family, utilising their training and experience in the best interests of both parties. Almost always, when medical information and the possible options are communicated sensitively and effectively, both the decision and the responsibility for it can be shared by the mother and her obstetrician.

4.3.4   There are limits to the accuracy and effectiveness of many diagnostic and therapeutic procedures during pregnancy and confinement and this should be discussed with the mother. For example, the methods for detecting fetal distress antenatally and during labour are not always reliable indicators of a poor outcome. The fine indices that determine whether the dynamic process of labour will culminate in a normal outcome are difficult to measure.

4.3.5   In caring for the pregnant woman an obstetrician must respect the woman's legal right to choose or refuse any recommended course of action and at the same time maintain the medical obligation to promote the wellbeing of mother and child.

4.4   Society's Responsibility

4.4.1   Society flourishes when professional and social relationships are good and it is important therefore to foster trust between Doctor and Patient, Medicine and the Public, and between the Law, the Medical Profession and the Public.

4.4.2 Conflicts between individuals leading to tension and disputes in medical management are less likely to occur in a society where the participants are working in harmony.

4.4.3 In so far as society is comprised of individual persons bound together to the common advantage, so it owes a duty of care both to its members and to its potential members. For neither mother nor society is it sufficient to consider a baby solely as a by-product of a sexual union or the fulfilment of her reproductive instinct. The end product of pregnancy is both an individual child and a new member of society. To regard it as anything less is a source of sadness, but not a justification for overriding maternal integrity or destroying the trust between doctor and patient.

4.5 Society's Stance

4.5.1 A woman's 'right to decide' must surely be balanced by her obligation to her dependent fetus and renders her morally accountable if knowingly the child is harmed by her decision or indecision.

4.5.2 In the United States of America pregnant women have been jailed for taking illicit drugs which might damage the fetus and the court judgments have stated that 'a child has a legal right to begin life with a sound mind and body' (*Smith v Brennan* 1960)[20]. While such action emphasises accountability, it can also be counter-productive as abusers may then be reluctant to attend for medical care or may conceal their pregnancies in case their defect comes to light.

4.5.3 It has been the practice in this country to offer services and provide incentives to encourage mothers towards caring for their unborn child rather than using threats of punishment or invoking laws (Bewley 1991). This help must be designed to enable women to give that care by providing adequate opportunities and pay, a comprehensive safety net and access to high quality antenatal services (Annas 1987).

4.5.4 The law and the ethics of the obstetrician are at one in recognising a duty towards the welfare of the fetus, which only exceptionally conflicts with the vital interests of the mother and her freedom of choice. It is in the common interest for society, and it is the object of obstetric care in particular, to assist the mother to fulfil her obligation.

4.5.5 The creation of an 'intentional crime of prenatal injury' would serve as a contemporaneous non-coercive threat only realisable on behalf of the child after delivery (Bewley 1991). This is unlikely to be of benefit in the management of the pregnancy.

4.5.6 It has been suggested tentatively that in extreme cases of competing claims between mother and fetus a judge could hear all the arguments and decide on the course of action (Kennedy 1990). Such a law giving the judge powers of pre-birth seizure would be seen by mothers as a threat, and by doctors as a restriction of clinical freedom, and would strike at the heart of the doctor-patient relationship.

4.5.7 Any change in approach to the mother must demonstrate that present methods have failed. The greater the restriction on the pregnant woman's freedom the greater must be the justification for interference; and the harm prevented must be more than the harm caused.

4.5.8 Present United Kingdom law protects the rights of the mother over the claims of the fetus. Resort to law in individual cases to overturn this presumption raises more difficulties than it solves.

4.6 Summary of Ethical Position

4.6.1 The management of pregnancy rests upon two sorts of obligation: moral obligation in the mother, professional obligation in the obstetrician. The latter is under the sanction of law; the former is not. Normally both responsibilities are exercised in concert.

4.6.2 Obstetricians must respect the woman's legal liberty to ignore or reject professional advice, even to her own detriment and that of her fetus. They are not thereby released from their duty of care. When that duty is discharged fully, as judged by objective professional standards, should ill nevertheless befall, the obstetrician also is under the protection of law. The protective function of law is to be valued more than the coercive.

5 CONCLUSIONS

5.1 The aim of those who care for pregnant women is to foster the greatest benefit to both mother and fetus with the least risk.

5.2 Occasionally problems arise when a pregnant woman and her doctor fundamentally disagree over action believed to be in the best interest of mother or fetus or when advice is in conflict with her religious scruples.

5.3 Although obligations to the fetus in utero increase as it develops, UK law does not grant it personal legal status. This comes from the moment of birth.

5.4 The law provides no restriction on a woman's freedom on account of her pregnancy. Any medical action requires her informed consent.

5.5 A pregnant woman has a natural duty and moral obligation to the welfare of her fetus as a future person and member of society.

5.6 Society should provide all the necessary services and incentives to help the pregnant woman to fulfil her obligation.

5.7 It is rare for a doctor to be faced with a conflict where judicial intervention on behalf of the fetus might be considered.

5.8 Such circumstances are usually unexpected and the requirement of haste leaves little time for the case to be properly prepared and decided.

5.9 Doctors must recognise that medical advice is based on evidence that is seldom infallible. It is the doctor's duty to provide appropriate information so that the pregnant woman can make an informed and thoughtful decision.

5.10 Where conflict arises the doctor should seek help and advice from other professional colleagues and, with the patient's agreement, it may be appropriate to involve other members or friends of her family.

5.11 A doctor must respect the competent pregnant woman's right to choose or refuse any particular recommended course of action whilst optimising care for both mother and fetus to the best of his or her ability. A doctor would not then be culpable if these endeavours were unsuccessful.

5.12 We conclude that it is inappropriate, and unlikely to be helpful or necessary, to invoke judicial intervention to overrule an informed and competent woman's refusal of a proposed medical treatment, even though her refusal might place her life and that of her fetus at risk.

GENERAL REFERENCES

- ACOG Committee on Ethics. (1987) Patient choice: maternal-fetal conflict. American College of Obstetrics and Gynecologists. Washington DC. No 551
- Annas, G.J. (1990) Foreclosing the use of force: AC reversed. Hastings Cent Rep 20:27.
- Annas, G.J. (1988) She's going to die: The case of Angela C. Hastings Cent Rep 18:23.
- Annas, G.J. (1987) Protecting the liberty of pregnant patients. New Eng J Med. 316, 1213.
- Bewley, S. (1991) Restricting the freedom of pregnant, drug-taking women: putting the fetus first? MA Thesis (University of London).
- Brodner, R.A. and Shuster, E. (1987) Fetal therapy: Ethical and legal implications of prenatal intervention and clinical application. Fetal Ther 2:57.
- Chervenak, F.A., McCullough, L.B. (1990) Clinical guides to preventing ethical conflicts between pregnant women and their physicians. Am J Obstet Gynecol 162:303.
- Elkins, T.E., Anderson, F.H., Barclay, M., Mason, T., Bowdler, N., Anderson G. (1989) Court-ordered caesarean section: An analysis of ethical concerns in compelling cases. Am J Obstet Gynecol 161: 150. Hewson, B. (1992) Mother knows best. New Law J p 1538.
- Johnson, D. (1987) A new threat to pregnant womens autonomy. Hastings Cent Rep 17:33.
- Kennedy, I.M. (1990) 'The woman and her unborn child: rights and responsibilities' in P Byrne (Ed) Ethics and law in health care and research. Chichester: John Wiley & Sons, pp 161-186. Reprinted in: Kennedy, I.M. (1991) Treat me right: Essays in Medical Law and Ethics 2nd Ed. Oxford, Clarendon Press pp 364-384.
- Kolder, V.E.B., Gallagher, J., Parsons, M.T. (1987) Court-ordered obstetrical interventions. New Eng J Med 316: 1192.
- Murray, T.H. (1987) Moral obligations to the not yet born: the fetus as a patient. Clin Perinatol 14:329.
- NHS Management Executive. (1990) A guide to Consent for Examination or Treatment.
- Nelson, L.J. and Milliken, N. (1988) Compelled medical treatment of pregnant women. JAMA 259:1060.
- Strong, C. (1987) Ethical conflicts between mother and fetus in obstetrics. Clin Perinatol 14:313.
- Swartz, M. (1992) Cambridge Quarterly of Health Care Ethics (Volume 1 No 1 Winter.)
- Walters, L. (1986) Ethical issues in intrauterine diagnosis and therapy. Fetal Therapy 1:32.

LEGAL REFERENCES

1. *Roe v Wade* (1973) 410 US 113.
2. *Re T (refusal of treatment)* [1992] 3 WLR 783.
3. *Sidaway v Board of Governors of the Bethlem Royal Hospital and the Maudsley Hospital* [1985] AC 871, 904 to 905.
4. *Malette v Shulman* [1990] 67 DLR (4th) 321.
5. *Airedale NHS Trust v Bland* [1993]1 All ER 821.
6. *Gillick v West Norfolk and Wisbech AHA* [1986] AC 12.
7. *Re F* [1990] 2 AC 1.
8. *Paton v BPAS* [1979] 1 QB 276.

9.   *Re F (in utero)* [1988] 2 All ER 193.
10. *Lowe* 96 LQR 29 at 30.
11. *Re S (Adult: refusal of medical treatment)* [1992] 4 All ER 671.
12. *Re T (Adult: refusal of medical treatment)* [1992] 411 ER 649.
13. *Re AC* [1990] 573 A 2d 1235.
14. *Re AC* (1987) 533 A 2d 611.
15. *Re F (Mental Patient: Sterilisation)* [1990] 2 AC 1.
16. A Grubb. 'Despatches' Vol. 3, No 3. Centre of Medical Law and Ethics, King's College, London.
17. Law Commission (1974) *Injuries to Unborn Children*. No 60, CMND 5709.
18. *McFall v Shimp* (1978) 10 Pa D and C 3d 90.
19. *Burton v lslington HA: de Martell v Merton and Sutton HA* [1992] 3 All ER 833.
20. *Smith v Brennan* [1960] 157Ad 2 497, 503.

ETHICS COMMITTEE

- Mr J R Friend MA DM (Oxon) FRCOG (Chairman)
- Revd Professor J M Beezley MD FACOG FRCOG
- Professor the Reverend Canon G R Dunstan CBE MA Hon DD Hon LLD FRCOG
- Mrs H Hayman MA, Chairman, Whittington Hospital NHS Trust
- Mr R H J Kerr-Wilson MA FRCS(Ed) FRCOG
- The Marchioness of Lothian, Patron, UK National Council of Women
- Professor A A Templeton MD FRCOG
- Mr J A A Watt, Solicitor, Senior Partner Hempsons
- Miss A Gawith, Secretary to the Committee

These guidelines were produced under the direction of the Ethics Committee of the Royal College of Obstetricians and Gynaecologists as an educational aid to obstetricians and gynaecologists. These guidelines do not define a standard of care, nor it is intended to dictate an exclusive course of management. Variations of practice taking into account the needs of the individual patient, resources and limitations unique to the institution or type of practice may be appropriate.

RCOG: Supplement to 'A Consideration of the Law And Ethics in Relation to Court-authorised Obstetric Intervention'

Royal College of Obstetricians and Gynaecologists
(1996)

INTRODUCTION

Since the original paper on court-authorised obstetric intervention was produced in 1994, further discussion and recognition of the place of advance directives in medical treatment have taken place. It was therefore felt appropriate by the College Ethics Committee to add a supplement to the original document in order to discuss problems which may arise with a pregnant woman who is incapacitated to the degree that she is not competent to make decisions concerning her treatment.

1 CLINICAL SITUATIONS

1.1 The incompetent pregnant patient with no advance directive.

1.2 The incompetent patient with whom the treatment has previously been discussed during the pregnancy and who, fully informed, has refused it in advance.

1.3 The incompetent patient with an advance directive relating to some form of treatment, eg life support or blood transfusion, but with whom there has been no opportunity for discussion during the pregnancy (and so may not have been fully informed):

1.3.1 Where pregnancy has been mentioned in the directive; 1.3.2 Where there is no mention of pregnancy in the directive.

1.4 The incompetent patient where there is only a presumption, however strong, of her refusal.

1.5 The timing of the clinical situation is also relevant. The mother's condition may either be that of transient vegetative state, or a continuing vegetative state when, after four weeks, it becomes increasingly unlikely that it is part of a recovery phase.

2 THE RESPECT DUE TO ADVANCE DIRECTIVES

2.1 The Law Commission, the House of Lords Select Committee on Medical Ethics and the BMA Guidelines all affirm that doctors are under duty to respect, in an advance directive, refusal of any procedure debarred to them by a patient's refusal of consent.

2.2 Doctors are not obliged to honour, in advance directives, a request for specific treatment which they would hold to be contrary to professional judgment or personal conscience.

2.3   Admittedly pregnancy presents difficulties:

2.3.1   The BMA *Code of Practice*, (BMA 1995)[1], at 7.4

'Women of childbearing age should be advised to consider the possibility of their advance statement or directive being invoked at a time when they are pregnant. A waiver covering pregnancy might be written into the statement.'

2.3.2   And at 10.5:

'If an incapacitated pregnant woman presents with an apparently valid advance directive refusing treatment, legal advice should be sought to clarify the position.'

2.3.3   The Report of the Law Commission (1995)[2] at 5.24, opens its discussion of advance statements by pregnant women with the case *Re S* (1993)[3], considered in the RCOG report on Court-authorised Obstetric Intervention (April 1994)[4]. In *Re S* the High Court effectively overruled the refusal of a pregnant woman to consent to a Caesarean section. The Law Commission then (at 5.25) reports that 'the majority of the US states with living will legislation set statutory limits to the effectiveness of any declarations during the maker's pregnancy'. It quotes a similar opinion from King's College London Centre of Medical Law and Ethics.

2.3.4   At once the Commission asserts robustly (5.25), 'We do not, however, accept that a woman's right to determine the sorts of bodily interference which she will tolerate somehow evaporates as soon as she becomes pregnant. There can, on the other hand, be no objection to acknowledging that many women do in fact alter their views as to the interventions they find acceptable as a direct result of the fact that they are carrying a child. By analogy with cases where life might be needlessly shortened or lost it appears that a refusal which did not mention the possibility that the life of a foetus (sic) might be endangered would be likely to be found not to apply in circumstances where a treatment intended to save the life of the foetus was proposed. Women of child-bearing age should therefore be aware that they should address their minds to this possibility if they wish to make advance refusals of treatment.'

2.3.5   Accordingly, at 5.26, 'The best way of balancing the continuing right of the patient to refuse such treatment with the public interest in preserving life is to create a statutory presumption in favour of the preservation of life.'

2.3.6   There follows a recommendation which is embodied in a proposed draft Statute: '9.(3) In the absence of any indication to the contrary, it shall be presumed that an advance refusal of treatment does not apply in circumstances where those having the care of the person who made it consider that the refusal (*a*) endangers that person's life; or (*b*) if that person is a woman who is pregnant, the life of the foetus.'

2.3.7   This recommendation reflects 'the one hypothetical exception' made by Lord Donaldson MR in the case Re T 'in relation to pregnancy to the right of a competent patient to refuse medical treatment.' He said 'The only possible qualification is a case in which the choice may lead to the death of a viable fetus'. (Quoted at 3.7.1 in the RCOG publication *Consideration of the Law and Ethics in relation to Court-authorised Obstetric Intervention*, 1994[4].)

3   THE ETHICS: THE CONSIDERATION OF DUTY

3.1   In the event of an adult patient being incompetent and in the absence of specific statutory authority[5], no-one else is in a position to give consent to treatment. It is often surmised wrongly that next of kin have power to give or refuse such consent. The doctor's duty is to act in the best interests of the patient as described by Wood J in *T v T* (1988)[6]:

> 'A medical adviser must, therefore, consider what decisions should be reached in the best interests of his patient's health ... a medical adviser is justified in taking such steps as good medical practice demands ... '

or the House of Lords judgment *Re F* (1989)[7], as reported by Kennedy and Grubb (1989)[8]treatment which is in the 'best interests' of a patient is justified under the common law on grounds of public policy (per Lord Brandon) or because of the principle of necessity (per Lord Goff), when the patient is incompetent. A doctor may even have a duty (per Lord Brandon) to administer treatment in such circumstances.

3.2   The underlying moral presumptions are first in favour of life, and secondly in favour of a mother's normal will to do what is best for the fetus. For example, in the absence of an advance directive and with neurological evidence of brain death in the mother, it would be appropriate to act on behalf of the fetus.

3.3   However, in the presence of an advance directive, or a presumed refusal on the part of the mother, the problem arises of conflicting duties to the pregnant woman and to the fetus. It is presumed that (unless the Law Commission's recommendation, quoted in 2.3.5 and 2.3.6 above, were enacted), the RCOG stands by its position as set out in the 1994 'Consideration' at 4.6.2 and 5.11, in refusing to intervene on behalf of the fetus against the mother's lawful refusal of consent. That position was stated notwithstanding the controversial judgment of Sir Stephen Brown in *Re S*, in which he authorised a Caesarean section despite the patient's refusal of consent.

3.4   It is now appropriate to consider the individual clinical situations.

3.4.1   The incompetent patient with whom the treatment has previously been discussed during the pregnancy and who, fully informed, has refused it in advance. In such a case, the mother's wishes should be respected in the same way as if she were conscious and competent. This may be at the expense of the fetus.

3.4.2   The incompetent patient with an advance directive relating to some form of treatment but with whom there has been no opportunity for discussion during the pregnancy:

(i)   Where pregnancy has been mentioned in the directive the same reasoning applies as in section 3.4.1.
(ii)   Where there is no mention of pregnancy in the directive: here the timing and content of the advance directive are relevant. If the document was drawn up before the pregnancy was known, and made no reference to pregnancy, the directive could be declared invalid because the circumstances at the critical time of decision were not clearly envisaged when the directive was made (following *Re T*, 1994, cited in the RCOG 'Consideration' at 3.6.3). The obstetrician, being uncertain of the intentions of the mother, would be free to allow more weight to the interest of the fetus. If the directive referred to pregnancy, or had been made after the pregnancy was known, that freedom would be denied.

3.4.3   The incompetent patient where there is only a presumption of her refusal (for example if she belongs to a religious sect with relevant scruples). In such circumstances, the obstetrician may be advised to act in the patient's 'best interests' as stated out of the Common Law in recent judicial pronouncements *T v T* [1988] and *Re F* [1989][6 and 7]. The previous wishes and feelings of the patient must be taken into account as well as the views of those who know her.

3.5   Relevant to any decision is the condition for which the patient is on life support. If the condition were one of a trauma from which the patient might reasonably be expected to emerge, her own interest would be higher than if she were in a persistent vegetative state or were brain stem dead. The medical discretion would be extended accordingly: to time the withdrawal of life support in the interest of the fetus in having as long in utero as is good for it.

4   CONCLUSIONS

4.1   In an emergency and in the absence of an advance directive the obstetrician should act in the best interests of the mother.

4.2   If the patient has an advance directive which specifies refusal of treatment during pregnancy this should be honoured even at the expense of the fetus (3.4.1 supra).

4.3   If the advance directive does not mention pregnancy specifically, then more weight may be given to the interests of the fetus unless the mother's condition was such that she was expected to recover within a reasonable time (3.4.2(ii) supra).

4.4   When the obstetrician has doubt or reservations then early consideration should be given to seeking legal advice (2.3.7 supra).

REFERENCES

1   Advance Statements about Medical Treatment. Code of Practice. Report of the British Medical Association. (April 1995).
2   The Law Commission (March 1995). *Mental Incapacity*.
3   *Re S (Adult: Refusal of Treatment)* [1993] Fam 123.
4   RCOG Guidelines, Ethics No 1, (April 1994). A consideration of the Law and Ethics in relation to court-authorised obstetric intervention.
5   England and Wales: The Mental Health Act 1983.
    Scotland: Mental Health (Scotland) Act 1984.
    N Ireland: The Mental Health (NI) Order 1986.
    Republic of Ireland: Health (Mental Services) Act 1981.
6   *T v T* [1988] Fam 52, [1988] 1 All ER 613.
7   *Re F* [1989] 2 All ER 545.
8   *Medical Law Text and Materials*, 1st Edition (1989) edited Kennedy and Grubb. Butterworth, London. p 606.

Appendix 7.1

Draft Particulars of Claim Restraining Force-feeding

IN THE HIGH COURT OF JUSTICE   CLAIM NO

FAMILY DIVISION

PRINCIPAL REGISTRY

B E T W E E N :

SUSAN PATIENT

Claimant

– and –

BLANKSHIRE HEALTHCARE NHS TRUST

Defendant

PARTICULARS OF CLAIM

1. At all material times the Claimant has been an in-patient at the Blankshire District Hospital which is managed by the Defendant.

2. The Claimant suffers from a condition which the medical staff at the said hospital have diagnosed as anorexia nervosa.

3. The Claimant does not accept that the said diagnosis is correct, and has received advice from her own medical adviser that there is insufficient evidence from her history, condition and prognosis for the said diagnosis to be established.

4. The Claimant retains the mental capacity to consent to or refuse medical treatment for her condition in that:

    (*a*) She is able retain and understand information about her condition and any treatment that might be proposed;
    (*b*) She is able to believe treatment information;
    (*c*) She is able to weigh such information to come to a decision.

5. The medical staff employed by the Defendant have informed the Claimant that they consider that she is unable to make decisions about her medical treatment for herself. Their opinion about her mental capacity is wrong for the reasons set out in the preceding paragraph.

6. The medical staff employed by the Defendant have also informed the Claimant that they consider it to be in her best interests to be given food and water by a naso-gastric tube, and that they intend to provide her with such treatment, regardless of whether she consents to it.

7. The Claimant has refused to consent to such treatment, as she is entitled to do and, further, it is not in her best interests to have such treatment imposed on her for the following, among other reasons:

    (*a*) She retains the capacity to make decisions about treatment for herself.

(*b*) There is no evidence, alternatively no evidence of which she has been made aware, that her life is in danger or that she is likely to suffer serious or permanent personal injury if she does not receive the proposed treatment.

(*c*) If treatment is imposed on her against her will, she will lose any trust in the medical profession, and become determined not to cooperate with any treatment plan.

(*d*) She has been advised by her own medical expert that the more appropriate immediate treatment would be a course of psychotherapy which she would be prepared to undergo.

8. In the circumstances the Defendant, through their servants or agents, their medical staff, are unlawfully threatening and intending to impose invasive medical treatment on the Claimant without her consent and against her best interests, and are thereby threatening and intending to commit a serious assault on her unless they are restrained from so doing.

9. This claim is of such importance and complexity that it should be dealt with in the High Court.

Appendix 7.2

Draft Directions Order in Feeding Case

IN THE HIGH COURT OF JUSTICE   **CLAIM No**

FAMILY DIVISION

PRINCIPAL REGISTRY

BETWEEN:

BLANKSHIRE HEALTHCARE NHS TRUST

Claimant

– and –

SUSAN PATIENT
[BY HER LITIGATION FRIEND
THE OFFICIAL SOLICITOR TO THE SUPREME COURT]

Defendant

DRAFT ORDER

UPON hearing counsel for the Claimant and counsel for the Defendant

AND UPON reading the claim form, the Statement of Truth of Joseph Manager, and the Application Notice dated

IT IS ORDERED that

1.   The identity of :
    (*a*) The Defendant
    (*b*) Any member of the Defendant's family
    (*c*) The Blankshire District Hospital
    (*d*) The Claimant
    (*e*) Any member of staff at the said hospital
    (*f*) Any witness of fact who gives oral or written evidence in this action
    be not disclosed in connection with this action.

2.   The title of this action shall be 'In re P (Adult patient: medical treatment)'

3.   The hearing of the action shall be in private.

4.   No judgement given in this action shall be published without leave of the Court.

5.   The costs of this application shall be costs in the action.

Appendix 7.3

Draft Injunction Restraining Force-Feeding

IN THE HIGH COURT OF JUSTICE   **CLAIM NO**

FAMILY DIVISION

PRINCIPAL REGISTRY

B E T W E E N :

SUSAN PATIENT

Claimant

– and –

BLANKSHIRE HEALTHCARE NHS TRUST

Defendant

DRAFT ORDER

UPON hearing counsel for the Claimant and counsel for the Defendant

AND UPON reading the application notice, the claim form, and the particulars of claim

IT IS ORDERED

1. That the Defendant, its servants or agents, be restrained from imposing any form of medical treatment or care, including naso-gastric feeding, on the Claimant without her consent until the trial of the action or further order of the court.

2. That the Defendant have permission to apply to discharge or vary this order on 24 hours notice to the Claimant and the Official Solicitor.

Appendix 7.4

DSM-IV: Diagnostic Criteria for Eating Disorders

Diagnostic and Statistical Manual of Mental Disorders (4th edn, 1995)
American Psychiatric Association

DIAGNOSTIC CRITERIA FOR F50.0 ANOREXIA NERVOSA

(A) Refusal to maintain body weight at or above a minimally normal weight for age and height (eg, weight loss leading to maintenance of body weight less than 85% of that expected; or failure to make expected weight gain during period of growth, leading to body weight less than 85% of that expected).
(B) Intense fear of gaining weight or becoming fat, even though underweight.
(C) Disturbance in the way in which one's body weight or shape is experienced, undue influence of body weight or shape on self-evaluation, or denial of the seriousness of the current low body weight.
(D) In postmenarcheal females, amenorrhea, ie the absence of at least three consecutive menstrual cycles. (A woman is considered to have amenorrhea if her periods occur only following hormone, eg estrogen, administration.)

Specify type:

Restricting Type: during the current episode of Anorexia Nervosa, the person has not regularly engaged in binge-eating or purging behavior (ie self-induced vomiting or the misuse of laxatives, diuretics, or enemas).

Binge-Eating/Purging Type: during the current episode of Anorexia Nervosa, the person has regularly engaged in binge-eating or purging behavior (ie, self-induced vomiting or the misuse of laxatives, diuretics, or enemas).

DIAGNOSTIC CRITERIA FOR F50.2 BULIMIA NERVOSA

(A) Recurrent episodes of binge-eating. An episode of binge-eating is characterized by both of the following:
  (1) eating, in a discrete period of time (eg, within any 2-hour period), an amount of food that is definitely larger than most people would eat during a similar period of time and under similar circumstances;
  (2) a sense of lack of control over eating during the episode (eg, a feeling that one cannot stop eating or control what or how much one is eating).
(B) Recurrent inappropriate compensatory behavior in order to prevent weight gain, such as self-induced vomiting; misuse of laxatives, diuretics, enemas, or other medications; fasting; or excessive exercise.
(C) The binge-eating and inappropriate compensatory behaviors both occur, on average, at least twice a week for three months.
(D) Self-evaluation is unduly influenced by body shape and weight.
(E) The disturbance does not occur exclusively during episodes of Anorexia Nervosa.

Specify type:

Purging Type: during the current episode of Bulimia Nervosa, the person has regularly engaged in self-induced vomiting or the misuse of laxatives, diuretics, or enemas.

Nonpurging Type: during the current episode of Bulimia Nervosa, the person has used other inappropriate compensatory behaviors, such as fasting or excessive exercise, but has not regularly engaged in self-induced vomiting or the misuse of laxatives, diuretics, or enemas.

F50.9   EATING DISORDER NOT OTHERWISE SPECIFIED

The Eating Disorder Not Otherwise Specified category is for disorders of eating that do not meet the criteria for any specific Eating Disorder. Examples include:

(1) For females, all of the criteria for Anorexia Nervosa are met except that the individual has regular menses.
(2) All of the criteria for Anorexia Nervosa are met except that, despite significant weight loss, the individual's current weight is in the normal range.
(3) All of the criteria for Bulimia Nervosa are met except that the binge-eating and inappropriate compensatory mechanisms occur at a frequency of less than twice a week or for a duration of less than 3 months.
(4) The regular use of inappropriate compensatory behavior by an individual of normal body weight after eating small amounts of food (eg self-induced vomiting after the consumption of two cookies).
(5) Repeatedly chewing and spitting out, but not swallowing, large amounts of food.
(6) Binge-eating disorder: recurrent episodes of binge-eating in the absence of the regular use of inappropriate compensatory behaviors characteristic of Bulimia Nervosa (see p 747 for suggested research criteria).

Draft Form for Refusal of Treatment to be Signed by the Patient

---

CONFIRMATION OF REFUSAL OF RECOMMENDED TREATMENT

Patient's name	Susan Patient	**Patient no.**	AB1000
Address	15 Acacia Avenue, Blankton, Blankshire BL15 5PW		
Ward	Elderberry		
Attending doctor	Dr James Concern		
Position	Consultant physician	**Date**	10th January 2000

STATEMENT OF PATIENT

I, the above-named patient, confirm that I have been advised by the medical practitioner whose name appears above that in order to prevent a deterioration in my health/permanent injury/ or death* I should receive the following treatment:

> *one or more blood transfusions as considered necessary by those providing me with medical treatment.*

I understand that if I do not receive this treatment my health may deteriorate and that I may suffer serious permanent injury or die as a result.* I confirm that I am not willing to consent to such treatment being given to me now or in the future in spite of this.

I have reached this decision of my own free will and have not been subjected to improper pressure or persuasion of any kind.

I understand that I may change the decision recorded in this document at any time while I remain conscious and mentally competent by telling a doctor or nurse, but that if I lose consciousness or my mental competence, I will not then be able to do so.

Patient's signature	Susan Patient
Witness' signature	Alison Carer
Witness position/address	Ward Sister, Elderberry Ward

STATEMENT OF ATTENDING DOCTOR

I, the above-named doctor, confirm that I have advised the above-named patient that the treatment specified above is required to prevent a deterioration in health/serious injury/death* and that in my opinion the patient understands the advice I have given and is competent to make an independent decision about this medical treatment.

Doctor's signature   J Concern   **Date**   10/1/2000

Delete as appropriate

Appendix 8.2

Draft Record of Refusal of Treatment to be Signed By Doctor

RECORD OF REFUSAL OF RECOMMENDED TREATMENT

Patient's name	Susan Patient	**Patient no.**	AB1000

Address   15 Acacia Avenue, Blankton, Blankshire BL15 5PW

Ward   Elderberry

Attending doctor   Dr James Concern

Position   Consultant physician

Date   10th January 2000

I, the above-named doctor, confirm that on the above date I have advised the patient whose name appears above that in order to prevent a deterioration in the patient's health/permanent/ injury, or death* he/she should receive the following treatment:

> *one or more blood transfusions as considered necessary*

I have advised the patient that if he/she does not receive this treatment his/her health may deteriorate and that he/she may suffer serious permanent injury or die as a result.*

In spite of this advice the patient has refused to give consent to this treatment being given.

In my opinion the patient has not lost the capacity to make a decision to consent or refuse this treatment, and I know of no facts which suggest to me that the patient is acting under the undue influence of others.

I have explained to the patient that he/she may change the decision recorded in this document at any time while remaining conscious and mentally competent by telling a doctor or nurse, but that if he/she loses consciousness or mental competence, he/she will not then be able to do so.

The patient has refused to sign a statement confirming his/her decision and has maintained that refusal in spite of being shown a copy of this document.

Doctor's signature   J Concern   **Date**   10/1/2000

Witness' signature   Alison Carer

Witness position/address   Ward Sister, Elderberry Ward

*Delete as appropriate

Appendix 8.3

Draft Specific Issue Order for Administration of Blood Products to Child

---

IN THE HIGH COURT OF JUSTICE   Case No WG 2000/001

FAMILY DIVISION

PRINCIPAL REGISTRY

BEFORE THE HONOURABLE MR JUSTICE GOODWILL

IN THE MATTER OF THE INHERENT JURISDICTION OF THE COURT

AND IN THE MATTER OF THE CHILDREN ACT 1989

B E T W E E N :

BLANKSHIRE COUNTY COUNCIL

Applicant

– and –

SUSAN PATIENT (A child)
(By her litigation friend the OFFICIAL SOLICITOR)
Respondent

– and –

JOSEPH PATIENT

Respondents

ORDER

UPON reading the application, and affidavits herein

AND UPON hearing the evidence of Mr and Mrs Joseph Patient, Dr Goodley,

AND UPON hearing counsel for the applicant and the Respondents

IT IS ORDERED that there be a specific issue order in respect of the child, namely that:

1. In an immediately life-threatening situation, when it is the professional opinion of those medically responsible for the said child, that she is in need of the administration of blood products, she shall be given such blood products without the consent of her parents.

2. In any situation which is less than imminently life-threatening, those medically responsible for the child shall consult with the parents and will consider at every opportunity all alternative forms of management suggested by the parents. In the event that those medically responsible for the child conclude, after such consultation, that there is no reasonable alternative to the administration of blood products, they shall be at liberty to administer such blood products without the consent of the parents.

Note: Taken from Re R (a minor) (medical treatment) [1993] 2 FCR 544. While phrased as a specific issue order it could be easily converted to an order under the inherent jurisdiction by the omission of the words 'that there be a specific issue order'.

Appendix 9.1

Practice Note (Official Solicitor: Vegetative State)
[1996] 2 FLR 375

The need for the prior sanction of a High Court judge
The termination of artificial feeding and hydration for patients in a vegetative state will in virtually all cases require the prior sanction of a High Court judge: *Airedale NHS Trust v Bland* [1993] AC 789, 805 per Sir Stephen Brown P, and *Frenchay Healthcare NHS Trust v S* [1994] 1 FLR 485.

The diagnosis should be made in accordance with the most up-to-date generally accepted guidelines for the medical profession. A working group of the Royal College of Physicians issued guidance on the diagnosis and management of the permanent vegetative state (PVS) in March 1996 ((1996) 30 J R Coll Physns 119-21). This has been endorsed by the Conference of Medical Royal Colleges. The working group advises that the diagnosis of PVS is not absolute but based on probabilities. Such a diagnosis may not reasonably be made until the patient has been in a continuing vegetative state following head injury for more than 12 months or following other causes of brain damage for more than 6 months. Before then, as soon as the patient's condition has stabilised, rehabilitative measures such as coma arousal programmes, should be instituted (see *Airedale NHS Trust v Bland* at 870–871 per Lord Goff). It is not appropriate to apply to court for permission to terminate artificial feeding and hydration until the condition is judged to be permanent. In many cases it will be necessary to commission reports based on clinical and other observations of the patient over a period of time.

Applications to court
Applications to court should be by originating summons issued in the Family Division of the High Court seeking a declaration in the form set out in para (5) below. Subject to specific provisions below, the application should follow the procedure laid down for sterilisation cases by the House of Lords in *Re F (Mental Patient: Sterilisation)* [1990] 2 AC 1, [1989] 2 FLR 376 and in the *Practice Note – Official Solicitor: Sterilisation* (June 996) [1996] 2 FLR 111.

Applications to court in relation to minors should be made within wardship. In such cases the applicant should seek the leave of the court for the termination of feeding and hydration, rather than a declaration. The form of relief set out in para 5 below should be amended accordingly.

The originating summons should seek relief in the following form:

It is declared that despite the inability of X to give a valid consent, the plaintiffs and/or the responsible medical practitioners:

(i) may lawfully discontinue all life-sustaining treatment and medical support measures (including ventilation, nutrition and hydration by artificial means) designed to keep X alive in his existing permanent vegetative state; and
(ii) may lawfully furnish such treatment and nursing care whether at hospital or elsewhere under medical supervision as may be appropriate to ensure X suffers the least distress and retains the greatest dignity until such time as his life comes to an end.

It is ordered that in the event of a material change in the existing circumstances occurring before such withdrawal of treatment any party shall have liberty to apply for such further or other declaration or order as may be just.'

The case will normally be heard in open court. The court will, however, usually take steps to preserve the anonymity of the patient and the patient's family (and, where appropriate, the hospital) by making orders under s 11 of the Contempt of Court Act 1981: *Re G (Adult Patient: Publicity)* [1995] 2 FLR 528. An order restricting publicity will continue to have effect notwithstanding the death of the patient, unless and until an application is made to discharge it: *Re C (Adult Patient: Publicity)* [1996] 2 FLR 251).

The parties
The applicant may be either the next-of-kin or other individual closely connected with the patient or the relevant district health authority/NHS trust (which, in any event, ought to be a party): *Re S (Hospital Patient: Court's Jurisdiction)* [1996] Fam 1, CA). The views of the next-of-kin or of others close to the patient cannot act as a veto to an application but they must be taken fully into account by the court: *Re G (Persistent Vegetative State)* [1995] 2 FCR 46.

The Official Solicitor should normally be invited to act as guardian ad litem of the patient, who will inevitably be a patient within the meaning of RSC Ord 80. In any case in which the Official Solicitor does not represent the patient, he should be joined as a defendant or respondent.

The investigation
There should be at least two independent reports on the patient from neurologists or other doctors experienced in assessing disturbances of consciousness. One of these reports will be commissioned by the Official Solicitor. The duties of doctors making the diagnosis are described in the report of the working group of the Royal College of Physicians as follows:

'They should undertake their own assessment separately and should write clearly the details of that assessment and their conclusion in the notes. They must ask medical and other clinical staff and relatives or carers about the reactions and responses of the patient and it is important that the assessors shall take into account the descriptions and comments given by relatives, carers and nursing staff who spend most time with the patient. The medical practitioners shall separately perform a formal neurological examination and consider the results of those investigations which have been undertaken to identify the cause of the condition. It is helpful for nursing staff and relatives to be present during the examination; their role as responsible witnesses who spend a much longer time with the patient than can the medical practitioners must be recognised.

It is to be emphasised that there is no urgency in making the diagnosis of the permanent vegetative state. If there is any uncertainty in the mind of the assessor then the diagnosis shall not be made and a reassessment undertaken after further time has elapsed. The most important role of the medical practitioner in making the diagnosis is to ensure that the patient is not sentient and, in this respect, the views of the nursing staff, relatives and carers are of considerable importance and help.'

The views of the patient and others
The Official Solicitor's representative will normally require to interview the next-of-kin and others close to the patient as well as seeing the patient and those caring

for him. The views of the patient may have been previously expressed, either in writing or otherwise. The High Court may determine the effect of a purported advance directive as to future medical treatment: *Re T (Adult: Refusal of Medical Treatment)* [1993] Fam 95, sub nom *Re T (An Adult) (Consent to Medical Treatment)* [1992] 2 FLR 458; *Re C (Refusal of Medical Treatment)* [1994] 1 FLR 31. In summary, the patient's previously expressed views, if any, will always be an important component in the decisions of the doctors and the court, particularly if they are clearly established and were intended to apply to the circumstances which have in fact arisen.

Consultation with the Official Solicitor
Members of the Official Solicitor's legal staff are prepared to discuss PVS cases before proceedings have been issued. Contact with the Official Solicitor may be made by telephoning 0171–911–7127 during office hours.

Practice Note replaces the Practice Note dated March 1994 reported at [1994] 1 FLR 654.

PETER HARRIS
Official Solicitor

Appendix 9.2

Draft Direction in PVS Case

IN THE HIGH COURT OF JUSTICE

FAMILY DIVISION

PRINCIPAL REGISTRY

Before ...   in Chambers

and in the Matter of the Supreme Court Act 1981

Between

Narnia Hospital NHS Trust	**Claimant**
and	
C S Lewis	**Defendant**

Draft/Directions Order

UPON HEARING Solicitor for the Claimant and Solicitor for the Defendant

AND UPON READING the documents filed herein

IT IS ORDERED THAT

1. The Official Solicitor be appointed as the Defendant's litigation friend;

2. For the purposes of these proceedings and during the trial:

    (*a*) the Defendant be referred to as Mr L;

    (*b*) any witness (other than an expert witness) who gives evidence, whether by affidavit or otherwise in writing, or orally, be referred to by the initial of their surname;

    (*c*) the hospital in which the defendant is being cared for be referred to as 'the hospital' and the claimant must be referred to as 'The Trust';

3. At the trial, any witness (other than an expert witness) who gives oral evidence in these proceedings be permitted not to disclose their name or address in open Court;

4. No person may disclose the identity of any party or witness in these proceedings (other than an expert witness), the Court considering non-disclosure necessary to protect the Defendant;

5. (i) There be permission to the Official Solicitor pursuant to Part 35.4 of the Civil Procedure Rules to instruct a report from Dr Aslan, a Consultant Neurologist;

    (ii) There be permission to the Official Solicitor to disclose to the said Consultant Neurologist all medical notes and documents filed herein;

6. The Official Solicitor do file and serve his report by 4 pm on the day prior to the hearing.

7. A Paginated Bundle to be lodged with the Court (Clerk of the Rules Department Room WG 5) at the Royal Courts of Justice, Strand, London WC2 by 4.00 pm on the day prior to the hearing;

8. The matter be listed for hearing before a High Court Judge of the Family Division at the Royal Courts of Justice, Strand, London WC2 on [*insert date for hearing*]

9. Costs reserved.

Appendix 9.3

Draft Order IN PVS Case

IN THE HIGH COURT OF JUSTICE   **Case No: FD00P11143**

PRINCIPAL REGISTRY

THE FAMILY DIVISION

BEFORE THE HONOURABLE MR JUSTICE WARDROBE

B E T W E E N :

An NHS TRUST   **Claimant**

– and –

Mr L

(by his litigation friend the Official Solicitor)   **Defendant**

DRAFT/ORDER

UPON HEARING Ms Lion, Counsel for the Claimant, and Ms Thompson, Counsel for the Official Solicitor

AND ON HEARING evidence from Dr X, Dr Aslan and Dr Hopkins,

and on reading the evidence filed herein

IT IS DECLARED THAT:

1. Mr L lacks the capacity of make decisions as to future medical treatment;

2. It is not in the existing circumstances in the best interests of Mr L for continued artificial nutrition and hydration to be provided;

3. The Claimant and/or the responsible attending medical practitioners, nurses and health care staff

    (*a*) may lawfully discontinue and withhold all life-sustaining treatment and medical support measures (including ventilation, nutrition and hydration by artificial means) designed to keep Mr L alive in the permanent vegetative state; and
    (*b*) may lawfully furnish such treatment and nursing care whether at hospital or elsewhere under medical supervision as may be appropriate to ensure Mr L retains the greatest dignity until such time as his life comes to an end.

AND IT IS ORDERED THAT:

1. In the event of a material change in the existing circumstances occurring before the discontinuance of such treatment each party shall have liberty to apply for such further or other declaration or orders as may be just;

2. No person shall disclose or publish in connection with these proceedings nor when publishing the text of the whole or any part of this order, save for the

purpose of caring for the Defendant or for the purpose of communications with any person exercising a function authorised by statute or by any court of competent jurisdiction, the name, address or photograph of:-

(*a*) the Claimant or its hospital;
(*b*) the Defendant or any family members;
(*c*) the responsible treating medical practitioners, nursing staff and care assistants or workers;
(*d*) any witness, other than an expert witness, who gives evidence in these proceedings whether by statement or otherwise in writing or orally; and

3. BY CONSENT the Claimant shall pay one-half of the costs of the Official Solicitor.

Dated this

Appendix 9.4

RCP: Criteria for the Diagnosis of Brain Stem Death

Review by a working group convened by the Royal College of Physicians of London April 1996

Endorsed by the Conference of Medical Royal Colleges and their Faculties in the United Kingdom

This review was first published in: The journal of the Royal College of Physicians Vol 29 No 5 September/October 1995

This review of the criteria used in the diagnosis of brain stem death (hitherto known as brain death) has been produced to update earlier documents on this subject published by the Conference of Medical Royal Colleges and their Faculties (Conference of Colleges) between 1976 and 1981 [1–4] and the relevant sections of the Department of Health revised guidelines published in 1983 [5].

The definition of death
It is suggested that 'irreversible loss of the capacity for consciousness, combined with irreversible loss of the capacity to breathe' should be regarded as the definition of death. The irreversible cessation of brain stem function (brain stem death) whether induced by intracranial events or the result of extracranial phenomena such as anoxia will produce the forementioned clinical state and therefore brain stem death is equivalent to the death of the individual. It is suggested that the more correct term 'brain stem death' should henceforth replace the term 'brain death' used in previous papers produced by the Conference of Colleges and the Department of Health.

The diagnosis of brain stem death
The clinical criteria for the diagnosis of brain stem death identified by the Conference of Colleges during the period 1976–1981 have been confirmed by all published series and have therefore been adequately validated.

(*a*) *The beating heart in brain stem death* – Even if ventilation is continued, both adults and children will suffer cessation of heart beat within a few days, very occasionally a few weeks, of the diagnosis of brain stem death.

(*b*) *Endocrinological and metabolic abnormalities* – Endocrinological abnormalities, such as diabetes insipidus, biochemical abnormalities, such as hypo- or hypernatraemia, and hypothermia may occur in patients following anoxic, haemorrhagic or traumatic cerebral injury. These endocrinological abnormalities may be consequences of brain stem failure and must be differentiated from causative abnormalities of endocrinological, biochemical or autonomic function.

(*c*) *Limb and trunk movements* – Reflex movements of the limbs and torso may occur after brain stem death. The doctor should be able to explain clearly the significance of these movements to relatives, who should understand that they are of a reflex and not a voluntary nature.

(*d*) *Investigations* – The accuracy of the clinical criteria for the diagnosis of brain stem death during the past 17 years provides justification for not including the results of neurophysiological or imaging investigations as part of those

273

criteria. At present there is no evidence that imaging, electroencephalography or evoked potentials assist in the determination of brain stem death
and, though such techniques will be kept under review, they should not
presently form part of the diagnostic requirements.

(e) *Children and the very young* – A report of a working party of the British
Paediatric Association in 1991 [6], supported by the Council of the Royal
College of Physicians suggested that, in children over the age of two months,
the brain stem death criteria should be the same as those in adults. There is
insufficient information on children under the age of two months and on
premature babies to define guidelines. A working party of the Conference of
Colleges on *Organ transplantation in neonates* in 1988 [7] recommended that
organs for transplantation may be removed from anencephalic infants when
two doctors who are not members of the transplant team agree that spontaneous respiration has ceased.

(f) *The persistent vegetative state* – Problems relating to the diagnosis and
management of the persistent vegetative state must not be confused with
those relating to brain stem death.

(g) *Peripheral neurological syndromes of critical care* – There is a range of
overlapping neuropathic, neuromuscular and myopathic syndromes which
may occur in the context of critical care and may cause problems in weaning
a patient from a ventilator. This is not true apnoea (respiratory centre
paralysis) and should not be taken as evidence of brain stem death.

Conditions under which the diagnosis of brain stem death should be considered

(1) There should be no doubt that the patient's condition is due to irremediable
brain damage of known aetiology (see Note 1).
(2) The patient is deeply comatose:
    (a) There should be no suspicion that this state is due to depressant drugs
(see Note 2);
    (b) Primary hypothermia as a cause of coma must have been excluded;
    (c) Potentially reversible metabolic and endocrine disturbances must have
been excluded as the likely cause of the continuation of coma. It is
recognised that metabolic and endocrine disturbances are a likely
accompaniment of brain stem death (eg hyponatraemia, diabetes insipidus) but these are the effect rather than the cause of that condition and
do not preclude the diagnosis of brain stem death.
(3) The patient is being maintained on the ventilator because spontaneous
respiration has become inadequate or ceased altogether (see Note 3).

*It is essential that these conditions be satisfied before the diagnosis of brain stem
death is considered or further investigated.*

Notes

1. It may be obvious within hours of a primary intracranial event such as severe
head injury, spontaneous intracranial haemorrhage or following neurosurgery
that the condition is irremediable. However, when a patient has suffered primarily from cardiac arrest, hypoxia or severe circulatory insufficiency with an
indefinite period of cerebral anoxia, or is suspected of having cerebral air or fat
embolism, it may take longer to establish the diagnosis and to be confident of the
prognosis. In some patients the primary pathology may be a matter of doubt and
a confident diagnosis may only be reached by continuity of clinical observation
and investigation.

2. Narcotics, hypnotics and tranquillisers may have prolonged duration of
action, particularly when hypothermia co-exists or in the context of renal or

hepatic failure. The benzodiazepines are markedly cumulative and persistent in their actions and are commonly used as anti-convulsants or to assist synchronisation with mechanical ventilators. It is therefore essential that the drug history should be carefully reviewed and any possibility of intoxication being the cause of or contributing to the patient's comatose state should preclude a diagnosis of brain stem death. It is important to recognise that in some patients anoxia may have followed the ingestion of a drug but in this situation the criteria for brain stem death will not be applicable until such time as the drug effects have been excluded.

3.   Relaxants (neuromuscular blocking agents) and other drugs must have been excluded as the cause of respiratory inadequacy or failure. Immobility, unresponsiveness, and lack of spontaneous respiration may be due to the use of neuromuscular blocking drugs and the persistence of their effects should be excluded by the elicitation of deep tendon reflexes or by the demonstration of adequate neuromuscular conduction with a conventional nerve stimulator Persistent effects of hypnotics or narcotics must be excluded as the cause of respiratory failure.

References

1   Conference of Medical Royal Colleges and their Faculties in the United Kingdom. Diagnosis of brain death. *Br Med J* 1976;ii: 1187–8.
2   Conference of Medical Royal Colleges and their Faculties in the United Kingdom. Diagnosis of brain death. *Lancet* 1976;ii: 1069–70.
3   Conference of Medical Royal Colleges and their Faculties in the United Kingdom. Diagnosis of death. *Br Med J* 1979; i: 332.
4   Conference of Medical Royal Colleges and their Faculties in the United Kingdom. Diagnosis of death. *Lancet* 1979; i: 261–2.
5   Health Departments of Great Britain and Northern Ireland. *Cadaveric organs for transplantation: a code of practice including the diagnosis of brain death.* **London**: HMSO, 1983.
6   British Paediatric Association. *Diagnosis of brain stem death in infant and children.* Report of a working party. London: BPA, 1991.
7   Conference of Medical Royal Colleges and their Faculties in the United Kingdom. *Organ transplantation in neonates.* London: Royal College of Physicians, 1988.

Members of the working group

Sir Douglas Black (Chairman); Professor Sir Leslie Turnberg President, Royal College of Physicians; Professor David London Registrar, Royal College of Physicians; Dr D Bates Consultant Neurologist, Royal Victoria Infirmary, Newcastle upon Tyne; Dr N Melia Observer, Department of Health; Dr C Pallis Reader Emeritus in Neurology, Royal Postgraduate Medical School, Hammersmith; Dr P F Prior formerly Consultant in charge of Clinical Neurophysiology, St Bartholomew's Hospital, London; Mr K Rolles Consultant Surgeon and Director of the Liver Transplant Unit, The Royal Free Hospital, London (representing the Royal College of Surgeons); Dr J C Stoddart formerly Consultant Anaesthetist, Royal Victoria Infirmary, Newcastle upon Tyne (representing the Royal College of Anaesthetists); Dr C R Kennedy Consultant Paediatric Neurologist, Southampton General Hospital; Professor J D Pickard Bayer Professor of Neurosurgery, University of Cambridge.

Appendix 9.5

RCP: The Permanent Vegetative State

Reproduced by permission of the Royal College of Physicians of London
Review by a working group convened by the Royal College of Physicians.
Endorsed by the Conference of Medical Royal Colleges and their Faculties in the
United Kingdom.

April 1996

This review was first published in: The Journal of the Royal College of Physicians
Vol 30 No 2 March/April 1996

Copyright © 1996 Royal College of Physicians of London

The working group was convened following a recommendation of the House of Lords Select Committee on Medical Ethics that PVS should be defined and a code of practice developed relating to its management [1].

Defining the vegetative state
The Working Group recognises that the commonly used acronym 'PVS' can denote either the '*persistent* vegetative state' [2] or the '*permanent* vegetative state' and could thus lead to confusion. It is therefore recommended that the following terms and definitions be used:

The vegetative state
A clinical condition of unawareness of self and environment in which the patient breathes spontaneously, has a stable circulation and shows cycles of eye closure and eye opening which may simulate sleep and waking. This may be a transient stage in the recovery from coma or it may persist until death.

The continuing vegetative state (CVS)
When the vegetative state continues for more than four weeks it becomes increasingly unlikely that the condition is part of a recovery phase from coma and the diagnosis of a continuing vegetative state can be made.

The permanent vegetative state (PVS)
A patient in a continuing vegetative state will enter a permanent vegetative state when the diagnosis of irreversibility can be established with a high degree of clinical certainty. It is a diagnosis which is not absolute but based on probabilities. Nevertheless, it may reasonably be made when a patient has been in a continuing vegetative state following head injury for more than 12 months or following other causes of brain damage for more than six months [3,4]. The diagnosis can be made at birth only in infants with anencephaly or hydranencephaly. For children with other severe malformations or acquired brain damage, observation for at least six months is recommended until lack of awareness can be established.

Criteria for diagnosis of permanent vegetative state
Preconditions

- There shall be an established cause for the condition. It may be due to acute cerebral injury, degenerative conditions, metabolic disorders or developmental malformations.

276

- The persisting effects of sedative, anaesthetic or neuromuscular blocking drugs shall be excluded. It is recognised that drugs may have been the original cause of an acute cerebral injury, usually hypoxic, but their continuing direct effect must be excluded either by passage of time or by appropriate analysis of body fluids.
- Reversible metabolic causes shall be corrected or excluded as the cause. Metabolic disturbances may occur during the course of a vegetative state and are an inevitable consequence of the terminal stage but should have been ruled out as causative.

Clinical criteria

1. There shall be no evidence of awareness of self or environment at any time. There shall be no volitional response to visual, auditory, tactile or noxious stimuli. There shall be no evidence of language comprehension or expression.
2. There shall be the presence of cycles of eye closure and eye opening which may simulate sleep and waking.
3. There shall be sufficiently preserved hypothalamic and brain stem function to ensure the maintenance of respiration and circulation.

These THREE clinical requirements shall ALL be fulfilled for the diagnosis to be considered.

Other clinical features are:

- There will be incontinence of bladder and bowel, spontaneous blinking and usually retained pupillary responses and corneal responses. The response to ice water caloric testing will be a tonic eye movement which can be conjugate or dysconjugate.
- There will not be nystagmus in response to ice water caloric testing, the patient will not have visual fixation, be able to track moving objects with the eyes or show a 'menace' response.
- There may be occasional movements of the head and eyes towards a peripheral sound or movement and there may be movement of the trunk and limbs in a purposeless way; some patients may appear to smile and the eyes may water, there may be a 'grimace' to painful stimuli. There may be startle myoclonus. These motor activities shall be inconsistent, non-purposeful and explicable as a reflex response to external stimuli. Deep tendon reflexes may be present and reduced, normal or brisk; plantar responses may be flexor or extensor; there may be clonus and other signs of spasticity. There may be roving eye movements.

Differential diagnosis (Table 1)
It is essential to distinguish the vegetative state from brain stem death, coma and the locked-in syndrome. The differentiation of these conditions is on clinical grounds; there is no evidence at present that electroencephalography, evoked potentials, computed tomography (CT) of the cranium or magnetic resonance imaging (MRI) of the cerebrum improve upon the clinical diagnosis. Patients who are in a permanent vegetative state may show changes of cortical atrophy and hydrocephalus on CT head scan, and positron emission tomography (PET) will show a reduction in cerebral metabolism; but neither finding is diagnostic of the permanent vegetative state.

The time course
There is evidence that the factors which influence the prognosis of patients in a continuing vegetative state are the cause of the condition and the length of time

for which it has continued. In patients who are in a continuing vegetative state following causes other than head injury there is very little hope of recovery of sentience after three months and none after six months. In patients who are in a continuing vegetative state after head injury the chances of recovery after six months are extremely low, and after 12 months non-existent [3, 4]. It is suggested that, whenever head injury is present, even when there is additional severe trauma, the longer of these time intervals be taken before the continuing vegetative state is termed 'permanent'.

Thus, the diagnosis of the permanent vegetative state should not be made before six months following non-head injury brain damage or 12 months following head injury.

Management of the patient in a vegetative state

Medical care – Prior to the diagnosis of a permanent vegetative state it is imperative that patients have a high quality of care with appropriate nursing or home care and that oxygenation, circulation and nutrition are maintained and complicating factors such as hypoglycaemia and infection corrected. Until there is firm scientific evidence that treatment, in terms of specific medical, physiotherapeutic or rehabilitative activities improves the outcome of patients in a continuing vegetative state it is a matter of clinical judgement as to the most appropriate measures, their application and the length of time they should be pursued. The medical staff must advise the relatives and carers of the situation during the continuing vegetative state.

Examination – When the diagnosis of a permanent vegetative state is being considered it is obligatory that the patient should be examined by two medical practitioners experienced in assessing disturbances of consciousness. They should undertake their own assessment separately and should write clearly the details of that assessment and their conclusion in the notes. They must ask medical and other clinical staff and relatives or carers about the reactions and responses of the patient and it is important that the assessors shall take into account the descriptions and comments given by relatives, carers and nursing staff who spend most time with the patient. The medical practitioners shall separately perform a formal neurological examination and consider the results of those investigations which have been undertaken to identify the cause of the condition. It is helpful for nursing staff and relatives to be present during the examination; their role as responsible witnesses who spend a much longer time with the patient than can the medical practitioners must be recognised.

Table 1 – Differentiation of vegetative state from other conditions

Condition	Vegetative state	Coma	Brain stem death	Locked-in syndrome
Self-awareness	Absent	Absent	Absent	Present
Cyclical eye opening	Present	Absent	Absent	Present
Glasgow coma Scale*	A4, B1–4, C1	A1–2, B1–4, C1–2	A1, B1–2, C1	A4, B1, C1
Motor function	No purposeful movement	No purposeful movement	None or only reflex spinal movement	Eye movement preserved in the vertical plane and able to blink volitionally

Experience of pain	No	No	No	Yes
Respiratory function	Normal	Depressed or varied	Absent	Normal
EEG activity	Polymorphic delta or theta – sometimes slow alpha	Polymorphic delta or theta	Electrocerebral silence or theta	Normal or minimally abnormal
Cerebral metabolism	Reduced by 50% or more	Reduced by 50% or more	Absent or greatly reduced	Minimally or moderately reduced
Prognosis	Depends on cause and length	Recovery, vegetative state, or death within 2–4 weeks	No recovery	Depends on cause though recovery unlikely

Glasgow coma Scale:	A	EYE OPENING	B	MOTOR FUNCTION	C	VERBAL
	1	No response	1	No response	1	None
	2	To pain	2	Extension	2	Grunts
	3	To voice	3	Flexion	3	Inappropriate words
	4	Spontaneously	4	Flexion	4	Confused

Re-assessment – It is to be emphasised that there is no urgency in making the diagnosis of the permanent vegetative state. If there is any uncertainty in the mind of the assessor then the diagnosis shall not be made and a re-assessment undertaken after further time has elapsed. The most important role of the medical practitioner in making the diagnosis is to ensure that the patient is not sentient and, in this respect, the views of nursing staff, relatives and carers are of considerable importance and help.

Final definitive diagnosis and decisions concerning life support
When the diagnosis of a permanent vegetative state has been established by (*a*) identification of the cause for the syndrome; (*b*) the clinical state of the patient; and (*c*) the lapse of time, recovery cannot be achieved and further therapy is futile. It merely prolongs an insentient life for the patient and a hopeless vigil for relatives and carers. The clinical team of doctors and nurses, augmented when necessary by colleagues, should formally review the clinical evidence. The decision, when made on full evidence that the situation is, in lay terms, 'hopeless' should be communicated sensitively to the relatives who are then given time to consider the implications, including the possibility of withdrawing artificial means of administering food and fluid [5,6,7]. At present the courts require, as a matter of practice, that the decision to withdraw nutrition and hydration, resulting in the inevitable death of the patient, should be referred to the court before any action is taken [8]. A decision to withdraw other life sustaining medication such as insulin for diabetes may also need to be referred to the courts because the legal position on this is uncertain. By contrast, decisions not to intervene with cardio-

pulmonary resuscitation or to prescribe antibiotics, dialysis and insulin are clinical decisions. Further, those responsible for the patient's care must take account of, and respect, the patient's own views when known, whether these are formally recorded in a written document (or advance directive) or not [9]. When the medical team is agreed on the course to be taken the relatives should be counselled and their views sought, but (subject to court involvement) the decision is for those professionals who have the responsibility for the care of the patient.

References

1   House of Lords. *Report of the Select Committee on Medical Ethics*. Session 1993–4. London; HMSO, 1994, (HL Paper 21-I)
2   Jennett B, Plum F. Persistent vegetative state after brain damage: a syndrome in search of a name. *Lancet* 1972;1:734–7.
3   Multi-Society Task Force on PVS. Medical aspects of the persistent vegetative state (first part). *N Engl J Med* 1994;330: 1499–1508.
4   Multi-Society Task Force on PVS. Medical aspects of the persistent vegetative state (second part). *N Engl J Med* 1994;330: 15 72–9.
5   BMA Medical Ethics Committee. *Discussion paper on treatment of patients in persistent vegetative state*. London: BMA, 1992.
6   Institute of Medical Ethics Working Party on the Ethics of Prolonging Life and Assisting Death. Withdrawal of life-support from patients in a persistent vegetative state. *Lancet* l993;337:96–8.
7   BMA Medical Ethics Committee. *BMA guidelines on treatment decisions of patients in a persistent vegetative state*. London: BMA, 1994.
8   Howard RS, Miller DH. The persistent vegetative state: information on prognosis allows decisions to be made on management. *Br Med J* 1995;310:341–2.
9   Doyal L. Advanced directives: like a will, everybody should have one. *Br Med I* 1995;310:612–13.

Members of the working group

Sir Douglas Black (Chairman); Professor D London Registrar, Royal College of Physicians; Dr D Bates Consultant Neurologist, Royal Victoria Infirmary, Newcastle Upon Tyne; Revd Professor G R Dunstan member of Royal College of Physicians Committee on Ethics; Dr K W M Fulford Consultant Psychiatrist, Warneford Hospital, Oxford; Dr E Gadd Observer, Department of Health; Mrs J Gaffln Executive Director, National Council for Hospice and Specialist Palliative Care Services; Professor A Grubb Professor of Health Care Law, King's College, London; Dr J S Horner Chairman, Medical Ethics Committee, British Medical Association; Rabbi Julia Neuberger Chairman, Camden & Islington Community Health Services; Professor J D Pickard Bayer Professor of Neurosurgery, University of Cambridge; Professor R O Robinson Professor of Paediatric Neurology, Guy's Hospital; Dr D L Stevens Consultant Neurologist, Gloucestershire Royal Hospital.

Appendix 9.6

BMA: Guidance on Treatment Decisions for Patients in Persistent Vegetative State

Revised June 1996[1]

Defining PVS

The persistent vegetative state (PVS) presents particular medical, ethical and legal dilemmas because of the extreme nature of the condition, the difficulties associated with diagnosing it accurately and the risks of premature diagnosis. It results from severe damage to the cerebral cortex, resulting in irreparable destruction of tissue in the thinking, feeling part of the brain. Patients appear awake but show no psychologically meaningful responses to stimuli. It is widely accepted that PVS patients are unconscious and incapable of suffering mental distress or physical pain although many reflex responses remain. Research studies have shown that the level of metabolic functioning of the cerebral cortex of PVS patients is the level associated with deep surgical anaesthesia. Greater detail is given in Jennett, B *Managing Patients in Persistent Vegetative State since Airedale NHS Trust v Bland* in McLean S (ed) *Death, Dying and the Law*, Dartmouth Press, 1996.

Management of PVS has been extensively discussed by bodies such as the House of Lords, the Law Commissions of England and Scotland, the Royal College of Physicians (RCP) and the BMA's Medical Ethics Committee (MEC). In the United States, a Task Force The Multi-Society Task Force on PVS. Medical Aspects of the Persistent Vegetative State The New England Journal of Medicine, Vol 33, No 21, 1994 pp 1499–1508 and The New England Journal of Medicine, Vol 330, No 22, 1994 pp. 1572–1579 examined various aspects of the condition in depth and these views informed the subsequent guidance issued by the RCP in 1996 (Royal College of Physicians, The Permanent Vegetative State, Journal of the Royal College of Physicians of London, Vol 30, No. 2, 1996, pp 119–121). In its document, the RCP distinguishes between 'continuing vegetative state' and 'permanent vegetative state'. The former describes a patient's diagnosis prior to confirmation of the permanence of the condition. For the present time at least, the BMA retains the term 'persistent' rather than 'permanent' but continues to keep the arguments and the evidence under review. The BMA regards PVS as distinct from other forms of profound mental impairment. It considers PVS to be sufficiently discrete and extreme that its management can be defined, without raising implications for other categories of severe handicap.

Misdiagnosis

Although it is impossible to make a confident diagnosis in all suspected PVS cases, positron emission tomography can be helpful in some. An enduring cause for concern, however, have been the intermittent reports of alleged 'recovery' from PVS. In the BMA's view, recoveries, where they can be verified, indicate an original misdiagnosis. The BMA calls for thorough review of all suspected PVS cases and more research to be carried out in this area.

Initial assessment and treatment

A diagnosis of persistent vegetative state takes time. During the period of initial assessment, it is appropriate to provide aggressive medical treatment. The BMA believes that it is vital that stimulation and rehabilitation should be available for patients suspected of being in a persistent vegetative state as soon as their condition is stabilised. Clinicians should give active consideration to the wide range of specific measures which might effect some improvement in each individual case. Even if few patients improve as a result of being included in coma arousal programmes, the appropriateness of this and other options for each individual must be explored at an early stage. It is for clinical judgement to decide as to the most appropriate measures and the length of time they should be pursued. (See also the RCP guidance on the diagnosis and management of PVS cases, ibid.)

It is good medical practice to provide artificial nutrition and hydration to sustain any patient whose prognosis is uncertain. Medical treatments, including artificial nutrition and hydration, may be withdrawn at a later stage, after legal review of the case, if they are considered futile.

Diagnosis
Current methods of diagnosing PVS cannot be regarded as infallible. Before a PVS diagnosis is made, all appropriate clinical steps must be taken to eliminate other possibilities and clinicians must be aware of the dangers of prematurely diagnosing the patient's condition as 'permanent'. The BMA has consistently recommended that the diagnosis of irreversible PVS should not be considered confirmed (and therefore treatment not be withdrawn) until the patient has been insentient for 12 months. The Association recognises that distinction can be drawn between different categories of PVS patient depending on factors such as the patient's age and the manner in which the damage to the brain occurred. For some categories, PVS can be diagnosed with considerable certainty within three months. **The BMA, however, recommends that decisions to withdraw treatment should only be considered when the patient has been insentient for 12 months**. The BMA believes that the minimum 12 month period currently provides an essential safety net.

The BMA recommends that the diagnosing clinician should seek views from two other doctors, one of whom should be a neurologist. **In any case of doubt as to whether the patient's condition is irreversible, decisions about possible withdrawal of medical treatment must be deferred**.

Review of treatment options
The BMA recommends that a high standard of nursing care, good nutrition and stimulation should be available to all unconscious patients. Rehabilitative measures should be continued until clinicians consider such measures can no longer benefit the individual patient. Specialised expertise should be sought to clarify this in each case.

If it is apparent at the end of the one-year period that the patient's condition is irreversible, consideration may be given to withdrawal of treatment. The decision should be based on the same principles as other medical decisions. Factors include a careful evaluation of all the evidence regarding the patient's diagnosis and prognosis, involvement of an independent specialist opinion, consideration of the anticipated benefits or burdens of the treatment, the patient's views if known and sensitive discussion with people close to the patient. In some cases, doctors may then recommend the withdrawal of all treatment including artificial nutrition and hydration. In England and Wales, an application must be first made to the courts. In Scotland, the legal situation is currently less clear cut (see below). For specific advice on the legal position, doctors can either contact the BMA's Ethics Dept or (for England and Wales) the Office of the Official Solicitor.

The views of the patient
In considering treatment options, doctors should consider the patient's own views and values, if known. These views may be ascertained through patients' relatives

or, in some cases, may have been recorded in an advance statement. The BMA has a booklet (available from BMJ publications) and a separate free guidance note on advance statements. If an advance statement instructs that the life of a PVS patient be prolonged indefinitely or curtailed before the one-year period, doctors should seek further advice. Treatment decisions for incompetent patients must be based on an assessment of the patient's best interests which includes careful consideration of the patient's former views.

The views of people close to the patient

It is good practice for the doctors to consult the wishes of people close to the patient although their views alone do not necessarily determine treatment. Relatives need time to accept and understand the prognosis. A decision to withhold life-prolonging treatment, such as artificial feeding, requires the co-operation of those emotionally close to the patient and those who provide the nursing care. In many cases health professionals and relatives agree about provision or withdrawal of treatment. Even so, in England and Wales, withdrawal of treatment from PVS patients is subject to court review. (See below.)

Views of health professionals

Decisions to withdraw life-prolonging treatment should be deferred if there is disagreement within the health team about the diagnosis or prognosis. Nurses must be consulted since they have particular expertise and close contact with patients and their families. It must be recognised that decisions to withdraw artificial nutrition and hydration from a PVS patient impose particular burdens and distress on nursing staff who are also often providing support for patients' families in addition to caring for the patient.

Conscientious objection

Any health professionals opposing the withdrawal of treatment on moral rather than clinical grounds, should not be marginalised or asked to act contrary to their conscience. They can be transferred to other duties. In some cases, the patient may be moved.

SUMMARY OF 'WITHHOLDING AND WITHDRAWING LIFE-PROLONGING MEDICAL TREATMENT: GUIDANCE FOR DECISION MAKING'[2]

Setting the scene for decision making

The primary goal of medical treatment is to benefit the patient by restoring or maintaining the patient's health as far as possible, maximising benefit and minimising harm. [Section 1.1]

If treatment fails, or ceases, to give a net benefit to the patient (or if the patient has competently refused the treatment), the primary goal of medical treatment cannot be realised and the justification for providing the treatment is removed.

Unless some other justification can be demonstrated, treatment that does not provide net benefit to the patient may, ethically and legally, be withheld or withdrawn and the goal of medicine should shift to the palliation of symptoms. [Section 1.1]

Prolonging a patient's life usually, but not always, provides a health benefit to that patient. It is not an appropriate goal of medicine to prolong life at all costs, with no regard to its quality or the burdens of treatment. [Section 1.2]

Although emotionally it may be easier to withhold treatment than to withdraw that which has been started, there are no legal, or necessary morally relevant, differences between the two actions. [Section 6.1]

Treatment should never be withheld, when there is a possibility that it will benefit the patient, simply because withholding is considered to be easier than withdrawing treatment. [Section 6.2]

Decisions involving adults who have the capacity to make and communicate decisions or those who have a valid advance directive
A voluntary refusal of life-prolonging treatment by a competent adult must be respected. [Section 9.1]

Where a patient has lost the capacity to make a decision but has a valid advance directive refusing life-prolonging treatment, this must be respected. [Section 10.1]

A valid advance refusal of treatment has the same legal authority as a contemporaneous refusal and legal action could be taken against a doctor who provides treatment in the face of a valid refusal. [Section 10.3]

Decisions involving adults who do not have the capacity to make or communicate decisions and do not have a valid advance directive and decisions involving children and young people

Adults
People have varying levels of capacity and should be encouraged to participate in discussion and decision making about all aspects of their lives to the greatest extent possible. The graver the consequences of the decision, the commensurately greater the level of competence required to take that decision. [Section 13.2]

In England, Wales and Northern Ireland no other individual has the power to give or withhold consent for the treatment of an adult who lacks decision-making capacity but treatment may be provided, without consent, if it is considered by the clinician in charge of the patient's care to be necessary and in the best interests of the patient. [Section 13.3]

In Scotland a tutor dative may be able to make treatment decisions on behalf of adults who lack decision-making capacity. [Section 13.4]

The same principles apply when decisions are taken in relation to a woman who is pregnant with a viable foetus and is unable to make or communicate decisions. The foetus has no legal status and the decision must be that which represents the best interests of the pregnant woman.

The extent to which the woman's likely wishes about the outcome of the pregnancy may be taken into account in determining her best interests is unclear. In order that these matters may be fully explored, legal advice should be sought. [Section 13.7]

Babies, children and young people
The same moral duties are owed to babies, children and young people as to adults. [Section 14.1]

Those with parental responsibility for a baby or young child are legally and morally entitled to give or withhold consent to treatment. Their decisions will usually be determinative unless they conflict seriously with the interpretation of those providing care about the child's best interests. [Section 15.1]

Treatment in a young person's best interests may proceed where there is consent from somebody authorised to give it; the competent young person him or herself, somebody with parental responsibility or a Court.

However, a young person's refusal may not, in law, necessarily take precedence over the consent of either parents or a Court. [Section 16.2]

Even where they are not determinative, the views and wishes of competent young people are an essential component of the assessment of their best interests and should, therefore, be given serious consideration at all stages of decision making. [Section 16.3]

The process of decision making
Where relevant locally or nationally agreed guidelines exist for the diagnosis and management of the condition, these should be consulted as part of the clinical assessment. Additional advice should be sought where necessary. [Section 17.2]

Where there is reasonable doubt about its potential for benefit, treatment should be provided for a trial period with a subsequent prearranged review. If, following the review, it is decided that the treatment has failed or ceased to be of benefit to the patient, consideration should be given to its withdrawal. [Section 17.7]

Before a decision is made to withhold or withdraw treatment, adequate time, resources and facilities should be made available to permit a thorough and appropriate assessment of the patient's condition including, where appropriate, the patient's potential for self-awareness, awareness of others and the ability intentionally to interact with them.

This should involve a multidisciplinary team with expertise in undertaking this type of assessment. [Section 17.8]

The benefits, risks and burdens of the treatment in the particular case should be assessed. [Section 17.10]

Although ultimately the responsibility for treatment decisions rests with the clinician in charge of the patient's care, it is important, where non-emergency decisions are made, that account is taken of the views of other health professionals involved in the patient's care and people close to the patient, in order to ensure that the decision is as well informed as possible. [Section 18.2]

Even where their views have no legal status, those close to the patient can provide important information to help ascertain whether the patient would have considered life-prolonging treatment to be beneficial. [Section 18.3]

Good communication, both within the health care team and between the health team and the patient and/or those close to the patient, is an essential part of decision making. Wherever possible, consensus should be sought amongst all those consulted about whether the provision of life-prolonging treatment would benefit the patient. [Section 18.4]

Decisions to withhold or withdraw conventional treatment, on the basis that it is not providing a benefit to the patient, should be made by the clinician in overall charge of the patient's care following discussion with the rest of the health care team and, where appropriate, those close to the patient. Where the clinician's view is seriously challenged and agreement cannot be reached by other means, review by a Court would be advisable. [Section 19.3]

Decisions about withholding or withdrawing artificial nutrition and hydration
In England, Wales and Northern Ireland, proposals to withdraw artificial nutrition and hydration from a patient who is in persistent vegetative state, or in a state of very low awareness closely resembling PVS, currently require legal review. [Section 21.1]

In Scotland the withdrawal of artificial nutrition and hydration from a patient in PVS does not require a Court declaration. [Section 21.2]

The Courts have not specified that declarations should be sought before withholding or withdrawing artificial nutrition and hydration from patients who are not in persistent vegetative state.

Although a body of medical opinion has developed that such action would be appropriate in some cases (such as some patients who have suffered a serious stroke or have severe dementia), UK Courts have not yet considered such a case.

This arguably leaves doctors in an area of legal uncertainty and therefore open to challenge. [Section 21.4]

The BMA believes that the following additional safeguards should be applied to decisions to withhold or withdraw artificial nutrition and hydration from patients whose death is not imminent and whose wishes are not known. [Section 22.1]

(*a*) All proposals to withhold or withdraw artificial nutrition and hydration whether in hospital or in the community should be subject to formal clinical review by a senior clinician who has experience of the condition from which the patient is suffering and who is not part of the treating team.
(*b*) In England, Wales and Northern Ireland, where it is proposed to withdraw artificial nutrition and hydration from a patient in persistent vegetative state or a state closely resembling PVS, legal advice should be sought and a Court declaration is likely to be required until such time as the Courts have stated otherwise.
(*c*) All cases in which artificial nutrition and hydration has been withdrawn should be available for clinical review to ensure that appropriate procedures and guidelines were followed. Anonymised information should also be available to the Secretary of State on request and, where applicable, the Commission for Health Improvement.

Once a decision has been reached to withhold or withdraw life-prolonging treatment
The basis for the decision to withhold or withdraw life-prolonging treatment should be carefully documented in the patient's medical notes. [Section 25.1]

Decisions to withhold or withdraw life-prolonging treatment should be reviewed before and after implementation to take account of any change in circumstances. [Section 25.2]

Decisions to withdraw or withhold life-prolonging treatment should be subject to review and audit. [Section 25.3]

Although not responsible for making the decision to withhold or withdraw treatment, those close to the patient are often left with feelings of guilt and anxiety in addition to their bereavement. It is important that the family is supported both before and after the decision has been made to withdraw or withhold life-prolonging treatment. [Section 26.1]

The emotional and psychological burden on staff involved with withdrawing and withholding life-prolonging treatment should be recognised and adequate support mechanisms need to be available and easily accessible before, during and after decisions have been made. [Section 26.2]

Notes
1 Extract from www.bma.org.uk
2 July 1999. The full document is available online at http://www.bmjpg.com/withwith/contents.htm

Appendix 9.7

International Working Part Report on the Vegetative State

Royal Hospital for Neuro-disability
February 1996

APPENDIX

Terminology
Terminology was one area where there was no clear agreement amongst the members of the Working Party and therefore recommendations are not made in the main body of the report. However, since terminology is so fundamental to the communication about the condition this Appendix explains some of the discussions in an attempt to provide a basis for other groups to reach a more satisfactory conclusion.

There was considerable discussion and marked differences in opinion among the Working Party as to whether there was one or several forms of Vegetative State. What was agreed was that there were at least several presentations within the diagnosis of Vegetative State.

Attempts were made to define and name these presentations. There was general agreement on the presentations but no agreement was achieved on the terminology to be used. There were members of the Working Party who wanted the term 'Vegetative State' to be included, whilst others wished to avoid the term altogether. There were some members who felt that there were distinct types of Vegetative State whilst others felt that there were only variations within a single state.

(*a*) The approaches attempted for those who were vegetative were as follows:
  (1) To describe the level of responsiveness: hyporesponsive or nil-reactive state; reflex responsive state; and localising responsive state. For those who wanted to include the term 'vegetative' then this could become hyporesponsive vegetative state; reflex responsive vegetative state and localising responsive vegetative state. One of the major arguments against this is that all reflex activities can be regarded as being a response and therefore the term may add to confusion.
  (2) To describe in terms of the reflex presentation: hyporeflexic state; primary reflexic state; localising reflexic state. For those wishing to include the word 'vegetative' this could be added before the word 'state'.
  (3) To simply term the presentations as Type I, Type II, Type III Vegetative State and avoid descriptive terms. There was concern from some members that this implied that Vegetative State was more than one diagnosis, a concept which they did not accept.
  (4) To name the terms in Stages (I, II, III) of the Vegetative State and avoid descriptive terms. Some felt that these were not necessarily 'stages' but specific entities.
  (5) To avoid the term 'Vegetative State' and describe in terms of 'Types' or 'Stages' of 'Profound Brain Damage'. There were strong arguments placed that this would not be helpful because it would include too broad a range of disorders and presentations.

(6) There were some who preferred the term 'Non-Relational' to replace the term 'Vegetative' ie Hyporesponsive Non-Relational State, Reflex Non-Relational State etc. This would then fit in with the use of the terms 'Inconsistent Relational State' and 'Consistent Relational State' for the non-vegetative conditions (see below).

(b) Several approaches were also discussed for those who had progressed from the Vegetative State but were still at a very low cognitive level. It was agreed that there were two basic levels - inconsistent and consistent responses. Within each of these categories terminology could be used as follows:

(1) To continue the theme of 'responsive state' as inconsistent and consistent responsive states. The term 'vegetative' could obviously not now be added to this group.

(2) To introduce the term 'relational state' to take over from the 'reflex states' described above.

(3) To accept the commonly used term 'low (or minimal) awareness states' (sub-dividing into inconsistent and consistent). The main reservation was that even cognitively unimpaired people may become temporarily unaware of their surroundings. This terminology, however, did have strong supporters.

(4) To accept another commonly used term of 'minimal responsive state'. The concern by some members was that reflex reactions can be regarded as minimal responses and that the term was not as definitive as was required.

The following tables put these terms together with the description of the clinical presentation:

COMA

Coma	Patient does not have a sleep-awake pattern (in absence of bilateral third cranial nerve lesion); may respond to painful stimulation by reflex pattern responses; displays no detectable signs of awareness.

VEGETATIVE PRESENTATIONS

Hyporesponsive State/ Hyporeflexic State/ Nil Reactive State/ Type I Vegetative State/ Type I Profound Brain Damage Stage I Vegetative State Type I Profound Brain Damage Stage I Profound Brain Damage	These patients have a sleep-awake pattern. They may respond on occasions by a reflex activity in a delayed fashion but are generally unresponsive to stimulation from the environment; displays no detectable signs of awareness.
Reflexic Responsive State/ Primary Reflexic State/ Type II Vegetative State/ Type II Profound Brain Damage Stage II Vegetative State Type II Profound Brain Damage Stage II Profound Brain Damage	Patient has sleep-awake patterns. The patient generally responds in mass extensor responses or startle responses to stimulation without habituation*. This may progress into flexor withdrawal responses. There may be roving eye movements but not tracking; displays no detectable signs of awareness; facial expressions may occur to stimulation.

Localising Responsive State/ Localising Reflexic State/ Type III Vegetative State/ Type III Profound Brain Damage Stage III Vegetative State Type III Profound Brain Damage Stage III Profound Brain Damage	Patient has sleep-awake patterns; single limb response to stimulation; withdrawal or intermittent localisation to touch, sound or visual stimulation may occur; tracking eye movements may occur but the patient does not focus on objects or people; may turn to sound or touch.

* The term habituate is scientifically defined as a decreasing effectiveness of a stimulus. Thompson and Spencer's definition of habituation is 'a response decrement as a function of stimulus repetition which does not result from either receptor adaptation or effector fatigue'. Thompson R F, Spencer WW. Habituation: A model phenomenon for the study of neuronal substrates of behavior. *Pschol Rev* 1966; 73: 16–43.

UNDECIDED*

Transitional State/ Borderline State/ Type IV Vegetative State/ Type IV Profound Brain Damage Stage IV Vegetative State Stage IV Profound Brain Damage	The patient has a sleep-awake pattern being awake for a major part of the day; generally more definite localising to visual, auditory or tactile stimulation; tracking eye movements following objects or people; may show emotional responses to presence of family; may smile or cry.

* Agreement was not reached as to whether this stage was vegetative or non-vegetative.

NON-VEGETATIVE STATES

Inconsistent Responsive State/ Inconsistent Relational State/ Inconsistent Low Awareness State/ Inconsistent Minimal Awareness State/ Inconsistent Minimal Responsive State Type V Profound Brain Damage	Patient has sleep-awake pattern; responds to simple commands inconsistently; remains totally dependent; profound cognitive impairments.
Stage V Profound Brain Damage Relational Responsive State/ Consistent Low Awareness State/ Consistent Minimal Awareness State/ Consistent Minimal Responsive State Type VI Profound Brain Damage Stage VI Profound Brain Damage	Patient has sleep-awake pattern; consistently responds to simple commands.

Overall Opinion

Although no overall agreement could be achieved the preferences with the largest amount of support were:

- Hyporesponsive Vegetative State.
- Reflex Responsive Vegetative State.
- Localising Responsive Vegetative State.
- Borderline or Transitional Vegetative State had equal number of supporters.
- Inconsistent Low Awareness State.
- Consistent Low Awareness State.

Conclusion

It has not been possible to obtain unanimous agreement from the Working Party on terminology. There seems to be a general acceptance that it will not be possible to remove the term Vegetative State. The terms with the greatest number of supporters were descriptive of the type of response (hypo-, reflex or localising) for the Vegetative State and the use of the term Low Awareness State sub-divided into those responses which were consistent and those which are inconsistent.

There is a clear need to have common agreement on terminology if the subject of the Vegetative State can be more fully examined and clinicians can communicate with each other.

INDEX

Index

Index